Sociocultural Theory and Second Language Learning

edited by
James P. Lantolf

OXFORD
UNIVERSITY PRESS

OXFORD
UNIVERSITY PRESS

Great Clarendon Street, Oxford OX2 6DP

Oxford University Press is a department of the University
of Oxford. It furthers the University's objective of excellence
in research, scholarship, and education by publishing
worldwide in

Oxford New York
Auckland Bangkok Buenos Aires Cape Town Chennai
Dar es Salaam Delhi Hong Kong Istanbul Karachi Kolkata
Kuala Lumpur Madrid Melbourne Mexico City Mumbai
Nairobi São Paulo Shanghai Taipei Tokyo Toronto

Oxford and *Oxford English* are registered trade marks of
Oxford University Press in the UK and in certain other countries

© Oxford University Press 2000

The moral rights of the author have been asserted

Database right Oxford University Press (maker)

First published 2000
Third impression 2004

ISBN 0 19 442160 0

Printed in China

To my mother and father

Contents

Introducing sociocultural theory

James P. Lantolf
The Pennsylvania State University

The chapters in the present volume all explore, in various ways, the implications for second language learning and teaching of a sociocultural theory of mind, as originally conceived of by L. S. Vygotsky, during the years immediately following the Russian Revolution. Such explorations lead to a view of learning and teaching which in many respects is very different from theories currently in favor in the mainstream SLA literature. My purpose in what follows is to outline the core statements of sociocultural theory, and then to preview their operationalization in the eleven chapters that comprise this volume. The discussion here is restricted to the central tenets of the theory. Those issues not germane to the scope of the present work, such as debates over concept formation in childhood and which modern incarnation of the theory is most faithful to Vygotsky's original ideas, I leave aside in the interest of space. Interested readers should consult the Bibliography (see, for example, Vygotsky 1978 and 1987; Luria 1979; Wertsch 1985a; Newman and Holzman 1993; Cole 1996).

Mediated mind

The most fundamental concept of sociocultural theory is that the human mind is *mediated*. In opposition to the orthodox view of mind, Vygotsky argued that just as humans do not act directly on the physical world but rely, instead, on tools and labor activity, which allows us to change the world, and with it, the circumstances under which we live in the world, we also use symbolic tools, or signs, to mediate and regulate our relationships with others and with ourselves and thus change the nature of these relationships. Physical as well as symbolic (or psychological) tools are artifacts created by human culture(s) over time and are made available to succeeding generations, which can modify these artifacts before passing them on to future generations. Included among symbolic tools are numbers and arithmetic systems, music, art, and above all language. As with physical tools, humans use symbolic artifacts to establish an indirect, or *mediated*, relationship between ourselves and the world. The task of psychology, in Vygotsky's view, is to understand how human social and mental activity is organized through culturally constructed artifacts.[1] Vygotsky conceived of the human mind as a functional system in which the properties of the natural, or biologically specified, brain are organized into a higher, or culturally shaped, mind through the integration of symbolic artifacts into thinking. Higher mental capacities include voluntary attention, intentional memory, planning, logical thought and problem solving, learning, and evaluation of the effectiveness of these processes.

Whether physical or symbolic, artifacts are generally modified as they are passed on from one generation to the next. Each generation reworks its cultural inheritance to meet the needs of its communities and individuals. For example, the cumbersome early computing machines which we were in awe of during the 1950s, today have become sleek and much more powerful devices that have increasingly found their way into the daily lives of communities in many parts of the world. Likewise, languages are continuously remolded by their users to serve their communicative and psychological needs.

A particularly powerful example in this regard is found in the impact of new metaphors on the way people think and behave. For instance, for nearly four decades researchers have conceived of and studied human minds as if they were computational devices, a perspective that would have been impossible until the development of computers during the middle years of the twentieth century.[2] As often happens throughout history, a development in one domain gives rise to a 'spin-off' in another (Wertsch 1998: 58–9). As a further example of a spin-off, consider the interesting work of David Olson on writing systems. Briefly, Olson (1994) shows how our commonly accepted view that 'writing maps onto preexisting models of language' (Wertsch 1998: 62) is misleading, since in fact, the relationship between writing and language models is the reverse. That is, the categories and structures (for example, sentences, words, phonemes) that are the focus of much linguistic theorizing are, in fact, spin-offs of alphabetic writing systems. For example, while early pictorial writing systems brought meaning into consciousness because these scripts 'provided a notion of saying the same thing each time they were scanned or recited', the graphemic or alphabetic system brought verbal form into awareness (Olson 1994: 258). Here 'saying the same thing' meant repeating the same forms. Hence linguistic categories such as 'words' were brought into awareness (Olson 1994: 259). Illich and Sanders (1988) point out that cultures which lack a writing system do not possess the concept 'word', which they claim arose only after the alphabetic system emerged in ancient Greece. The alphabetic system is also noteworthy for what it leaves out of consciousness as much as for what it brings into awareness. Graphemic writing has had a notoriously difficult time indicating such linguistic features as intonation, stress, volume, length, and other markers of the illocutionary aspects of utterances. Is it, then, merely an accident that these features, until relatively recently, have not been central to linguistic theorizing? Generative theory, for instance, is a theory of possible sentences, and as it turns out, sentences are an aspect of language that alphabetic writing can easily make explicit. Something similar can be said with respect to the sounds of speech. It is interesting to note that while syntax and phonology continue to be viewed as core areas of language and thus of linguistic analysis, pragmatics is often relegated to the margins of linguistics, if not pushed completely into other disciplines such as communication theory, philosophy, or sociology. Such is the power of (the spin-off of) *written words*!

Genetic domains

Since we inherit cultural artifacts from our ancestors, who in turn inherit these artifacts from their ancestors, Vygotsky reasoned that the only adequate approach to the study of higher mental abilities was historical. As such, he proposed four *genetic* domains for the proper study of higher mental functions: *phylogenetic* domain, concerned with how human mentation came to be distinguished from mental processes in other life forms through the integration of mediational means over the course of evolution; *sociocultural* domain, concerned with how the different types of symbolic tools developed by human cultures throughout the course of their respective histories affected the kinds of mediation favored, and with it the kinds of thinking valued, by these cultures (for example, the impact of such artifacts as numeracy, literacy, and computers on thinking); *ontogenetic* domain, where focus is on how children appropriate and integrate mediational means, primarily language, into their thinking activities as they mature; *microgenetic* domain, where interest is in the reorganization and development of mediation over a relatively short span of time (for example, being trained to criteria at the outset of a lab experiment; learning a word, sound, or grammatical feature of a language).

Although sociocultural theory recognizes four genetic domains, most of the research has been carried out in the ontogenetic domain where focus has been on exploring the ways in which abilities such as voluntary memory are formed in children through the integration of mediational means into the thinking process. In one well known experiment (see Vygotsky 1987), young children were forbidden to utter specific color terms when describing a series of objects placed before them. They were also instructed not to repeat the same color term more than once. In order to help the children, Vygotsky provided them with a set of colored cards, which, if used correctly, could cue them as to the forbidden colors as well as reminding them which terms not to repeat. He found that young children could not integrate the cards into the task and recourse to the cards only confused the children further. Older children had no difficulty integrating the colored cards and in fact were only able to avoid the forbidden colors by referring to the cards. Adolescents and adults, on the other hand, did not require the cards at all since they were able to rely on memory to avoid the forbidden color terms.

The point of the above experiment was to demonstrate the developmental nature of mediation from a stage in which any type of assistance was useless, to a stage in which external forms of mediation would improve task performance, to a final stage in which external mediation had been internalized. The fact that the adolescents and adults in Vygotsky's experiment did not require mediation in the color naming task does not imply that this is a general property of adult consciousness in all tasks, since there are clearly tasks in which even adults require external forms of assistance. A typical example, provided by Wertsch (1998), is when an adult is asked to multiply two sets of high numbers (for example, 245×987). Most of us are unable to carry out this task internally and must rely on paper and pencil to complete the arithmetic operation. If the numbers are even higher and, say, include decimals, we might even require use of a more powerful artifact, such as a calculator.

Luria (1981) carried out a series of studies in which he showed how language came to function as a means for children to mediate their own physical behavior. In this research, children were instructed to press a bulb whenever they saw a green light come on in the apparatus set before them and to stop pressing the bulb when a red light came on. Very young children were not only unable to follow the instructions, but in fact, tended to press more vigorously when the red light turned on. Older children were able to perform the task appropriately but only under the verbal direction of someone else, who cued them to press or stop pressing (the same verbal regulation produced no effect in the youngest children). Still older children were able to regulate their own pressing behavior by externally telling themselves when to press and when not to. Finally, the oldest group of children participating in the experiment had internalized the mediational means afforded by language in this case and thus were able to regulate their own pressing behavior appropriately in the absence of externalized verbal utterances. In this way, Luria was able to demonstrate how language comes to play a central role in inhibiting and initiating behavior—essential aspects of planning.

Although most formational research has focused on the ontogenetic domain, there has been some work carried out in the other three domains as well. Vygotsky himself wrote about the mediational differences in the phylogenetic separation of humans and higher primates. Rather than carrying out his own research, however, he relied heavily on the work of researchers such as Yerkes and his colleagues. While Vygotsky's writings here argue for marked mediational differences between humans and apes, more recent research has shown that differences may not be as clearly defined as Vygotsky assumed. With regard to the sociocultural domain, some work has been carried out on the impact of literacy on cultural and social development (see the discussion of Olson 1994 above), but certainly a great deal more research is required in this area. With regard to microgenesis, the majority of the research in this domain, until very recently, had been represented by the work of A. R. Luria (1973, 1981). The research of McNeill (1992) and his colleagues on the link between gesture and speech clearly falls within the domain of microgenesis (see p. 204 and below).

In addition, some of the work on second language learning, as represented in the present volume, falls within this domain as well; however, in this case, the concern is more about the reformation rather than the formation of mediational means.

With regard to reformation processes, one of the most frequently cited cases within sociocultural psychology is Luria's (1976) investigation of the consequences of collectivization and schooled literacy on Uzbek peasants. Luria demonstrated that those Uzbeks who had been schooled, even for a short period of time, were able to shift from their earlier practical situationally-based thinking strategies to logical and taxonomic patterns of thinking. Thus, when presented with a task which asked participants to group objects according to some common property, unschooled Uzbek peasants argued that objects such as *hammer*, *saw*, *log*, and *hatchet* should be grouped together, roughly on the grounds that hammers, saws, and hatchets were of no use without an object on which to employ them. When shown a picture of three adults and one child and asked which one did not belong, an unschooled peasant responded that they all belonged together because 'Three men are working, you see, and if they have to keep running out to fetch things, they'll never get the job done, but the boy can do the running for them' (Luria 1976: 55). And when asked to solve the following syllogism: 'Cotton can grow only where it is hot and dry. In England it is cold and damp. Can cotton grow there?' one unschooled Uzbek responded with 'I don't know'... 'I've only been in the Kashgar country; I don't know beyond that' (Luria 1976: 108). On the other hand, Uzbeks who had spent a year or two in school had no difficulty solving the above, and similar, tasks as most educated Westerners would. As a consequence, these individuals not only grasped principles of categorical classification and deductive inferencing, but tended to use these as their chief modes of thinking. Thus, their mental system had been reformed as a result of their participation in a culturally specified activity known as schooling. Learning of a second language, under certain circumstances (see the chapter by Pavlenko and Lantolf in the present volume), can lead to the reformation of one's mental system, including one's concept of self (see also Lantolf 1998).[3]

Since none of the chapters in the present volume addresses issues of deformation, I will only briefly consider this interesting and important aspect of sociocultural theory and research. In addition to work on the ontogenetic formation of children, sociocultural research has also been concerned with understanding the nature of mind through work with physically and mentally impaired children. This research has a practical as well as a theoretical slant. On the practical side, researchers were able to help children learn how to carry out normal physical and mental activities, but through the use of alternative mediational means (for example, tactile signs to help blind-deaf children communicate). On the theoretical side, researchers were able to test their hypotheses about how normal minds function by observing the effects of introducing alternative forms of mediation on mental and physical activity (see Vygotsky 1993)[4]. Luria took the lead in working with individuals whose mental systems had unraveled as a result of cerebral damage arising from physical trauma, disease, or illness such as stroke (see Luria 1973, 1979). Here he was able to help cerebrally impaired adults overcome deficits through the introduction of alternative mediational means into a damaged mental system. Luria found, for example, that a patient exhibiting problems of narrative coherence was able to overcome the symptom by writing the fragments of a story on slips of paper, at which point he was able to rearrange them into a coherent narrative (Luria 1973). Through such research Vygotsky and Luria were not only able to verify the propositions of their theory but they were also able to help people recover from trauma. In many ways, then, work on deformation of mental systems is linked to research carried out on the reformation of such systems.

Yet another means of exploring the consequences of deformation of mediational means is under experimental conditions, in which the researcher sets a task for the individual and then introduces an interruption or complication. At this point the individual generally begins to explore ways of (re)mediating the activity through integration of different mediating artifacts. In second language research, the early study by Frawley and Lantolf (1985) compared the performance of intermediate and advanced ESL speakers and showed how in the face of a difficult narrative task, the performance of the intermediate speakers breaks down and they subsequently lose control, or self-regulation, over the mediational means provided by their second language and become controlled, or regulated, by the task set before them. More advanced speakers are able to control the mediational means afforded by the second language in guiding themselves through the task; in fact, to be an advanced speaker/user of a language means to be able to control one's psychological and social activity through the language. This of course also applies to a first language. As children develop they gain increasing control over the mediational means made available by their culture, including language, for interpersonal (social interaction) and intrapersonal (thinking) purposes. In both circumstances, individuals move through stages in which they are controlled first by the objects in their environment, then by others in this environment, and finally they gain control over their own social and cognitive activities. These stages are usually referred to in sociocultural theory as object-, other-, and self-regulation. The reader should recall Luria's bulb-pressing experiment in which young children were first unable to exercise any voluntary control over their pressing behaviors. These children are said to be object-regulated by the devices in the experiment. Somewhat older children were able to respond appropriately to the lights; however, only when instructed to do so by someone else; hence, these children are said to be other-regulated. Those children who were able to instruct themselves verbally when to inhibit or initiate their bulb-pressing behavior are said to be self-regulated, although unlike in the case of adolescents or adults (who generally have no difficulty in carrying out such experiments and therefore require little or no overt verbal instruction from themselves or anyone else) they had to overtly instruct themselves in this activity.[5]

Unit of analysis

Sociocultural theory clearly rejects the notion that thinking and speaking are one and the same thing. It also rejects what some now call the communicative view of language (see Carruthers and Boucher 1998), which holds that thinking and speaking are completely independent phenomena, with speaking serving only as a means of transmitting already formed thoughts. Sociocultural theory argues that while separate, thinking and speaking are tightly inter-related in a dialectic unity in which publicly derived speech completes privately initiated thought.[6] Thus, thought cannot be explained without taking account of how it is made manifest through linguistic means, and linguistic activities, in turn, cannot be understood fully without 'seeing them as manifestations of thought' (Bakhurst 1991: 60). To break the dialectic unity between speech and thought is to forego any possibility of understanding human mental capacities, much in the same way, as Vygotsky observed, that independent analysis of oxygen and hydrogen fails to generate an explanation of water's capacity to extinguish fire. What is needed, then, is a unit of analysis that preserves the dialectic unity of the elements (thinking and speaking).

Vygotsky proposed the *word* as this unit, because, in the word, meaning, the central component of thought, and linguistic form are united. In making his argument, Vygotsky distinguishes between the stable, or conventional, meaning of a word and its *sense*, or personal, and contextualized, meaning that emerges from particular ways people deploy words in mediating their mental activity. It is in a word's sense that the microcosm of consciousness is to be uncovered.

Not all scholars working within sociocultural theory have agreed with Vygotsky's designation of the word as the unit of analysis for the study of mediated mind. Wertsch (1985a: 197), for instance, suggests that it is difficult to perceive mediated processes such as memory or attention in the sense of a word. Vygotsky's colleague, A. N. Leontiev (1978), early on rejected word sense as too psychological and thus too far removed from the concrete activity of people in their world. Zinchenko (1985), building on Leontiev's claim, and at the same time drawing on Vygotsky's own writings, argues that the appropriate unit of analysis is *tool-mediated goal-directed action*. This unit, according to Wertsch (1985a: 207–8), preserves the dynamic nature of intermental and intramental organization and functioning, while at the same time it encompasses those precise functional systems that for Vygotsky defined human mental ability—memory, problem solving, attention, intention, planning, orientation, evaluation. The tool, as Wertsch (1998) points out, can be a physical artifact, as in the case of a pole for pole vaulting, or symbolic, as in the case of utterances produced during conversations with others and with the self. This perspective on the unit of analysis for the study of mind leads naturally to consideration of the overall theoretical framework which informs sociocultural research, and this is known as *activity theory*.

Activity theory

Activity theory is a unified account of Vygotsky's original proposals on the nature and development of human behavior. Specifically, it addresses the implications of his claim that human behavior results from the integration of socially and culturally constructed forms of mediation into human activity. Luria (1973, 1979) refers to the system that results from the integration of artifacts into human activity, whether that activity be psychological or social, as a *functional system*. Mind, according to Luria, is not, properly speaking, the activity of the biologically given brain, but is a functional system formed when the brain's electro-chemical processes come under control of our cultural artifacts: foremost among these is language. Vygotsky argued that if psychology was to understand these functional systems it had to study their formation (i.e. their history) and activity and not their structure. Vygotsky's ideas were eventually crystallized by A. N. Leontiev in his theory of activity, and while researchers since the time of Leontiev's original formulations have modified aspects of the theory, his fundamental claims continue to reside at its core. Activity in Leontiev's (1978) theory is not merely doing something, it is doing something that is motivated either by a biological need, such as hunger, or a culturally constructed need, such as the need to be literate in certain cultures. Needs become motives once they become directed at a specific object. Thus, hunger does not become a motive until people decide to seek food; similarly, literacy does not become a motive for activity until people decide to learn to read and write. Motives are only realized in specific *actions* that are goal directed (hence, intentional and meaningful) and carried out under particular spatial and temporal *conditions* (or what are also referred to as *operations*) and through appropriate *mediational means*. Thus, an activity comprises three levels: the level of motivation, the level of action, and the level of conditions. Activities, then, can only be directly observed, by others, at the level of conditions. However, the motives and goals of particular activities cannot be determined solely from the level of concrete doing, since the same observable activity can be linked to different goals and motives and different concrete activities can be linked to the same motives and goals. The illustrations given below should make these important points clear.

I will begin with Leontiev's informative example of the hunting practices of some tribal cultures and then consider some more recent examples taken from the education and L2 learning literature. Hunting, according to Leontiev, has its basic motive in the biological need to satisfy hunger. The actual form the hunt takes is culturally specified. In some cultures, it is a collective activity in which some members of the community are assigned the responsibility of beating the bush mediated by such artifacts as sticks, hands (clapping), voices (shouting), and drums, in order to scare and drive the prey (the immediate goal of the hunt) toward other members of the community given the task of slaying it with the use of other artifacts, such as spears, and bows and arrows. Yet other members are given the responsibility of butchering and distributing the carcass to the general community, often according to a hierarchically specified code. The hunt then is an activity that can only be realized in the concrete actions of the hunters under specific conditions. For those participating in the hunt, their actions have meaning because they are linked to the activity's motive, satisfying hunger, and its immediate goal, slaying an animal. The beaters make sense of their actions, making noise to frighten the animal, by connecting this behavior to the motives and goals of the hunt. This is important because the beaters' actions are only indirectly linked to the primary goal, which is the slaying of an animal.

As I have stated earlier, activities are differentiated from each other by their objects and motives and not necessarily by their concrete realization as actions. Thus, the same activity can be realized through different actions and with different forms of mediation. For example, not all cultures engage in collaborative hunting. In some cultures, all aspects of the hunt are carried out by the same individuals, say through stealthfully stalking and killing the prey with a bow and arrow, spear, or rifle. In yet other cultures, the need to consume food is realized in the action of purchasing groceries at a supermarket. At the level of motive, these actions are all part of the same activity, even though they appear different in their overt manifestation. On the other hand, what appear to be the same actions can be linked to a different motive and thus constitute different activities. In the case of the beaters, it might turn out that they discover beating the bush rhythmically is fun and so they continue to engage in this action even when the community has no need for food. Thus, what was originally part of the activity of hunting now becomes an activity in its own right, because it is linked to a different motive—the motive of fun. Beating the bush now has new meaning. One might suspect that sport hunting arose under similar circumstances.

Wertsch, Minick, and Arns (1984), in a cross-cultural study, provide another example of how activity theory can inform our understanding of human mental and social behavior. In this study, the researchers compared the interactional activity that arose between rural Brazilian mothers and their children and urban school teachers and their students in a puzzle-copying task. The object of the task was for the adult-child dyads to copy a barnyard scene depicted in a model. The researchers hypothesized that given the contrasts between rural and urban cultures in Brazil there would be differences in the way the dyads carried out the copying activity. Briefly, the researchers found that indeed clear differences emerged between the rural and urban dyads with regard to how the children were mediated by their respective caregivers. In the case of the urban dyads, the adults preferred to offer the children strategic clues by first orienting them to the model and telling the child to construct a similar scene. Along the way, the teachers suggested that the children look at the model before selecting the appropriate animal, fence, or what have you, to place in their own scene. In no case did the teachers pick up any pieces for the child, nor did they offer direct commands such as 'Pick up the duck and put it in this spot.' Instead they created a linguistic scaffold which allowed the child to figure out for him- or herself what to do at each point along the way. Thus, they would produce utterances such as 'Now look at the model.' 'Are you sure this is the correct place?' 'What comes next?' According to the researchers, there are three important features of this activity that need to be highlighted: the children made mistakes along the way, because they were offered strategic rather than directive help; the children carried out all of the actions themselves; by directing the children's attention to the model, the teachers were not just helping the children to copy the specific scene but they were instructing them in how to work with models.

The rural dyads behaved in a markedly different way. The mothers maintained responsibility for most of the moves throughout the task. They only rarely directed the children's attention to the model, opting instead to look at the model themselves. They used much more directive rather than strategic language. Thus, they tended to say things like 'Now pick up the duck and put it here.' In a sense, the rural mothers used their children as tools to construct an accurate copy of the model, without imparting to their children an understanding of what the task was about. Under such direct adult regulation, however, the rural children made significantly fewer errors in copying the model than their urban counterparts. Nevertheless, because most of the task remained under adult control, the children failed to learn much about how to orient themselves toward and copy models.

Comparing the relative performance of the rural and urban dyads from the perspective of activity theory, we note that the teachers made every effort to ensure that the goal of the activity (copying a model) became shared by their students. This did not happen in the rural dyads, where the mothers preferred not to share the goal. With regard to the actual conditions under which the children selected and placed pieces in their scene, the teachers consistently tried to shift responsibility for the decisions underlying this behavior to their students, while the mothers by and large determined which pieces to select and where to place them, directing their child's behavior through linguistic means.

In attempting to explain these differences, the researchers suggest that the rural and urban dyads operated from different underlying motives, which gave rise to very different objects of activity. They reasoned that in the particular rural communities under study economic considerations are the driving motive. That is, these communities rely on the production and sale of artifacts such as pottery, clothing, and the like. In the production process, errors in performance often result in the loss of money either because materials have to be discarded when an error is made, or time is lost because a process must be undone and begun anew from the point where the error was made. Hence, the leading activity for the rural dyads was error-free performance, and the way to ensure this was for the mothers to control as much of the activity as possible and share as little as possible with their children. The goal was not simply to copy the model but to produce an *error-free* copy of the model. In the urban dyads, the motive underlying the activity was educational—i.e. that children need to learn to think independently. To realize this, the teachers had to share responsibility for decision making with their students. This of course meant that in some cases, children would make inappropriate decisions, thus leading to erroneous performance. But in this case, errors were not seen as costly but as necessary conditions for the taking on of responsibility for one's actions. The point is that while the rural and urban dyads engaged in the same task—copy the model—they were not engaged in the same activities, because even though pieces were selected and placed, the motives and goals underlying this behavior differed.

The unstable nature of activities

Activities, whether in the workplace, classrooms, or other settings, do not always unfold smoothly. What begins as one activity can reshape itself into another activity in the course of its unfolding. Cobb (1998), for example, in his studies of children learning arithmetic reports a case in which the children began a project on measuring by playing shoestore, which required that they learn how to measure feet with the appropriate template. After a time, the children shifted their attention to measuring other kinds of objects and quickly lost interest in the shoestore activity. However, in order to measure objects such as chairs, tables, blackboards, and the like, they were not able to use the foot templates and had to discover a new set of measuring tools. Hence, a shift in activity gave rise to the need to discover different mediational tools for carrying out what had now become the activity of measuring objects in the world.

Thorne (1999) considers the impact of internet mediation on foreign language learner communicative activity. Using log file records and participant reports, Thorne provides evidence that learner communicative interaction is reconfigured when it is synchronously mediated through the internet. Students report feeling 'less culpable' for their on-line utterances; moreover, they express feelings of a lack of supervision, even though they are aware that their instructor is on-line. Thus, the internet environment creates among the students a certain sense of freedom which allows them to say things they would probably not say in face-to-face interaction. At one point, in their interactions, some students began to use what some people take to be obscene language—a clear violation of the rules of the educational setting, but apparently not a violation of the chat world, at least not according to some students, who had experience with digitized culture. The teacher then stepped out of the role of electronic eavesdropper and back into the role of teacher and confronted the students producing the illegal language face-to-face. This move clearly changed the nature of the activity because for one thing the rules mediating chat discussions are different from the rules mediating discussion in the educational setting. Thorne argues that the shift in the mediational means from verbal face-to-face interaction that might occur in the normal language classroom to electronically mediated interaction, in which the students were no longer facing each other physically, changed the activity of communicating and thus opened up a set of options not available in the other venue. To be sure, it occasionally gave rise to negative speech behavior, but by and large, this different form of mediation enhanced creative language use in which fun and wit were valued and which fostered dynamic engagement (see van Lier's chapter) with others instead of comprehensible input and information exchange.

All of this means that in any given classroom setting (or any setting for that matter), not only can activities change from one moment to the next, but different activities might be underway at any given time, despite the fact that all of the participants display the same or similar overt behaviors in a task. A student might not care if she learned the language, as long as she passed tests and received an acceptable grade for the course, which, in turn, could enhance her chances of obtaining a good job or gaining admission to a choice graduate school, while other students engaging in the same task might well be oriented to the goal of learning the language because, for example, they find it intrinsically interesting. Gillette (1994) reports that some of the students in her university French class had personal histories in which anything foreign, in this case, non-American, was devalued and therefore not worthy of knowing. Thus, the so-called learning strategies they deployed were not directed at learning the language, but at coping with the 'imposition' of having to study a foreign language. Others of Gillette's students reported histories in which the family was intently interested in different cultures and their languages. These students showed strong evidence of strategies specifically directed at learning the language. Even if students in the same class engage in the same task they may not be engaged in the same activity. Students with different motives often have different goals as the object of their actions, despite the intentions of the teacher. A person who devalues foreignness may carry through on a pedagogical task with the sole aim of complying with the immediate demand of the teacher. Again, as Gillette's (1994) work shows, under such circumstances language learning is not likely to occur. Students, then, play a major role in shaping the goal and ultimate outcomes of tasks set for them by their teachers. Thus, from the perspective of activity theory, while task-based instruction could yield positive learning outcomes, there can be no guarantees, because what ultimately matters is how individual learners decided to engage with the task as an activity.

As people participate in different culturally specified activities they enter into different social relations and come into contact with, and learn how to employ and ultimately appropriate, different mediational means. One outcome of activities such as collaborative hunting is a division of labor in which people begin to think of themselves as beaters, slayers, butchers, distributors, consumers, etc. In classrooms we also observe a division of labor, not only the obvious one between teacher and students, but among students. For example, Cole (1996) discusses a study on reading activity in an afterschool cooking club in which teams of children were given the opportunity to bake a cake according to a recipe. In some teams one child took on the task of coordinating the integration of ingredients while the other had the task of reading the recipe. If both children had read and coordinated, baking the cake would have, in all likelihood, proven to be more difficult to achieve.

Among culturally motivated activities are included work, education, accumulation of wealth, play, and the like. Play is an especially important activity in Vygotsky's theory of development, because it is in play that children create, usually in collaboration with other children, a zone of proximal development (see p. 17) in which they perform beyond their current abilities (see Vygotsky 1978 and 1997). So when children play house, mommy and daddy, or some particular profession, such as a doctor, a sports figure, etc., they engage in activities that are not just about having fun, but allow children to project into the future. Thus, play is an important activity for child development. The ways in which they play house, or the kinds of jobs and professions they play at are determined by their cultures. Child language scholars have, for some time, recognized the importance of play with language in the acquisition process (see Weir 1962; Kuczaj 1983). Second language researchers have begun to document the appearance of language play among child and adult learners (see Peck 1980; Saville-Troike 1988; Cook 1997, 2000; Lantolf 1997; Broner and Tarone 1999; and Sullivan, in this volume).

Internalization and inner speech

The convergence of thinking with culturally created mediational artifacts, above all those which are linguistically organized (for example, conversations, metaphors, narratives, poetry, writing, etc.),[7] occurs in the process of *internalization*, or the reconstruction on the inner, psychological plane, of socially mediated external forms of goal-directed activity. Internalization is in essence the process through which higher forms of mentation come to be. Internalization, then, assumes that the source of consciousness resides outside of the head and is in fact anchored in social activity. At first the activity of individuals is organized and regulated (i.e. mediated) by others, but eventually, in normal development, we come to organize and regulate our own mental and physical activity through the appropriation of the regulatory means employed by others. At this point psychological functioning comes under the voluntary control of the person.

Internalization is not the wholesale transfer of external mediation to a preexisting internal plane. This would indeed sustain the Cartesian dualism that Vygotsky and other materialists oppose. On the contrary, sociocultural theory argues above all that specifically human psychological processes do not preexist inside the head waiting to emerge at just the right maturational moment. This requires a bit of clarification, given what has already been said about natural mind and our biological capacities. Kozulin (1998), relying on the extensive cross-cultural research of Michael Cole, notes that as far as we know, all humans are capable of classifying objects, which may well be a biologically specified ability. However, not all humans classify objects according to the same schema. In some cultures, classification of objects is based primarily on the objects' functional role in everyday practical activity, while in others they are classified according to formal schema internalized in school.[8] Thus, while biology provides a foundation for classification, the concrete schemata deployed by individuals to classify entities in their world is culturally constructed. Therefore, attempts to ground explanations of mental development in the isolated individual are inadequate. A materialist account holds that internalization is a process through which mental actions are formed on the basis of external, materially based, social actions. Internalization, then, is the process through which a person moves from carrying out concrete actions in conjunction with the assistance of material artifacts and of other individuals to carrying out actions mentally without any apparent external assistance. This, however, does not mean that mental activity is free of mediational support. Indeed, there is support only now it is internally situated.

Consider the difference between the expert and novice pool player, as discussed by Wertsch (1998). In order to determine what the result of a particular shot is likely to be, the novice must actually play the shot and rely therefore on the external material support of the cue stick, the balls, and the table. The expert, on the other hand, is able to determine the outcome of the shot internally before actually playing it. In fact, the expert need not even be in the presence of pool playing equipment to make such a determination. He or she can 'visualize' the shot on the psychological plane. This is so because the expert has internalized what was at one time the external material support provided by the cue stick, balls, and table.

In a revealing series of studies, Wertsch (see summary in Wertsch 1985a: Chapter 6) showed that in learning to solve certain cognitive tasks, such as reconstructing a wooden puzzle according to the specifications of a model, the behavior of young children (ages two to seven) initially was under the mediational control of the child's parent. Gradually, control passed from the parent to the children as they appropriated the language used by the parent as a means of mediating their own mental and indeed physical activity. At this point, the children's speech also shifted from an exclusively social to a shared psychological function, but as in the case of the novice pool player, the psychological function was still linked to the specific external circumstances in which the puzzle solving occurred. The children's speaking activity, therefore, was in some respects social in that it occurred in the presence of the other person, but it was importantly psychological to the extent that it was not directed at the other person; rather it was oriented to the children themselves as they instructed themselves in selecting the appropriate piece from the pieces pile, placing the piece in the puzzle, and in evaluating the correctness of their moves.

Importantly, the self-directed language attested in Wertsch's research and numerous other studies (see Diaz and Berk 1992), takes on an elliptical quality. That is, it most often consists of utterances that are not fully syntactic. In fact, it looks like one half of a dialogue between individuals with a close personal relationship. For instance, utterances such as the following are frequently attested in self-directed speech in English: *What? Next, an orange one*, *Wait, No, I can't … Done*, etc. This speech, in which we ask ourselves questions, answer these questions, tell ourselves to interrupt a particular activity, tell ourselves we are wrong or that we cannot do something, and that we have completed a task, is generally referred to as *private speech*; that is, speech that has social origins in the speech of others but that takes on a private or cognitive function. As cognitive development proceeds, private speech becomes subvocal and ultimately evolves into *inner speech*, or language that at the deepest level loses its formal properties as it condenses into pure meaning. According to Vygotsky, it is in the process of privatizing speech that higher forms of consciousness arise on the inner plane and in this way our biological capacities are organized into a culturally mediated mind.

Once mental processes grow inward and private speech evolves into inner speech, mental activities need not remain, and for most people, they do not remain, as exclusively internal mental operations. In the face of difficult tasks, and here difficulty is ultimately determined by the individual, these processes can be reexternalized as the person attempts to regain control over them in performing the task. Frawley and Lantolf (1985) refer to this process as *reaccessing* earlier stages of development.[9] If a task is especially difficult, and if the person decides that it is important enough to persist in the task, the person has the option of seeking help from other people. In this way, psychological processes once again become social as the person seeks out other mediation. Alternatively, the person may seek assistance not in some other person, but in particular artifacts made available by the culture. Hence, the person may decide to consult a book, use a calculator or computer, or even a horoscope as a means of obtaining needed mediation.[10]

Inner speech and gesture

The work of David McNeill (1992) and his colleagues has been instrumental in drawing our attention to the significance of gesture not only in social interaction but also to the central role it plays in cognitive activity. Briefly, McNeill's claim is that inner speech is not only composed of a verbal aspect but has a gestural side to it as well. His work has shown that not only is gesture an indispensable part of our communicative activities with others but it is also a key feature in our communicative activities with ourselves. He has demonstrated how meaning is manifested not only verbally but also gesturally, not as a substitute for a verbal sign but as a complement to it. In other words, much of what we mean is only partially constructed through linguistic means. It is also partially constructed through gesture. Thus, when we interact with others we read not only their verbal signals but their gestural signals as well and in some cases the gestural signals may even override our verbally expressed intentions.

To illustrate, I recall an incident in which a generative-transformational linguist was engaged in dinner conversation about grammatical movement. At one point, the linguist uttered the word 'movement' and simultaneously his right hand moved through the air from right to left and with a low to high trajectory, thus tracing the grammatical form of constituent movement in the theory. The English word 'movement' specifies neither directionality nor trajectory, but this was a crucial aspect of the meaning the speaker intended to project, and he did it through the integration of his verbal and gestural signs.

Yet another incident I observed illustrates how gesture is used in its cognitive function. During a television interview, a well known owner of a professional American baseball team was talking about how one builds a winning team. In the jargon of baseball, a metaphorical expression used to refer to the field on which the game is played is 'diamond', presumably because the field is laid out in the shape of a marquis-cut diamond. At one point, in discussing the various positions for which quality players were required, the owner stopped in mid-utterance and proceeded to produce a series of filled pauses as follows, 'and uh, and uh, and uh.' He was clearly engaged in a lexical search. Eventually, he looked down at his hands which were configured in such a way as to indicate the shape of a marquis-cut diamond. At which point, he uttered 'oh, on the diamond' and continued his discourse.

Zone of proximal development

The site where social forms of mediation develop is the 'zone of proximal development.' This metaphor, originally proposed by Vygotsky as a way of capturing the process through which institutionalized schooling impacts on intelligence, as measured by IQ tests, has become perhaps the most well known and widely adopted construct of the theory. According to Vygotsky, all higher mental abilities appear twice in the life of the individual: first on the intermental plane in which the process is distributed between the individual, and some other person(s) and/or cultural artifacts, and later on the intramental plane in which the capacity is carried out by the individual acting via psychological mediation. It must be emphasized again that the ZPD is not a physical place situated in time and space; rather it is a metaphor for observing and understanding how mediational means are appropriated and internalized.

Vygotsky's definition states that the ZPD is the difference between what a person can achieve when acting alone and what the same person can accomplish when acting with support from someone else and/or cultural artifacts. In light of our earlier discussion of internalization and appropriation, the reader should be able to appreciate the controversies that have arisen in conjunction with how the ZPD is to be construed. Some researchers have assumed that the ZPD necessarily involves interaction between an expert and a novice in which the expert eventually transmits an ability to the novice through social interaction. This view of the ZPD, in my opinion, has received substantial support from the work of Wertsch and his colleagues on parent and child joint puzzle-solving interactions. This is not to say that on theoretical grounds Wertsch himself sanctions such a perspective; however, because of the nature of his empirical research, it is not too difficult to understand how the expert/novice interpretation became the accepted interpretation. In fact, L2 research that I have participated in underpins this belief as well (see Aljaafreh and Lantolf 1994). Be that as it may, several scholars are now calling for a broader understanding of the scope of the ZPD to include more than just expert/novice interaction (see Kuutti 1996; Engestrom and Middleton 1996; Wells 1996, 2000; Swain and Lapkin 1998).

If we do not lose sight of the key ingredient—mediation—I believe that a more robust and useful way of thinking about the ZPD can be sustained. It seems clear that people working jointly are able to co-construct contexts in which expertise emerges as a feature of the group. This is important, since without such a possibility it is difficult to imagine how expertise of any kind could ever arise; unless of course we were to assume an *a priori* biological endowment that specified the precise properties of the ability in question. But are we willing to accept that biology alone is responsible for the rise of literacy, numeracy, the invention of computers, legal systems, etc.? The ZPD, then, is more appropriately conceived of as the collaborative construction of opportunities (in his chapter van Lier discusses these as *affordances*; Swain and Lapkin 1998 call them 'occasions for learning') for individuals to develop their mental abilities.

Even in those cases in which experts and novices do come together, as in a teaching situation, novices do not merely copy the experts' capabilities; rather they transform what the experts offer them as they appropriate it. The key to transformation resides in *imitation*, which along with collaboration in the

ZPD, 'is the source of all the specifically human characteristics' of development (Vygotsky 1987: 210). Imitation in the ZPD, unlike copying (the verbatim mimicking of what the expert appears to do), is a complex activity in which the novice is treated not as a repeater but as a communicative being (Newman and Holzman 1993: 151–2). As an example of imitation, consider the following interaction between an adult and a child taken from a study by Bloom, Hood, and Lightbown as presented in Newman and Holzman:

Child: (opening cover of tape recorder) open, open, open
Adult: Did you open it?
Child: (watching tape recorder) open it
Adult: Did you open the tape recorder?
Child: (watching tape recorder) tape recorder

(Newman and Holzman 1993: 151)

The child creates something new (open > open it; tape recorder) as a result of imitating portions of the adult's utterances. Notice that the child does not produce an exact copy of the adult's speech and importantly the exchange is both communicative and instructional.

As often happens in traditional school settings, however, the expert (for example, language teacher) may well insist that the novice (for example, student) produce an exact copy of what is offered. In such circumstances, little if any account is taken of the student's ZPD, and while the novice with sufficient effort may succeed in accurately reproducing the expert's model, imitation, in Vygotsky's sense, is not operative. Moreover, the expert/novice interface in such a situation is rarely if ever communicative.[11] The reader will encounter several examples of genuine imitative interactions in the chapters that follow; importantly, many of these occur between and among learners with only marginal intervention from the teacher.

The present volume

Because sociocultural research seeks to study mediated mind in the various sites where people engage in the normal activities affiliated with living, it undertakes to maintain the richness and complexity of 'living reality' rather than distilling it 'into its elementary components' for the purpose of constructing 'abstract models that lose the properties of the phenomena themselves' (Luria 1979: 174). On this account, explanation of human activities is about observation, description, and interpretation guided by a theory that is careful not to compromise 'the manifold richness of the subject' (*ibid.*: 178). As Bruner, in his introduction to Luria (1987), puts it,

Explanation of any human condition is so bound to context, so complexly interpretive at so many levels, that it cannot be achieved by considering isolated segments of life in vitro, and it can never be, even at its best, brought to a final conclusion beyond the shadow of human doubt.

(Luria 1987: xii)

While the eleven chapters included in the present volume are squarely situated within the research tradition discussed by Luria and Bruner—theory-guided observation and interpretation of people engaged in the activity of teaching, learning (in educational or other settings), and using second and foreign languages—each chapter foregrounds specific features of sociocultural theory and backgrounds others. The nine empirically grounded chapters mesh nicely with previous work carried out by sociocultural scholars in such ordinary venues as an after-school cooking club in New York (Cole and Traupmann 1981), a milk processing plant in New York (Scribner 1985), village shops in rural Nepal (Beach 1995), Russian immigrant communities in Israel (Kozulin and Venger 1994), tailor shops in Liberia and butcher departments in American supermarkets (Lave and Wenger 1991), a gas turbine manufacturing company in Japan (Engestrom 1999), airliner cockpits (Hutchins and Klausen 1996), and of course, classrooms.

All of the chapters in the present volume deal in some way with the fundamental concepts of mediation and activity theory. Moreover, several of the chapters work with the constructs of inner speech and private speech (Donato, Pavlenko and Lantolf, Verity, and McCafferty and Ahmed), the zone of proximal development and scaffolding (Donato, Swain, Ohta, Verity, and van Lier), and regulation and control (Verity, Ohta, Thorne, van Lier). Nine of the chapters present empirically-based studies and two are theoretical discussions of the potential benefits derived from relating socio-cultural theory to other theoretical perspectives. Seven of the empirically-based chapters (Donato, Kramsch, Ohta, Roebuck, Sullivan, Swain, and Verity) focus on language learning and teaching in classroom settings, and two (Pavlenko and Lantolf, McCafferty and Ahmed) investigate the processes and consequences of learning other languages in domains beyond the classroom.

The first chapter, by Donato, deals with four major themes: private speech, mediation, scaffolded learning in the zone of proximal development, and activity theory. As part of an introductory graduate course on sociocultural theory, Donato apprenticed his students into the theory by asking them to carry out a series of small-scale classroom research projects. Several of these projects are discussed and commented on in the chapter. The first is on the appearance of private speech during grammar instruction in an ESL class. According to Donato, it is important for teachers to recognize that students frequently need the opportunity to mediate their own learning privately; additionally, students often make their appeals for assistance through private speech, which, because it is not fully social, may not be fully appreciated for what it is by the teacher.

The second set of studies looks at mediational processes between teachers and students in a college-level elementary French class and a third-year high school Spanish class in the US. These studies bring to light important differences between purely instructional talk on the part of the teacher and instructional conversations between teachers and students in which students have the opportunity to regulate the conversation in ways they cannot when teachers engage in instructional talk. As it turns out, however, only a small portion of teacher/student talk was found to entail instructional conversations.

The study on scaffolding analyzed videotapes made in an elementary school Japanese class in which the students move from single-word responses to teacher-initiated interactions to more complex language which allows them to scaffold each other's learning. The study spans three different class levels. All three studies, according to Donato, provide evidence of a shift away from what Sfard (1998) calls the 'acquisition' metaphor to a new 'participation' metaphor. The chapters by Pavenko and Lantolf, and van Lier, respectively, introduced on pp. 23–5, also consider language learning from the perspective of the participation metaphor.

The final study examined in Donato's chapter involves an overt application of activity theory to classroom language learning. The focus is on small-group work carried out in an ESL setting in which the researcher shows how the same task is interpreted differently by different groups and thus becomes in each case a different activity, with a different goal and different mediational strategies. Donato argues that it is important for teachers to concern themselves more with students' orientation to tasks than to task outcomes and that consequently, tasks need to be seen as 'emergent interactions' rather than as recipes for ensuring specific kinds of language performance.

Continuing Donato's theme of scaffolding and learning in the zone of proximal development, Ohta's chapter presents a close analysis of two college-level students of Japanese who co-construct a zone of proximal development which allows them to scaffold their performance as they carry out an eleven-item translation task. In analyzing the videotaped interaction between the students, Ohta shows how each student either bids for or offers assistance. The bids can be manifested as explicit requests for help, or they can be rather subtly deployed through such markers as vowel lengthening and changes in intonation. Importantly, the assistance offered, according to Ohta, is developmentally sensitive to the requester's growing ability to use the language required to carry out a specific task. She also documents the grammatical learning that the students achieve as a consequence of their interactions, which is evidenced, among other things, by shifts from other-regulated to self-regulated error correction. The learners develop increasing independence in the use of a difficult sentence structure through activities that move from a focus on form to a focus on meaning.

Roebuck, in her chapter, addresses the relevance of activity theory not only for language pedagogy, as does Donato, but also considers its importance for research. She extends the earlier work of Coughlan and Duff (1994) on the fluid nature of cognitive activity among university-level classroom L2 learners of Spanish as they undertake to complete a classroom task. Roebuck argues that it is important for teachers and researchers to distinguish between *tasks* and *activities* (explained above). Specifically, she discusses the processes through which learners position themselves as individuals in carrying out a written recall of a newspaper article in the second language, and contends that neither teachers nor researchers can assume that their particular orientation to a task is the one that learners (or participants) will adopt. Moreover, learners' orientation, that is, what they think the task is about, and what counts as its successful completion, can change as the activity of carrying out the task unfolds. This is because learners, and in fact, non-learners as well, often reinterpret the meaning and intent of a task and, importantly, their abilities relative to the task on-line rather than prior to engaging with it. For instance Roebuck reports that some learners oriented themselves to the goal of writing a recall of the newspaper article, while others used the writing activity as a means not of telling someone about the contents of the article, but of comprehending what the article was about. Roebuck further shows how shifts in orientation, as well as the externalization of cognitive strategies for completing the task (for example, lexical search) often unfold on the page in a form of private speech known as *private writing*.

In her chapter, Swain examines mediation from the perspective of collaborative dialogue in a French immersion and an adult ESL classroom. She argues that collaborative dialogue is a key form of mediated learning. The French immersion study demonstrates how young learners, through collaborative dialogue, are able to organize and mediate their own learning without the intervention of the expert teacher. Thus, she argues that through their dialogic interaction, the students do not negotiate meaning; rather they negotiate learning (see also the chapter by Sullivan). The ESL study extends to language learning the work that Talyzina (1981) and her colleagues carried out in the former Soviet Union which focused on the positive effects of learners verbalizing strategies for doing geometry problems. Specifically, the study Swain reports on shows that overt collaborative verbalization of meta-cognitive strategies such as predicting, planning, and monitoring can be a more effective means of mediating learning than just instruction in learning strategies alone.

Sullivan's chapter considers the way in which communicative language teaching (CLT) is implemented in a non-Western setting. In particular, she focuses on the role of playful behavior in mediating the interaction that unfolds in an adult English as a foreign language classroom setting in Vietnam. This is especially important from a sociocultural perspective, since as we have seen, Vygotsky argued that play fulfills an important role in mental development. Sullivan also challenges some common Western assumptions about effective language teaching: decenter the teacher in favor of individual learners;

communication is primarily about information exchange and meaning negotiation; incorporate authentic materials into pedagogical practices; and learning is 'work,' as evidenced in notions of small-group and pair work. Her chapter is also relevant to activity theory, since, as the theory maintains, different actions, linked to the same goal, can give rise to similar outcomes. In this case, CLT is linked to play between teacher and learners and among learners rather than to work among the members of small groups or pairs of students. The goal, however, is invariant—to learn the language.

Continuing the theme of mediation, the chapter by Kramsch discusses the ways in which second language learners explore the reformation of identity through the mediational means of a new language. Unlike in Sullivan's study, however, Kramsch's is situated in a Western communicatively-based classroom setting. Kramsch integrates Vygotsky's approach to semiotic mediation with C. S. Peirce's theory of signs and Bakhtin's concept of dialogism with the aim of bringing to light the ways in which learners, to some degree at least, experience new identities as authors, narrators, interpreters, and critics through their second language. Briefly, signs are about more than just meaning and reference; that is they are not just *symbols*, the usual understanding of a sign in linguistics, but they are also *indexes*. A symbol is a sign that derives its meaning from the system which supports it and must be agreed upon by its users. Thus, the English word *table* has meaning to the extent that it is part of a system of other symbols, such as *dog*, *house*, *chair*, and the like, and speakers of this language have agreed to use the term to designate a specific kind of object in the world and no other. An index, on the other hand, is a sign which has a 'real' link to its object. The fact that smoke indexes, or points to, fire is a well known example of indexing. When the fire disappears, so does its index, smoke. Linguistically, *I* used in a dialogue is an example of an index, since it points to the person speaking. When the person is no longer speaking, in a sense, she/he disappears, and the *I* also ceases to function as an index, or it may index some other speaker. *Dialogism* not only highlights the importance of interaction and context, but crucially, proposes that structure cannot be separated from language use. Language use does not just press structural properties into service; it reconstitutes them through communicative and cognitive activities. In other words structure and practice 'co-determine one another' (Linell 1998: 36). Kramsch proposes that learning a second language is not about simply learning new linguistic forms, but it is about learning how to construct, exchange, and interpret signs that have been created by someone else. She shows how ESL students, both through writing and in dialogic interaction about writing, (co-)construct new mediational means (symbols and indexes) through a second language that impacts on their identities.

The next two chapters, by Pavlenko and Lantolf and by Verity, share a common interest in identity reformation, and in this respect are linked to Kramsch's chapter. Similarly to Kramsch's, both chapters focus on people who enter into and must find ways of engaging with unfamiliar cultural surrounds. Both chapters also examine the ways in which individuals in such circumstances undertake to reconstruct their identities. In Verity's case it is an identity as an expert language teacher, while in Pavlenko and Lantolf's study, it is an identity as a member of a new culture.

Pavlenko and Lantolf consider the powerful role that personal narratives play as mediating artifacts as people undertake to reform an identity. The documentation for their study is provided by the written narratives of individuals, largely academics, who have abandoned their original cultural surround and have struggled to take on a new surround along with its new mediational artifacts. They show how the process, at least for the people considered in their study, moves through stages of loss to stages of recovery. The former is marked by such phenomena as the weakening of one's linguistic system as a tool not only for social interaction, but as a tool for mediating one's own thinking processes, including above all one's inner voice. The latter is characterized by the appropriation of a new voice, and along with it, a new sense of identity, from the voices of those encountered in the new cultural circumstances. As the authors discuss, one of the major problems confronted by those passing through such a reformation process in a second culture relates to the need to construct a new history, or a new narrative, which can be relied upon as a mediational means to make sense of the events in the new circumstance.

Verity's study is based on a series of self-reflections contained in a daily journal in which the author documents her sense of loss and recovery of self-regulation as an expert language teacher upon entering Japanese educational culture. The journal evidences the author's struggle to construct a zone of proximal development which would allow her to scaffold herself, rather than seek external other-regulation, into a new identity as an expert teacher in accordance with a new set of cultural norms. For Verity, it was crucial for her to hear her own voice rather than the voice of others, because the problem she was confronting was not so much one of taking in new information as it was of restructuring her current knowledge. Much of the writing contained in Verity's journal can be considered private writing, and while similar in function to the strategic writing of writers, scholars, composers, etc. explored by John-Steiner (1985), it also served as self-acknowledgment, in a concrete form, of the author's sense of lost expertise. It also enabled her to overcome this sense of loss and ultimately to restructure her professional identity as an expert language teacher.

The chapter by McCafferty and Ahmed is also about private speech, not in its verbal but in its gestural manifestation. Speakers not only use gestures to repeat meanings that they externalize verbally, but they also use gestures to manifest meaning that is not verbally expressed. The authors report on one aspect of a larger and on-going cross-linguistic study of Japanese and English L2 learners. Informed by the research of David McNeill and his colleagues, the chapter discusses the appropriation of American metaphoric gestures that emerged in discussions of the concept of marriage by Japanese L2 naturalistic and classroom learners of English.

The topic of marriage is an especially appropriate one, given the marked differences in the way Japanese and American cultures construct this social institution. Metaphorics are one type of gesture in the taxonomy developed by McNeill. They represent abstract concepts, such as knowledge, language, narratives, questions, and the like. For instance, in American culture the cupping of the hand with the palm facing upward is a metaphorical gesture for a question. In comparing the gestural behaviors of classroom and naturalistic learners of English, McCafferty and Ahmed reveal that the naturalistic learners develop culturally appropriate metaphorics and other gestures of the abstract, which their classroom counterparts do not. The authors suggest that the appropriation of American metaphoric gestures by Japanese naturalistic learners implies that these individuals must also have shifted their conceptualization of marriage at the inner speech level, given the connections between inner speech and thought proposed in sociocultural theory. They also acknowledge another potential explanation to account for the performance of the naturalistic learners—appropriation of metaphorics is merely a way for the Japanese learners to signal their attempt to fit in to the American milieu on some surface level, without necessarily modifying their conceptual understanding of marriage. As the authors suggest, however, it is entirely possible that in attempting to do nothing more than 'fit in' the naturalistic Japanese learners eventually end up changing their concept as well.

The volume concludes with two chapters that consider ways in which sociocultural theory links up with other theories of language learning and language teaching. In his chapter, Thorne discusses the relevance of sociocultural theory for a general theory of second language learning. To carry out his project, he brings Vygotsky into contact with the writings of his contemporary, Mikhail Bakhtin as well as with the late twentieth century work of social philosophers, Pierre Bourdieu and Jurgen Habermas and the cognitive psychologist, Ragnar Rommetveit, among others. He argues for the need to build a pluralistic approach to second language acquisition, which integrates historically situated, and thus contingent, understandings of human activity with universalist oriented neurobiological research.

Van Lier, for his part, focuses on the development of an ecological perspective on language learning and teaching grounded in the principles of sociocultural theory and constructivist models of human activity. He brings Vygotsky's ideas on mediation into close contact with the work of psychologists such as J. J. Gibson, Gregory Bateson, and Uri Bronfrenbrenner. This leads him to develop an ecological metaphor of language learning and teaching which he proposes as an alternative to the familiar input–output metaphor. An ecological perspective compels us to reconceptualize learning as always and everywhere contextualized. Thus, not only do language and learner matter, but so do place, time, others, goals, and motives. In an ecological approach, because everything is connected to everything else, one cannot look at any single entity in isolation from the others, without compromising the integrity of the very processes one is trying to understand and foment. Similarly to Kramsch, van Lier also finds the integration of Peirce's notions of icon, index, and symbol a useful way of expanding Vygotsky's notion of language as a psychological tool.

Van Lier also argues for the need to consider new research and teaching methodologies which are appropriate for dealing with ecosystems and cautions against transferring the methodologies developed within the input–output metaphor in which teaching is seen as providing input and learning as taking in input, negotiated or otherwise. To this end, he considers the zone of proximal development as an especially promising way of organizing teaching/ learning activities in the classroom ecosystem, because learning, under the new metaphor, is about developing an ability to engage with, and participate in, a particular environment, whether it be the classroom or another cultural setting. For van Lier, this means that the learners, with support from the teacher and other learners, must assume control of their own participatory activities. Teaching must become much more flexible that it currently is. It must break from the notion of ready-made lessons that are rigidly adhered to in favor of improvisation. This does not mean an 'anything goes' approach, since teaching in the ZPD means developing a sensitivity to students' current abilities and their potential development.

Notes

1 Some sociocultural theorists have posited that changing tools, either physical or symbolic, will lead to a change in an activity. As will become clear in the discussion of activity theory below, an activity has a complex structure and merely changing the means (without altering its motive and goal) through which it is realized will not in itself give rise to a change in the activity. To be sure, changing tools may change the appearance of an activity, but this does not mean that its fundamental structure is altered.

2 Somewhat earlier, the dominant metaphor for the mind had been the telephone switchboard and going still further back to the time of Descartes, the mind was frequently thought of as the inner workings of a clock.

3 See Scinto (1987) for a study of the role of schooled literacy on cognitive development during onotogenesis.

4 Originally Vygotsky viewed the gestures of deaf children as arising from the natural, or biological mind and thus considered them to be a detriment to the development of higher, culturally mediated, mental systems. Later, however, he realized that deaf individuals did not merely gesture but relied

on a sophisticated and culturally constructed sign system to mediate their communicative and psychological activities.

5 For an interesting set of studies on the regulation of mediational means during ontogenesis, see the research of Wertsch (1985a: Chapter 6) and Wertsch and Hickman (1987). Also, see Wertsch, Minick, and Arns (1984) for a study on intercultural differences in the development of regulation.

6 It is interesting to note that recent work in mainstream cognitive science by people such as Carruthers and Clark supports a (meta)cognitive of speech—a viewpoint that is not radically different from that proposed by Vygotsky and his colleagues nearly a century ago. See Carruthers and Boucher (1998) for an informative collection of papers on this topic.

7 For an interesting and detailed discussion of the role of symbolic artifacts in thinking from a cross-cultural perspective, see Shore (1996).

8 Kozulin (1998: 113) reports on a study in which a young Ethiopian immigrant to Israel was asked to group familiar musical instruments. The young man could not conceive of any way of grouping them other than on the basis of which instruments were played together and on which social occasions they were played. Grouping them as a schooled Westerner might on the basis of the sound source (for example, wind instruments, strings, percussion, etc.) was not relevant in the context of Ethiopian culture. According to Kozulin, if the Ethiopians were to function appropriately in modern Israeli culture, they would have to learn how to classify according to a different scheme that was appropriate for their new context.

9 On the development of expertise and the differences between novice and expert performance see Dreyfus and Dreyfus (1986).

10 Wertsch (1998) has recently proposed the concept of *mastery*, or knowing how to do something, as an alternative to internalization. According to Wertsch, mastery, unlike internalization, recognizes that most mediated activity does not occur solely on the internal plain, but is almost always partially external. Although Wertsch's proposal is attractive to some degree, it does not explain the link between inner speech and mediation. Space does not permit me to pursue this interesting issue further here. For a fuller discussion of some of the problems associated with internalization and ways of dealing with them that differ from Wertsch's, see Newman, Griffen, and Cole (1989).

11 For a summary of an interesting series of studies on the relative successes of the US and Soviet educational systems in compelling their students to appropriate the official story of the 'colonization' or 'liberation' of their respective countries, see Wertsch (1998).

1 Sociocultural contributions to understanding the foreign and second language classroom

Richard Donato
University of Pittsburgh

Introduction[1]

Each week, as we gathered around the long conference table of the seminar room and immersed ourselves in sociocultural theory ... our group began to see more and more the usefulness of the fundamental theoretical tenets posited by Vygotsky and his followers. Through our discussions, we constructed the understanding that words construct thinking, that language is the principal mediational means available to individuals engaged in social interaction, and that human learning and development are inherently embedded in social relations. Then one week, when our discussion turned to the topic of discursive interactions in foreign language classrooms, one of the more practice-minded members of the group raised an interesting issue. 'Yes,' she wondered aloud, 'but can you have an instructional conversation in French I?'

(Sanford 1996)

The preceding extract is taken from a final paper of a student in a doctoral seminar on sociocultural theory and classroom language learning taught in the Department of Instruction and Learning at the University of Pittsburgh. The seminar, entitled *Sociocultural perspectives on foreign language learning, teaching and research*, was intended to introduce doctoral students in foreign language education to various concepts within sociocultural theory as interpretive tools for understanding the dynamics of life and learning in a foreign language classroom. Additionally, a course goal was to enable future classroom-based researchers to analyze classroom interactions as they unfolded in real time and to appraise experimental and quasi-experimental studies for their relevance to actual classroom practice (see Lantolf 1999). Finally, a rather ambitious yet essential goal was to understand the far-reaching educational implications of the claim that human mental functioning is related to the cultural, institutional, and historical settings in which human action is mediated by tools made available through participation in these societal contexts (Wertsch, Tulviste, and Hagstrom 1993; Wertsch 1998). Achieving this last goal became all the more complex when faced with the standard theories of language development that feature the individual as a generic and autonomous knower using individualistic and inaccessible cognitive processes—topics about which these students were familiar. Overcoming the dichotomy between the individual and the social, understanding deeply the differing and incommensurable theoretical perspectives in language acquisition studies, and drawing implications for language education research and instruction were themes that arose frequently and vigorously throughout the course.

The purpose of this chapter is to present, through the perspectives of the students in this seminar, how an array of language teaching professionals pursuing a doctoral degree in foreign language education made use of the interpretive tools of sociocultural theory to examine the dynamics of classroom foreign language instruction and learning. In what follows, I briefly describe the nature of the course followed by summaries of student projects.[2] The studies have been selected to represent various instructional contexts (primary, secondary, and tertiary foreign and second language classrooms) and ages of learners (elementary school children to adults). Each study is followed by a commentary highlighting the contribution of sociocultural theory to the question posed, a brief appraisal of the study, and areas for further inquiry. I conclude with a discussion of a few of the major themes of sociocultural theory emerging from the student projects and compare them to traditional understandings of scientific research on language learning. Through the lens of these students' classroom-based projects, I hope to provide insight into areas where new connections between sociocultural theory and classroom research can be made. In this way, I attempt to uncover how sociocultural theory can begin to unravel the complexities of instructional interactions in language classrooms. In the spirit of collective activity (Petrovsky 1985), discursive interanimation (Vološinov 1973; Bakhtin 1981), and the co-constructed nature of learning and development (Donato 1994; Swain 1995; Wells 1996), I allow the voices of my students to tell the story.

Apprenticing students into sociocultural theory

The students

The seminar was composed of eight doctoral students and two post-doctoral students interested in learning about sociocultural approaches to foreign language instruction and research. Seven of the doctoral students were completing degrees in foreign language education and one was enrolled in the doctoral program in French literature. This student also served as the teaching assistant co-ordinator in the University's Department of French and

Italian. Among the seven doctoral students in foreign language education, two had extensive full-time ESL and EFL teaching experience, two were international students who had taught EFL in their respective countries, one was a Japanese language instructor in a local university, one was a Chinese language instructor at the University, and one was a high school teacher of Russian. Two of these students (the Russian teacher and one ESL instructor) were full-time students in foreign language education, taught courses in language teaching methodology and served as supervisors for the clinical experiences of pre-service language teachers. The students represented a variety of teaching backgrounds and cultures and brought to the seminar a wide array of experiences in language instruction and teacher supervision. All students but one had taken courses on mainstream second language acquisition theory and research and experimental research design. The students also possessed intimate knowledge of language teaching but were relatively novice concerning sociocultural theory. As will be shown, their questions about instruction were anchored in the realities of classrooms. Thus, their investigations of language teaching become all the more interesting and revealing of how sociocultural theory can address salient issues of language instruction.

The seminar

The class was divided into two parts. The first part of the class (approximately four weeks) reviewed five research traditions specifically applied to foreign language/ESL classroom—correlational studies, case studies, survey research, experimental research, and ethnographic research. These five traditions were studied for their underlying epistemologies and ontology. During the course, students addressed issues of rigor in research, generalizable findings vs. the situated nature of learning (Rogoff and Lave 1984; Lave and Wenger 1991; Miles and Huberman 1994), the biological and natural and the cultural and historical perspective on development (Vygotsky 1986), and the assumptions research makes about teaching and learning (Phillips 1995). Students were challenged to take seriously lessons from the sociology of science. That is, they discovered that it may be unwise to interpret paradigm shifts in educational research in terms of the succession of disciplinary truths, the emergence of more refined and exacting methods, and a continually improving 'state of the art' (Luke 1996).

After our discussion of research in mainstream Western social science, we moved to sociocultural theory and Vygotskyan perspectives on learning and development (for example, Vygotsky 1986; Lantolf and Pavlenko 1995). The class was organized around four themes: (a) language, cognition, and communities; (b) language-based theories of learning and semiotic mediation; (c) private speech; and (d) activity theory. As one course requirement, students conducted a classroom-based study on a self-selected topic from a sociocultural perspective. The students were instructed to motivate their study theoretically, observe one or more classes, record and transcribe interactions, and stay close to the discourse in their analysis. During conferences about their projects, students formulated questions and connected these questions to class discussions, readings, and their own teaching background. They also experienced first-hand the recursive process of describing, analyzing, and interpreting qualitative data (Wolcott 1994).

The outcome of this seminar was eight research projects from a sociocultural perspective on a variety of classroom-based topics, in diverse instructional contexts, and with learners of different ages. In the interest of space, I will consider only five of these studies. As a prelude to reading and understanding these studies, it is important to point out that although the studies are empirical, they are not experimental. The studies reported here follow a research paradigm associated with naturalistic inquiry. Studies within this research tradition do not control variables or introduce treatments on subjects. Rather, they seek to understand the complexity of the classroom through such research methods as case studies, discourse analysis, ethnographies, narrative inquiry, grounded theory, and biography. (See Bailey and Nunan 1996 for a collection of research studies within this framework.) Additionally, they are constructed within their own theoretical and philosophical frameworks and subject to their own standards of quality and verification (Creswell 1998). Attempts to evaluate these studies on standards from the quantitative paradigm (for example, generalizability), are unfair and inaccurate. Further, Ellis (1997: 34) has argued that investigations of classroom learners need to be conducted on classrooms, not just in classrooms. Following Ellis' suggestion and the long tradition of research within the qualitative paradigm, naturalistic investigations of classrooms are, therefore, not flawed studies. In contrast to experimental methods, naturalistic inquiry holds as its primary objective to preserve the instructional completeness of classroom events, including the discursive interactions that occur there, to illuminate the topic under investigation (Creswell 1994).

The studies that follow will be organized around three sociocultural themes: (a) private speech; (b) language-based theories of learning and semiotic mediation; and (c) activity theory. While reading these studies, the three central themes will be explained, illustrated, and applied to the issue of classroom language learning. Additionally, the studies will show how sociocultural theory can contribute to a richer understanding of the foreign and second language classroom in which these graduate students work.

Classroom-based research projects

Private speech

In his study, Smith (1996) applies the concept of private speech to an area not yet researched in the literature—direct instruction during grammar lessons in an ESL class. Citing the work of McCafferty (1994a), Frawley and Lantolf (1985), and Appel and Lantolf (1994), Smith operationalizes private speech as 'a verbal attempt to gain self-regulation during problem-solving tasks, distinguishable from the interpersonal communication into which it is often interwoven, and the result of stress that can accompany the task of constructing meaning in L1 or L2'. (See Diaz and Berk 1992, for a fuller discussion of the features of private speech.) Smith examines a grammar class of high intermediate ESL students and claims that private speech is revealed in one learner as she struggles with understanding the grammatical explanation and examples of the teacher. He builds his argument from theory and data. From theory, he argues that because interlocutors naturally seek to establish coherent discourse (for example, Gricean co-operative principles), private speech can arise in, and be mistaken for, a discussion. His data, collected during a grammar lesson on gerunds and infinitives, involve the instructor explaining the difference between the two structures *mean* + infinitive and *mean* + gerund (for example, *She meant to go to the library* vs. *She meant going to the library*). At the close of the teacher's presentation, one student still expressed difficulty understanding the distinction between *mean* + infinitive for expressing intention and *mean* + gerund for expressing clarification. In the following protocol, Smith shows how the teacher skillfully worked with the student as she struggled to comprehend the relevant sentences. The teacher does not respond negatively to the student's confusion, marked linguistically by repetitions, hesitations, and incomprehensible utterances, all aspects of her private speech, according to Smith. He states further that the teacher does not react like a 'lifeguard ready to dive in as soon as the student goes under' or, perhaps more appropriately, as soon as private speech surfaces.

Protocol 1: I'm puzzling through now.

1   S: I'm puzzling through now.
2   T: OK.
3   S: (laughs)
4   T: OK ... does this help to make any more sense?
5   S: So, could you change ...?
6   T: OK, yes?
7   S: Could you change the verb?
8   T: OK.
9   S: (Laughs) because ... (laughs) ... because ...
10 T: Which verb do you want to change?

11 S: Well ... so the ... uh ... the teacher ... you know ... uh ... I ... I
12   believe that 'mean' has many meanings. Some ... some ... some ...
13 T: OK.
14 S: It means ... means ... means ... 'I mean ... I mean to do this,' means
15   the, you know, ... I have some ... I found some meaning to do this
16   somethin'.
17 T: Uh huh.
18 S: But the ... uh, on the other hand, the 'means' just mean, you know,
19   explain their meaning.
20 T: Yeah.
21 S: Well, so the ... I believe that ... this ... in this case the teacher meant,
22   you know, uh, just meaning, but the, uh, you know, have a serious
23   idea, uh, could you ... could you change the verb?
24 T: You wanna change the verb 'mean'? Is this the verb you wanna
25   change?
26 S: Yes, please
        (The teacher goes on to explain that the verb 'to mean' plus
        infinitive or gerund controls the different meanings.)
27 T: The trouble is ... (laughs and students join in laughing) ... if I
28   change the verb, I can't teach you the teaching point.
        (The teacher provides more examples and other students help to
        explain the difference.)
29 S: I see. Uh huh ... Oh!
30 T: Does this help?
31 S: Yes. Great.

(Smith 1996)

In Protocol 1, Smith shows how, through a series of backchannel cues (i.e. expressions that encourage the speaker to continue such as, *Yeah*, *OK*, and *Uh huh*), the teacher assumes the status of listener allowing the student to make public her problem-solving talk (lines 6, 8, 13, 17, 20). Smith also states that the protocol represents in reality two puzzles—the student's attempt to understand the meaning of the verb (lines 1, 11–12, 18–19, 21–23) and the teacher's effort to assist and still maintain the lesson objective (lines 27–28). Together teacher and student construct this understanding and Smith concludes that this co-construction process is triggered through the externalization of the student's thinking and the tolerant and persevering responses of the teacher.

Commentary 1

Smith's study contributes to understanding the intersubjective nature of learning (Rommetveit 1985), the relationship between speaking and thinking (Vygotsky 1986), and the pedagogical importance of recognizing that students mediate their thinking in private speech as they 'puzzle through' difficult concepts and communicative encounters (Diaz and Berk 1992; Ahmed 1994; Antón and DiCamilla 1998). Two areas not sufficiently explored in the study, yet clearly suggested by the protocol, are a careful linguistic analysis of private speech (Appel, 1986; DiCamilla and Lantolf 1994) and a critical discussion of the dichotomy between private speech and social speech. As Wells (1998) has pointed out, 'all speech in a dialogic context has both functions simultaneously ... action taken with others is always both social and individual' (*ibid.*: 349). That is, overt speech in the social context of problem solving is made public for both the speaker and the hearer. Nevertheless, this study reveals that it is unwise to assume that all classroom talk is composed of 'between-person' meanings to be sent and received. Indeed, the student announced to the class that 'she was puzzling through now', indicating her need to work through her problem aloud.[3] The private verbalizations (see Swain this volume) of the learner appear to serve several functions. They indicate, at the same time, appeals for assistance, statements of student's private orientation to the explanation (line 1, line 11–12, and line 21), the externalization of one's thinking and problem solving, and evidence that a learner's seemingly incomprehensible utterances can serve as a cognitive tool for mediating and navigating a learner and teacher to eventual shared understandings and problem solutions (see Roebuck this volume). Finally, this study suggests that a fruitful line of inquiry within the private speech research agenda is to examine more fully the concept of private speech during teacher-fronted instruction. Classroom discourse is all too often analyzed for its social, communicative value (Johnson 1995) leaving the cognitive function of instructional talk relatively unexamined (Frawley and Lantolf 1985; Platt and Brooks 1994; Lantolf 1997).

Language-based theories of learning and semiotic mediation

A second group of studies examined classroom discourse as a mediational tool for language development, in particular regarding the use of Instructional Conversations (Tharp and Gallimore 1988, 1991; Goldenberg 1991). Instructional conversations are based on Vygotsky's notion that the origins of learning, development, and human action may be traced to conversation and the semiotic mediation that these conversations provide the novice.[4] Further, Vygotsky's theory of learning and development implies that learning is also a form of language socialization between individuals and not merely information processing carried out solo by an individual. Advocates of instructional conversations find inspiration for their research in the concepts of scaffolding (Wood, Bruner, and Ross 1976), guided participation (Rogoff 1990), and language-based theories of learning (Green 1983a, 1983b; Cazden 1988; Donato and Adair-Hauck 1992; Brooks 1993; Aljaafreh and Lantolf 1994; Gee 1994; Wells 1994; Lantolf and Aljaafreh 1995; Hall 1995a and b).

Instructional conversations reflect Vygotsky's instrumental method (Yaroshevsky 1989) which includes two important ideas about language and learning. First, on the interpsychological plane, children learn to use sign systems, notably language, as psychological tools to communicate and share cultural meanings. Second, on the intrapsychological plane, the use of these cultural signs affects the child's learning and cognitive development. Through signs children learn, therefore, to organize their inner and outer worlds. Instructional conversations are said to be instrumental to cognitive development in the sense that they reconstruct informal conversations (for example, a parent verbally mediating a child to complete a task) within a formal educational setting. For example, a classroom episode can be *conversational* in its attention to coherence, distributed turn taking, spontaneity and unpredictability, and its focus on new information. These conversations can also be *instructional* because teachers shape the discussion toward a curricular goal, build or activate background knowledge in students, engage at times in direct instruction or modeling, and promote more complex language and expression by using questions to help students expand, elaborate, or restate. Instructional conversations are relevant to language classrooms because they socialize students into language learning in pragmatically rich contexts that facilitate language growth and development and provide opportunities for experiencing how language is used outside of the classroom. As a framework for analyzing classroom talk, instructional conversations capture a wider range of communicative and cognitive functions of talk than current models of input, output, and interaction.

Can you do this in French I?

Attempting to answer the question posed in the student's comments at the beginning of this paper, 'Yes, but can you have an instructional conversation in French I?', two studies (Sanford 1996; Todhunter 1996) explore the question of instructional conversations in elementary and intermediate foreign language classes. The motivation for these two studies was the observation that all studies of instructional conversation had been carried out in an L1 setting or with fairly advanced ESL learners during text-based discussions. The question remained, can an instructor have an instructional conversation in the L2 that is topically coherent, extended, and meaningful in a beginning foreign language class where students have limited linguistic resources? For this reason, Sanford and Todhunter searched for instructional conversations in elementary and intermediate foreign language classrooms. Sanford's (1996) study was carried out in a first semester college French language course; Todhunter's (1996) study was conducted in a high school (grades 11 and 12) third-year Spanish class. In both classes the instructors were relatively novice (an MA teaching assistant and an intern earning an instructional certificate in foreign language teaching) and their students were fulfilling language requirements for high school and college graduation.

Using the categories for identifying and coding instructional conversations as outlined by Tharp and Gallimore (1991) and Dalton and Sison (1995),[5] the studies reveal that instructional conversations take place in the target language but not as the core lesson or consistently throughout the class period. Additionally, in both the college and high school language class, instructional conversations were located outside the planned lesson and were only marginally connected to the lesson objective. In the case of the high school classroom, Todhunter found that across several episodes of the interactive practice (Hall 1995a and b; Hall and Brooks 1996) she labeled 'working with new vocabulary', the teacher followed a predictable pattern: (a) management (or setting up the vocabulary practice exercise); (b) exercise (or completing textbook exercises using the new vocabulary); and (c) extension (or spontaneous questions and comments by students and teacher embedded within the practice exercise). Todhunter's data show how the teacher and students engage in communication that is conversational and also instructional *only* when they departed from the traditional, textbook-based forms of contextualized language practice most commonly associated with foreign language classrooms. That is, management talk and extension activities are the sites of instructional conversations and not the 'contextualized' exercises of the textbook. Todhunter states that 'interestingly, it is management interactions and extension activities that show features of instructional conversation most consistently and impressively.' Another notable finding is that these instructional conversations occurred five times during a 4.8 minute vocabulary practice exercise. Although the extension activities accounted for 46 per cent of the total vocabulary practice, their marginal position in the teacher's presentation made them disjointed and fleeting. That is, they were not consecutive but linked to the practicing of the vocabulary word in question. In one case, an instructional conversation located within an extension activity lasted only 32 seconds before being interrupted by the onset of the new word for repetition and practice.

Protocol 2: ¡Es la mentira!

(End of exercise)
32 T: Extrañar.
33 Ss: (repeating aloud) Extrañar.

(Beginning of extension activity)
34 T: Yo extrañé mucho a ustedes ayer *(sic.)*.
35 S1: ¿Por qué?
36 T: Porque me gusta estar en la escuela.
37 S2: ¡Es la mentira!
38 T: Yo fui a Expomart ayer para muchas entrevistas para empleos.
39   ¡Para el trabajo, no? En otras ciudades para enseñar.

40   Entrevistas. ¿Qué son 'entrevistas'?
41 S3: Interviews.

(Beginning of exercise)
42 T: Sí. Imaginarse.
43 Ss: (repeating aloud) Imaginarse.

(Todhunter 1996)

Todhunter points out that this 32 seconds of discourse satisfies the requirements of instructional conversation because student comments are not elicited solely by the teacher (lines 35 and 37), students share the responsibility for directing the discourse (line 35), the teacher's responses are contingent upon student-initiated utterances (lines 36, 38–40), the talk is guided by the global topic of the teacher's absence on the previous day (line 34), and the teacher directly provides the word *interview* in Spanish (lines 38–40). The instructional conversation concludes with the teacher redirecting attention to the exercise by announcing the next vocabulary word to practice, *to imagine*. The problem Todhunter raises is that, although close to half of the discourse generated in a five-minute vocabulary exercise qualifies as instructional conversation, these coherent, multi-party conversations are disconnected and are not sustained. Thus, the pragmatic appropriateness of the larger discourse into which these instructional conversations are embedded is questionable. The issue seems to be, therefore, for this Spanish 3 class, not the presence or absence of instructional conversation, but rather its detached, sporadic nature, and lack of continuity across the teacher's planned lesson.

Sanford (1996) finds similar instructional conversations in a first semester French course. During activities that are ostensibly communicative, Sanford argues that very little instructional conversation takes place. Rather, he states, when the teacher steps out of her position of authority and talks to the class as a co-participant in the interaction, instructional conversations emerge.[6] In the following protocol, the teacher digresses from her routine Inquiry-Response-Evaluation (I-R-E) interaction (Mehan 1979) for 53 seconds during student reports after a paired-interview activity. During this brief period, Sanford observes that an instructional conversation took place in elementary language classes.

Protocol 3: Okay, but ... can you do that in French I?

= indicates linked utterances
44 T: Dites-moi ... quelles sont les caractéristiques d'un Bélier?
45 S1: Ah ... elles sont sérieuses.
46 T: Oui, les Béliers sont sérieux, et=
(Student 2 announces to the class that Russell, who is an Aries, had lots to drink thus indicating that he is not serious.)
47 S2: =Russell bu beaucoup.

48   S3: Elle (pointing to Annie) est ... comment-allez. ... uhm ...
            comment dit-on 'stubborn'?
49   T: Pourquoi? Annie est têtue? Non. 'Stubborn'?
50   S3: Yeah ... ah ... oui, 'stubborn'. comment=
51   T: =Têtue.
52   S3: Elle (pointing to Annie) très têtue.
(laughter)
53   T: Non, elle n'est pas têtue. Elle sait ce qu'elle veut.
54   C'est pas vrai Annie?
55   S4: (Annie speaks to Bill) Tu es stupide.
(laughter)
56   T: De quel signe es-tu, Bill?

(Sanford 1996)

The instructional conversation in Protocol 3, according to Sanford, is characterized by high student participation (four students interacting with each other and the teacher), a thematic focus (line 44), utterances linked topically to the larger theme of the discourse, one student self-correction (line 52), direct teaching of the word 'stubborn' in French (lines 49–51), and feedback by the teacher prompting linguistic elaboration by the student (lines 49, 53, and 54). He also notes that the obdurate pattern of teacher–student–teacher exchange had been replaced by a pattern where the teacher responds to comments of one student (line 46), poses questions of another (lines 49 and 53–54), and allows for student self-selected turns. He concludes that 'the traditional pattern of classroom interaction has become blurred because for one brief moment students and teachers alike become equal members of the classroom discourse community.' In both of these studies, the students have set out in search of instructional conversations and have located them for brief periods of time outside the planned lesson and during spontaneous detours that traditionally are not considered instructional (see Brooks 1993).

Scaffolding in the FLES classroom
Takahashi's (1998) study, conducted in an elementary school Japanese class and, based on the work on scaffolding by Wood, Bruner, and Ross (1976) and Donato (1994), investigated how student utterances developed over time in a collaborative context. Using a data set from a larger four-year study of Japanese language learning in an American elementary school (Donato, Antonek, and Tucker 1994; Donato, Antonek, and Tucker 1996; Tucker, Donato, and Antonek 1996), Takahashi looks at videotapes of classroom interactions across three years and at intervals of approximately nine months—September 1994, May 1995, and March 1996. The students were in a combined kindergarten–first grade class and first and second grade class. Therefore, over the three years of data collection, a cohort of students remained constant.

Takahashi's analysis indicates that as students progress in their language learning they become better able to provide mutual assistance during classroom activities. In addition, students demonstrate spontaneity with the language, for example, bursting into Japanese song, telling each other vocabulary words when needed, and collectively scaffolding (see Donato 1994) each other's production. In the first-year data, Takahashi shows that students were mainly producing one-word utterances that were repetitions after the teacher, and that the consistent pattern of classroom interaction was teacher–student(s)–teacher. That is, students only responded when asked to do so by the teacher. By year two, she notes that, in addition to more complex language, the children added unexpected comments to the teacher's utterances and assisted and scaffolded[7] each other actively during production. The following protocol shows how a child is assisted during a student-fronted presentation by the other children while attempting to describe a picture from a story. A secondary focus of this particular lesson was to have students practice different modes of the verb such as *eats*, *wants to eat*, and *does not eat*.

Protocol 4: I want, I want, I want …

(Teacher shows a picture of a boy eating an apple.)
57   T: Hai.
58   S1:   Denisu wa ringo o tabemasu. Masu!
59   T: Denisu wa ringo o tabemasu, ii desu ne. Mary? (Mary = S2)
(Teacher shows a picture of a boy who is thinking about eating an apple.)
60   S2:   Denisu wa ringo o tabe …
61   T: Tabe …?
62   S2:   Tabemasu.
63   S3:   (directed to S2) Tabetai. Tabemasu. Tabemasen.
(Teacher begins singing the 'I want' song.)
64   T: Remember this song? Tai, tai, tai.
(The students begin singing along with the teacher.)
65   T/Ss: Tai tai, tai, nomitai, tabetai, hon yomitai, netai, kaitai, terebi mitai.
66   T: Haaaai, tabetai! Ii desu ka? Tabetai.
67   Ss: Tabetai.
68   T: Tabetai, hai, Mary?
69   S2:   Denisu wa ringo o tabetai.
70   T: Hai, ii desu ne!

(Takahashi 1998)

The interaction begins with the child producing a sentence containing the verb form *eats* (line 58) rather than the *wants to* construction (line 67), in this case the appropriate verb form for the picture she is describing. Another child is then observed to begin spontaneously supplying the various forms of the verb (line 63) followed by the teacher leading the class in a song where the verb *wants to eat* and other similar verb constructions were embedded (lines

64–65). After this active assistance by the teacher and the other children, the student produces the correct verb form (line 69), uses the topicalizing and direct object particles *wa* and *o* correctly, and supplies the direct object *apple*. Takahashi states that 'although the child's actual developmental level did not allow her to accomplish this linguistic task, guidance from her peers and her teacher allowed her to outperform her present competence' (see Cazden 1981). According to Takahashi, the protocol illustrates clearly that in this Japanese class, learning and teaching were realized as a co-constructed process within the children's zones of proximal development. Additionally, the protocol represents a good example of how learners can and do scaffold each other's performance. This claim is based on the fact that the children were not solving a problem collaboratively, but rather assisting a classmate who was engaged in a student-fronted presentation. That is, no child intended to assume full responsibility for the child's presentation, only one child was given the task of retelling the story, and no child showed a desire to take control of the presentation from the student speaker. The goal of the assistance from the other children was to 'hand over control of the task to the learner' (Wells 1998: 346) and not to distribute the task among class members. An important lesson of this protocol is that, as Wells suggests, to define forms of peer assistance requires a knowledge of the task, goals of the participants, and instructional context (Donato 1988).

In the third year data, Takahashi notes similar interaction patterns of teacher scaffolding and student assistance. She also observes that teacher assistance has been reduced and that students play a more active role during the class. Classroom participation is characterized by extended sequences of student–student exchanges and children taking on the scaffolding role of the teacher. In the interest of space, I will not provide the protocol but in one interaction children were observed to mediate lexical recall by initiating the singing of a class song. Following this help, the children were observed to engage in the co-construction of a complex Japanese structure dealing with the existence of animate objects and resulting in one child producing the sentence *Akachan wa tsukue no ue ni *i-mas-u**. (The baby *is* on top of the desk.)

That the child ends his utterance with the singing of *i-mas-u* reveals the mediating effects of the song on the child's ability to recall and construct this utterance. It is also noteworthy that the assistance provided by the children was also similar to that observed in the teacher at an earlier time. This observation indicates that the children are not learning only Japanese from their teacher but also, through her dynamic assistance (Tharp and Gallimore 1988; Rogoff 1990), ways of mediating their own and each other's learning. Takahashi states that while in 1994 children's utterances were primarily echoes of what the teacher said, by 1995 and 1996 the children produced self-initiated utterances, took turns with each other more regularly, and collaboratively constructed sentences through mutual assistance. Her study is also a good example of how interaction within the zone of proximal development changes over time (in this case three years) and how the assistance once offered by the teacher is internalized by the children and now used as a tool to provide mediation to each other.

Commentary 2

The three research projects cited above are noteworthy for several reasons. First, concepts drawn from sociocultural theory provided access to a range of language learning phenomena not easily captured under experimental conditions. Indeed, several of the findings dealing with the occurrence of spontaneous instructional conversations in lessons would not easily be detected in narrowly controlled conditions of an experimental study. Spontaneity and digression from task demands are not desirable and acceptable behaviors during experimental studies, even if learners in the classroom frequently behave in this way (Foster 1998; Lantolf 1999). Second, the longitudinal focus of Takahashi's study provides a profile of in-class discourse development that reflects language growth and target language classroom participation patterns over time. Longitudinal studies of classroom discourse development across several years of instruction are rare in the literature and these data are much needed particularly in the area of early language learning (Donato, Antonek, and Tucker 1996).

Third, aside from these important findings, one implicit yet prevailing perspective on learning merits attention. Each of these three projects shifts the governing concept of learning away from the acquisition metaphor toward metaphors of participation. As Sfard (1998) points out, the dichotomy between metaphors of acquisition and participation—having or possessing something by a recipient vs. becoming a participant in various aspects of practice, discourse, activity, and community—cannot be reduced to simplistic distinctions between the individual and the social. Clearly, the social is not absent in the acquisition metaphor (see for example, Gass 1997) and acquisition in the form of internalized social practices and conversation is not absent from the participation metaphor (Hall 1995b; Bruffee 1994). Thus, it may also be unwise to adopt one metaphor over the other (Sfard 1998).

The issue here is not the validity of metaphorical projections of development *per se*, but the lack of awareness that all sociocognitive phenomena are constructed and explained in metaphors in the first place. Entailed in this lack of awareness is the danger of overlooking far-reaching implications about learning that derive from the adoption of one metaphor or another. For example, if one adopts as the dominant metaphor of acquisition—the 'taking in' and possessing of knowledge—as indices of achievement, then failure to achieve may be explained away by reference to an individual's low aptitude, lack of motivation, or inappropriate learning strategies. If one adopts the participation metaphor, alternate reasons for an individual's failure to achieve could be posited, such as the individual's marginalization from a community of practice, insufficient mediation from an expert, or scant access to a learning community. Further, the acquisition metaphor requires independent evidence of what was learned after instructional treatment, often taking the form of a post- or delayed post-test. In contrast, the participation metaphor finds evidence for learning in an individual's growing and widening activity in a community carried out through shared practices of discourse with expert participants. From this perspective, in the classrooms investigated by Todhunter, Sanford, and Takahashi, it can be said that learning was made visible through the increasing participation and emergent communication of these learners with their teachers and each other, an observable feature of these classroom interactions that cannot be denied. Whether one accepts the participation view for evidence of language development is, therefore, a matter of one's preferred metaphorical projection.

What is striking about the preceding research projects, and also for sociocultural research in general, is that, as Sfard states, 'until recently, no real attempt to transgress the boundaries of the acquisition metaphor was made. The metaphor just did not look like a metaphor at all' (*ibid.*: 7). Edwards (1997) echoes this claim when he states that 'the objection to cognitive science is not that it pursues a metaphor ... of human nature as if we were digital computers, but that it tends to proceed as if that were not metaphorical' (*ibid.*: 31). The research studies above represent, therefore, an act of transgression, perhaps unwittingly so, to understand learning in a new way and with new conceptual and interpretive tools. This non-conformity is not a trivial matter and represents divergent ontologies that 'draw on two radically different answers to the fundamental question. "What is this thing called learning?"' (Sfard 1998: 7).[8] This terminology is not a case of 'old wine in new skins' but a perspective that fulfills a different educational goal and defines learning in a different way. Adopting participation as the prevailing metaphor for learning 'defies the traditional distinction between cognition and affect, brings social factors to the fore, and thus deals with an incomparable wider range of possibly relevant aspects' (Sfard 1998: 12) as stated in the opening of Commentary 2.

Activity theory

A final research project I will present involves the application of activity theory (Wertsch 1981) to an intermediate ESL writing class. Inspired by the work of Coughlan and Duff (1994), Wang (1996) observes how the same small-group task is realized in different ways depending on how the group members operationalize the goal of the activity. That is, as Wang shows, classroom group work is best conceived as internal goal-directed actions of the students rather than passive adherence to external task demands (Brooks and Donato 1994). Wang also documents the teacher's frustration at not understanding why her students could not follow directions and why they approached the task in different and unpredictable ways.

The task required students to rank order a list of seven effects of excessive TV viewing, from the most immediate to the most remote effect (for example, eyestrain, getting fat, less reading, lack of communication in the household, loneliness, more violent crime). Wang analyzes the discussion of two groups as they report their consensus ranking back to the teacher. The protocols show clearly the role of student agency (Shieh and Donato 1996) in defining the goal of the activity and the unique situational definitions (Wertsch 1985a) the students brought to the task. The first protocol involves the teacher questioning the group concerning their placement of 'more violent crimes' as a more immediate effect of TV viewing before 'getting fat'.

Protocol 5: Group A Violent crime and eyestrain

71   T: OK, you said that you are organizing them by immediate to
72   remote?
73   S1: Yes.
(Teacher points to 'more violent crime' which is placed before 'eyestrain'.)
74   T: Uh, but this one … is this one immediate or remote?
75   S2: I said in between but …
76   T: Oh, you said in between=
77   S2: It (more violent crime) could be immediate but 'eyestrain' or 'get
78   fat' in some way they are remote but they are also immediate.
79   T: But what is the relationship here (pointing to 'more crime')? I mean
80   what do you see would be the relationship between watching TV
81   and more violence?
82   S2: Well you take children for example. Uhm, there is some influence
83   on children in a long term effect. They can become a criminal or
84   more violent. This is also a sociological problem.
85   T: OK, so, I guess my question is why do you want to put this one
86   ('more crime') which seems to be more remote in between this
87   ('eyestrain') and this ('get fat')?
88   S2: OK, well, because we consider we don't agree with most of them.

(Wang 1996)

In this interaction the teacher expresses confusion concerning the rank-ordering of 'violent crimes' before 'weight gain' (line 74). The discussion with the group (lines 75–87) indicates that the students have not approached the task as the teacher intended because they do not agree with the items on the list (line 88). Wang states that the goal of the students was not to ratify the teacher's perspective of the task, that is, her privileged rank-ordering of the list visible in the discourse (lines 85–87). The last line (line 88) of the protocol reveals that, as agents of their own learning activity, students alter rigidly constrained classroom tasks.

The second group orients itself differently to the same rank-ordering task. In this protocol, one student decides to rank-order the list from 'more remote to more immediate' rather than to conform to the task requiring the opposite ordering procedure, i.e. 'from immediate to remote.'[9]

Protocol 6:   Group B   This immediate–remote thing

```
 89   T:   OK, now, let's go to the other group and see is there any other you
 90         would change here?
 91   S3:  Uh, yes, we agree … 2-3-1-6-7-4-5.
 92   S2:  (student from group A) What … what … what?
 93   S3:  2-3=
 94   T:   =OK, 2, 3 (writing on the board)=
 95   S3:  =1-6-7-4-5.
 96   T:   OK, so …
 97   S3:  Remote=
 98   T:   Two … what was two? Oh, OK, crime? so you are going from,
 99         you said you, what's the organization pattern here?
100   S3:  We organized from remote to immediate … and … yeah, because
101         2-3-1-6 are very far I think.
102   T:   Are very … ? (keeps writing at the board)
```
(As the teacher transforms the numbers into words on the board, the following conversation takes place between two students in Group B.)
```
103   S4:  (to S3) are eyestrain more remote or more crime?
```
(S4 causes S3 to redefine the task to conform with task requirements)
```
104:  S3:  Yea, yea, yea, one (eyestrain) … one is close … one is the first.
105:  S4:  Uh huh, yes.
106   S3:  Yea, one is the uh=
107   S4:  =is immediate.
```
(The teacher overhears the conversation.)
```
108   T:   One, uh, one is =immediate= rather than remote.
109   S3:  =immediate=
110   S4:  =immediate= … rather than remote=
111   T:   OK, where do you want to move this one to? Oh, excuse me, you
112         said you want to go from remote to immediate (sounds of
            confusion).
113   S3:  Yea, I think so. (The class laughs. S3 addresses S4.) But that you,
114         you, you are agree with my opinion?
115   S4:  (laughing) Yes, yes, yes.
116   S3   Yea! (The class and S3 all laugh.)
117   T:   OK. Well, maybe we'll just forget about this immediate–remote
118         thing and just do things that could go together naturally.
```

(Wang 1996)

Protocol 6 reveals that one student (S3) has reversed the ordering procedure of the task (line 100), the group has not reached consensus in the same way as the first group (lines 113–14), and the teacher has redefined the task for herself and the class (lines 117–18) based on the group's redefinition of the task. It is also interesting to note differences in group reporting. Group B reports to the teacher using numbers as if speaking in code (lines 91, 93, and 95) and demonstrates their failure to act as a cohesive group by their overt lack of agreement, whereas Group A reaches consensus by 'agreeing to disagree' with the task. The two distinct goals—the first, to transform the contents of the task and, the second, to change the rank-ordering rules—arouse the teacher to change the task for the class by abandoning the 'immediate–remote thing' in favor of 'just things that go together naturally' (lines 117–18). Wang concludes, therefore, that 'we see in the two student groups and in the teacher three emergent and differing operational compositions [of the same classroom task].'

Commentary 3

Several important conclusions from this study can be made. First, tasks are not generalizable because activities vary according to participants and circumstances. Second, tasks do not manipulate learners to act in certain ways because participants invest their own goals, actions, cultural background, and beliefs (i.e. their agency) into tasks and, thus, transform them. Third, a seemingly irrelevant, trivial task can, in fact, supply important forms of mediation helping students to gain control over language and task procedures. As Wang demonstrates, tasks are not externally defined on the basis of task procedures but internally defined on the basis of participant goals, desires, and motivations (Coughlan and Duff 1994). Finally, she states that teachers need to focus less on task outcomes and more on students' orientations and multiple goals during the conduct of classroom tasks (Brooks and Donato 1994). Here again we see an orientation toward participation as the predominant metaphor for learning rather than independent measures of the accumulation of knowledge. Classroom language learning tasks are thus best seen as uniquely situated, emergent interactions based on participants' goals and subgoals and not merely task objectives and invariant task procedures. This line of research makes a valuable technical and practical contribution to the work of task-based instruction (Ellis 1998; Crookes and Gass 1993a, 1993b).

Conclusion

This brief overview of five studies has demonstrated the usefulness of sociocultural theory for examining important and relevant psychological, affective, linguistic, social, and individual conditions of foreign and second language classrooms. As Ellis has argued (1998: 56), technical knowledge (acquired deliberately though empirical study) and practical knowledge (acquired implicitly and intuitively through practice) need to be aligned through investigations of classrooms that treat experimental research findings as provisional specifications to be experienced and observed in practice. The research projects I have summarized provide examples of the intersection of practical knowledge, technical knowledge, and theory for analyzing the reality of classroom language learning. Three themes emerge from these studies that directly address the question of the contribution of sociocultural theory to advancing both practical and technical knowledge in the field of foreign and second language instruction.

First, sociocultural theory underscores the importance of conceptualizing language learning as a developmental *process mediated by semiotic resources* appropriated from the classroom (Wertsch 1991, 1998). These semiotic resources include print materials, the physical environment, gestures, and, most notably, classroom discourse. This theme contrasts sharply with cognitive approaches based solely on the acquisition metaphor of development, which rigidly ascribes language learning to various internal mental processes such as, the construction of interlanguage representations, encodings and decodings between individuals, input processing and attentional operations by the learner, or the biological unfolding of linguistic universals. Within the cognitive–acquisition perspective, the individual is seen as the sole channel through which knowledge is gained. Within a sociocultural framework, however, learning, including the learning of second languages, is a semiotic process attributable to participation in socially-mediated activities. Additionally, this mediation becomes the eventual means for mediating the individual's own mental functioning. Through socially-mediated activity and the eventual 'individual(s)-acting-with-mediational-means' (Wertsch, Tulviste, and Hagstrom 1993), the social and the individual planes of human psychological activity are interwoven. As Vygotsky (1981) states, 'humans' psychological nature represents the aggregate of internalized social relations that have become functions for the individual and form the individual's structure' (*ibid.*: 164). Semiotic mediation is clearly seen in Smith's study of a learner 'puzzling through' in talk about a verb construction, in the linguistic assistance provided by high school and college teachers and students during instructional conversations, and in the collaboratively constructed utterances of an elementary school Japanese class where the language is simultaneously the tool and the object of learning (Swain 1995, 1998).

A second theme involves the *role of instruction* as central to second language development in the classroom. When read and interpreted in light of classrooms, sociocultural theory is both overarching and emerging in its application to language instruction. The theory spans the continuous period of oral and written language development from the time a learner speaks her first words in the L2 through adulthood. At the same time, the theory focuses on instruction within the zone of proximal development beyond the learner's actual developmental level, as witnessed in the elementary Japanese class. In the high school and college classroom, we observed how a hiatus from the teacher's planned lesson leads to an instructional conversation that serves as local opportunities for discourse development (Brooks 1993). In the ESL classes, we saw how teaching is a collaborative achievement not easily reduced to implicit or explicit instruction (Donato and Adair-Hauck 1992), programmed input to the learner, or the individual's unassisted and unmediated discoveries about language form and function.

Since sociocultural theory emphasizes that during instruction awareness of the structure and function of language is developed by using it socially, the theory adds greater clarity to the issue of modified interaction and the negotiation of meaning in classroom settings. Rather than individuals who are constrained by their lack of comprehension, teachers and learners are afforded opportunities to mediate and assist each other in the creation of zones of proximal development (Vygotsky 1978) in which each party learns and develops. More specifically, the utterances of a teacher and other students in a foreign language class are more than linguistic input to be made comprehensible. They are essentially social practices of assistance that shape, construct, and influence learning within interactional and instructional contexts (Donato 1988, 1994; Swain 1995, 1998). In this way, the negotiation of meaning in a social context is subordinated to the creation of a meaning in a collaborative act where the gap between the intermental/social and intramental/individual is bridged. By shifting the focus to discursive collaboration (Brooks and Donato 1994; Donato 1994; Swain 1995; Antón and DiCamilla 1998) during instruction, we begin to understand how interactions within a social instructional network are responsible for an individual's cognitive and linguistic development. As Vygotsky points out (1989: 61) 'social interaction actually produces new, elaborate, advanced psychological processes that are unavailable to the organism working in isolation.'

Third, sociocultural theory is about language classrooms where *agency* matters. That is, learners bring to interactions their own personal histories replete with values, assumptions, beliefs, rights, duties, and obligations. In the study of activity theory, we observed the interplay of perspectives on one particular task and the divergent ways two groups of students played out their agency within the constraints of a language task. In so doing they reinterpreted and transformed their learning and teaching activity. Further, we observed a student who desired to change her teacher's grammar example, elementary school children who spontaneously mediated recall through an instructional song, and learners who expressed their feelings (*That's a lie.* and *You are stubborn.*) in the target language. A central concern in sociocultural theory is that learners actively transform their world and do not merely conform to it. This depiction of the learner goes beyond isolated individuals who grapple for higher mental ground separated from the cultural institutions and historical conditions in which they learn. Where mentalist theories assume that language learning can be understood without taking into account the active and purposeful agent, sociocultural theory maintains that no amount of experimental or instructional manipulation (for example, structured input, controlled teacher talk, required information exchange tasks, etc.) can deflect the overpowering and transformative agency embodied in the learner.

So what are the lessons learned from participation in this seminar? As the instructor for the course, I realize that I experienced many of the concepts reflected in our discussions and in the studies discussed above. The students and I engaged in instructional conversations where research questions emerged and classroom-based studies took shape. Each week we built a learning community made possible through our growing participation in each other's work, shared experiences as teacher and researchers, and the intertextual resources provided through our readings. Expertise was relative, not embodied in a single member of the group, and scaffolded assistance and mediation were encouraged, expected, and valued. Both students and instructor co-constructed understandings and insights on the nature of language learning as a collaborative achievement and the value of sociocultural theory for understanding the powerful relationship between social interaction, social context, and language. My hope is that this chapter will provide a resource for other graduate seminars on second-language classroom research who draw on, investigate, and contribute to the lessons of sociocultural theory. One important lesson of sociocultural theory that we learned is that learning and development, including foreign and second languages, is situated. Situatedness means that learning unfolds in different ways under different circumstances. The circumstances include the specific concrete individuals each with their different histories, the signs they use, and the assistance they provide and are provided. The students and I experienced first-hand the validity of these assertions.

Notes

1 I would like to thank the following people for their insightful comments on earlier drafts of this chapter: Frank B. Brooks, Florida State University, Dawn McCormick, University of Pittsburgh, Robert J. J. Shieh, University of Pittsburgh, and G. Richard Tucker, Carnegie Mellon University. I would also like to thank my graduate students at the University of Pittsburgh for creating with me a zone of proximal development for exploring socio-cultural perspectives on the language classroom.

2 The graduate student projects reported in this chapter are small-scale studies of the language classroom by researchers-in-training. As such, the projects were intended to introduce students to procedures for data collection, analysis, data display, discussion, interpretation, etc. The

projects should not be confused with refereed studies (the study by Takahashi is an exception and has appeared in *Foreign Language Annals* 1998). For the purposes of this chapter, however, the studies provide a valuable source of data for identifying areas where sociocultural theory was believed to be a useful interpretive tool for understanding classroom language learning among a diverse group of practicing language teaching professionals.

3   In a study of private speech during teacher-fronted instruction McCone (1993) found that undergraduate chemistry students externalized their problem solving with American teaching assistants, whereas with international teaching assistants they tended to ask for problem solutions.

4   Based on Vygotsky's notion of the dialogic origin of competence, Bruner (1996) has described a curriculum as an 'animated conversation'. See also van Lier (1996) for a discussion of the curriculum as interaction in which conversation is a significant form of pedagogical action.

5   Tharp and Gallimore (1991) define an instructional conversation as verbal interactions that share both conversational features (for example, responsiveness, joint participation, thematic focus, and few known-answer questions) and instructional goals (for example, outcomes-based, direct teaching, assistance in the development of more complex language and concepts, and on-going teacher assessment).

6   It is important to note that teachers may never totally abandon their position as authorities in classrooms. Sanford's observations indicate, however, that at times during a discussion the teacher willingly assumed the role of non-knower allowing students to be the source of information (see Protocol 3). This is not surprising given that the teacher was an international student and native speaker of French, who genuinely was concerned about learning various aspects of American culture from her students.

7   Wells (1998) has argued that scaffolding may not be an appropriate metaphor for student-to-student assistance when no transfer of responsibility between expert and novice is intended. Rather, he suggests that 'collaborative problem solving' is a better term to describe some types of student-assisted interactions, citing collaborative writing as one such task.

8   A response to this query may be 'Through participation in these interactions, the children provide evidence of higher levels of achievement.' A follow-up question might be 'Can these students perform unassisted at a later time indicating the acquisition of new knowledge?' (i.e. participation does not count as evidence of having or possessing anything). The response might be 'Belonging, participating and communicating is evidence of knowing' (Sfard 1998: 7). Depending on the metaphor one adopts, responses will vary in radically different ways to the issue of learning. Further, these differing perspectives explain why dialogue between those embracing one metaphor or the other is difficult to achieve. (See the

discussion between Firth and Wagner and others published in the *Modern Language Journal* for instances of the tension and misunderstandings between 'participation' and 'acquisition' metaphors.)
9 Note that even in open-ended activities, students still exercise their intentions in ways that defy instructional expectations.

Appendix 2.1: Protocol translations

Protocol 2: That's a lie!

(End of exercise)

32 T: To miss.
33 Ss: (repeating aloud) To miss.

(Beginning of extension activity)

34 T: I missed all of you a lot yesterday.
35 S1: Why?
36 T: Because I like to be in school.
37 S2: That's a lie!
38 T: I went to Expomart for many interviews for jobs. For
39   work, right? To teach in other cities.
40   Entrevistas. What are 'entrevistas'?
41 S3: Interviews.

(Beginning of exercise)

42 T: Yes. To imagine.
43 Ss: (repeating aloud) To imagine.

(Todhunter 1996)

Protocol 3: Okay, but … can you do that in French 1?

= indicates linked utterances

44 T: Tell me …What is the personality of an Aries?
45 S1: Ah … they are serious.
46 T: Yes, Aries are serious, and=
(Student 2 announces to the class that Russell, who is an Aries, had lots to drink thus indicating that he is not serious.)
47 S2: =Russell drank a lot.
48 S3: She (pointing to Annie) is … how go … uhm …
        how do you say 'stubborn?'
49 T: Why? Annie is 'têtue?' No. 'Stubborn'?
50 S3: Yeah … ah … oui, 'stubborn.' how=
51 T: =Têtue.
52 S3: She (pointing to Annie) very stubborn.
(laughter)

53   T: No, she is not stubborn. She knows what she wants.
54   Isn't this true Annie?
55   S4:   (Annie speaks to Bill) You are stupid.
(laughter)
56   T: And what sign are you, Bill?

(Sanford 1996)

Protocol 4: I want, I want, I want …

(Teacher shows a picture of a boy eating an apple.)
57   T: Yes.
58   S1:   Denis is eating an apple. (Child marks present with *masu*.)
59   T: Denis is eating an apple. Very good. Mary? (Mary = S2)
(Teacher shows a picture of a boy who is thinking about eating an apple.)
60   S2:   Denis *eat apple … (Mary does not complete the verb form.)
61   T: Eat …?
(Teacher provides base verb and signals verb ending necessary for want with rising intonation.)
62   S2:   Is eating.
63   S3:   (directed to S2) Wants to eat. Is eating. Does not eat.
(Teachers begins singing the 'I want' song.)
64   T: Remember this song? Want, want, want.
(The students begin singing along with the teacher.)
65   T/Ss: Wants, wants, wants. (Children and teacher sing 'wanting verbs'.)
             Tai tai, tai, nomitai, tabetai, hon yomitai, netai, kaitai, terebi mitai.
66   T: Yes (emphatically), wants to eat! Right? Wants to eat.
67   Ss: Wants to eat.
68   T: Wants to eat, yes, Mary?
69   S2   Denis wants to eat an apple.
70   T: Yes, very good!

(Takahashi 1998)

2 Rethinking interaction in SLA: Developmentally appropriate assistance in the zone of proximal development and the acquisition of L2 grammar

Amy Snyder Ohta
University of Washington

Introduction

There is a growing interest among teachers and researchers in understanding how language development occurs through situated interaction, not in laboratories, but in classrooms, tutoring sessions and other teaching–learning settings. Recent work has prioritized examining developmental processes from a holistic perspective, as they occur moment-by-moment in the interaction of learners (Frawley and Lantolf 1985; Donato 1988, 1994; van Lier 1991; Brooks 1992; Hall 1995a, 1995b; Lantolf and Aljaafreh 1995; Ohta 1995, 1997, in press; Antón and DiCamilla 1998; Swain and Lapkin 1998). This work has considered learners as neither processors of input, nor producers of output, but as speaker/hearers involved in developmental processes which are realized in interaction. L2 acquisition, in this scheme, is not considered to be wholly resident in the mind of the language learner, such that it can only be inferentially accessed by the researcher, but the learner-and-environment are seen in a holistic perspective (van Lier this volume). In this approach, previously sharp edges defining who is 'speaker' and who is 'hearer' become blurred; speaker/hearers collaboratively produce utterances which they jointly own. And, language acquisition is realized through a collaborative process whereby learners appropriate the language of the interaction as their own, for their own purposes, building grammatical, expressive, and cultural competence through this process. Here, the language learning 'task' is an entity which is transformed through its instantiation into the activity of particular learners (Coughlan and Duff 1994). In order to better understand the role of interaction in L2 development, researchers have begun to study both how native speakers or more proficient 'experts' support 'novices', as well as how L2 learners collaborate with one another as they work on assigned language learning tasks in their L2 classrooms.

Recent work has demonstrated the gains produced through a collaborative process called scaffolding (Bruner 1975; Cazden 1988), through which assistance is provided from person to person such that an interlocutor is enabled to do something she or he might not have been able to do otherwise. Research on scaffolding in language learning has shown how learners working together reach a higher level of performance by providing assistance to one another (Brooks 1992; Donato 1994; Ohta 1995, 1997, 1999, in press; Antón and DiCamilla 1998). The construct of the zone of proximal development (ZPD) specifies that development cannot occur if too much assistance is provided or if a task is too easy. Development is impeded both by helping the learner with what she or he is already able to do, and by not withdrawing assistance such that the learner develops the ability to work independently. The idea of scaffolding has also been described through another metaphor, that of 'assisted performance' (Tharp and Gallimore 1991; Poole and Patthey-Chavez 1994). The term assisted performance captures both the 'assistance' provided and the results of that assistance in facilitating 'performance'; the effects of assistance are evident in the performance of the one assisted.

While research on learner–learner interactive processes has shown how collaboration may result in provision of developmentally appropriate assistance, the interactional mechanisms involved in the obtaining or providing of assistance during language learning tasks have been little examined. In order to be truly helpful, learners must somehow discern when assistance will be of use. This paper investigates the interactional cues to which peers orient in order to provide developmentally appropriate assistance. In this investigation, theoretical constructs from Vygotskian psycholinguistic theory are applied to illuminate the role of assisted performance in the developmental processes of two learners completing an oral translation task in a university-level Japanese language class. In completing the task, Hal and Becky, two learners of Japanese, engage in form-focused collaborative activity that revolves around concerns for grammatical accuracy. In their interaction, the learners negotiate language form and the giving/receiving of form-related assistance. Micro-analysis of the mechanisms of this assistance reveals that Hal, in helping Becky, is not oriented to her linguistic errors in general, but to her subtle bids for help with what she is specifically struggling with. Hal does not help whenever Becky struggles, but episodes of assistance are most concentrated when she indicates she needs assistance, which she does with subtle interactional cues. Hal's responsiveness to these bids results in help that is both develop-mentally appropriate and timely. It is only after Becky attains a level of proficiency with the task that Hal intervenes, unbidden, to correct linguistic errors that persist. Through the process of receiving developmentally appropriate assistance, Becky, who had the greater difficulty with the task, dramatically improves in her use of a difficult construction. In addition, Hal, the partner who assisted Becky, also evidences development through this process. The most important finding of this study is that the provision of developmentally appropriate assistance is not only dependent upon attention to what the peer interlocutor is able to do, but also upon sensitivity to the partner's readiness for help, which is communicated through subtle interactional cues. In addition, as shown by previous studies, analysis of microgenesis illuminates internalization processes, here, internalization of grammatical structure. As the learners' activity proceeds, Becky evidences increasing independence in her construction of L2 sentences, eventually using them appropriately in a form-focused communicative task which follows the translation task. Finally, through the process of analysis, the importance of learner engagement as a vehicle for the L2 internalization process also becomes apparent. Here, Hal's close attention to Becky's interactional cues, and the collaborative engagement of both as they attack the translation task, transforms the 'task', which does not appear to be particularly optimal for promoting collaboration or interaction in the L2, into an opportunity for language development. The results confirm the importance of investigating how different sorts of tasks may function in the language learning process by examining how those tasks are actualized in the activity of learners (DiNitto 1997; Foster 1998; Swain and Lapkin 1998; Samuda 1999; Roebuck this volume).

Second language acquisition: a sociocultural perspective

A holistic perspective on developmental questions in SLA has been gained through a sociocultural approach to language development, based upon the work of psycholinguist L. S. Vygotsky and his present-day interpreters (Vygotsky 1978, 1981, 1987; Wertsch 1985a; Newman and Holzman 1993). Analyses of situated L2 interaction from a Vygotskian perspective consider how learners acquire interactional competence, including the acquisition of vocabulary, syntax, and pragmatics. The approach entails use of a holistic qualitative methodology which sheds light on learning processes as they occur in interactive settings. First, I will present theoretical constructs which facilitate analysis of interactive data, leading the researcher directly to questions of language development. My interest is to expand the examination of L2 interactive discourse by using analytic constructs which facilitate understanding of how learners acquire L2 competence through social interaction.

For Vygotsky, learning is a socially situated activity. What a learner at first accomplishes only in a social setting, she or he will eventually be able to do independently. The social locus of cognitive and linguistic development is outlined in Vygotsky's general genetic law of cultural development.

Any function in the child's cultural development appears twice, or on two planes. First it appears on the social plane, and then on the psychological plane. First it appears between people as an interpsychological category, and then within the child as an intrapsychological category. This is equally true with regard to voluntary attention, logical memory, the formation of concepts, and the development of volition ... . [I]t goes without saying that internalization transforms the process itself and changes its structure and functions. Social relations or relations among people genetically underlie all higher functions and their relationships.

(Vygotsky 1981: 163)

While Vygotsky was speaking of children, this principle is being successfully applied to the SLA context. Through social interaction, L2 constructs (whether vocabulary, grammatical structures, etc.) appear on two psychologically real planes, first the interpsychological or 'between people' plane, which is developmentally prior to the intrapsychological, or mental, plane. In other words, social processes allow the language to become a cognitive tool for the individual. These planes of functioning are dynamically interrelated, linked by language which mediates social interaction on the interpsychological plane, and mediates thought on the intrapsychological plane.

The mechanisms of internalization: assisted performance in the zone of proximal development

Meaningful social interaction functions as a mechanism through which the transformation of the L2 from interpsychological to intrapsychological functioning occurs. The making of meaning in social interaction is a cognitive process, or, as Burgess (1993: 26) states, 'an act of mind', that unites the social with the individual. It is the interpenetrated nature of the social and cognitive that allows the study of human cognitive processes, including second language acquisition processes, through analysis of the language of social interaction. In other words, because of the intimate connection between thought and language resulting from language's function as a mediator of human cognition, interaction provides a window into developmental processes (see Frawley and Lantolf 1984, 1985 and Lantolf and Ahmed 1989). Language acquisition—internalization of the language of social interaction from interpsychological to intrapsychological planes—occurs through a dynamic transformative process called microgenesis (Wertsch 1985a). Microgenesis is cognitive development that occurs moment by moment in social interaction. Microanalysis of learner discourse in its sequential context allows the researcher to examine this process in flight. Internalization of social interactive processes happens in the zone of proximal development (ZPD) (Vygotsky 1978; Wertsch 1985a), the interactional space within which a learner is enabled to perform a task beyond his or her own current level of competence, through assisted performance. For the analyst, according to Lantolf and Aljaafreh,

> Determining a learner's ZPD is an act of negotiated discovery that is realized through dialogic interaction between learner and expert. In other words, the learner and expert engage each other in an attempt to discover

precisely what the learner is able to achieve without help, and what the learner can accomplish with assistance ... . Importantly, the help negotiated between the novice and expert is graduated and contingent in the sense that it moves from more explicit to more implicit, or strategic, levels, and is offered only when needed and is withdrawn once the novice shows signs of self-control and ability to function independently (Aljaafreh and Lantolf 1994: 468) or even rejects help when it is offered (Wertsch and Hickmann 1987).

(Lantolf and Aljaafreh 1995: 620)

While for Vygotsky, the partner providing assistance was assumed to be an adult, and the learner, a child, researchers have applied these ideas to a broad range of teaching and learning situations, including foreign language learning situations (van Lier 1991). Lantolf and Aljaafreh (1995) examined interaction between adult ESL learners and a non-native, but more expert, tutor. Learners were shown to progress in the ZPD through developmentally sensitive assistance in tutoring sessions. Researchers have also applied Vygotsky's ideas to peer interaction where there is not a clear 'expert'. Studies of peer interaction in a foreign language have found that differential competence among peers allows a ZPD to emerge in groups (Donato 1994) or pairs (Brooks 1992; Ohta 1995, 1997; Antón and DiCamilla 1998) of adult learners, when no true 'expert' is present. In their examination of peer learning in a French immersion class, Swain and Lapkin (1998) show how dyadic collaboration during a story reconstruction task results in increased accuracy in the French used by middle-school students. Donato (1994: 46) examines how L2 development occurs through a triadic planning task, finding that 'the speakers are at the same time individually novices and collectively experts, sources of new orientations for each other, and guides through this complex linguistic problem solving.' Ohta (1995) examined a collaborative pair-work task, comparing student language use in teacher-fronted and pair-work contexts. In pair-work, emergence of a ZPD results in both students performing at a higher level of competence.

The research described above has shown how the ZPD functions in different L2 learning settings using different sorts of tasks. More research is needed to better understand the nature of effective assistance in peer learning situations. Lantolf and Aljaafreh's description of effective help as being 'graduated' (moving from implicit to explicit as the expert determines the appropriate level of help) and 'contingent' (offered only when needed, and withdrawn when the novice shows signs of independent functioning) applies to the expert–novice tutoring situation they describe, but its applicability to other situations needs to be examined. Unlike teaching or tutoring situations, in peer language learning tasks, no one peer is responsible for helping another or facilitating another's development. While previous studies have shown that peer interaction may result in the emergence of a ZPD, and that peers do help one another, the nature of help provided by peers, the mechanisms through which that help is sought and provided, and the impact that effective help has on the acquisition of a grammatical structure have not been closely examined. The data to be examined here provide a context for further investigation of these areas.

Methodology

The data

The data are audio and video recordings of a second year university-level Japanese language class. Data were transcribed for analysis using conventions from conversation analysis and first-language acquisition research (Ochs 1979). Transcription conventions are shown in Appendix 2.1.

The participants

Analysis focuses upon the participation of two learners, given the pseudonyms 'Hal' and 'Becky'. Hal is a 33-year-old MBA student who studied Japanese in his native Taiwan as an undergraduate before coming to the US for graduate school where he began studying Japanese again, beginning with the second-year course. Becky is a 20-year-old Filipina-American undergraduate who was in her second year of language study at the time of recording.

The lesson

Three language learning tasks are relevant to the analysis, a role-play task, a translation task, and a communicative interview task that concluded the lesson. Analysis focuses on the translation task, which was particularly difficult for one of the participants, Becky. All three tasks occurred during a portion of class devoted to introduction and practice of a desiderative construction. The structure of the lesson is broadly outlined in Figure 2.1:

Role-play pre-work (teacher-fronted practice making requests using the desiderative form of the benefactive construction)

Role-play task done in pairs, with follow-up performances

Grammar lecture (in English) on sentences using *hoshii*, followed by teacher-fronted practice in forming target sentences

Translation task done in pairs

Follow-up communicative interview task

Figure 2.1: Organization of the lesson

In order to more clearly explain the relationships of the tasks to one another, an explanation of the Japanese desiderative construction will first be provided. The tasks will then be explained in further detail.

The Japanese desiderative construction

In English, the concept of desire may be expressed in sentences such as (1).

(1)   I want the teacher to buy me a pencil.

In Japanese, ideas such as that shown in (1) are expressed using the desiderative construction, shown in (2):

(2)   Watashi wa   sensei ni   enpitsu o   katte hoshii.
      I   TOP teacher DAT   pencil ACC   buy want.
      I want the teacher to buy me a pencil.

In both (1) and (2), what is desired is the doing of an action—the speaker wants the teacher to buy a pencil for him/her. In the Japanese version, the one who desires the action to be performed is marked with the topic marker *wa*, while the subject of the embedded clause, the one who is to do the 'buying', is marked with the dative marker *ni*. The desiderative can also be used in benefactive constructions as shown in (3), to make requests:

(3)   Enpitsu o   katte itadaki-tai n desu ga.
      Pencil ACC   buy receive-DESIDERATIVE-COP CONJ
      Would you buy me a pencil?
      (literally, 'I would like to receive the buying of a pencil but ...')

Here, the *te*-form of the verb *buy* is combined with the helping verb *itadaku*, *receive*, conjugated with the desiderative affix *-tai* as *itadakitai*, want to receive. To express this request, neither the one who desires the pencil nor the one who is to do the action of pencil buying are explicitly mentioned, but the utterance will function as a request in its appropriate context, with the helping verb used to show that the pencil will be received by the speaker, and the desiderative affix used to show the speaker's desire that the action be performed.

The tasks

The first task presented in this lesson is a role play that incorporates the request shown in (3), above. In a previous lesson, learners had extensive practice forming benefactive sentences, but using the desiderative affix to make requests is new. After form-focused practice making these requests, learners were guided in a two-turn request sequence that included a request and an affirmative or negative response. Then, learners practiced and expanded this role play in pairs. As they did so, they produced a variety of their own requests, practiced ways to express their willingness or unwillingness to comply with the request, and added a range of other turns to their role plays (Ohta 1995[1]). In the role-play task, the request form learners were guided to use is shown in (4a) and (4b), below. (4a) shows the structure of the request, with elided topic and dative phrases shown in parentheses, and *Vte* indicating the *te*-form of a Japanese verb. (4b) is an example of a target request.

(4a)   (Watashi wa)   (sensei   ni)   Vte itadakitai n desu ga.
      (I   TOP) (teacher   DAT)   verb-receive   COP CONJ.

(4b)   Sushi o tsukutte itadakitai n desu ga.
     Would you make me sushi?

As in (3), in (4ab) the topic and dative phrases are elided because they are understood from context.

The translation task, which is the focus of analysis in this chapter, presented a greater challenge to the students because it required them to include the topic and dative phrases elided in the role play. The translation task sheet, Activity 1 shown in Appendix 2, lists the 'person who wants someone to do something' and 'what she or he wants who to do'. Students were to combine these components into sentences using the desiderative as shown in the model on the activity sheet. No broader communicative context was provided for any of the sentences. The vocabulary used was, for the most part, familiar. (5a) lists the sentence structure learners were guided to use in the translation task, with blanks left for topic and dative phrases, and *Vte* indicating that an appropriate verb in *te*-form is to be inserted. (5b) is an example of a sentence using this structure:

(5a)   —————— wa ——————ni Vte hoshii to omotteimasu.
     ——————TOP——————DAT verb phrase CMP think.

(5b)   Kato-san wa okusan ni tabako o yamete hoshii to omotteimasu.
     Mr. Kato TOP wife DAT cigarettes ACC quit want CMP think.
     Mr. Kato would like his wife to quit smoking.

While using different verb phrases, the sentences shown in (4) and (5) are similar structurally. In (4a) and (4b), a request is formed using a benefactive construction that combines the *te*-form of the verb with the helping verb *receive* in the desiderative form. (5a) and (5b) are desiderative sentences which use the adjectival *hoshii* instead of a helping verb. In both sentences, *wa* marks the person who would like to have something done for him or her. The person to perform the action is marked with *ni*. Neither of these phrases, however, is explicitly stated in (4). The translation task required students to construct the whole sentence, including topic and dative phrases. Particle choice is difficult, because *wa* and *ni* are used differently depending on the meaning of the predicate. Compare, for example, the benefactive sentence in (6) with the desiderative sentence in (7). Students have had extensive practice using sentences such as (6) in previous lessons:

(6) Hal wa   Becky ni   enpitsu o   katte ageta.
     Hal TOP   Becky DAT   pencil ACC   buy gave.
     Hal bought Becky a pencil.

(7) Hal wa   Becky ni   enpitsu o   katte hoshii.
     Hal TOP   Becky DAT   pencil ACC   buy desire.
     Hal wants Becky to buy him a pencil.

In the benefactive construction shown in (6), *wa* marks the person who performs the action, and *ni* marks the recipient of the action. In contrast, in the desiderative construction shown in (7), the *wa* marks the person one who desires the action to be performed, and *ni* marks the subject of the embedded clause who performs the action. Particle selection, therefore, makes the task particularly difficult.

The third task presented was an interview task, Activity 2 on the worksheet in Appendix 2. The teacher had the students interview each other regarding an imaginary situation in which the teacher has offered to the students whatever they want, asking each other what they want the teacher to buy for them. Following this interview, the teacher asked students to report about themselves or a classmate to the class. This task required learners to use the desiderative construction, including specifying agent and patient as was done in the translation task. In other words, the structure used in the translation task was used in the follow-up communicative interviewing task, but in a context in which students asked and answered questions of each other, without translating, and using their own ideas.

Translation task evaluation

The translation task presented is a decontextualized grammar practice task that does not provide any communication practice in terms of information exchange. Skehan's (1996) framework for implementing task-based instruction provides four criteria (*ibid.*: 38) for optimal task design, suggesting that meaning should be primary, that there should be some relationship between the task and the real world, that task completion should have some priority, and that assessment should be measured by task outcome. The translation task does not meet these criteria. The task only prioritizes meaning in the sense that students must translate from English to Japanese. The task does not involve the information exchange or decision making described as being critical to L2 development (Pica, Kanagy, and Falodun 1993). All information is laid out in the task, and the task for students is simply to translate the sentences into Japanese using the pattern given. The task also involves no relationship to the real world, except for the world of a classroom where students are asked to do decontextualized grammar practice tasks, not any sort of non-pedagogical setting where Japanese might be used. Completion of the task is a priority in the sense that the teacher expects students to do the task and actively monitors the working pairs. However, completion is not prerequisite to some higher goal. Assessment is not measured by task outcome as a whole, but by the grammatical correctness of the translated sentences. This judgment is left to the students themselves as they go through the task under the observation of the circulating teacher. Finally, the structure of the task does not, in itself, suggest a collaborative structure. Students are told to work in pairs, but are free to make their own decisions about how to work together.

Analysis

Analysis proceeded using procedures for discourse analysis, including particular attention to Hal and Becky's interaction. Hal and Becky's interaction was examined for evidence of assisted performance, with the focus of analysis on episodes in which help was or was not provided. Particular attention was paid to sequential development in terms of what preceded and followed provision or nonprovision of assistance.

A Vygotskian analytic framework was used to illuminate the nature of the language development processes in the data set. The analysis made use of Vygotsky's general genetic law of cultural development which considers the transformation of cognitive constructs from the interpsychological to intrapsychological space, and the ZPD, which proposes how this transformation occurs through a process of developmentally sensitive assisted performance. These constructs illuminate the role of collaborative interaction in L2 development, in particular allowing examination of assistance and internalization processes. Table 2.1 describes features of interaction which allow the analyst to study these processes.

Construct	Focus of analysis
Mechanisms of assistance	Analysis examines the sequential structure of episodes of assistance, examining what triggers suppliance of assistance.
Appropriate assistance	It is not assumed that all assistance is helpful. 'Appropriate assistance' is defined as assistance which leads to language development, with language development defined as gains in learner performance on the sentence-construction task, and maintained in the subsequent communicative task. Analysis focuses upon changes in performance and how these changes relate to the assistance provided.
Internalization processes	This is examined through analysis of microgenesis (Wertsch 1985)— of how language structure is appropriated for individual use. Internalization of linguistic structure is visible through increasing independence of appropriate task performance.

Table 2.1: Examining sociocultural constructs related to assistance and internalization

The analysis first examined the notion of assistance in order to consider the appropriateness of assistance, and the mechanisms through which assistance was obtained or given. Then, analysis turned to internalization processes—to the learners' L2 development.

Results

Preliminary overview of the data: What is accomplished?

In presentation of the results, focus will be upon Becky's L2 development, since her progress was most dramatic. The task contains prompts for eleven sentences. The teacher has the students make sentences orally, in pairs, referring to the model grammatical structure written on the task sheet. Becky and Hal do the task twice, alternating turns, so each of them translates all eleven sentences. A preliminary overview of the data shows that the students make impressive gains in their ability to construct the sentences, gains which persist in the interview and reporting task used to follow up the grammar-translation task. Becky's first attempt to construct a sentence takes 18 turns, through which she produces the sentence *My brother wants my father to take him to Japan*, as follows:

(1) 1 B: Otoosan, (.) watashi wa=
          Father ((honorific)), (.) I=

   2 H: =(What she want?)

   3 B: uh, what she wants you// to do

   4 H: Your father. Your father. // (Understand?)

→ 5 B: Oh, watashi no oko ((laughs)) watashi no chichi wa,^ (.)
          niho:n (.) ah (..) niho::n
          Oh, my oko ((laughs)) my dad (.) Japan (.) ah (..)Japan

   6 H: E   to

   7 B: Ni? E.   *to ((either* ni *or* e *is correct))*

   8 H: Nihon e?   *To Japan?*

   9 B: Oh nihon ni,   *Oh to Japan,*

   10 H: Oh nihon ni?   *Oh to Japan?*

   11 B: [Niho:n ni:,^ (.)   *To Japan:^ (.)*

   12 H: [Nihon ni.   *To Japan*

   13 B: tsurete: hoshii to omotte imasu.
          wants ((somebody)) to lead ((him)) to Japan.

   14 H: Tsurete itte hoshii to omo//tte imasu.
          ((adds the missing verb 'itte' (go) to Becky's utterance))

   15 B: Tsurete itte?   *To take along?*

   16 H: Hai.   *Yes.*

17   B: Tsurete: itte hoshii to omotte imasu.
     ((Becky repeats Hal's line 14 utterance))

18   H: Hai.   *Yes.*

Instead of *My brother wants my father to take him to Japan*, what Becky produces is a sentence that means *My father wants (someone) to take him to Japan*. However, Hal does not help Becky to fix the sentence in terms of adjusting its overall meaning, but helps more locally. He helps with lexical choice (line 4) and particle selection (line 6), and, following the completion of the sentence, helps her to correct the verb phrase in line 14. Hal's contributions result in a sentence that is structurally better formed, but which does not convey the meaning of the original. And, Hal's performance early on is only slightly better. In fact, one wonders what is going to be accomplished here— it seems we have two students who are not paying much attention to meaning, and who ignore or do not notice most of their interlocutor's errors. However, in spite of this, by the end of the activity, both students produce sentences with the appropriate meanings fluently and correctly. Here is the last sentence produced by Becky. (Excerpts are numbered in the order of the translation task, with 1 denoting the first sentence translated, 2, the second, through 22, the last sentence of the task.)

(21)   1   B: Yoshida san wa,^ (.) uh- okusan ni,^ (.) tabako o yamete hoshii
                 to omotte imasu.
                 Yoshida-san wants (.) uh- his wife (.) to quit smoking.

       2   H: Hai.   *Yes.*

Becky and Hal both improve dramatically, developing the ability to produce the sentences fluently and correctly. While the task at first seems unpromising, these students accomplish a great deal. And, as I said earlier, the gains we see in excerpt 21 persist into the communicative task that follows.

Developmentally appropriate assistance: bids for help

In the ZPD a learner performs above his or her level of individual competence with the assistance of another; development occurs as the learner acts with increasing independence. In the interaction between Hal and Becky, Hal's assistance is quite effective. Analysis of the data focused upon how he was able to provide such effective help. The answer was found in subtle inter-actional details, discernable because of the detailed transcription of the data, which notes articulatory and suprasegmental features such as intonation contours, glottal stops, and vowel elongation, as well as documenting the temporal evolution of the interaction through noting, for example, filled pauses, restarts, and overlap between speakers. Narrow transcription allowed examination of interactive and cognitive processes (Ochs 1979). Results of analysis show that the help which leads development does not occur in a haphazard or random way, but both Becky and Hal bid for and provide assistance in an orderly and developmentally sensitive manner. Hal and Becky obtain help by explicitly asking for assistance, but also bid for help with more subtle cues which show their readiness for assistance. The relevance of these cues is evident as interlocutors orient to their use and respond accordingly, as will be shown below.

In general, neither student interrupts the other to provide help, or provides help when their interlocutor is clearly continuing. This is consistent with analyses of turn taking which reveal that, overwhelmingly, one speaker talks at a time, with minimal overlap evident, a feature of turn taking that results from the interlocutor's projection of possible completion points (transition relevance places) in their interlocutor's talk (Sacks, Schegloff, and Jefferson 1974; Levinson 1983). In Hal and Becky's interaction, help may be offered when it is clear that the interlocutor is not continuing. In the present data, 'continuing' and 'not continuing' are shown through particular interactive cues described in Table 2.2. Transcription conventions showing these features are in square brackets, as well as being listed in Appendix 2.2:

Continuing	1) Final syllable uttered with 'continuing' intonation [,] and a glottal stop [^], and/or 2) filled pauses (including laughter, fillers such as *ano* or *uh*, and restarts), and/or 3) rapid rate of speech [> <].
Not continuing	1) Rising 'question' intonation [?], or 2) elongating the final syllable of the last word uttered [:], with question intonation or a sing-song flat intonation, and/or 3) slowed rate of speech [< >].

Table 2.2: Signaling 'continuing' or 'not continuing'

In excerpt 8 below, continuing (marked with c) is indicated in line 1 and a not continuing bid for help in line 4 (marked with b). Cues indicating continuing/not continuing are underlined.

(8) c 1 H: Sumisu-san <u>wa,</u>^ (.) sensei <u>ni,</u>^ (.)
           Smith TOP,^ (.) teacher DAT,^ (.)

     2 B: Hai doozo.   *Yeah, go ahead.*

     3 H: Kan- ((laughs)) Sumisu san- Sumisu san wa,^ sen- sensei ni,^
           Chin- ((laughs)) Mr. Smith- Mr. Smith TOP tea- teacher DAT

b 4   [kanji taku<u>sa:n</u>?
           [kanji many?

     5 T: [Un. ((T is standing by))   *Uh-huh.*

     6 H: Takusan?   *Many?*

     7 T: Mo- motto ne?   *Mo- more, right?*

Even though Hal pauses after *Sumisu-san wa* and stops after *sensei ni* in line 1, Becky does not provide assistance. Hal's intonation and use of the glottal stop are cues that he will continue, and Becky prompts him to do so.

Hal explicitly bids for help in line 4, looking at the teacher, and saying *kanji takusa:n?* with an elongated final vowel and question intonation, requesting confirmation in line 6.

In excerpt 5, below, Becky has difficulty choosing the correct word for *younger brother.* In line 2 she utters the possessive marker *no* with continuing intonation and a glottal stop. Using falling intonation on the word *kanojo* (used here to mean *girlfriend*), Becky pauses briefly—but Hal does not intervene. As she continues the word search (line 2), she comes up with the correct choice, *otooto.* During her word search Becky uses filled pauses, restarts, and a rapid rate of speech (line 2), which function in keeping the floor. In line 3, although her particle choices are incorrect, note how each postpositional phrase is marked with a glottal stop and rising intonation. Although she uses incorrect grammatical particles to mark topic (younger brother—*otooto*), and the giver of the favor (girlfriend—*kanojo*), Hal does not help.

(5)   1 H: Goban?   *Number five?*

c 2 B: Imooto: (.) ɴo:,^ (.) kan<u>ojo</u>. (.) <u>Huh?</u> >Hai Imo-omo-<uh:
<u>otooto</u> ((laughs))=
Younger sister's girlfriend (.) Huh? Yeah young- yo- uh:
younger brother ((laughs))

c 3   =Otooto ɴo kanojo w<u>a</u>,^ shukud<u>ai</u>^ (.) o,^ shi<u>te</u>,^ hoshii-
hoshi t<u>o</u>,^ omotte imasu. (.) (unintelligible) Hai.
Younger brother's girlfriend wants (.) ((someone)) to do his
homework.

As shown, Becky and Hal generally do not provide help when it is clear that the interlocutor is continuing, except for excerpts 6 and 15 (to be discussed later), where Hal explicitly corrects Becky's misuse of the particle *no.*

When Becky signals 'not continuing' by elongating the vowel in the last syllable she utters (underlined below), with a flat intonation contour, Hal provides assistance, as in line 5 of excerpt 1, repeated below:

(1)   b 5 B: Oh, watashi ɴo oko ((laughs)) watashi ɴo chichi wa,^ (.)
niho:n (.) ah (..) ni<u>ho::n</u>
Oh, my oko ((laughs)) my father ((familiar)) (.)
Japan (.) ah (..) <u>Japa::n</u>

6 H: E   *to [destination marker]*

In line 6, Hal responds by providing the particle *e.* Another example occurs in excerpt 7, where Becky again receives significant help from Hal.

(7)   b 1 B: Un. Hai. Yooko. Ah-Lee san wa,^ <u>Yooko::</u> (.)
Un. Yeah. Yooko. Ah- Lee-san ᴛᴏᴘ <u>Yooko::</u> (.)

→   2 H: Yoko-san.

b 3 B: <u>sa:n</u>

→   4 H: Ni.   *((dative marker))*

c/b   5 B: <u>Ni:</u>,^ (.) Garufure:heh ndo <u>how do you say will become?</u>
            DAT *(.) girlfrie:nd <u>how do you say will become?</u>*

      6 H: Garufurendo ni,^?   *Girlfriend ((dative marker))*

b   7 B: Ga-garufurendo [<u>ni:::</u>   *Gir-girlfriend <u>((dative marker))</u>*

→   8 H: [ni nari?
                                        [DAT *become*]

After marking the topic phrase *Lee san wa* with continuing intonation and a glottal stop (line 1), she elongates the final syllable of the name Yooko, elongating the final vowel with flat intonation. Hal provides help in line 2. Again in line 3, Becky elongates the final vowel. Hal again responds by providing help—the postpositional particle in line 4. Then, in line 5, when Becky utters *ni* with continuing intonation and a glottal stop, Hal does not provide assistance until she explicitly asks for it. In line 7, Hal begins constructing the sentence together with Becky, uttering *ni* in overlap with Becky. And, as she elongates the vowel, Hal adds a form of the verb. Each of these bids for help as described above functions as the first pair part of an adjacency pair, the second pair part of which is the provision of help.

Hal's assistance to Becky is developmentally cued, contingent on Becky's need for assistance. Hal not only provides help, but also withholds it, even when Becky bids for help as shown above. As in other adjacency pair sequences, a second pair part is not always provided. As Becky's accuracy improves, Hal provides less assistance, letting Becky solve her own problems. Lines 12 and 13 of excerpt 11 (the last sentence of the activity, and the sixth Becky has translated) show this process. Becky uses the same bidding strategy, but Hal does not intervene. Becky then solves her own problems with particle selection (this is discussed further in a later section). Hal only helps when Becky's difficulty with conjugating the adjective *hayai* causes a complete breakdown and she comes to a stop, saying *oh darn* (particle errors are in small caps, bids for help are underlined).

(11) b 12 B: (   )Yoshida sa:n (.) wa,^ (.) shujin   <u>NO</u> (.) uh shujin
                <u>NO</u>?
                (   ) *Yoshida-san (.)* TOP *(.) husband* <u>POS</u>*(.) uh husband*
                <u>POS</u>*?*

      b 13   shujin <u>NO</u> uc<u>hi::</u> (.) ah shu- (.) shujin <u>ni:</u> (.) haya:- (.)
                hayatte,^ (.) uchi ni haya- oh darn.
                husband <u>POS</u> *hou<u>se::</u> (.)ah hus- husband* DAT: *(.) earl- (.)*
                early (.) home earl- oh darn.

        14 H: Ku.
               ((adverbial ending needed when placing hayai *before a*
               verb))

Hal's assistance to Becky is developmentally sensitive, in Lantolf and Aljaafreh's (1995) terms, 'graduated and contingent'. Hal's sensitivity to interactional cues and Becky's growing ability to act independently result in the giving and withholding of help in a developmentally sensitive manner.

From interpsychological to intrapsychological: Becky's gains

When Hal and Becky begin the task, the performance of both contains errors—neither is able to translate the sentences correctly. In excerpt 1 (shown earlier), we witnessed a myriad of errors. Becky initially marked the topic, *watashi* (I), correctly with *wa* (line 1), but chose the wrong word for father, *otoosan* (father, honorific). When Hal corrected her lexical error (line 4), Becky then overcompensated, not only changing to the word *chichi* (father, humble), but also changing the formerly correct topic marker *wa* to the possessive marker *no*. This results in the phrase *watashi no chichi*, which means *my father*, an expression that is redundant since the word *chichi* (father, humble) refers to the speaker's own father. Along with this change, Becky moved the topic marker *wa* from its formerly correct location (marking *watashi* (I)), to mark the benefactor, *chichi* (father), with *wa*, which is incorrect—she should have used the dative marker *ni*. And, as noted earlier, Hal does not correct any of Becky's particle errors, even though they impede meaning. Instead, he picks up on the elongated final syllable of *niho::n* in line 5, providing her with the marker which shows destination, *e*. Becky uses *ni*, which serves an equivalent function. In line 10, Hal repeats Becky's correct use of *ni* to mark destination, and works to construct the sentence with her (note how Becky and Hal say *Nihon ni* in overlap in lines 11–12). In line 13, Becky completes the sentence, but neglects to use the verb *itte* (go), as needed. After Becky finishes, Hal repeats the verb phrase, adding *itte* in line 14. Becky repeats the verb phrase in line 15, and then restates the end of the sentence, correcting her error, in line 17. In excerpt 1, Becky cannot correctly form the sentence. And, in general, Hal tends to ignore Becky's errors, and in his own attempt, makes plenty of errors of his own. Looking over their early interaction, one wonders what will be accomplished—it appears that the task may function merely to reinforce Becky's misunderstanding of how various grammatical particles are used.

In excerpts 2, 3, and 4, similar problems occur. In excerpt 2, Hal marks the benefactor, *haha*, with *wa*, perhaps picking up Becky's error from excerpt 1.

(2)   1 H: Watashi wa,^ (.) haha WA,^ (.) atarashii- (.) atarashii
             konpyuutaa o^ (.) katte hoshii to,^ omoimasu.
             *I want (.) my mother wants (.) ((someone)) to buy a ne- (.) new
             computer.*

      2 B: motte imasu.   *((repeats verb ending from task sheet)).*

And, Becky does not correct that error, but corrects a stylistic point, that Hal uses *omoimasu* instead of *omotteimasu*, as indicated on the task sheet. In translating the third sentence, Becky makes the same errors she made in excerpt 1. The first time ni is used correctly to mark the benefactor is by Hal in excerpt 4, underlined below:

(4) 1 H: Hai hai hai. Unn, yon-yonban.
            Yeah yeah yeah. Unn, num- number four.

     2 B: Hai doozo.   *Okay, go ahead.*

→   3 H: Sensei <u>ni</u>,^ (.) Shoku- shokudai o,^ (.) setsumei (.) setsumei
            shite,^ (.) hoshii n tto omotteimasu.
            I want the teacher DAT *to explai- (.) explain the (.) home-
            homework.*

     4 B: Hai.   *Okay.*

Becky, however, does not use this *ni* in her subsequent translation of the fifth item. What draws her attention to Hal's correct particle use is his translation in excerpt 6, shown below. In line 2, Hal asks Becky for help saying *So how do you say?* Hal's difficulty is with the word *to marry*. This word, *kekkon suru*, is the only word that is new in this sentence as compared to previous sentences. Instead of providing the word Hal seeks, Becky answers his general plea for help by beginning the sentence in line 3. But, as Becky begins the sentence, she uses the possessive *no* instead of topic-marking *wa*, repeating the same error she made in excerpt 1, and Hal made in excerpt 2. After Becky's line 3 error, Hal takes over in line 5, explicitly correcting Becky's particle error by replacing *no* with the topic marker *wa*, and continuing on to use *ni* correctly as well. The relevant particles are underlined below, with incorrect particles shown in small caps.

(6) 1 B: Sachiko. Tanaka-san. Oh, that's yours. Hai doozo.
            Sachiko. Mr. Tanaka. Oh, that's yours. Go ahead.

     2 H: So how do you say?

→   3 B: Tanaka: sa:n no::,^ Tanaka//san
            Mr. Tanaka pos:: *Mr. Tanaka*

→   4 H: Tanaka san <u>wa</u>,^ (.) Tanaka san <u>wa</u>,^ Sachi- sachikko-san ni,^
            ka- (.)
            Mr. Tanaka top. *Mr. Tanaka wants Sachiko to ma-*

     5 B: ((laughs))

     6 H: Kekkon-kekkon shite hoshii n tto,^ omoimasu.
            Wants (her) to marry him.

Becky's line 3 help, though incorrect, serves an important function. Through providing help, she becomes highly engaged in Hal's construction of the sentence. This engagement promotes Becky's noticing of Hal's particle choices.

In line 4, Hal translates the sentence himself, using the correct particles. This is the first time that either student has used both *wa* and *ni* correctly. In line 4, he first corrects Becky's use of *no*, saying just *Tanaka-san wa*. He then restarts, marking the benefactor, Sachiko, with *ni*. He has difficulty in pronouncing *to marry* (*kekkon suru*), mispronouncing the first syllable at the end of line 4. Becky's laughter provides Hal with time to reflect, and he self-corrects in line 6, completing the sentence.

The power of the interaction in excerpt 6 is evident in excerpt 7, shown below, where Becky now must construct a sentence. Here, she uses *wa* correctly, and bids for help with other particles. Becky now recognizes her own particle errors, and bids for help extensively in structuring the sentence, resulting in a collaborative process through which Hal provides the particles and relevant verb form.

(7) 1   B: Un. Hai. Yooko. Ah-Lee san wa,^ Yooko:: (.)
          Un. Yeah. Yooko. Ah- Lee-san TOP *Yooko*

    2   H: Yoko-san.

    3   B: sa:n

→ 4   H: Ni.   *((dative marker))*

    5   B: Ni:,^ (.) Garufure:heh ndo how do you say will become?
          DAT *(.) girlfriend. How do you say will become?*

    6   H: Garufurendo ni^?   *Girlfriend ((dative marker))*

    7   B: Ga-garufurendo [ni:::   *Gir-girlfriend ((dative marker))*

→ 8   H: [ni nari?   *((dative marker)) become?*

    9   B: Narite?   *Become? ((misconjugation of te-form))*

  10   H: Nari like natte.   *((gives correct te-form of narimasu))*

  11   B: Natte. What's natte?

  12   H: Narimasu.

→ 13   B: Oh. [Natte hoshii to omotte imasu.
          Oh. [become his girlfriend.

  14   H: [Natte.   *Become.*

  15   T: Oh soo desu ne.   *Yes, that's right.*

Becky's bids for help show a new awareness of how her sentences have deviated from the grammatical structure being studied. What she learned from excerpt 6 has allowed her to reflect and to work toward change. As Becky bids for help, Hal feeds her the sentence, word by word. He provides the particle *ni* in line 4 to mark the benefactor. In line 8, his engagement is evident as he collaboratively constructs the sentence with Becky in overlap, stating a form of the verb *naru*, *to become*, after which Becky experiments with making the *te*-form needed in line 9. In response to her line 9 question intonation, Hal provides the correct form *natte* in line 10, which Becky uses to complete the sentence in line 13. And, along with getting help from Hal, Becky also turns to the teacher for confirmation in lines 18, 22, and 24, with the teacher confirming that the particles and verb are correct:

16	B:	Lee san.	Lee san wa Yooko san::
		Lee.	*Lee* TOP *Yooko san:::*
17	H:	ni.	*((dative marker)).*
→ 18	B:	ni?	*((dative marker))?*
19	T:	Un. So so.	*Yeah. That's right.*
20	B:	Garufurendo:: (.)	*Girlfriend:: (.)*
21	H:	ni	*((dative marker))*
→ 22	B:	ni?	*((dative marker))?*
23	T:	Un.	*Yeah.*
→ 24	B:	natte: hoshii to omotte imasu.	*I want her to become.*
25	T:	So so so.	*Right.*
26	H:	Hai hai hai.	*Yeah yeah yeah.*
27	B:	Uhhh. ((discovery intonation)) Natte.	*Uhhh. Become.*

The teacher does not provide new information or intervene, but confirms in response to Becky's questions. As Hal provides each particle, Becky queries the teacher, and the teacher confirms his correct choice, and Becky moves on to the next word in the sentence, as she and Hal collaboratively build the sentence with the teacher's support. The result is a vertical construction. Faerch and Kasper (1986: 263) have expressed concern that vertical constructions result in a 'piecemeal' type of interaction that they feel might not be helpful for language development—their concern is that, particularly if vertical constructions are long, 'there is a risk that learners forget the formal elements and hence create no basis for establishing new syntactic structures'. We will see, however, as analysis continues, that this vertical construction functions as an important resource in Becky's developmental processes.

The next time Becky translates a sentence, shown in excerpt 9, she returns to using *no* instead of *wa* to mark topic. When Becky fails to continue in line 3, Hal neither corrects her, nor provides the next particle (line 4), but he repeats the name *Yamada-san* with falling intonation, prompting Becky to continue. Becky restarts, correctly using *ni* (underlined, in line 5) and completes the sentence.

(9)	1	B:	Wa:tashi: NO (.) Yamada:: (.)
			I POS (.) *Yamada.*
	2	H:	san.
	3	B:	san.
→	4	H:	Yamada san.

5 B: Yamada san <u>ni</u> nama- watashi no namae ni,^ wa- uh oboe//te=
     Yamada-san DAT *nam- my name* DAT, TOP- *uh remem//ber=*
     ((Yamada to remember my name))

6 H: Oboe.   *Remember ((stem))*

7 B: =hoshii to omotte imasu.   *((I)) want ((him)) to.*

Hal's engagement in Becky's sentence construction is evidenced not only by
how he provides Becky with words (*san* in line 2), and repeats sentence
components (*Yamada-san* in line 4), but also how he collaboratively completes
the sentence with Becky, uttering part of the verb in overlap with Becky
(line 6). Clearly, he is engaged in interaction as Becky works to complete her
sentence.

In excerpt 11, the last sentence of Becky and Hal's first pass through the
task, Becky corrects her own particle errors for the first time (errors are in
small caps, with other relevant particles underlined). A portion of this episode
was shown earlier to illustrate Hal's withholding of help. Here, the entire
episode is given, with analysis focusing on Becky's developmental processes.
The sentence Becky is working to construct here is:

Yoshida-san wa   shujin ni   hayaku kaette hoshii to   omotteimasu.
Ms. Yoshida TOP husband DAT early   return   desire CMP think.
Ms. Yoshida would like her husband to return home early.

The excerpt proceeds as follows: in line 1 Becky misuses both *wa* and *no*, but
Hal does not correct her. In line 3, she self-corrects, marking *Yoshida-san*
with *wa*, but she also changes marking of *shujin wa* (which was wrong) to
shujin no, which is still incorrect. After several turns related to the use and
meaning of the word *hayai* (lines 4–11, omitted here), Becky begins the sentence
again, with the same particles she used earlier in line 3. Her use of question
intonation in line 12 reveals her uncertainty about the use of *no*, but Hal does
not intervene. He also does not intervene when she bids for help in line 13,
elongating the final vowel in the word *uchi* (house) and pausing. Becky then
successfully self-corrects, her discovery of the problem evidenced by her use
of the word *ah*, a change-of-state token (Heritage 1984) which shows her
new understanding. At this point, she says *shujin ni*, using the correct particle.

(11)   1 B: [Ok Yoshida san <u>NO</u> shujin <u>WA</u>,^ (.) ne?
           [Ok Yoshida-san <u>POS</u> *husband* <u>TOP</u> *(.) ne?*

      2 H: [Ok,   Hai.

→   3 B: Oh Yoshida san <u>wa</u>,^ (.) shujin <u>NO</u>,^ (.) uchi: <u>ni</u>,^ (.)
           um kitte,^ (.)
           Oh Yoshida san <u>TOP</u>, *(.) husband* POS *(.) house* <u>DAT</u> *(.)*
           um come (.)

           ((interaction concerning use of *hayai* [early] deleted to save space))

→   12 B: ( )Yoshida sa:n (.) <u>wa</u>,^ (.) shujin   <u>NO</u>,^ (.) uh shujin <u>NO</u>?
               ( ) Yoshida-san (.) TOP (.) husband POS(.) uh husband POS?
→   13   shujin <u>NO</u> uchi:: (.) ah shu- (.) shujin <u>ni:</u> (.) haya:- (.)
               hayatte,^ (.) uchi <u>ni</u> haya- oh darn.
               husband POS house:: (.)ah hus- husband DAT (.) earl- (.)
               early (.) home DAT earl- oh darn.
    14 H: Ku.
               ((adverbial ending needed when placing 'hayai' before a verb))

Here Becky reaps the fruit of the collaborative work which occurred in previous sentence-construction episodes. She is finally ready to solve the problem on her own. The interaction shows the uneven process of transformation of the structure from the interpsychological plane to the intrapsychological plane. And, as noted earlier, we also see how Hal becomes less responsive to Becky's bids for help. His unresponsiveness is evidence of his discernment that even though she bids for help, he has provided enough help in the past that she should be able to perform without assistance, and she does.

Becky's self-correction in excerpt 11 marks a developmental turning point for Becky. As Hal and Becky repeat the task, each doing different sentences, Becky shows a new awareness of the structure which she applies to her performance, and produces sentences with greater confidence and fluency. After she uses particles incorrectly in excerpt 13 (not shown), Hal explicitly corrects her in excerpt 15. She is using the wrong particles in line 1, but shows no evidence of difficulty—she does not bid for help, but shows signs of continuing. Instead of letting her continue, Hal's explicit correction occurs in line 2. Then, in line 3, Becky uses *ni* correctly. Hal's engagement is evident in his overlapped production of the dative phrase. Finally, in line 6, Becky repeats the entire sentence with fluency.

(15)   1 B: Watashi <u>NO</u>,^ (.) sensei <u>WA</u>,^. (..)
               I POS (.) teacher TOP. (.) ((My teacher))
→   2 H: Ie ie. Watashi <u>wa</u>.   *No no. I TOP.*
      3 B: Watashi wa [sensei <u>ni</u>,^   *I top teacher DAT*
      4 H: [sensei ni,^   *teacher DAT*
      5 H: Hai.   *Yes.*
      6 B: Watashi wa,^ sensei ni,^ (.) shukudai o setsumei shite,^ hoshii
               to,^ omo:tte imasu.
               I want the teacher (.) to explain the homework to me.

Explicit correction helps Becky here—it reminds her of what she has already discovered in excerpt 11. After Hal restarts the sentence correctly, Becky uses *ni* in line 3 without his assistance. Hal's correction is appropriately timed for Becky. He did not correct her earlier use of particles, but does so now, reminding her of what she, herself, has already discovered.

Becky applies her new knowledge by analyzing her own performance. In excerpt 17, she catches her own error—she began with *Sachiko* instead of the topic, *Tanaka-san*. She restarts in line 2, producing the sentence fluently, using the correct particles.

(17) 1 B: Sachiko oh no.

   2   Tanaka san wa,^ Sachiko san ni,^ (.) kekkon shite hoshii to omoimasu.
          Mr. Tanaka wants Sachiko (.) to marry him.

Becky's fluent, correct sentence production continues through her last two turns at making sentences. In excerpt 21, her last chance to make a sentence during this task, Becky performs fluently and correctly:

(21) 1 B: Yoshida san wa,^ (.) uh- okusan ni,^ (.) tabako o yamete hoshii to omotte imasu.
          Yoshida-san wants (.) uh- his wife (.) to quit smoking.

   2 H: Hai.   *Yes.*

Finally, in the communicative task following pair work with Hal, Becky is asked by another student what she wants the teacher to give her for her birthday. She answers in (a) below:

(a) B: Wa- watashi wa: (.) sensei ni (.) uh: atarashii kaban o katte hoshii to omotteimasu.
     I want the teacher to buy me a new purse.

After the task, the teacher nominates her to report what one of her classmates wants. She reports what Hal said he wanted in (b) below:

(b) B: Ano (..) u:::m. (.) Hal-san wa sen- sensei ni atarashii kam- (.) kam- kamkoodaa o katte hoshii desu.
     Hal wants the teacher to buy him a new camcorder.

While she stumbles over the unfamiliar pronunciation of *kamukoodaa* (camcorder) in (b), she marks receiver and giver of the action correctly in both sentences, both when talking about herself and talking about another.

Becky's progress is summarized in Table 2.3. The numbers from 1–21 in the left-hand column refer to Becky's turns in the sentence-construction task. C1 and C2 refer to her two utterances in the communicative task. The first row indicates each of the phrases of the target structure (Topic phrase, Dative phrase, Object—or destination or dative—phrase, and verb phrase). For each phrase, the table shows whether Becky produced the phrase correctly, made a grammatical error, self-corrected, or bid for assistance. Here, only bids for assistance related to *grammatical structure* are listed. Explicit correction from Hal is also noted. In addition, Hal's assistance is shown through shading of a particular cell. Shading indicates any sort of assistance, including assistance with lexical items. In cells where there is shading but a bid for assistance is not noted, the assistance did not relate to grammatical structure. For example, in the first cell of row 1, the cell is shaded. Becky's error is in the use of *no* for *wa*, but Hal's assistance was with word choice. The last row of the chart sums up the number of untreated errors, bids and assistance, explicit correction, self-correction, and correct uses. Instances where Hal provided a particle or recast Becky's utterance are also noted.

#	Topic phrase (*wa*)	Dative phrase (*ni*)	Object (*o*) Destination (*ni/e*) Dative phrase (*ni*)	verb phrase (*Vte + hoshii*)
1	Uses *no* for *wa*	Uses *wa* for *ni*	Bid + help	Hal recasts
3	Uses *no* for *wa*	Uses *wa* for *ni*	Deletes *o*	Deletes main verb
5	Uses *no* for *wa*	Deletes *ni*	Correct	Correct
6	Hal explicitly corrects *no* to *wa*[2]	(#6 is Hal's turn to construct a sentence, not Becky's. Becky started the sentence for Hal at his request, and he corrected her.)		
7	Bid + help	Bid + help	Hal provides	Bid + help
9	Uses *no* for *wa*	Correct	Uses *ni/wa* for *o*	Correct
11	Self-corrects *no* to *wa*	Self-corrects *no* to *ni*	Self-corrects— adding *ni* after first omitting	Bid + help (adverb) Self-corrects (verb)
13	Uses *no* for *wa*	Uses *wa* for *ni*	Miscorrects *ni* to *o*	Correct
15	Hal corrects *no* to *wa*	Correct	Correct	Correct
17	Self-corrects	Correct. Hal also says in overlap.	Correct	Correct
19	Correct	Correct	Correct	Correct
21	Correct	Correct	Correct	Correct
C1	Correct	Correct	Correct	Correct
C2	Correct	Correct	Correct	Correct
Summary	5 untreated errors (*no* for *wa*— #1, 3, 5, 9, 13) 1 'bid + help'—#7 2 explicit correction —#6, 15 2 self-correction— #11, 17 4 correct— #19, 21, C1, C2	4 untreated errors— #1, 3, 5, 13 1 self-correction—#1 1 'bid + help'—#7 7 correct— #9, 15, 17, 19, 21, C1, C2	3 untreated errors— #3, 9, 13 1 'bid + help'—#1 1 provided—#7 7 correct— #5, 15, 7, 19, 21, C1, C2	1 untreated error— #3 1 recast—#1 2 'bid + help' (1 self-correct)—#7, 11 9 correct— #5, 9, 13, 15, 19, 21, C1, C2

Note: *no* is the genitive marker; *wa* is the topic marker; *ni* is the dative marker; *o* is the accusative marker. Destination may be marked with *ni* or *e*.

Table 2.3: Summary of errors, self-correction, bids/receipt of help (shaded areas indicate Hal's assistance), and correct production

As shown in the summary, Becky at first uses the wrong particles, consistently misusing *no* for *wa* in the topic phrase, and *wa* for *ni* in the dative phrase. She also occasionally has difficulty with object phrases, and has some difficulty with verb phrases. She bid for and received help from Hal at least once for each phrase type. And, in #15, Hal explicitly corrected her most persistent error, the use of the genitive marker *no* for the topic marker *wa* in the topic in #6 (which is Hal's turn, but in which Becky started the sentence for him, shown earlier), after she bid for help once in #7, and self-corrected in #11.

Hal's assistance supported Becky where she was struggling the most. Most of the help is concentrated in Becky's first six sentences, where Hal provided assistance for 12 out of 25 cells in the table. Hal's help, though, did not prevent Becky from making early errors, but allowed her to work to solve her own problems to the extent to which she was able, and functioned as an important resource for Becky as she worked through the task. In addition, it is clear that treatment of all errors was not needed for development to occur. Hal's assistance (in addition, of course, to other models provided through instruction, etc.) was sufficient.

Becky's internalization of L2 grammar

Becky's appropriation process is visible through analysis of the interaction, which shows her increasing autonomy (Wertsch 1985a), according to the levels of internalization outlined by Aljaafreh and Lantolf (1994) in Table 2.4. Hal first provided particles in response to Becky's bids for help (excerpts 1, 7), then provided a correct model (excerpt 4), and then corrected Becky when she gave him wrong information (excerpt 6). His help became more implicit in response to Becky's gains. In Excerpt 9, he prompted by providing the word prior to the problematic particle, and in excerpt 11 he stood by as Becky solved her own problems. When repeating the task, Hal used explicit correction to guide her performance (excerpt 15). Overwhelmingly, the help provided was tailored to Becky's developmental level. That the help was appropriate is evidenced by the fact that *the help was effective*—the data show that the help provided led to L2 development.

Of course, the development which occurred in this classroom setting does not guarantee that the structure is acquired for all time—Becky has not yet reached 'Level 5,' where she would be able to use the target structure correctly in a broader range of contexts. What the data do show are microgenetic processes as they occur moment by moment in this particular classroom activity. During task performance itself, we, in fact, see that as Becky improves, her performance is variable and includes regression. Regression is expected as a natural part of the developmental process (Lantolf and Aljaafreh 1995); even as the learner grows in L2 competence, L1 and L2 attrition studies are reminders that no level of mastery is impervious to regression (Seliger and Vago 1991; de Bot 1996). I do not claim that Becky has fully mastered this construction, but that she is on her way. Through her collaborative and independent activity, Becky has moved to 'Level 4', where she is able to correct her own errors, and to use the structure independently in a particular context. Becky would need further experience with the structure in a broader range of contexts in order to build optimally upon what she accomplished in this particular lesson.

Levels of internalization from interpsychological to intrapsychological functioning	
Level 1	The learner is unable to notice, or correct the error, even with intervention.
Level 2	The learner is able to notice the error, but cannot correct it, even with intervention, requiring explicit help.
Level 3	The learner is able to notice and correct an error, but only with assistance. The learner understands assistance, and is able to incorporate feedback offered.
Level 4	The learner notices and corrects an error with minimal, or no obvious feedback, and begins to assume full responsibility for error correction. However, the structure is not yet fully internalized, since the learner often produces the target form incorrectly. The learner may even reject feedback when it is unsolicited.
Level 5	The learner becomes more consistent in using the target structure correctly in all contexts. The learner is fully able to notice and correct his/her own errors without intervention.

Table 2.4: Transition from interpyschological to intrapsychological functioning
(Aljaafreh and Lantolf 1994)

Conclusion

Examination of interaction from a Vygotskian perspective illuminates developmental processes as they are realized via assisted performance. Vygotsky called for analytic approaches which capture the dynamic whole of the process being examined (Zinchenko 1995; Vygotsky 1987). The general genetic law of development and ZPD work hand-in-hand to provide a framework which illuminates developmental processes in the data. The analysis provides evidence of how classroom interaction promotes L2 development in the ZPD. As a result of collaboration, Becky becomes able to accomplish with ease what she initially could not do without assistance. These gains remain in the follow-up interview task, both during task performance, and when Becky reports her findings to the teacher.

The analysis details how Hal provided help when Becky needed it most by orienting to subtly articulated cues through which Becky communicated whether or not she was continuing; orientation to these cues allowed Hal to work collaboratively with Becky. Teamwork and mutual sensitivity are essential in assisted performance. For the analyst, narrow transcription is necessary, as fine details may be found to be pivots upon which the analysis turns. In this case, transcription of details such as vowel elongation, false starts, filled pauses, and intonation contours clarified the cues to which Hal oriented in his provision or nonprovision of assistance. Hal's apparent intuitiveness is grounded in his responsiveness to these subtle cues. And, as a result of assistance, not only did Becky's performance improve, but Hal became less responsive to her bids for help, withdrawing support as Becky increased in ability to come to her own solutions.

Clearly the nature of effective assistance in the ZPD varies depending upon a variety of factors, including the expertise of the helper (whether 'expert' or 'peer'), the nature of the task, the goals of the participants, and the developmental levels of the learners. For example, the tutor in Aljaafreh and Lantolf's (1994) study began with more implicit help as he worked to establish what a tutee could do unaided, with help increasing in explicitness according to what the student could not do, and then became less explicit as the learner developed autonomy. In the present study, where the task involved peer practice of a structure new to the students, help was responsive to interlocutor bids which quickly established the parameters of the ZPD by showing the learner's own awareness of what was difficult. Hal's efforts, therefore, were concentrated on helping Becky with problems that she herself noticed. In this way, his help was maximally effective. Other careful analyses of the collaborative interaction of language learners are needed to clarify how assisted performance in the ZPD is realized for a broader range of L2 learners. To understand how different tasks may have an impact on L2 development, analyses of various tasks as realized in learner–learner interaction are essential.

The results also speak to the impact of task design on classroom learning. Task design, while important, ultimately cannot determine the nature of the activity engaged in by learners. The translation task used here did not incorporate characteristics considered essential in a state-of-the-art foreign language curriculum (Pica, Kanagy, and Falodun 1993; Skehan 1996), and would likely be rejected by many language teachers for its lack of a communicative purpose. In spite of these design problems, however, Becky and Hal transformed the task into L2 activity that pushed them forward in their ability to use a difficult grammatical construction. Here, we see how two learners create their own language learning activity. Becky and Hal's progress resulted from their high investment in the task, and their persistence at pushing onward even though it was difficult, and pushing each other to create with language. Learner engagement is clearly of primary importance. Analyses of learner *activity* during task implementation are essential to understand the relationship between task design and how tasks are instantiated by particular learners. The productivity of learner interaction cannot necessarily be determined by looking at task design, but tasks themselves may be transformed as each learner applies him or herself in instantiation of a unique activity (Coughlan and Duff 1994). Foster (1998) has shown that what transpires during learner activity may be quite different from what an analysis of task design might lead one to expect. Further investigation of what learners actually do with classroom tasks, and how learner activity relates to their language development, is needed before research can be said to show the value of particular task types over others. Such studies will give teachers a better idea of how learners may implement different sorts of tasks, as well as giving researcher and teacher alike a better understanding of the situated processes of L2 development.

Notes

1 Ohta (1995) provides a detailed analysis of this activity.
2 The remaining cells in row 6 are blank because this was Hal's turn, not Becky's. Becky produced the topic phrase using the wrong particles in response to Hal's request for help. Hal then corrects the particles and goes on to finish constructing his sentence.

Appendix 2.1: Transcription conventions

WA, GA, NI, etc.	When particle is spelled out in small caps, it indicates an error.
Underlining	portion highlighted for reader attention
^	glottal stop
,	'continuing' intonation
?	'question' intonation
.	falling intonation
[	onset of overlap
//	turn in the next line starts here
:	elongation of a sound
(.)	brief pause
=	latched utterances
TOP	topic marker
DAT	dative marker
ACC	accusative marker
POS	genitive marker
COP	copula
CONJ	conjunction
CMP	complementizer

Appendix 2.2: Worksheet used in class

Activity 1:　Ｖてほしい Practice
〜は…にＶてほしい（と思っています）

Person who wants someone to do something	What s/he wants who to do
I	Father will take me to Japan.
I	Mother will buy me a new computer.
I	Older brother will tell me how to use computer.
I	My teacher will explain the homework.
Younger brother	His girlfriend will do his homework.
Tanaka	Sachiko will marry him.
Lee	Yoko will become his girlfriend.
Smith	Her teacher will teach her more Kanji.
I	Ms. Yamada will remember my name.
Yoshida	His wife will quit smoking（たばこ）.
Yoshida's wife	Her husband will come home early.

Activity 2:　先生に何を買ってほしいですか。

Your Japanese teacher has generously offered to buy each of you *whatever you want* for your birthday. (On a teacher's salary?? Clearly this is a joke!) Anyway, interview five classmates, and find out what they want 先生　to buy them for their birthday:

名前：　　　　　　　　　　　　　　買ってほしい物：

_____　　　_____

_____　　　_____

_____　　　_____

_____　　　_____

3 Subjects speak out: How learners position themselves in a psycholinguistic task[1]

Regina Roebuck
University of Louisville

Introduction

Tasks are often used in experimental psycholinguistic research to elicit performance data from subjects because they are believed to be both controllable and measurable. Part of the perceived controllability of tasks, however, stems from the belief that subjects, although so named, can be manipulated by the intentions of the researcher and, in particular, by task instructions. Thus, subjects are treated as objects and are denied the agency attributed to true subjects.

The purpose of the present discussion is to consider the construct of *subject* in the context of psycholinguistic research, looking specifically at how subjects are construed in both natural science-based and hermeneutic models. It will be argued that natural science-based methodologies effectively allow researchers to marginalize subjects by eliminating those who show intentionality or by failing to recognize the intentionality and individuality of others. The theory of activity, a component of sociocultural theory, however, is predicated on the belief that people are uniquely constructed individuals, and that human activity is a complex process, determined by the context and the goals and sociocultural history of the participants. Thus, researchers working in this and other hermeneutic frameworks challenge the assumption that individuals and their activity in tasks can be controlled.

Drawing on data from written recall protocols, it will be shown that subjects involved in the same *task* are necessarily involved in different *activity*, since they bring to the task their unique histories, goals, and capacities (as has been argued by Coughlan and Duff 1994). The discussion will consider not only the cognitive activity of producing a written recall protocol, but also that of positioning the self as a co-participant in the experimental interaction, and will provide evidence that learners, because they are agents, realize both kinds of activity in different ways, according to the needs and goals of the moment. One such need, as will be shown here, is that of protecting the self from the scrutiny of a researcher who is still perceived by some as an instructor.

Sociocultural psychology and methodology

Psychology has seen the rise of three distinct theoretical paradigms since its beginnings as a scholarly discipline. The first generation (to use Mehler and Noizet's 1973 term) was that of the Behaviorist or Neo-Behaviorist school, in which psychology was the study of objectively described 'inputs and outputs to an idealized human individual' (Harré 1995: 143). The second generation, the result of the (first) cognitive revolution, is that of cognitive or computational science, expounded by Miller and Johnson-Laird (1976) and others, and influenced by Chomsky's syntactic theory (1972). This paradigm focuses on the investigation of the unobservable mental processes which are believed to constitute cognition.

Both generations have tacitly embraced the model and methods of the natural sciences, with an emphasis on prediction, reductionism, and the formulation of universal laws governing causal relationships. Although differing in focus and epistemology, the Behaviorist and computational schools are grounded in the positivist or empiricist model of the classical physical hard sciences and privilege quantitative methods (Van Langenhove 1995). Human beings are likened to material objects and are thought to be controllable and passive spectators to either their overt reactions to verbal and physical stimuli, or their running of covert and inaccessible cognitive processes (Harré 1995). Similarly, in both paradigms, the role of language and language use in cognition is neglected, reduced to either mere behavioral reaction or simple speech manifestations of underlying, abstract linguistic structure (A. A. Leontiev 1981).

Third generation psychology, first evident in the work of Bruner (1973) and Blakar and Rommetveit (1975), has also been called the second cognitive revolution (Harré and Gillett 1994). This psycholinguistic paradigm departs from its predecessors in two significant ways. One, it treats psychological and linguistic processes as a unified phenomenon. The focus of investigation shifts from an analysis of abstract mental processes to a psychological analysis of speech and thought (A. A. Leontiev 1981). Moreover, this approach emphasizes utterance or discourse, as opposed to idealized sentences, taking into account the sociocultural context and, importantly, utilizing a hermeneutic model of analysis. In the West, this approach is known as Discursive (Harré and Gillett 1994), Sociotextual (Frawley 1987), Dialogical (Rommetveit 1991, 1992; Wold 1992a) and Sociocultural (Wertsch 1985a, 1991) Psycholinguistics.

Although he lived and died in the early part of this century, Vygotsky's ideas should be understood as contributing to third generation psychology. Expanded upon by colleagues and students such as A. N. Leontiev, A. A. Leontiev, Gal'perin, Luria and others, they formed the basis of Soviet speech-activity theory, of which sociocultural theory is an offspring.

Sociocultural theory is a theory of mind, based on Vygotsky's belief that the properties of the mind can be discovered by observing mental, physical, and linguistic activity, because they are *intrinsically* related. According to Vygotsky, the essence of consciousness is the way in which humans constantly construct their environment and its representation by engaging in various forms of activity (Wertsch 1985a: 188). Vygotsky saw consciousness as a process through which people dynamically organize and realize higher mental functions such as voluntary attention, voluntary memory, intention, planning, and the resulting physical behavior. This organization is not, as cognitive scientists in the Cartesian tradition would argue, a preexisting, underlying system of abstract representations that determines our behavior. Rather, Vygotsky argues, behavior and consciousness arise and exist together. Therefore, consciousness may be observed in the organization of human behavior.

To understand the organizational properties of consciousness, Vygotsky turned to the political and social writings of Engels, who stressed the importance of physical tools in mediating and controlling objects in the physical environment. Vygotsky analogized this concept to the case of consciousness, where both the activity and the tools are psychological, arguing that the most powerful psychological tool is an elaborate semiotic system, that is, language. Observing that language was crucially relevant to the problem of consciousness, Vygotsky wrote that:

> The problem of speaking and speech belongs to the set of psychological problems in which the main issue is the relationship among various psychological functions, among the various forms of the activity of consciousness.
> (Wertsch 1985a: 195)

In the case of mental activity, Vygotsky argued that it was the word or, more precisely, word meaning, which was crucially involved in the dynamic organization of consciousness. The role of symbolic mediation in consciousness was also observed by Wittgenstein (1953), who stated that 'thinking is the activity of operating with signs' (cited in Harré and Gillett 1994: 50).

Vygotsky's original ideas about semiotic mediation have been extended considerably by the speech-activity theorists in the former Soviet Union (A. N. Leontiev, A. A. Leontiev, Luria) as well as by researchers in the West such as Scribner and Cole (1973, 1981), Kozulin (1986, 1990), Wertsch (1985a, 1991), Frawley (1987), and Harré and Gillett (1994). Harré and Gillett argue that it is not merely the individual word or concept that makes up consciousness, but rather it is the discourse. Similarly, Frawley proposes that mind is a sociotextual process. These analyses are alike in that they see mind as a discursive process. The emphasis on discourse unites the essential features of mind as originally proposed by Vygotsky and as currently explained by sociocultural researchers in third-generation psycholinguistics: consciousness implies language or symbol use, process, and activity in social space.

First, the notion of discourse reinforces Vygotsky's idea that mental activity is made up of 'individual and private uses of symbolic systems' (Harré and Gillett 1994: 27). Also, like Vygotsky, discursive psychology emphasizes that consciousness is mental activity achieved through discourse, whether public or private, and not underlying or hidden abstract processes. Finally, the notion of discourse or sociotextual activity embodies the socioculturally embedded nature of mind and the symbolic system. It situates speakers and thinkers in social, historical, political, cultural, and interpersonal contexts. On the one hand, this means that mind is realized in the act of discourse, private or public. On the other, this means that mental activity, the operation of a symbolic system, is to a large extent determined by the sociocultural history of the person and the discourses to which she has access. Mind is, then, a symbolically organized social construction, determined by and, thus visible in, discourse (Harré and Gillett 1994: 86).

Third generation psychology eschews the natural science model, particularly, its reductionism and need for prediction and universals. Instead, researchers in this framework follow a hermeneutic model, focusing on the search for meaning and knowledge of particulars through detailed, interpretive explanations of persons and their mental and physical activity (Van Langenhove 1995). For Vygotsky, word meaning was crucial to understanding the interfunctional organization of mental and physical activity and was thus the correct unit of analysis for the study of consciousness and the meaning-making that it entails (Wertsch 1985a). Similarly, Harré and Gillett (1994), Frawley (1987), and Rommetveit (1992) look to linguistically constructed social discourse in the investigation of mind.

The subject in sociocultural research

It has been argued that what is missing from first and second generation theories of psychology is a focus on the individual. Much of this is due to what Danziger (1990: 68) refers to as 'the triumph of the aggregate' in psychology. In early psychological research, all participants, experimenters and subjects alike, were thought of as collaborators. Furthermore, the discipline focused on individual human beings. Eventually, however, the focus of psychology switched from a description of 'a human mind', that is, the mind of a particular individual, to 'the human mind', that is, a quantified collective. Thus, psychology began to attribute characteristics not to individual subjects, but to a population or populations. In large part this was due to the rise of statistical methods in other fields, such as criminology and social sciences, as well as the use of the questionnaire as a methodological tool, which was then brought into psychology. As a consequence, Danziger argues, social acts and psychological phenomena became

> not to be understood in terms of the local circumstances of their individual agents but in terms of a statistical magnitude obtained by counting the number of heads, and the number of relevant acts and dividing the one by the other.
>
> (Danziger 1990: 76)

This equation severs the crucial link between an individual and her actions and thus eliminates the agency, or the subjecthood, of individual subjects.

This is not surprising, since methods based on the natural sciences assume that subjects, like objects in the material world, lack motive and intentionality. Instead, in both behavioral and computational psychologies, human beings are understood to be mere spectators of processes over which they have no control (Harré 1995).

These methodological assumptions are evident in some of the ways in which investigators regard their subjects. Often, subjects are seen as objects to be manipulated by the task instructions and the investigator's intentions. Moreover, researchers routinely remove subjects who appear to violate instructions, unaware that all participants in a study necessarily behave as individuals, engaged in unique instantiations of human activity.

Sociocultural theory focuses on human individuals and, in doing so, the possibility that an individual will act according to her own intentions.[2] As Van Langenhove notes,

> one of the big differences between physical entities and human beings is that the behaviour of people has a meaning for the people themselves and is mainly intentional.
>
> (Van Langenhove 1995: 23)

According to Vygotskian thought, then, human beings are agents who act upon the world and engage in activity, constructing their environment in unique ways. Particularly, the theory of activity, a component of sociocultural theory, maintains that human behavior is a complex process, and the properties of any given activity are determined by the sociohistorical setting and by the goals and sociocultural history of the participants (A. N. Leontiev 1981). Activity, then, necessarily differs between, and even within, individuals.

Along these lines, Coughlan and Duff (1994) have argued that the behavior found in experimental conditions is neither constant nor controllable because it is an instantiation of activity. They posit a clear distinction between *task* and *activity*, and propose that tasks are merely 'behavior blueprints', motivated by the researchers' agenda and imposed on subjects. In comparison, activity is the

> behavior that is actually produced when an individual (or group) performs a task. It is the process, as well as the outcome of the task, examined in its sociocultural context.
>
> (Coughlan and Duff 1994: 175)

Coughlin and Duff illustrate this through a comparison of across-learner and within-learner performance on a standard oral picture description task. They find that in each case, the task yields visibly different activity, which they attribute to small, yet important, differences in the material circumstances of the activity, as well as in the learners' perception of and orientation to the conditions of the task. Specifically, Coughlan and Duff discovered that some of the differences might have arisen from the on-going struggle experienced by the learners, as they attempted to realize an anti-social and contrived experimental task under the guise of a conversational interaction with another person, namely the researcher.

The role of orientation—that is, how subjects approach a task—in determining task performance is one commonly overlooked by social science researchers in general. It is often assumed that subjects will simply adopt the orientation prescribed by the researcher. However, orientation, like the other features of activity, is contextually derived and a crucial part of the context is the individual herself. Thus, it is impossible for a researcher to pass on an orientation (usually in the form of directions for completing the task) to the subject. The necessary discrepancy between the orientation of the researcher and that of the subject is a major reason why task performance—that is, activity—is not predictable. However, task and activity are both part of experimental and instructional conditions.[3] The task represents what the researcher (or the instructor) would like the learner to do, and activity is what the learner actually does. Thus, activity is how learners—as agents—construct the task.

This discussion is not meant to imply that task-generated data, either from an individual or from a group of individuals, are useless in the line of psychological inquiry. On the contrary, such data are potentially quite revealing, as long as they are treated as instances of realized activity potential, and not simply as a monolithic performance on a standardized task. In second language research it is often deemed necessary, for the purpose of the experiment, to assume that subjects are homogeneous individuals engaged in the same activity (i.e. doing the same thing) in compliance with the wishes of the researchers. Often the suggestion that this may not be the case threatens the supposed validity of the test instrument and the experiment itself, or causes certain subjects to be removed from the study. However, investigation pursued in the framework of activity theory is not threatened in this way, because it anticipates, and thus has the potential to explain, task-generated activity in a principled and theoretical way.

It has been argued, then, that some schools of psychology, with their reliance on a statistical model that by definition excludes individuals, treat subjects as grouped objects who lack agency and intentionality and who can be led to perform tasks according to the researchers' wishes. However, the data to be presented here, consistent with Coughlan and Duff's findings, will provide evidence that this cannot be the case. Thus, the data will reveal learners acting like agents, that is, actively engaged in creating their own diverse enterprises. Furthermore, evidence will be presented that suggests that the learners were involved in two concurrent tasks (which in turn result in two sets of intertwined activities). First, activities relevant to the cognitive problem of producing a written recall protocol will be considered. Subsequently, evidence will be provided to show that the learners were also engaged in the activity of maintaining and constructing the frame of a social interaction, even in the context of a written experimental task. Particular attention will be paid to the way in which some learners repositioned themselves (and thus reframed the interaction) in response to a difficult cognitive task. Since symbolic mediation is the organizational principle of human activity, one way of investigating and explaining mental functioning in the framework of activity theory is through an examination and analysis of the language activity that tasks generate. Such will be the approach to the data that follow.

The data

The data presented here come from an earlier study, discussed at length in Roebuck (1998), involving the production of written recall protocols by 27 elementary and five intermediate students of Spanish at the university level. The learners read and immediately recalled three experimental texts which were chosen to represent differing degrees of difficulty, as a result of either the text language or the content.[4] There were two newspaper reports, one each in the L1 and L2, dealing with political issues in Latin America, of which it was hoped that the students would have no more than general knowledge. The third text was an expository text in English regarding physics, and was considered to be challenging because of its content. Difficult texts were chosen in accordance with Vygotsky's Genetic Method, in which it is proposed that psychological processes can be best studied as they emerge (Vygotsky 1978). One way to accomplish this is to confront the person with a difficulty or with disruptions in the flow of the task (Lantolf and Appel 1994a). This allows the researcher to observe how changes (i.e. development) occur as a result of the interference.[5]

Retaining the excludable

The written recall protocols were rich with language that suggested that the activity in which the learners were engaged was as individual as the learners themselves. Before examining particular linguistic features, however, we first consider the case of one learner, Brian M., whose unique intentionality was made evident during the administration of the experiment by his own admission that he had not followed the instructions correctly.

Participants are frequently eliminated from experimental research on the basis of not having followed the task directions. This is based on the assumption that all subjects can and should adhere to task instructions, an assumption which Coughlan and Duff have shown to be false. A quantitative study of reading comprehension would in all likelihood have excluded this learner from analysis, because his performance would be considered too different from that of the group. However, when examined alongside the recalls that the learner produced 'as per the directions', this particular protocol sheds light on the relationship between an individual's perception of a task, his own experience, and his orientation to the series of recalls that he was asked to produce.

After the administration of the first of the three experimental texts, this learner indicated that he had misunderstood the directions and had, he felt, made a terrible mistake in completing the recall task. Specifically, he had read and written about only the *first* of the three paragraphs that made up the Spanish newspaper text. Thus, the learner's assessment of the task at hand was significantly different from that of the others, as he thought he was responsible for reading and recalling a much shorter text. This difference in assessment manifested itself in an orientation unseen in the other recalls: that of producing a literal translation of the original text. This can be seen by comparing his recall protocol, given in (1), with the first paragraph of the target text shown in (2)[6]:

(1)   Miami United States of America 28th. President George Bush on Friday the 23rd passed the controversial law known as the Torricelli Law on the last days of his electoral campaign ^in order to maintain _____ over the Cuban community.

(Brian M., Text A)

(2)   Miami, EEUU. 28 octubre. El presidente de Estados Unidos, George Bush, firmó viernes 23 en Miami la controvertida Acta para la Democracia en Cuba, conocida como *ley Torricelli*. Bush transformó la firma de la ley en unos de los últimos actos de su campaña electoral en Florida, en un intento por mantener a su lado a la comunidad de origen cubano.

(Text A)

Miami, US. October 28th. The President of the United States, George Bush, signed, Friday the 23, in Miami, the controversial Act for Democracy in Cuba, known as the Torricelli law. *Bush transformed the signing of the law into one of the last acts of his electoral campaign in Florida in an attempt to keep on his side the community of Cuban origin.*

(Translation of Text A)

Orientation to a given activity is based in large part on a person's assessment of the situation (Talyzina 1981). Thus, it seems plausible that the orientation towards memorization was made feasible based on having to read only one short paragraph. What is interesting, however, is that this learner appears to have approached the recall of the second experimental text (the English expository text) with the same mnemonic orientation, even though he knew then that it entailed reading a seemingly much longer text. This carryover, arguably, may be seen as a result of the relative success of the initial orientation. The second time, however, the learner was only able to copy down the first few lines of each paragraph of the original text. This is understandable, given that this text was considerably longer. Perhaps this lack of success accounts for his failure to carry his mnemonic orientation to the third text he was asked to read and recall.

Thus, the learner, Brian M., by his own admission, failed to follow task instructions for the first protocol. Yet, his data are valuable as they shed interesting light on the complex relationship between assessment, previous experience, orientation, and even learning within the context of the experimental task. They confirm Talyzina's (1981) original claim that people orient themselves to tasks based on their assessment of the proposed activity and their abilities to complete it. Researchers, however, often miss differences in orientation less obvious than that just shown, because they fail to allow for the possibility that learners will behave in ways other than that what is expected of them.

Problem-solving activity

One way to discover the features of human activity is through an examination of the linguistic forms which mediate it. This type of inquiry follows from Vygotsky's fundamental theoretical insight that speech, in addition to its communicative function, bears a private, self-oriented function, and is thus used to organize and carry out mental activity (Vygotsky 1986). When faced with cognitive difficulties, speakers often make external their inner order as speech in an attempt to achieve and maintain control of their mental activity in the task (Wertsch 1979; John-Steiner 1992; Appel and Lantolf 1994). Researchers working within the framework of sociocultural theory have found that this overt, organizing speech for self, referred to as *private speech* or *private writing*, differs in form from communicative speech, in that it is more abbreviated and manifests seemingly aberrant formal properties: i.e. the use of affective markers, odd pronominalization, tense and aspect (Frawley and Lantolf 1985) epistemic modality (Ahmed 1988; DiCamilla and Lantolf 1994), focus (Frawley 1992; Roebuck 1998), the use of certain gestures (McNeill 1992; McCafferty 1996, 1998) and some forms of vague language (Roebuck 1998).

An analysis of the linguistic features of the recall protocols, and particularly of the private writing features, reveals that the learners in this study were engaged in problem-solving activity which differed not only among them but also within them. That is, individual learners approached the task in diverse ways, and even reoriented themselves to different activity throughout the task.

At the outset, many learners appeared to be predominantly, if not entirely, oriented towards the reader-directed task of relating the content of the experimental texts, as can be seen in the example in (3), which represents the beginning of a fairly complete and accurate recall of the Spanish newspaper article.

(3)   On the 28th of October in Miami, Florida, George Bush signed a law
       that prohibits American owned business in other countries from trading
       with Fidel Castro's Cuba. [...]

(Clay, Text A)

Some learners, however, were actively engaged in the activity, not of trying
to reproduce the target text, but of trying to comprehend the text through the
act of writing about it. This can be seen in the following example (4),
whereby the writer avails herself of the private speech feature *focus* in order
to better understand the target text:

(4)   a. The law called Rotticelli [sic] was recently passed
       b. by Bush in October ^(Friday 23)
       c. with the support of Robert Roticelli [sic] from New Jersey.
       d. It is a very controversial law.
       e. And some guy from Florida.
       f. It will get rid of the trade embargo between Cuba and the
          United States.
       g. It will get rid of the taxes also [...]

(Sunanda, Text A)

Focus is a feature of private speech first discussed by Frawley (1992) who
proposed that, when faced with a cognitive problem, speakers continue referring
to the same item without changing topic in an attempt to resolve the problem.
Thus, this learner is not involved in simply relating information about the
law in question. Rather, she is primarily involved in generating the relevant
details by writing about it, or more specifically, by focusing on it via her external
linguistic tools, a move which allows her to bring forth more information.

Other learners were initially oriented to the activity of knowing and
remembering certain information, in order to facilitate the primary activity
of relating that information as part of a coherent recall text. There were
several examples in which learners copied down bits of information in the
top margin before writing the main text of the protocol. In most cases, this
information consisted of names, numbers, and dates. However, one learner
apparently availed himself of this pre-recall writing to prepare for the
subsequent recall of the English expository text, by listing in order the main
topics of the experimental text. Thus, the learner not only externalized relevant
information, but he also ordered it in such a way as to plan the writing of the
recall text. His initial orientation, then, was to prepare for writing the recall.

Learners, then, did not act homogeneously at the outset of the task. Moreover,
several learners exhibited shifts in activity during the actual writing of the
protocol. For some, the shift was temporary, for others, it was definitive. One
learner apparently interrupted her recall activity in order to engage in a
lexical search. She carried out this search in the margin of the page on which
she was writing. In this example, given in (5), the learner was momentarily

engaged in the activity of resolving the meaning of the Spanish word *viernes* (Friday):

(5)   l
      m
      mier
      j
      viernes

(Meredith, Text A)

Clearly, this learner knew that *viernes* was a day of the week, but did not know exactly which one. There is evidence of editing in the protocols, suggesting that the learner first generated a lexical item which she found to be unsatisfactory. She thus undertook a lexical search externally, by writing down the first letter of the days of the week one by one until arriving at *viernes*. She was then able to resume the activity of relating the experimental text.

Another learner shifted her activity in the middle of writing the protocol, but was unable to return to her initial activity of relating the text as a coherent one (6).

(6)   It was the 28th of October, a Friday. George Bush wants to have a compact or something of that sort for the Democracy of Cuba. He also wants the 3rd world countries not to deal w/ Fidel Castro. The representative of N.J. and Senator of Florida were not invited. Canada, France and Mexico opposed his ideas. Bush needs support. He wants that all of Cuba will be united under liberty.
      600 citizens?
      Torricelli - N.J. Senator?

(Samantha, Text A)

This learner began the protocol recalling information, but at some point abandoned the goal of producing a coherent discourse and instead contented herself with writing down the remaining information she was able to generate in the form of a list. Thus, the learner altered her activity definitively, although in so doing converted it into one she was able to sustain.

When considered in light of other private writing features of the protocols, these examples show that the task of producing a recall protocol was a difficult one for most learners. Most importantly, they show that the learners responded to the task in individual and dynamic ways, availing themselves of different linguistic tools and cognitive strategies. In doing so, each learner was engaged in activity that differed in some cases substantially from that of the others and, in many cases, from what the researcher might have predicted.

Thus, the learners' cognitive states, and more importantly, the differences among individuals with regard to their cognitive state and their resulting activity, are made visible through the language which mediated their activity.

The private writing features evident in their protocols allow us to discover the diversity of the activity in which the learners were engaged, and by extension, the unique struggle of every learner to complete a difficult task successfully. These learners, then, perhaps inadvertently, confirm that it is misguided to strip them of their subjecthood by lumping them together and attempting to manipulate their behavior through *a priori* assumptions and simple task instructions.

Positioning the self

The private writing features provide strong evidence that learners, in spite of being treated as objects, acted as agents engaged in shaping the problem-solving activity in which they were involved. We now turn to consider the learners' agency in relation to a different though related task: that of maintaining the frame of the social interaction in which they were involved, and particularly, that of positioning the self in the context of the experiment.

Psychological or psycholinguistic experiments are instances of social interaction. They are jointly constructed by participants who at the same time position themselves in relation to each other and the interaction itself. As has been argued by Hall (1995a) and others, social interaction is jointly and dynamically constructed by individuals who use their linguistic resources to align themselves with others and to position themselves in the activity. Furthermore, social interaction entails a frame, that is, a set of shared expectations on the part of the participants as to what the interaction ought to entail (Goffman 1974; Tannen 1993a). Thus, social interaction is a discursive practice through which persons create, express, and position themselves, according to their own sociocultural histories, needs, and expectations.

While positioning is largely thought of as a conversational phenomenon (Davies and Harré 1993), the written data in this study provide evidence that individuals may use written means to position themselves, in this case, in the social interaction brought about by the experimental task. Thus, the definition of discursive practice ought to be expanded to include all the symbolically mediated ways in which people construct social and psychological realities.

By agreeing to participate in the study and by accepting the assigned tasks, the learners appeared to indicate that they initially operated in a discursive space in which they were positioned as 'subjects in an experiment'. It is also likely, however, that their position might have been characterized better still as part of a 'student in a university setting' frame, since the learners were physically located in their Spanish classrooms. They were also following the instructions, as it were, of a person who was either their own instructor or known to them to be an instructor. Thus, it could be argued that some learners operated in a frame in which they were not only expected to do what was asked of them, but in which they could also expect to be graded or judged on their ability to complete the assigned tasks successfully.

Some learners, however, appeared to challenge this frame by inserting their own voices into the text and by repositioning themselves in the task. In doing so, they changed the frame of the interaction and, thus, the nature of the activity of constructing and maintaining the interaction. Before considering examples of this, however, it should first be pointed out that the learners who reframed the task at the level of social interaction were precisely some of the students having the most difficulty with the experimental texts. Therefore, it is suggested that some learners changed the frame of the task when the self—as associated with the protocol—was in danger of losing face. That is, when the task of writing a recall protocol became dangerously difficult—and therefore a threat to the self—some learners responded by repositioning themselves in relation to the task and the perceived threat.

Some of these learners inserted their voices in what appeared to be attempts to distance themselves from the content of their protocols. Studies in private speech have shown that speakers express their attitudes regarding the truth value of their statements by the use of certain metacomments, modals, vague language, and other indications of their uncertainty (Frawley and Lantolf 1985; DiCamilla and Lantolf 1994; Roebuck 1998). Use of these and other devices allows the speaker to distance herself from information of which she is not entirely sure. Examples of this phenomenon can be seen in the following examples (7–10):

(7) I think it had something to do with emposing [sic] some sort of trade restrictions on Cuba [...]

(Dan, Text A)

(8) This congress, which would have 80 members, would be established anyway I think because the article says the vote was only to prove to opposing forces that the country supports the new regime [...]

(Brian A., Text B)

(9) The article stated that the Bill acted to increase the strife of Cubans trying to apply for citizenship?

(Meredith, Text A)

(10) Statistical (?) stability is [...]

(Nathan, Text C)

Learners, then, inserted their voices into the recall text and in this way revealed their uncertainty with regard to propositions and individual words alike. Other features of private speech, such as irregular tense marking, provide evidence that many learners were unsure of the content of the target texts. However, metacomments such as these can be taken as evidence of the learners' conscious effort to distance themselves symbolically from a protocol (or parts of a protocol) which they believed to be in some way defective. In this way, the learners repositioned themselves in the interaction, so that they were far removed from the protocols at the center of the researcher's investigation. Thus, the learners were able to salvage the self symbolically, albeit at the expense of their own protocols.

The data presented two cases where learners inserted their voices into the task and in so doing questioned the conditions of the experiment. Hence, they called attention to the shortcomings, not of their own recalls, but of the experiment itself, and were thus able to shift attention, if not blame, to conditions outside their control. One learner did this by commenting on the time frame of the experiment. At the end of the protocol, he made several dashes and then wrote the phrase 'Out of time' (11):

(11)   Static vs. dynamic balance, when in static balance a tripod-like three
        limbs in contact with the ground is necessary. Center of gravity has to
        be over the legs and tipping at all can't be present - - -
        Out of time

                                                                (Jason, Text C)

The ending to this protocol suggests that the learner wished to indicate to the researcher that he would have been able to continue, if he had been allowed the time. It may be argued, then, that this learner inserted his voice in order to ask the researcher to see him as controlled not by the difficulty of the readings or even by his own limitations, but rather by the time constraint, which he may have seen as the lesser evil. The learner, therefore, repositioned himself from being a student asked to perform under normal conditions, to one asked to perform under unfair conditions. The latter, he may have hoped, would be judged less harshly.

Finally, one learner, Brian A., attempted to reposition himself and to reframe the task entirely by putting himself on par with the researcher. While he did well on the recalls of the Spanish and the English newspaper articles (not surprisingly since he was an advanced student of Spanish), he was apparently unable to recover much of the content of the English expository text. In fact, he was unable to construct a cohesive or coherent recall. Presumably, this is because he was not able to extract or construct much information from the text at the time of reading. His tactic, however, was to criticize the article by referring to it as having its sentences jumbled about or as being 'discombobulated', as seen in examples, (12) and (13), respectively. Finally, at the bottom of the page, he remarks that the text was a 'Cruel thing to make students read' (14).

(12)   This article, with all its sentences jumbled around [...]

                                                                (Brian A., Text C)

(13)   THE INTERIM WAS VERY DISCOMBOBULATED [...]
        [caps in original]

                                                                (Brian A., Text C)

(14) Then, --- In order to understand walking and running, remember to
       keep balance in mind.
       I think this was the last sentence.
       [space of about four inches]
       A cruel thing to make students read.

(Brian A., Text C)

His final comment can only be interpreted as a criticism of both the article and the researcher's decision to ask the learners to read it. With this statement, he reformats the task in a way that no other learner was able or chose to do: he positions himself as an equal of the researcher and thus is able to exclude himself and his protocol from the focus of the investigation.

What these last examples illustrate then, is that learners, concurrent with their problem-solving activity, were also engaged in the ongoing activity of constructing and maintaining an interaction in which the self needed to be positioned. While some learners may have continued with the compliant 'subject of an experiment' or 'university Spanish student' frame initiated by the researcher/instructor, they were all free to reposition themselves at any time. This some did actively and according to their own reasons, histories and resources, and, as a result, reframed the social activity in which they were involved. What is especially interesting to the present discussion is that those who most vividly asserted themselves in the interaction did so in an apparent attempt to distance themselves from the protocols they had written. Thus, these learners relinquished their agency, that is, they rejected their role in producing their own protocols, arguably in order to escape judgment on the part of the researcher/instructor.

Before concluding the discussion it is interesting to note that in spite of the difficulty of the task, no learner refused outright to complete it. This is important because it indicates that while learners transformed the task to meet their abilities and even sought to reposition themselves in the task, all conceded final authority to the researcher. This was probably so because the primary frame of the interaction may have been that of the university setting, where all were enrolled as students. Thus, their overriding goal may have been that of complying, at least in some way, with the requests of the researcher/instructor.

Conclusion

It has been suggested that, in some psychological frameworks, experimental subjects are marginalized by assumptions about their individual ability to determine their own behavior. However, while some investigative models treat subjects as objects by ignoring their agency, the data presented in this discussion have provided evidence that this procedure is misguided.

The data presented here have provided evidence in support of a premise of the theory of activity, namely, that examples of human behavior are individual instantiations of activity. By examining the private writing and other features of the protocols it was argued that the learners in the study were each engaged in their unique struggles to complete the task at hand. Specifically, the learners' activity or activities included memorization, translation, recall, and reconstruction, all as the result of a single blueprint task of recalling first and second language texts.

It was further shown that the diversity and uniqueness of the problem-solving activity had a correlate at the level of social interaction. The private writing and other features of the protocols collected in this study revealed pertinent information about the ways in which the learners initially positioned themselves in the task, and importantly, about the ways in which some repositioned themselves as they progressed through the task. Thus, the learners' attempts to reframe the task can be seen as further evidence of the dynamic nature of activity.

It was suggested that the repositioning came about as a result of the difficulty that some learners encountered upon trying to complete the task. It seems reasonable to propose that this particular task gave learners a sense of what they were not able to do with the language. Many appeared to have felt overwhelmed by the difficulty of the task and their own limitations as second language learners. Thus, by inserting their individual voices into the recall texts, some learners attempted to reframe the task such that they themselves were not the object of scrutiny. The learners may have felt especially justified in doing so in the case of the English expository text which, while in their native language, presented some with an unexpected degree of difficulty which they, understandably, did not want to attribute to their own proficiency or lack thereof.

This discussion, then, has argued for an awareness of subjects as individual agents involved in shaping their activity based on their own particular goals, motives, and sociocultural histories. While cause–effect relations may be observed in natural science, the study of human beings must focus on conscious individuals as they act upon themselves and their environment. Therefore, it cannot be assumed that subjects will do what is asked or expected of them. The goal of the researcher, then, is to discover rather than predict, subjects' activity.

Notes

1   An earlier version of this chapter was presented at the 1997 Annual Meeting of the American Association for Applied Linguistics, March 8–11, Orlando, Florida. Thanks are extended to James P. Lantolf, Merrill Swain, and Aneta Pavlenko for their thoughtful comments and insightful discussion of the data presented here.

2　See Lantolf and Pavlenko (1998) for a discussion of the differences between causes and reasons, and the importance of considering the latter instead of the former when dealing with human behavior.

3　Foster (1998), however, finds that the predictions of the laboratory do not always transfer to the classroom setting.

4　The task instructions were as follows: on the following page there is a text in Spanish. You will be given four minutes to read the text—you may read it as many times as you wish, but you may not take notes. After the four minutes are up, you will be asked to turn the page over and to write down in ENGLISH everything that you can remember about what you have just read. You will have six minutes to write.

5　Note that in this way sociocultural methodology may differ from socio-cultural pedagogy. That is, pedagogical tasks are chosen because they lie within the learners' range of capabilities, or zone of proximal development. However, tasks which lie beyond the learners' current capabilities may be chosen when attempting to discover how people respond to problems and difficulties.

6　Text A= the Spanish newspaper article; Text B = the English newspaper article; Text C = the English expository text.

4 The output hypothesis and beyond: Mediating acquisition through collaborative dialogue[1]

Merrill Swain
*The Ontario Institute for Studies in Education of
The University of Toronto*

Introduction

This chapter is about 'the output hypothesis and beyond'. In this chapter, 'the beyond' is collaborative dialogue. And what is 'collaborative dialogue'? It is knowledge-building dialogue. In the case of our interests in second language learning, it is dialogue that constructs linguistic knowledge. It is what allows performance to outstrip competence. It is where language use and language learning can co-occur. It is language use mediating language learning. It is cognitive activity and it is social activity.

But those are the claims I would like to end this chapter with. To get there, I will take the following steps. First, in order to locate collaborative dialogue in theoretical and empirical claims about second language learning, I will examine very briefly current views on the role of interaction—and its components of input and output—in second language learning. Second, I would like to shift the frame of reference somewhat by considering interaction from the perspective of a sociocultural theory of mind. Third, I will consider several recent studies from this perspective. These studies suggest that at least some actual language learning can be seen to be occurring in the dialogues of participants, and that, as well as the separate consideration of input and output, a profitable focus of analysis of language learning and its associated processes may be dialogue.

Background

I begin with a brief overview of recent views of the role of interaction in second language learning. To a considerable extent, contemporary thinking and research about interaction have emphasized its role as a 'provider of input' to learners (cf. Gass 1997). This focus has its origins in Krashen's comprehensible input hypothesis—the hypothesis that the *cause* of second language acquisition is input that is understood by the learner. Input, it is argued, can be made comprehensible in a number of ways. Long, in the early 1980s (for example, 1981, 1983b), proposed that one way input is made comprehensible is through 'interactional modification', that is, through modifications to learners' input as a consequence of their having signaled a lack of comprehension.

As Pica (1994) points out, this 'modification and restructuring of interaction that occurs when learners and their interlocutors anticipate, perceive, or experience difficulties in message comprehensibility' has been referred to as *negotiation*. Through negotiation, comprehensibility is achieved as interlocutors repeat and rephrase for their conversational partners. Pica points out that negotiation is not the only type of interaction that might lead to learning. 'But', she states, 'negotiation, with its emphasis on achieving comprehensibility of message meaning ... has sparked and sustained considerably more interest in the field of SLA' (*ibid.*: 495). As I will try to show later in this chapter, a form of interaction which, for the present, I am calling collaborative dialogue, also deserves to be examined for its contribution to second language learning.

In research on negotiation, then, the focus has been on input, and how to make it comprehensible. Because of the theoretical framework in which this research has been embedded, it has been seen as enough to demonstrate that negotiation leads to greater comprehensibility of input. Virtually no research has demonstrated that the greater comprehensibility achieved through negotiation leads to second language learning. Indeed, it has only been recently (Ellis, Tanaka, and Yamazaki 1994) that evidence has been provided suggesting a causal link between comprehensible input and second language acquisition, and that evidence was concerned only with the acquisition of the meaning of concrete nouns.[2] Clearly there is scope for more research exploring the relationship between comprehensible input and second language learning.

However, if we are to understand more fully the language learning that occurs through interaction, the focus of our research needs to be broadened. We need to look beyond the comprehension of input to other aspects of interaction that may be implicated in second language learning. For example, Lightbown and Spada (1990), Lyster and Ranta (1997), Doughty and Williams (1998), and others have explored how interaction provides opportunities for learners not only to negotiate the message of the input, but, in doing so, to focus on its form as well. Other researchers, for example, Aljaafreh and Lantolf (1994) and Nassaji and Swain (2000), have explored the nature and type of feedback that will be most helpful to learners during interaction at different stages of their acquisition of a language form. Van Lier (present volume) has moved beyond the concept of 'input' to 'affordance', examining social interaction from an ecological perspective.

As van Lier's perspective implies, interaction is more than a source of comprehensible input, or input as feedback. Interaction also provides learners with the opportunity to use the target language, that is, to 'output'. Van Lier, along with others (for example, Kramsch 1995a), would not approve of the continued use of the term 'output', claiming that it limits our understanding of second language learning to an information-processing perspective rather than permitting us to broaden the perspective to one in which all social activity forms a part of the learning environment. But in this chapter I will continue to use the term 'output' in ways it has already been considered in the published literature. However, later in this chapter I will alter my use of terminology to signal a broadening of the scope of output as communicative activity, to understanding it also as cognitive activity.

Output and SLA

Output might theoretically play several roles in second language learning. Relative to the potential roles of input in second language learning, those of output have been relatively underexplored.

The basis for my initial claim that perhaps output plays a role in second language learning (Swain 1985) was our research with French immersion students which showed that in spite of six or seven years of comprehensible input—some might say, 'acquisition-rich input'—in French, the written and spoken French of these students included numerous grammatical and syntactic deviations from native-speaker usage. Furthermore, our observations in grades 3 and 6 immersion classes suggested that although students used French in class, little of it included extended discourse, and, generally speaking, teachers did not 'push' their students beyond their current level of interlanguage as the teachers interacted with them.

As I have argued elsewhere (Swain 1995), it seems to me that the importance of output to learning could be that output pushes learners to process language more deeply—with more mental effort—than does input. With output, the learner is in control. In speaking or writing, learners can 'stretch' their interlanguage to meet communicative goals. To produce, learners need to do something. They need to create linguistic form and meaning, and in so doing, discover what they can and cannot do. Output may stimulate learners to move from the semantic, open-ended, strategic processing prevalent in comprehension to the complete grammatical processing needed for accurate production. Students' meaningful production of language—output—would thus seem to have a potentially significant role in language development. These characteristics of output provide a justification for its separate consider-ation, both theoretically and empirically, in an examination of the value of interaction for second language learning.

One role for output in second language learning is that it may promote 'noticing'. This is important if there is a basis to the claim that noticing a language form must occur for it to be acquired (Ellis 1994). There are several levels of noticing, for example, noticing something in the target language because it is salient or frequent. Or, as proposed by Schmidt and Frota (1986), in their 'notice the gap principle', learners may not only notice the target language form, but notice that it is different from their own interlanguage. Or, as I have suggested, learners may notice that they do not know how to express precisely the meaning they wish to convey at *the very moment of attempting to produce it*—they notice, so to speak, a 'hole' in their interlanguage.

Certainly, for many of the learners we have recorded as they interacted while working together on tasks (for example, Swain and Lapkin 1995; Kowal and Swain 1997), we have observed that those learners noticed 'holes' in their linguistic knowledge and they worked to fill them by turning to a dictionary or grammar book, by asking their peers or teacher; or by noting to themselves to pay attention to future relevant input. Our data showed that these actions generated linguistic knowledge that was new for the learner, or consolidated their existing knowledge. In line with van Lier, one might hypothesize that learners seek solutions to their linguistic difficulties when the social activity they are engaged in offers them an incentive to do so, and the means to do so. The important point, however, in this context, is that it was the act of attempting to produce language which focused the learner's attention on what he or she did not know, or knew imperfectly.

Another way in which producing language may serve the language learning process is through hypothesis testing. It has been argued that some errors which appear in learners' written and spoken production reveal hypotheses held by them about how the target language works. To test a hypothesis, learners need to *do* something, and one way of doing this is to say or write something.

For example, in doing a task that required students to recreate in writing a text they had just heard (a difficult text consisting of five sentences), Rachel and Sophie (pseudonyms), two grade 8 French immersion students working together, wrote the sentence: 'Même les solutions écologiques causent quelquefois des nouvelles menaces' (*Even ecological solutions sometimes cause new threats.*) In their written text, *des* was crossed out and replaced by *de*. On the basis of this written work, we might have concluded that this modified output—reflected in the change from *des* to *de*—represents the students' current hypothesis about the form a partitive should take in front of an adjective. We might further have argued that this process of modification represents second language acquisition (Pica *et al.* 1989; Swain 1993). However, our understanding of what Rachel and Sophie produced is immensely enriched by our being privy to their dialogue as they constructed the phrase *des nouvelles menaces.*

Example 1:

1 Rachel: Cher[chez] nou..des nouveaux menaces.
         (**Look up new [as in] new threats.**)
2 Sophie: Good one!
3 Rachel: Yeah, nouveaux, des nouveaux, de nouveaux. Is it des nouveaux
         or de nouveaux?
4 Sophie: Des nouveaux or des nouvelles?
5 Rachel: Nou[veaux], des nou[veaux], de nou[veaux].
6 Sophie: It's menace, un menace, une menace, un menace, menace ay ay
         ay! [**exasperated**].
7 Rachel: Je vais le pauser.
         (**I'm going to put it on pause [ie the tape-recorder].**)
         [**They look up 'menace' in the dictionary.**]
8 Sophie: C'est des nouvelles! [**triumphantly**].
9 Rachel: C'est féminin … des nouvelles menaces.

(Kowal and Swain 1997)

In the text the students had heard, the phrase was actually *de nouveaux problèmes*, but Sophie and Rachel made rephrasing the text a main feature of their work. For them, two comparatively proficient students, this was a self-chosen means of making the activity more challenging; here we see them 'stretching' their interlanguage. In turn 1, Rachel has used the noun *menaces* as a synonym for *problèmes*, and Sophie, in turn 2, congratulates her on this. But the phrase *des nouveaux menaces* is not well-formed. To be well-formed, the partitive *des* needs to be changed to *de* because it precedes an adjective, and *nouveaux* should be *nouvelles*, because *menaces* is a feminine noun. In other words, by producing *des nouveaux menaces*, Sophie and Rachel have created for themselves a phrase that they can now reflect on. In effect, it has given them the opportunity to notice gaps in their linguistic knowledge. And this opportunity has arisen directly from having produced a phrase new to them.

Often, as researchers or teachers examining such a phrase, we can only hypothesize that Rachel's output in turn 1 represents a hypothesis about the target language. However, in this case, we are able to conclude that what Rachel said, did indeed, represent a hypothesis, as we then see Rachel and her friend Sophie put the phrase through a set of tests.

Rachel wonders if the partitive form she has produced is correct. In turn 3, she verbalizes the possibilities out loud to see what sounds best, and then explicitly formulates her question: 'Is it *des nouveaux* or *de nouveaux*?', that is, 'Should the partitive be *des* or *de*?' She continues to test out her hypothesis in turn 5.

Sophie however is caught up with whether this new word that her friend has introduced is masculine or feminine. This is important because if *menaces* is masculine, then the form of the adjective should be *nouveaux*; if it is feminine, then the form of the adjective should be *nouvelles*. As we can see in turn 6, Sophie, too, tests alternatives, hoping that her saying it out loud will guide her to the correct choice.

They resolve the issue by turning to a readily available tool, their dictionary, and discovering that *menaces* is feminine. Triumphantly they give the implications of this discovery, that is, that the adjective should be *nouvelles*: in turn 8, Sophie provides the correct form of the adjective, and in turn 9, Rachel confirms Sophie's choice and provides the reason for that choice—that *menaces* is a feminine noun. In their delight with this discovery, the issue of the partitive is laid aside, though later they return to it and change it from *des* to *de*.

To sum up, we have seen in this example that Sophie and Rachel, in trying to produce a phrase, came to recognize what they did not know. They formed hypotheses, tested them out, and finally, turned to a tool that would provide them with a definitive answer, their dictionary. Together what Sophie and Rachel have accomplished is the construction of linguistic knowledge; they have engaged in knowledge building. Furthermore, unlike in the sort of 'negotiation' sequence discussed by Pica, Sophie and Rachel have not engaged in this knowledge building because they misunderstood each other. They have done so because they have identified a linguistic problem and sought solutions. In their dialogue, we are able to follow the (cognitive) steps which formed the basis of their written product. Here, their output, in the form of collaborative dialogue, is used to mediate their understanding and solutions.

Collaborative dialogue and SLA

Output of the sort we saw Rachel and Sophie engage in is an important part of the learning process. Wells (2000) points out that 'One of the characteristics of utterance, whether spoken or written, is that it can be looked at as simultaneously process and product: as "saying" and as "what is said" '(*ibid.*: 73). In 'saying', the speaker is cognitively engaged in making meaning; a cognitive act is taking place. 'Saying', however, produces an utterance that can now be responded to—by others or by the self. Wells suggests that it is frequently in the effort of 'saying' that a speaker 'has the feeling of reaching a fuller and clearer understanding for him or herself' (*ibid.*: 74). Furthermore, 'what was said' is now an objective product that can be explored further by the speaker or others.[3]

The two faces of an utterance—the cognitive activity and the product of it—are present in both output and collaborative dialogue. Collaborative dialogue is dialogue in which speakers are engaged in problem solving and knowledge building.[4] It heightens the potential for exploration of the product. What I would like to show, through examples, is that collaborative dialogue mediates joint problem solving and knowledge building. But first I wish to make two brief digressions: one is about terminology and one is about theoretical perspectives.

First, about terminology: the continued use of the terms 'input' and 'output' has recently come under question. Kramsch (1995a), van Lier (present volume) and others have pointed to the inhibiting effect of the 'conduit metaphor' on the development of a broader understanding of second language learning. As Steve Thorne (personal communication, February 1998) asked me: 'Is your new, expanded output worthy of a new label?' He goes on to wonder 'whether output, even given its new momentum by revisiting it through collaborative dialogue, will have the escape velocity to "move beyond" its original identity ... ?' He ends by noting that he regrets not having thought up such a term yet. And so do I.[5]

I am sympathetic to the view that metaphors guide our work, in ways in which we are often unaware. In an article analyzing two metaphors for 'learning'—the 'acquisition metaphor' and the newer 'participation metaphor'— Sfard (1998) concludes that the conceptual frameworks generated by each offer 'differing perspectives rather than competing opinions' (*ibid.*: 11), incommensurability rather than incompatibility. This provides me with some hope that differing perspectives will be seen as enriching and complementary.

Having said that, I now intend to avoid using the term output for the rest of this chapter, replacing it with such labels as 'speaking', 'writing', 'utterance', 'verbalization', and 'collaborative dialogue'. This is an interim solution, one that will last until my own understanding of differing perspectives deepens enough for the appropriate terminology to emerge.

The second digression is to outline, in the briefest of forms, why the concept of dialogue might be important in considering second language learning, and how it is different from a consideration of comprehensible input and/or output. Vygotsky (1978, 1987) and others (for example, Wertsch 1985a; Cole 1996) have articulated a sociocultural theory of mind. The main premise of a sociocultural theory of mind is that cognitive functions such as voluntary memory, reasoning, or attention are mediated mental activities, the sources of which are activities external to the learner but in which he or she participates. Through a process of internalization (Gal'perin 1967; Arievitch and van der Veer 1995), external activities are transformed into mental ones. In other words, as Stetsenko and Arievitch (1997) state: 'psychological processes emerge first in collective behaviour, in co-operation with other people, and only subsequently become internalized as the individual's own "possessions" ' (*ibid.*: 161). This process is mediated by semiotic tools. Language is one of the most important semiotic tools.

Vygotsky argued that just as physical tools such as a hammer and saw allow us to accomplish qualitatively different physical activities than we might without such tools, so do semiotic tools allow us to accomplish qualitatively different mental activities than those we accomplish without them. Physical and semiotic tools mediate our interaction with the physical and social environment. Language, as a particularly powerful semiotic tool, mediates our physical and mental activities. As a cognitive tool, it regulates others and ourselves. And, as we have seen, it can be considered simultaneously as cognitive activity and its product.

How does this help us to interpret Sophie and Rachel's dialogue? First, it suggests that their 'collective behaviour' may be transformed into individual mental resources. This means that the knowledge building Sophie and Rachel have collectively accomplished may become a tool for their further individual use of their second language.[6] Initially socially constructed, their joint resolution may serve them individually.

Second, and importantly, their knowledge building was mediated by language—by a dialogue in which they drew attention to problems and verbalized alternative solutions—'des nouveaux, de nouveaux', 'un menace, une menace'. This verbalization, this 'saying', provided an object ('what is said') to reflect upon—'*Is it* des nouveaux *or* de nouveaux?'; '[*Is it*] des nouveaux *or* des nouvelles?' That is, this verbalization objectified thought and made it available for scrutiny. The use of English here is significant.[7] They use English, their first language, to *ask* the question, putting in relief the object of their attention. As the dialogue continued, Rachel and Sophie conveyed the outcome of that reflection and scrutiny—'C'est des nouvelles', 'C'est feminin … des nouvelles menaces.'

The problem Sophie and Rachel addressed in this dialogue was a language-based problem—one which arose as they tried to express the meanings they had in mind. To sum up, what is occurring in their collaborative dialogue—their 'saying' and responding to 'what is said'—is language learning (knowledge building) mediated by language (as a semiotic tool).

Finally, this theoretical perspective suggests that what we, as researchers, are observing in Rachel and Sophie's dialogue, is both social and cognitive activity; it is linguistic problem-solving through social interaction. As Donato and Lantolf (1990) pointed out, developmental processes that are dialogically derived and constituted 'can be observed directly in the linguistic interactions that arise among speakers as they participate in problem-solving tasks' (*ibid.*: 85).

Language as a mediating tool

In other educational domains such as mathematics and science, language has been shown to mediate the learning of conceptual content. Newman, Griffin, and Cole (1989), for example, have studied children and teachers 'at work' in diverse content areas such as social studies, science, and arithmetic. Their research reveals learning as a process of 'joint constructive interaction' mediated by language and other cultural tools.

The Russian developmental psychologist, Nina Talyzina, demonstrated in her research the critical importance of language in the formation of basic geometrical concepts. Talyzina's research was conducted within the theoretical framework of Gal'perin (1902–1988), himself a contemporary of Vygotsky. With Nikolayeva, Talyzina conducted a series of teaching experiments (reported in Talyzina 1981). The series of experiments dealt with the development of basic geometrical concepts such as straight lines, perpendicular lines, and angles.

Three stages were thought to be important in the transformation of material forms of activity to mental forms of activity: a material (or materialized) action stage, an external speech stage, and a final mental action stage.[8] In the first stage, students are involved in activities with real (material) objects, spatial models, or drawings (materialized objects) associated with the concepts being developed. Speech serves primarily as a means of drawing attention to phenomena in the environment (*ibid*.: 112). In the second stage, speech 'becomes an independent embodiment of the entire process, including both the task and the action' (*ibid*.: 112). This was instructionally operationalized by having students formulate verbally what they carried out in practice (i.e. materially)—a kind of on-going think-aloud verbalization. And in the final mental action stage, speech is reduced and automated, becoming inaccessible to self-observation (*ibid*.: 113). At this stage, students are able to solve geometrical problems without the aid of material (or materialized) objects or externalized speech.

In one of the series of instructional studies conducted by Talyzina and her colleagues, the second stage—the external speech stage—was omitted. The students in the study were average-performing, grade 5 students in Russia. The performance of students for whom the external speech stage was omitted was compared to that of other students who received instruction related to all three stages. The researchers concluded that the omission of the external speech stage inhibited substantially the transformation of the material activity into a mental one. They suggest this is because verbalization helps the process of abstracting essential properties from nonessential ones, a process that is necessary for an action to be translated into a conceptual form (*ibid*.: 127). Stated otherwise, verbalization mediates the internalization of external activity.

Talyzina further noted that 'the development of mental actions and concepts is not an end in itself ... [They] are subsequently employed in solving a variety of problems' (*ibid*.: 133). Often, in confronting a new problem requiring the application of already developed mental actions and concepts, students were observed to begin to apply them at the external speech stage, or even at the material stage. In collaborative dialogue, verbalization, which mediates the internalization of meanings created and the externalization of those meanings, is naturally and spontaneously evoked.

Holunga (1994), one of our former Ph.D. students, conducted a study concerned with second language learning, but it has many parallels to those carried out by Talyzina and her colleagues. Holunga's research involved adults who were advanced second language learners of English. The study was set up to investigate the effects of metacognitive strategy training on the oral accuracy of verb forms. The metacognitive strategies taught in her study were predicting, planning, monitoring, and evaluating (Brown and Palincsar 1981). What is particularly interesting in the present context is that one group of her learners was instructed, as a means of implementing the strategies, to talk them through as they carried out communicative tasks in pairs. (See Example 4, p. 107–8.) This group was labeled the metacognitive with verbalization, or MV, group. Test results of this MV group were compared to those of a second group who was also taught the same metacognitive strategies, and who carried out the same communicative tasks in pairs. However, the latter group was not instructed to talk about the metacognitive strategies as they implemented them. This group was called the metacognitive without verbalization, or M, group. A third group of students, included as a comparison group (C group), was also provided with language instruction about the same target items, i.e. verbs. Their instruction provided opportunities for oral language practice through the same communicative tasks completed by the other students, but the students in this group were not taught metacognitive strategies. Nor were they required to verbalize their problem-solving strategies.

Each group of students in Holunga's study received a total of 15 hours of instruction divided into ten lessons. Each lesson included teacher-led instruction plus communicative tasks to be done in pairs. The main activity of a lesson occurring near the end of the 15 hours of instruction was a task described as 'a linguistically unstructured communicative task; that is, there was no one overt grammatical focus' (*ibid*.: 93). In this task each student dyad was given a list of names representing applicants for a university scholarship. Based on the information provided about each applicant, they were to decide who should get the scholarship.

The success of the instructional treatments can be seen in the qualitatively distinct ways student dyads from the different groups approached this task. Example 2 is from a pair of students, T and R, who were in the M group. T and R's dialogue in general resembles those of student dyads from the C group.

Example 2

1   T: Who begins?

2   R: Me. Just a minute. Oh yeah, don't forget the teacher said to error correct. Ready … ummm. First guy, Albert Smit, age 45. No way. He can't qualify. He's too old. He's married and he has a social life. He must to spend his time with his family. So I think he not really interesting in study because it's his wife. If he don't get scholarship, he will go back to work.

3   T: I agree. Basil. He is 19. It's not possible to give him the scholarship. He have no motivation to get the scholarship. Also his character does not look like a good person.
4   R: Yes, he has bad behaviour. He probably will spend more time with his girlfriend. Okay. No for people one and two. Next person.

(Holunga 1994: 108)

The strategy training relating to error correction of the verb system that T and R had received prior to doing this task is not much in evidence in their dialogue. Although in turn 2 R reminds T that the teacher has just told them to correct their errors, they pay no further attention to that externally-imposed objective. Their dialogue is conversational: they focus on meaning and not on form.

As we see in Example 3, evaluation took the form of praise. As R says in turn 1, '… our discussion is good. We talked very well.' T, in turn 2, understands this to refer to content, not form: 'Yes. It's very interesting.' And in spite of being told to focus on verb errors, T's 'I can't' in turn 4 is accepted and responded to by R's empathetic comment in turn 5, 'It's too difficult.'

Example 3

1   R: So far our discussion is good. We talked very well.
2   T: Yes. It's very interesting.
3   R: We didn't correct. Remember what the teacher said?
4   T: Oh yeah. For me I can't.
5   R: It's too difficult.

(Holunga 1994: 109)

The interaction between R and T is typical of that seen in 'negotiation of meaning' tasks: meaning is focused on and error is ignored in an attempt to create an effective social interaction. Although S and G of Example 4 also maintain an effective social interaction, and attend to the meaning inherent in the task, their dialogue is strikingly different from R and T's.

In Example 4, S and G begin the task by working out what they are supposed to do. In turn 4, S explains: 'We have to speak about these people and justify our position.' But, not only do they focus on the substantive content of the task, they talk about what verb form—'a conditional'—they might need to do the task, and why—'… not just the past. We have to imagine our situation now.' We have to give our opinions now. This implementation of the strategies of planning and predicting has led them to verbalize not only the verb form needed but the function it will be serving in the current context, and to provide a concrete example (see turn 6).

Example 4

1   G: Let's speak about this exercise. Did you read it?
2   S: Yes.

3 G: Okay. What are we suppose to do?

4 S: We have to speak about these people and ummm justify our position … you know our decision … our decisions about actions in ummm the past.

5 G: No. I think not just the past. We have to imagine our situation now. We have to give our opinions now.

6 S: So, for example, I choose Smit because he need it. No … it's a conditional. I would give Smit … I would choose Smit because he need the money. Right. I WOULD give …

7 G: Needs it.

8 S: Yes, because he need it.

9 G: Yes, but no. He needs. 's', you forgot 's'. He needs.

10 S: Did I? Let me listen the tape. (Listens to the tape.) Yes … yes. He needS. I have problem with 's'. I paying so much attention to conditionals I can't remember 's'. Can you control … your talking?

11 G: It's a big problem. I still must remember 'had had'. But we try.

12 S: Yes, We try. But I don't know.

13 G: We don't try … you know we don't get better. We don't improve. We must practise to change old ways.

14 S: Okay. Maybe good idea to listen to tape after we each talk.[9]

(Holunga 1994: 98)

As G and S continue with the task, G in turn 7 corrects S's 'need' to 'needs it'. Interestingly, S responds to G's meaning 'Yes, because he need it', not understanding that G is responding to a grammatical error. G in turn 9 first responds 'Yes' to S's meaning, but she perseveres with her focus on form, 'but no', going on to give the correct form again and telling S how to correct it: 'He needs. "s", you forgot "s".' This focuses S's attention, and with some scepticism, she plays back the tape. She hears her error, corrects it, and in turn 10 provides an explanation for her error 'I paying so much attention to conditionals I can't remember "s".' Having agreed that 'It's a big problem', G in turn 13 comments on the importance of practice: 'We must practise to change old ways'. S suggests in turn 14, based perhaps on what she has just experienced, a way that they can effectively monitor their language use for errors: 'Maybe good idea to listen to tape after we each talk'.[10]

S and G's verbalization as seen in Example 4 serves several functions. For both speaker and hearer, it focuses attention; it externalizes hypotheses, tests them, and supplies possible solutions, and it mediates their implementation of such strategic behavior as planning and evaluating. Through their collaborative effort, they produce the appropriate verb form accurately, and propose a concrete plan to monitor its accuracy in future use. Speech comes to serve as 'an independent embodiment of the entire process, including both the task and the action' (Talyzina 1981: 112).

The students in this study were tested individually, first by being asked a series of discrete-item questions in an interview-like format, and second by being asked three open-ended questions in which learners would give their opinions, tell a story, and imagine a situation. The questions were designed to elicit specific verb forms concerning tense, aspect, conditionals, and modals, and were scored for the accuracy of their use. A pre-test, post-test, and delayed post-test were given. The delayed post-test was administered four weeks after the post-test.

The data were analyzed statistically as four separate tests: the first 40 discrete-item questions as one test, and each of the open-ended questions as three separate tests. Initial analyses were conducted to determine if there were significant gains in the accurate use of verb forms as a result of the instructional treatment, and if post-test scores were maintained. The analyses revealed that the MV group made significant gains from pre- to post-tests in all four tests; the M group made significant gains in only the discrete-item questions. And the C group showed no improvement on any of the four tests. Furthermore, both the MV and M groups' level of performance at the post-test level was maintained through to the delayed post-tests four weeks later.

A second set of analyses was conducted to determine if there were statistically significant differences among the groups (using an analysis of co-variance with pre-test scores as the covariate). The results indicate that both experimental groups performed better than the comparison group on all four tests. Furthermore, the MV group's performance was superior to that of the M group on both the discrete-item questions and the third open-ended question which required the use of conditionals.

In summary, although those students who were taught metacognitive strategies improved the accuracy of their verb use relative to a comparison group that received no such instruction, students who were taught to verbalize those strategies were considerably more successful in using verbs accurately.[11]

Interpreting these findings through the lens of Talyzina's theoretical account suggests that for the MV group, external speech mediated their language learning. Verbalization helped them to become aware of their problems, predict their linguistic needs, set goals for themselves, monitor their own language use, and evaluate their overall success. Their verbalization of strategic behavior served to guide them through communicative tasks allowing them to focus not only on 'saying', but on 'what they said'. In so doing, relevant content was provided that could be further explored and considered. Test results suggest that their collaborative efforts, mediated by dialogue, supported their internalization of correct grammatical forms.

Verbalization was initiated through social interaction. The basis of their task solution was dialogue. Dialogue mediated their co-construction of strategic processes and of linguistic knowledge. Through such collaborative dialogue, the students engaged in knowledge building.

The role of dialogue in mediating the learning of such substantive areas as mathematics, science, and history is generally accepted. Yet, when it comes to the learning of language, the mediating role of dialogue seems less well understood. Perhaps this is because the notion of 'language mediating language' is more difficult to conceptualize and it is more difficult to be certain of what one is observing empirically.

Dialogue as a mediator of second language learning has found support in our current research (for example, Swain 1997; Swain and Lapkin 1998). The students we have been studying are grade 8 French immersion students who, although fluent, have a distance to go in their production of grammatically accurate French. We are interested in finding ways to move these students beyond their current interlanguage.

We have had students engage collaboratively in a variety of tasks (Kowal and Swain 1997; Swain and Lapkin 1998) which, through task design, we anticipated would encourage them to focus on form in the French they were producing. Spontaneously, in carrying out the task, students engaged in dialogue. Given the theoretical framework I have already outlined, our focus has been to examine closely the content of the students' dialogue. We have noted instances in the dialogue of language-related episodes (Swain and Lapkin 1995; 1998) in which language is a focus of attention. In these episodes, the students' dialogue mediated their learning. Language-related episodes may be thought of as serving the functions of external speech in the external speech stage outlined by Gal'perin and Talyzina. As with the other examples in this chapter, Example 5 is illustrative.

In Example 5, Kathy and Doug (pseudonyms) are in the process of writing out a story based on a set of pictures they have been given (see Swain and Lapkin 1998 for details of the task). In the part of their dialogue provided below, they are working out how to write the second half of a sentence which begins with *Yvonne se regarde dans le miroir* ... (Yvonne looks at herself in the mirror...).

Example 5

1   Kathy: Et brosse les cheveux.
    (**and brushes her hair.**)
2   Doug: Et les dents.
    (**and her teeth.**)
3   Kathy: Non, non, pendant qu'elle brosse les dents et ...
    (**No, no, while she brushes her teeth and ...**)
4   Doug: Elle se brosse...elle SE brosse.
    (**She brushes ... she brushes [emphasizes the reflexive pronoun].**)
5   Kathy: Pendant qu'elle se brosse les dents et peigne les cheveux.
    (**While she brushes her teeth and combs her hair.**)
6   Doug: Ya!

7   Kathy: Pendant qu'elle … se brosse … les cheveux, I mean, no, pendant
            qu'elle se PEIGNE les cheveux.
            (While she … brushes … her hair, I mean, no, while she COMBS her
            hair.)
8   Doug: Ya.
9   Kathy: Et se brosse…
            (And brushes …)
10 Doug: Les dents.
            (Her teeth.)
11 Kathy: Pendant qu'elle SE peigne les cheveux et SE brosse les dents.
            (While she combs her hair and brushes her teeth [emphasizes the
            reflexive pronouns].)

(Swain and Lapkin 1998)

In Example 5, we see Kathy and Doug co-constructing the second half of the
sentence that Kathy is writing down. They end up with the correct, *pendant
qu'elle se peigne les cheveux et se brosse les dents* (while she combs her hair
and brushes her teeth), but not without struggling with which verb goes with
which noun, and the reflexive nature of the particular verbs they are using.
Kathy starts off with *brosse les cheveux*, a phrase that translates well from
the English *brushes her hair*. But Doug's offer of *et les dents* (and her teeth) in
turn 2 seems to suggest to Kathy that *brosse* should be used with *les dents*,
while *peigne* should be used with *les cheveux* (see turns 3 and 5). Doug
quickly reacts to Kathy's use of *brosse* in turn 3 by pointing out through
emphasis that *brosse* is a reflexive verb: *elle SE brosse*. Kathy incorporates
this information in turn 5 for *brosse* and for *peigne* in turn 7 even though her
emphasis in turn 7 is on using the verb that best accompanies *les cheveux*. In
turn 11, Kathy turns her focus to the form of the verbs as reflexives, thus fully
incorporating Doug's contributions to this conversation.

This dialogue between Doug and Kathy serves to focus attention and to
offer alternatives. Through dialogue they regulate each other's activity, and
their own. Their dialogue provides them both with opportunities to use
language, and opportunities to reflect on their own language use. Together their
jointly constructed performance outstrips their individual competencies. Their
dialogue represents 'collective cognitive activity which serves as a transitional
mechanism from the social to internal planes of psychological functioning'
(Donato 1988: 8).

In our research we are beginning to tackle the issue of how to demonstrate
that these language-related episodes (LREs) are occasions for second language
learning. In one study (LaPierre 1994; see also Swain 1998), dyad-specific
post-test items were developed based on recordings of the dialogues of each
pair of students as they worked through a dictogloss task. Students' responses
on the post-test showed a 70 to 80 per cent correspondence with the
solutions—right or wrong—that they arrived at in their dialogues. The post-

test was administered a week to ten days after task-completion. We interpret these test results as a strong indicator that their dialogue mediated, in these cases, the construction of linguistic knowledge.

In another study (Swain and Lapkin 1998, 2000) students were given pre- and post-tests. As a research methodology, this did not work very well because, as it turns out, it is impossible to predict what pairs of students will talk about. We tried to predict what they would talk about by giving the 'same' task to another group of students and building a pre-test based on the language-related episodes of those students. Even though we gave the students the very same task, and even though the students were French immersion students from the same grade level and even the same school, as we examined what our student dyads chose to discuss, it was obvious that 'the same task' is *not* 'the same task' for different pairs of students (cf. Coughlan and Duff 1994). Each pair focused on different aspects of language, and did so in different ways—an important message to researchers and teachers alike (Kowal and Swain 1994, 1997; Swain 1995; Swain and Lapkin 1998). For researchers, this principle makes problematic the use of a pre/post-test design if one is attempting to trace language learning specific to the dialogue of individual student pairs. In a relatively small number of instances where a language-related episode happened to relate to a pre- and post-test item, we were able to demonstrate that the LRE was an occasion for second language learning (Swain and Lapkin 1998). For teachers, this finding serves yet again as a reminder that what one intends to teach may only indirectly, if at all, be related to what is learned. Students set their own agendas.

Conclusion

In this chapter, the concept of output has been extended to include its operation as a socially-constructed cognitive tool. As a tool, dialogue serves second language learning by mediating its own construction, and the construction of knowledge about itself. Internalization of process and knowledge is facilitated by their initial appearance in external speech.

From a research perspective, we need to find new methodologies to unravel this layered complexity. We also need to recognize that research in which students' activity is accompanied with verbalization is not a neutral environment. Verbalization is not just a research tool; it has important consequences for learning.

From a pedagogical perspective, the position argued in this chapter offers additional reasons for engaging students in collaborative work. It suggests that tasks which encourage students to reflect on language form while still being oriented to meaning making—that is, tasks which engage students in collaborative dialogue of the sort illustrated in this chapter—might be particularly useful for learning strategic processes as well as grammatical aspects of language. In many of the research tasks used in the study of negotiation, this reflective, problem-solving orientation is not demanded. The focus is instead on communication where 'attention is principally focused on meaning rather than form' (Nunan 1989: 10). However, it is certainly feasible for a communicative task to be one in which learners communicate about language, in the context of trying to produce something they want to say in the target language.

In sum, collaborative dialogue is problem-solving and, hence, knowledge-building dialogue. When a collaborative effort is being made by participants in an activity, their speaking (or writing) mediates this effort. As each participant speaks, their 'saying' becomes 'what they said', providing an object for reflection. Their 'saying' is cognitive activity, and 'what is said' is an outcome of that activity. Through saying and reflecting on what was said, new knowledge is constructed. (Not all dialogue is knowledge-building dialogue.) In this way, our students' performance outstripped their competence.

From a sociocultural theory of mind perspective, internal mental activity has its origins in external dialogic activity. The data presented in this chapter provide evidence that language learning occurs in collaborative dialogue, and that this external speech facilitates the appropriation of both strategic processes and linguistic knowledge. These are insights that a focus on input or output alone misses.

Notes

1   Alister Cumming, Rick Donato, Birgit Harley, Claire Kramsch, Jim Lantolf, Sharon Lapkin, Helen Moore, Steve Thorne, and Gordon Wells have each read earlier drafts of this chapter. I am grateful for their useful and critical comments.

2   Ellis, Tanaka, and Yamazaki (1994) claim that they have provided 'the first clear evidence that access to modified input promotes acquisition' (*ibid*.: 481). However, they conclude cautiously as follows: 'Although our studies support a causative relationship between negotiated interaction and acquisition, we acknowledge ... the fact that different aspects of language ... may not be acquired in the same way. Our studies examined only vocabulary acquisition, and only the acquisition of the meaning of concrete nouns. It does not follow that negotiated interaction will promote the acquisition of other aspects of the L2 or even that it is important in other aspects of vocabulary acquisition' (*ibid*.: 482). Since then, several other studies have demonstrated a relationship between negotiating meaning and the acquisition of some particular aspect of language. For example, Mackey (1995) found that negotiation was related to the acquisition of question forms.

3   Wertsch and Stone (1985) claimed that 'One of the mechanisms that makes possible the cognitive development and general acculturation of the child is the process of coming to recognize the significance of the

external sign forms that he or she has already been using in social interaction' (*ibid.*: 167). This would seem to be equally so for adults. Consider, for example, the first-time use of a term like 'mediation', and the fully elaborated meanings it may come to have after years of interaction within the discourse communities that use the term.

4   Bereiter (1994) proposed the term 'progressive discourse' for dialogue in which 'understandings are being generated that are new to the local participants and that the participants recognize as superior to their previous understandings.' (*ibid.*: 9).

5   Alister Cumming (personal communication, June 1998) suggested the term 'purposeful language production'.

6   Possibly the subsequent writing of their joint product supports the process of internalization/appropriation (Donato, personal communication, June 1998).

7   The use of the first language to mediate second language learning creates a situation where the use of language as a mediating tool is particularly clear. Notable examples appear in Brooks and Donato 1994; Brooks, Donato, and McGlone, 1997; Antón and DiCamilla 1998; Swain and Lapkin 1998.

8   Talyzina discussed a stage which occurs between the external speech stage and the final mental stage. That stage, 'an external unvoiced speech stage', appears to be a transition between the other two stages during which external speech goes 'underground'. It is the beginning of inner speech, the final mental stage.

9   As Helen Moore pointed out (personal communication, June 1998), a lot of teacher educators would say that the focus on form seen in this dialogue would be inhibiting. Perhaps what is key are (a) roles (may work better with peers than with teachers) and (b) goals (T and R may see the activity as an opportunity to socialize; S and G see the activity as a learning exercise, not a socializing one).

10 S's comment makes clear the difficulty of focusing on both 'saying' and 'what was said' simultaneously.

11 Birgit Harley (personal communication, April 1998) and Helen Moore (personal communication, June 1998) wondered whether the focus on language detracted somewhat from content. Perhaps it did (tests only measured the accuracy of verb use), but it is clear that it did *not* detract from the students' *engagement* with the task. Furthermore, in an informal analysis that Pauline Gibbons conducted (personal communication, April 1998), more language functions are apparent in Example 4 compared to Example 2.

5 Playfulness as mediation in communicative language teaching in a Vietnamese classroom

Patricia N. Sullivan
University of California, Santa Cruz

Introduction

The social context of second language learning is fundamental to Vygotskian sociocultural theory; the theory is predicated upon understanding the importance of interaction between people for the formation of mental activities (Vygotsky 1978). Two basic tenets of Vygotskian sociocultural theory are activity theory (Wertsch 1979), which reflects the fundamental idea that motives for learning in a particular setting are intertwined with socially and institutionally defined beliefs; and mediation, which proposes that human mental activity is mediated by tools and signs, the foremost tool being language. In this chapter I build on these concepts, with an example of language playfulness as mediating the interaction between participants (teacher and students) and the language being learned. I incorporate not only an examination of pedagogical practices and discourse between students, but also a discussion of how these classroom practices and classroom discourse are related to broad sociohistorical values.

By 'social context', I am referring not only to the classroom setting and the ways students interact within it, but also to the historical and cultural context of the world outside the classroom. In a sociocultural approach to second language learning, one takes as a starting point that classroom practices are situated in particular cultural environments (Breen 1985b; Kramsch 1985; Brooks 1992; Holliday 1994), and that within these environments, the definition of 'good teaching' is socially constructed. Furthermore, a critical educational perspective emphasizes that schooling is not a neutral process, but is tied to history, power, and ideology (Fairclough 1989; Giroux and McLaren 1989; Pennycook 1989). To simply assume, then, that what works well in one educational setting will work well in another is to ignore the interrelatedness of history, culture, and pedagogy, and ignore the argument that ELT methodology is associated with an Anglo-Saxon view of communication (Phillipson 1992; Pennycook 1994a).

In this chapter I bring together history, culture, and pedagogy by examining playfulness as mediation in Communicative Language Teaching (CLT) in a classroom in Vietnam. I begin with a historical overview of CLT followed by a reflection on cultural values that are embedded in descriptions of CLT methodology.

Communicative Language Teaching

CLT has its beginnings in the 1970s. It was associated with the work of the Council of Europe, and followed on the development of English language courses specifically aimed at the increasing numbers of Third World students preparing to work in fields such as science and engineering in Britain (Howatt 1984). The development of these courses, which led to the coinage of the term English for Specific Purposes (ESP), grew out of the movement away from viewing language purely from a formal structural perspective, and toward a view that focuses on language use. The ideas of Halliday (1970), Labov (1970), Hymes (1972), and Widdowson (1978) were all instrumental early in this movement. The focus on ESP was further defined with the publication of Munby's (1978) *Communicative Syllabus Design*.

During the 1980s, CLT continued to develop, through various perspectives. While Munby's design was clearly a syllabus, CLT was also seen in terms of methodology. According to Brumfit (1984: 122) 'syllabuses in themselves, while important, inevitably result in fragmentation insofar as they are specific, and they must be seen as servants of integrated goals and bases for integrated methodology.' He emphasizes that the 'processes of classroom activity ... must be given greater prominence' (*ibid.*: 122), and proposes a model for language-teaching methodology that consists of goals, means, and methods. Littlewood (1981) proposed that the concept of teacher as 'instructor' is inadequate in that the teacher's role is also that of overseer of learning, classroom manager, consultant, and co-communicator. Sometimes the teacher performs in the familiar role of presenting new materials, but other times the teacher lets learning take place through independent activity such as pair work. Savignon (1983: v), in her discussion of CLT, refers to the term communicative competence, as coined by Hymes, which 'came to be used in language teaching contexts to refer to the ability to convey meaning, to successfully combine a knowledge of linguistic and sociolinguistic rules in communicative interactions.' From Richards' and Rodgers' (1986) perspective, CLT is an approach rather than a method.

Howatt (1984: 279) distinguishes between 'strong' and 'weak' versions of CLT. The weak version 'stresses the importance of providing learners with opportunities to use their English for communicative purposes', while the strong version 'advances the claim that language is acquired through communication'. A syllabus based on the weak version, in other words, would integrate communicative activities in the classroom to develop second language use, while a syllabus based on the strong version would see second language knowledge as an outcome of communicative activity, not as a prerequisite to it. Prabhu's (1987) project in Bangalore, India was based on a strong view of CLT. As he states (1987: 3) 'The stimulus for the project was a strongly-felt pedagogic intuition ... that the development of competence in a second language requires not a systematization of language inputs or maximization of planned practice, but rather the creation of conditions in which learners engage in an effort to cope with communication.'

Though Howatt distinguishes between strong and weak versions, much of the literature does not reflect the theoretical basis of the strong version. In fact, the weak version seems to dominate in that descriptions of CLT commonly emphasize ways that the teacher can develop activities that provide learners with the opportunity to communicate using what students have learned in the second language. This is not a new phenomenon. In 1984, Howatt commented that 'the weak version ... has become more or less standard practice in the last ten years' (1984: 279). The weak version lends itself to being easily incorporated by teachers who have followed the presentation, practice, production model of language teaching, as they are able to fit the communicative activity into the production stage (Holliday 1994).

In the years since the late 1970s and early 1980s definitions and descriptions of CLT have varied. Currently in North America books commonly refer to CLT classroom practices as those, for instance, that use authentic material, link classroom language learning to life outside the classroom, emphasize communication through interaction among students, and have a learner-centered, content-centered focus. According to Brown (1994: 81), 'at the heart of current theories of communicative competence is the essential interactive nature of communication ... thus, the communicative purpose of language compels us to create opportunities for genuine interaction in the classroom.' Brown goes on to list important aspects of interactive classes, such as (a) doing a significant amount of pair work and group work, (b) receiving authentic language input in real-world contexts, and (c) producing language for genuine, meaningful communication.' Holliday (1997) also describes the 'popular perception' of CLT as including the following: (a) primacy given to oral practice, (b) practice equally distributed in the classroom, (c) group or pair work for enabling equal distribution of practice, (d) most useful in classes under 20 seated in a U-shaped arrangement, and (e) better managed by native speakers in multilingual class groups. These types of descriptions are ubiquitous in English language teaching material in the Anglo-Saxon world, and have become synonymous with CLT.

Values underlying CLT

In the last twenty years, CLT has been adopted—and adapted—in a number of ELT institutions around the world. But apart from the example of the

Bangalore project mentioned above, much of the research on CLT has been conducted either with native English-speaking teachers, or with non-native English-speaking teachers in North America, Great Britain, or Australia, regions that share cultural and historical similarities, and for which English is an 'inner circle' (Kachru 1986) language. The terminology that developed to describe classroom activities in CLT, such as 'meaningful communication' and 'interaction', is thus linguistically and historically linked to 'Western', and particularly Anglo-Saxon, nations. I contend that the emphasis on 'communicative purposes', which reflects the 'weak' version of CLT, has been narrowly conceived. What, for instance, defines 'genuine' communication in the classroom? In line with Pennycook's (1994a) argument of Western domination, I argue that classroom activities espoused by CLT have come to represent Anglocentric culture and Anglocentric goals of communication, and that these cultural values are being exported as part and parcel of CLT methodology.

When discussing culture and value systems, it is difficult not to focus the discussions in terms of one culture as 'the other'. One way to help counteract this, however, is to reexamine one's own culture. I therefore turn now to a discussion of ways in which 'Western' historical and cultural approaches to 'good communication' are embedded in pedagogical practices based on the common terms used currently to describe CLT.

A major emphasis in current descriptions of CLT is on the use of group work as a way to enhance classroom communication. Though Prabhu (1987) advocated against 'group work', (in the sense of small-group work) and the Bangalore project did not incorporate it, group work now seems to be a requisite part of CLT practices. (See Jacobs 1996 for a discussion of the appropriacy of group activities in Southeast Asia.) At first glance, the terms 'pair work' and 'group work' pertain simply to numbers of people working together; that is, two for pair work, and maybe three, four, or five for group work. It is also clear from a CLT perspective that the terms are not just referring to the size of a group, but to a value decision on how best to teach and learn languages. The terms encompass a reaction against classrooms that are teacher-centered and removed from student needs, and instead, represent a move towards a student-centered, interactive classroom. However, also embedded in the terms 'group work' and 'pair work' are notions of choice, of independence and freedom, of privacy, and of equality. These concepts of 'pair work' and 'group work' are clear examples of the embeddedness of values in classroom practices.

Choice, independence, freedom, privacy, equality

Choice is demonstrated in pair work and group work when students are instructed to 'find a partner'; that is, the students are encouraged to choose whom to talk to, and sometimes even what to talk about. In addition, students may be given the choice about whether to tell the teacher or the class about what was said in the group. This exemplifies the notion of privacy. Only members of the group are privy to what is said, and they may choose not to tell the whole class what they talked about. In addition, the concepts of freedom and independence also underlie group work. Within their groups students are 'free' from the teacher's control, at least as far as control of what is said. They are told to work independently, and they are encouraged to give their own opinions to their partners. Lastly, the value of equality underlies group work. When peers talk in small groups, the hierarchy of a teacher-led class is reduced.

The above values, of course, are ideal, and as such are not always realized: even in a student-centered class in which students are working in groups, the teacher is in charge. The teacher has the final word, and there is a natural hierarchy and power difference. Students are not free to step outside the bounds of appropriate classroom behavior; they are usually not allowed to swear at other students, for instance, or act in violent ways. Nevertheless, the values of choice, independence, and equality are quintessential American values (cf. Bellah *et al.* 1985) that underlie the concepts of group work and pair work.

Work

In addition to the values of choice, independence, privacy, equality, and freedom, another core notion underlying the CLT approach is the concept of work. CLT terms include 'pair work', 'group work', 'task-based learning', 'co-construction', 'scaffolding', and 'collaboration'. Each of these terms incorporates the notion of work. We work at tasks just as we work when collaborating. The word 'collaborate', in fact, literally means 'co-labor' or 'work with'. We collaborate on jobs, on tasks, on assignments; the term 'collaborate', however, is not commonly used when talking about play. If the terms 'pair work' and 'group work' were changed to 'pair play' or 'group play', we would have a very different image of the purpose of groups.

Information exchange and technology

In addition to values such as freedom, independence, and equality, and, second, the notion of work, there is a third area embedded within the world of CLT: information exchange and technology.

Within a CLT framework, the work of language learning is done through an exchange of information. In an 'information-gap' exercise, for instance, students must get information from each other in order to complete a task. As with pair work, information-gap activities carry the goal of equality: students participating in the activity are put on equal terms by being given only a portion of the necessary information. In some cases even the teacher becomes 'equalized' by not having any more information than the students. The value of information exchange and the goal of equality are brought out in a recommendation by Pica (1987: 17): 'What is needed are activities whose outcome depends on information exchange and which emphasize collaboration and an equal share of responsibility among classroom participants.' The underlying message is that unequal, hierarchical relationships are not conducive to learning languages, or at least are not as communicative or interactive.

Another notion underlying information exchange is that 'reality' is crucial to language learning. In an American CLT classroom, students are encouraged to give real information about real events, and to do real tasks that relate to the real world. While bringing 'outside reality' into an ESL class in the United States may be helpful for English language learning, the notion of 'authenticity' as part of a communicative pedagogy in international settings has become controversial (cf. Widdowson 1994; Breen 1985a; Kramsch and Sullivan 1996). Whose reality is 'real'? What context is 'authentic'? That which is authentic or real in one context may be inappropriate in another. In fact, the very idea of basing language study on the notion of 'reality' is a cultural decision.

In addition to information exchange, the underlying notion of technology in language learning is evident in the use of terms such as 'input' and 'output'. Such a notion of communication is implicitly based on an engineering model, reflecting the conduit metaphor of message transmission. Platt and Brooks (1994) question the mechanistic view of information input–output models, 'acquisition-rich' environments, and 'negotiated exchanges of message meaning'. 'The mechanistic nature of information and the theory's application to human communication is ... evident in the writing of Wiener, who originated Cybernetic Theory and assigned the terms "input" and "output" to the communication process' (*ibid.*: 498). 'We found that speech activity functions far beyond, and in a more complex manner than, merely the exchange of information' (*ibid.*: 508). By continuing to use these technological terms we perpetuate the image of a self that performs independently of the social setting.

These three areas—CLT as it incorporates choice, freedom, and equality, CLT as work, and CLT as technology and information exchange—are all representative of the values that underlie the practice of CLT in North America. If we are going to approach CLT and communication from a sociocultural perspective, we cannot assume that the values that underlie CLT are universal. We must take into consideration cultural, historical, and institutional factors on a local level.

Confucian values

Today, as Vietnam joins the world of international business, there is a strong need and desire for English skills, and along with that, a feeling among Vietnamese teachers that they want to learn the newest and best methods of teaching. Many have taken part in workshops on CLT methodology in an effort to update their teaching skills, though many have also complained that the new methods just do not work for them (cf. Sullivan 1996a). When CLT is exported to Vietnam, a country whose history includes a strong Confucian heritage, conflicts arise (for discussions of Chinese conflicts with CLT, see Sampson 1984; Ting 1987; Burnaby and Sun 1989; Craven 1991; Graf 1991). Underlying values of Vietnamese Confucian society conflict with those that are represented by CLT. Confucianism emphasizes dependency and nurture rather than independence; it emphasizes hierarchy rather than equality; and there is more of an emphasis on mutual obligation of members of a group than on individualism (Bond and Hwang 1986; Cheng 1987; Scollon and Scollon 1994).

While at first glance, it would seem that the idea of 'group work' would fit well in a society with Confucian roots, in fact, the American practice of forming small groups works against Confucian precepts. Grouping in a classroom serves to divide up a class, not bring it together. The American notion of group work stems from a value placed on individuality, freedom, and choice, as I have just pointed out. In the United States, students are put into groups in order to bring out their individuality. This can conflict with the ideal of group harmony. One Vietnamese teacher who had tried to break up his class into small groups, and found that it did not work well, discussed the purpose of groups with me. He said, 'A group is made up of people who must agree. A member of a group would not want to destroy the atmosphere of the group by not agreeing. If they don't agree, they will say their reason, but then join the group. The very purpose of the group is consensus, or at least all agreeing to disagree' (Sullivan 1996a: 209). This differs considerably from an American teacher who might say that the purpose of grouping is to allow students to express their own opinions. Conflicts with CLT activities such as group work, as shown in this example, may, in fact, be less tied to a particular pedagogical approach than to broader historical and cultural values.

The varied definitions of the purposes of groups as described above can be related to two approaches to knowledge. The 'Western' perspective is that knowledge is based on reason, observation, critical analysis, and Aristotelian logic. A rationalist thinks of knowledge as 'truth' or information that one possesses in a particular field. The more information one acquires, the more knowledgeable one becomes. Knowledge, from this perspective, is a collection of discrete instances of truths that are historically linear and progressive. Poster (1989: 30) cautions, 'Since Descartes, theorists have assumed that a rational voice was also a universal one, [one that would] speak for humanity.' This perspective is, as Poster says, not only ethnocentric, but problematic since rationalists are in positions of power. Cheng (1987) contrasts a rationalist's perspective of knowledge with the Chinese view. The latter have a view of ontology in which form and substance cannot be separated. 'Reality is the totality of all things' (1987: 27). In this interrelatedness view there is an emphasis on the relationship between whole and part. True knowledge is not just a factual record of information, but is an understanding of life that enables one to achieve a more harmonious relationship between nature and society: knowledge is not isolated from individual life or society. 'A mere intellectual knowledge, that does not transform the person for a better living, is considered a waste of time' (To Thi Anh 1974: 95). In a Confucian view of social relationships, the development of 'self' entails the participation of the 'other'. One needs to communicate with others in order to achieve good human relations. This, in turn, helps develop the nature of the individual. The individual and the social are intertwined with rights and responsibilities, with certain relationships paramount: 'those between sovereign and subject, father and son, elder brother and younger brother, husband and wife, and friend and friend' (Bond and Hwang 1986: 215). These relationships are hierarchically ordered. Harmony is realized if each member conscientiously follows the requirements of his or her role. 'One cannot understand an individual unless one understands the network of relations, and one cannot understand the network of relations unless one understands the individual' (Cheng 1987: 31–32).

Broad sociohistorical values are unconsciously embedded in the ways people interact with each other. If any language learning approach is to be advocated worldwide it must be broad enough to allow it to be appropriated by any who use it. In particular, if a language learning approach is to be based on 'communication', it must be applicable to all types of communication. As researchers, if we try to force classroom discourse into categories and terminology that only represent 'Western' values and approaches to communication, we are limiting our analysis of that discourse. As one way of broadening the term 'communicative' in CLT, I discuss playfulness as an aspect of language learning.

Playfulness in classroom language learning

Though it is difficult to define 'play', (cf. Cook 1997) most people would agree that play entails fun. It is often accompanied by laughter. In the context of this chapter, playfulness includes teasing and joking, puns and word play, and oral narratives. As an observer in EFL classrooms in Vietnam, I was continually struck with the amount of laughter among students (cf. Kramsch and Sullivan 1996). University level foreign language classrooms in the United States seemed, in comparison, quiet and serious, even when they utilized games. (For a discussion of educational differences, see Sullivan 1996b.)

Within the framework of CLT, language play as a classroom activity among adults is often thought of in terms of planned events such as role plays or word games, activities which occur in both 'Western' and Vietnamese FL classes. Spontaneous play, on the other hand, is often viewed as a distracter in the classroom, as an action arising from 'not being on task'. It is this spontaneous social playfulness that I am focusing on, not in terms of distraction, but as mediation of the learning process of adult language learners.

The role of play in sociocultural theory

In Vygotskian sociocultural theory, play in children is seen as much more than an activity that gives pleasure. The role of play in the development of language is viewed as one that creates a zone of proximal development in which the child behaves 'beyond his average age, above his daily behavior' (Vygotsky 1978: 102). Imagination in play is a psychological process that is not possible in very young children; play represents a specifically human form of conscious activity in which the child is learning to act in a cognitive, rather than visual, realm. The imaginary situation that is created through play is rule-based. 'What passes unnoticed by the child in real life becomes a rule of behavior in play' (1978: 95).

Spontaneous play in the language learning of older children and adults has not been studied much (see review by Lantolf 1997). When Vygotsky refers to the play of older children and adults, he speaks of play in terms of athletic games, not spontaneous play (Vygotsky 1978). Vygotsky's developmental perspective of play, however, is the theoretical basis of Lantolf's study of the use of language play among adult L2 learners of English and Spanish (Lantolf 1997). In this study Lantolf looks at play carried out as an individual activity, involving such actions as talking to oneself in the L2, repeating phrases to oneself or 'hearing' in one's head the words or phrases from class or laboratory. Lantolf reports that these activities 'seem to have a positive effect on the learner's confidence to use their L2' (*ibid.*: 32).

The language playfulness that is described in this study is not an individual activity, but verbal play within the social context of the classroom. The playful exchanges are a socially mediated activity that stand between the individuals (students and teacher) and the language being learned. The students are not demonstrating passive responses to the teacher's playfulness, but are jointly engaged in it themselves. These playful exchanges serve as tools that result in awareness of language meaning and form.

Underlying Vygotsky's theory is a preference for verbal, as compared to non-verbal, forms of mediation (Wertsch 1991). As Wertsch notes, this is related to his own cultural background, and reveals a cultural bias against some non-western cultures that involve more nonverbal socialization practices (cf. Rogoff 1990). In Vietnam, however, an analysis of mediation in terms of verbal expression is appropriate in light of the atmosphere in the classroom. In the next section of this chapter I present and discuss examples of play in a particular classroom setting.

Playful learning in a Vietnamese classroom

Data collection

The data described below come from research conducted in Vietnam during 1993 and 1994. During that time I was an observer in 22 different classes, in addition to being a regular participant-observer in two focal classes over a period of two months. The classes I observed were, for the most part, university level English classes, though my observations also included an adult evening center, a business college, two French language classes, one Chinese language class, and one Vietnam history class. In the two focal classes I audiotaped all classes and transcribed all classroom discourse. I videotaped both classes. In addition, I interviewed teachers, administrators, test developers, government officials, and students, often checking and rechecking my initial observations on educational practices with them. I examined written material that included history, policies, curricula, methodology, and linguistics. From this data collection have come extensive field notes, tapes, and transcribed data from which I base my observations of the appropriation of CLT.

Student profile

The class I refer to below is a second year university level English language classroom in Vietnam, taught by a teacher who describes his teaching as 'communicative'. At the time of the data collection the students were about 20 years old. For most, this was their fifth year of English; they had had three years of English in secondary school, and one previous year at the university. All had chosen English as their major area of study. They were in English classes for about 15 hours per week, with separate classes in reading, writing, grammar, speaking, and listening. The excerpts I refer to are from the oral skills class.

Having a teacher with a lively, entertaining style, the classroom contained much laughter and light-hearted joking. Students seem engaged throughout the three-hour long morning classes. Though the teacher varied the activities during the morning, generally he sat in front of the students conducting whole-class practice from the textbook. Students were sometimes asked to express their own opinions on issues, but usually this was not the objective. In their study sessions outside of class the students had animated discussions of their personal opinions, but the classroom was viewed by both students and teachers as a place to practice the language and to check on understanding more than as a place for individual expression (cf. Sullivan 1996a: 199–206).

Physical set-up of the classroom

In analyzing classroom discourse it is crucial to consider the physical set up of the classroom. In this class, the teacher generally sits in front of his students.

The students sit closely together on shared benches, so closely that their arms rub and their books and papers overlap. Even if they wanted to do 'independent' work, it would not be possible. Nor is it physically possible for the teacher to hover over an individual's desk, speaking to that student alone. There is barely room to walk between rows of benches, and any speaking to one person would, by necessity, be speaking to all those around the same bench. The physical set-up is most conducive to a teacher-fronted class, with the teacher guiding and leading all students as a whole class.

The students who share benches and who share their answers are not engaged in what Americans call pair work or group work, since, as I have described earlier in this chapter, simply sitting together or even deciding what to write together does not alone constitute the American notion of 'group work'. The students sharing benches, who often check with each other as they write their answers in their textbooks, and who also call out their answers together as they respond to the teacher's questions, exemplify Confucian values of dependence, nurture, and obligations of group membership. The physical constraints of seating serve to embody the underlying value that the good of the group outweighs the good of the individual, rather than the American value of individualism. This teacher has adapted CLT to a whole-class, teacher-fronted format, one that does not emanate from the values of choice, work, or information exchange, but instead emanates from a value of group harmony. He brings the students together through teacher-led playful practice.

A heritage of play with language

In the Vietnamese class as described above, as in other classes in my data collection, imitation, repetition, and memorization were a part of learning, as was playful oral interaction. Wordplay, one-upmanship and oral impromptu playfulness are, in fact, a part of the Vietnamese cultural heritage. There is an ancient tradition of oral verse, called *hat doi*, used for making friends, beginning courtships, and establishing relationships, that is based on impromptu clever verses and couplets that are called out among farmers in the fields (Nguyen 1980). A woman, for instance, who is walking down a path, might call out or sing out a verse to a man in the fields. He might, in turn, respond, matching her tune and style. This teasing can turn into a battle of wits with each trying to outdo the other. If they are mutually attracted, they might meet or later even marry.

Though *hat doi* poetic exchanges are not practiced as such in the classroom, the heritage is evident. This teacher would often play with words by transposing sounds, turning *teacher* for instance, into *cheater* in a pun. Or he would change the meaning of a sentence by the pronunciation of *aunt* (British) as *aunt/ant* (American). He would bring in double meanings to liven up a grammar practice. After a student's sentence, *My uncle's garden is the biggest*, for example, (during a textbook exercise practicing the superlative), the teacher said, *Your uncle's garden is not as big as mine*. The laughter that followed this statement indicated that students immediately understood the innuendo, though the teacher had to gloss for me that by *mine* he meant my (our) *Uncle Ho*, referring to Ho Chi Minh.

The teacher's quick responses in the language classroom are related to a cultural historical tradition of verbally outwitting others through impromptu couplets and verses (cf. Ellis 1996). Vietnam, as a country steeped in a tradition of oral language, puts great emphasis on such activity, and this carries over to all aspects of life and learning, including the second language classroom. Impromptu wordplay such as this is part of the discourse of both teachers and students, often through echoing voices and repeating phrases in a form akin to poetic chanting. Though my observations were in the north of Vietnam, the ubiquity of wordplay in classrooms was brought out to me by a Vietnamese student in the United States who told me that he missed the puns and plays on words that were so common in his schooling in southern Vietnam.

Oral narrative play

It is not only the teacher's play with single words, phrases, and *double entendre* that are common in my classroom data. Playfulness in language use among students abounds. One example is the way the whole class participates in jointly forming playful narratives.

In the following example, the teacher is leading a whole class discussion from their British textbook.[1] The book asks the students to discuss the advantages and disadvantages of controversial statements about medical care. The statement that the teacher has just read is: 'The tax on cigarettes should be increased to pay for the health care needed by smokers.' The book clearly frames the discussion in terms of personal opinion and information exchange, and I would guess that an American teacher might ask students to get into groups, discuss the effects of tax increases, and possibly have students report back to the whole class. In this Vietnamese class, however, the discussion turns into a story-telling, playful exchange for the enjoyment of the whole class.

The teacher begins by joking that he is lucky that he does not have to pay any tax even though he is a smoker. Then one student picks up on the topic to tell about her father who smokes. She begins:[2]

1   S1: My father himself try and [try to stop] smoking
2   T: [(   )]
3   S1: One time he uh he uh had some uh medical medical [(   )]
4   T and Ss: [some medicine]
5   S1: Yeah and he tried to stop smoking but he can't because after he uh one time he got ill very serious and he (   ) and the doctor (   ) from his lungs
6   T: OK.
7   S1: so he had to stop smoking but
8   T: He can not
9   S1: Yeah he couldn't
10 T: He couldn't. OK
11 S2: After that he was more interested in [eating]
12 Ss: ((laugh))   [eating]
13 S2: in eating and uh he smoked more
14 Ss: ((laugh))
15 S3: He smoked more
16 S4: He is more addicted to smoking
17 T: He is more [addicted] to eating
18 Ss: [addicted]
19 S1: But it can't it couldn't make him stop eating
20 T: Yes. He doesn't lose (a problem) but he gains another
21 Ss: ((laugh))

The above excerpt demonstrates the playful narrative aspect typical of this Vietnamese classroom discourse. Though one student begins by telling a personal story about her father, her story is soon taken over by S2 (line 11) who embellishes the story, changing the tone from the discussion of a serious illness to a playful narrative. Students 3 and 4 add to the story while the others in the class chime in by repeating words and laughing. The teacher also joins in the fun (line 17 and 20). Student 1, who began the story, does not seem offended that her story has been taken over by her classmates, as evidenced by smile, her laughter (as shown on the videotape), and her joining the telling of the story (line 19).

The type of oral classroom interaction demonstrated above does not incorporate individualism, privacy, or collaboration on a task in terms of 'work'. It does not demonstrate the goal of speaking to 'understand oneself' that has roots in 1970s American sensitivity groups. This is not 'information exchange'. The point is neither to discuss advantages or disadvantages of taxation, nor is it to discuss the consequences of taxation. Rather, it is a rhapsody of voices, with playful attention to the sounds and meanings of words. The word 'addicted', for instance (lines 16–18), is first called out by a student, then picked up by the teacher, and, at the same time is repeated by multiple overlapping student voices. The activity of calling out answers in a spontaneous way and making up stories along with other students is not necessarily to give information, but to engage in verbal pleasure. 'Getting at truth' is not the goal of classroom interaction. Rather, it is language practice—not the dry practice of recitation without meaning, but lively practice, often with non-referential meanings of words. In this type of discourse, the 'meaning' does not come from personal revelation nor 'reality', but is in the interaction between teachers and students, and between the students themselves. Students work together as in a performance, for their own pleasure. The discourse is often rhythmic and repetitive, reminiscent of the Vietnamese heritage of oral verse, with jointly-called out overlaps and repetitions that are more aptly described as 'audience participation' than 'choral response'.

The oral narrative described above could be analyzed as 'collective scaffolding' (Donato 1994), 'co-construction of text', or 'building on a common topic'. It could also be described in terms of output that allows a student to try out language, promoting 'noticing' (Swain 1985, 1995). Each of these terms and concepts, however, is historically and semantically tied either to the notion of work or to technology. I think it more appropriate to give emphasis to the notion of play as a mediator of classroom language learning.

Performance and aesthetics in oral language

The playfulness of language in the examples given above is not one tied exclusively either to Confucianism, to Asia, or to Vietnam. Numerous studies in the United States point to the aesthetics of language and of learning. Shirley Brice Heath (1983) examines the speech of 'Trackton' children in the piedmont Carolinas, revealing a rich heritage of language steeped in the tradition of storytelling. 'From a very early age, Trackton children learn to appreciate the value of a good story for capturing an audience's attention ...' (1983: 166). 'Trackton children can create and tell stories about themselves but they must be clever if they are to hold the audience's attention and to maintain any extended conversational space in an on-going discourse' (1983: 167). Jordan and Au (Jordan 1982; Jordan, Au, and Joesting 1983) describe the overlapping 'talkstory' speech of Hawaiian children. According to Tharp and Gallimore,

> the group discussion pattern for Hawaiian children's instructional conversations is characterized by rapid-fire responses, liveliness, mutual participation, interruptions, over-lapping volunteered speech, and joint narration. Children build on one another's responses to create a pattern of 'group-speech'.
>
> (Tharp and Gallimore 1988: 157)

Bauman (1986: 2) argues for 'an integrated vision of the social and the poetic in the study of oral literature' as he draws on performance theory in his discussion of oral storytelling. Foster (1989) also draws on performance theory as she demonstrates how a Black college teacher invokes a style of teaching that draws on rhythm and intonation as a call for active vocal response from students. Foster's description of the classroom reveals values similar to those I have ascribed to the Vietnamese setting: 'The teacher's attention is directed at the group; the group, not the individual, is the organizing principle behind the speech events. Cooperative not competitive behavior is stressed, and the interactions among participants are marked by social equality, egalitarianism, and mutuality stemming from a group, not an individual, ethos' (1989: 23). Tannen (1989) points out that intonation and rhythm are an aspect of classroom discourse.

> The experience of a perfectly tuned conversation is like an artistic experience. The satisfaction of shared rhythm, shared appreciation of nuance, mutual understanding that surpasses the meaning of words exchanged ... goes beyond the pleasure of having one's message understood. It is a ratification of one's way of being human and proof of connection to other people ... successful conversation is an aesthetic experience.
>
> (Tannen 1989: 152)

Revisiting a definition of CLT

Though current definitions of CLT often focus on classroom practices such as group work, pair work, information gap activities, and the use of authentic materials, the definitions of CLT in the early 1980s when it was in a formative stage, are more broad. Breen and Candlin (1980), for instance, define the essentials of a communicative curriculum as 'a process which grows out of the interaction between learners, teachers, text, and activities' (*ibid.*: 95). They emphasized that the classroom

> can serve as a focal point of the learning–teaching process ... [it] no longer needs to be seen as a pale representation of some outside communicative reality. It can become the meeting place for realistically motivated communication-as-learning, communication about learning, and meta-

communication. A communicative methodology will therefore exploit the classroom as a resource with its own communicative potential.

(Breen and Candlin 1980: 98)

This broad definition of CLT is applicable to a variety of styles of communication. It fits with the findings of Holliday (1997), who, after analyzing six classrooms in China and India, concludes, among other things, that successful communicative involvement incorporates activities with texts more than oral practice, that group and pair work do not in themselves ensure communicative involvement, and that the teacher-fronted class does not in itself conflict with communicative goals.

Using common CLT classroom practices such as group work and pair work as a basis for assessing communicative language teaching can be limiting. In fact, if CLT classroom observation checklists and schemes (such as the COLT as developed by Spada and Frohlich 1995) are used as indications of communicative teaching, the Vietnamese class discussed in this chapter emerges as mostly 'uncommunicative' since the class is generally teacher-fronted with whole-class responses, and there is little group work, pair work, or use of authentic material. By using Breen and Candlin's focus on interaction in a definition of CLT, the aesthetic nature of rhythmically-tuned responses and the formation of playful narratives can be recognized as an important part of learning, whether in Vietnam or the Anglo-Saxon world.

Conclusion

While it is clear from much research that one good way to encourage communication is to arrange learners in small groups, we should not be limited by this. By analyzing the example of classroom discourse given in this chapter through the notion of play as a mediated activity, rather than through common CLT terms such as 'group work' or 'teacher-fronted class', we are encouraged to view it on its own terms rather than try to fit it into an Anglo-Saxon ideological system. 'The main criterion [of a sociocultural approach to mediated action] is that the analysis be linked in some way to specific cultural, historical, or institutional factors' (Wertsch 1991). Wertsch adds that 'the universalism that has come to dominate so much of contemporary psychology makes it extremely difficult to deal in a serious, theoretically motivated way with human action in context' (*ibid.*: 18). The discussion in this chapter is rooted in the idea that communicative language teaching represents an Anglocentric view that is often seen as universal, and that 'in order to understand the individual it is necessary to understand the social relations in which the individual exists' (Wertsch 1991: 26).

Examination of the use of CLT in 'non-core' countries such as Vietnam requires us to confront the historical embeddedness of English terms and to reflect on Anglocentric values that are being exported within a framework of 'communicative' classroom activities. By broadening the definition of CLT to one that can include teacher-led, playful oral narrative styles, for instance, we are encouraged to recognize the many ways that CLT is being appropriated throughout the world.

Notes

1 The book being used by this class was the intermediate level of *Headway* by John and Liz Soars, published by Oxford University Press, 1990. The particular excerpt referred to is on page 47.
2 I use the following discourse markers: [   ] = overlapping speech; (   ) = indecipherable speech; ((   )) transcriber's comments.

6 Social discursive constructions of self in L2 learning[1]

Claire Kramsch
University of California, Berkeley

Vygotsky's ideas have inspired SLA researchers and language teachers mostly through the cognitive, psycholinguistic aspects of his work. In this chapter I focus on Vygotsky's semiotic analysis, and I draw inspiration from his theory of the semiotic mediation of practical activity through linguistic signs. I first outline the principles of his theory of signs as they apply to foreign language learning. I suggest how they can be supplemented by C. S. Peirce's triadic theory of signs and Bakhtin's notions of addressivity and dialogism. I then show on a concrete classroom writing exercise how a neo-Vygotskyian semiotic analysis can help define the learning of a language as a dialogic process of sign making, exchanging, and interpreting that constructs the self as it constructs the other.

Language learning: a case of semiotic mediation

Traditional theories of language and language acquisition are predicated on a clear dichotomy between the individual and the social. Language, and the psychological processes of language *acquisition*, are thought to reside in the head; communication, and the social processes of language *use*, are thought to reside in the social context. Language can be studied *in* its social context, but language itself is seen as a system of arbitrary signs or symbols that are given social existence through their reference to a context which is itself outside of language.

As Lantolf explains in the Introduction to this volume, Vygotsky puts such a theory on its head. In sociocultural theory, linguistic signs and psychological processes do not precede their use in social contexts; on the contrary, it is social activity, and its material forms of social and cultural mediation, that precedes the emergence of individual forms of consciousness. For Vygotsky, psycholinguistic processes are the reconstruction in the mind of the individual of the mediated social interactions that this individual has experienced on the social plane. This mediation occurs through signs of various sorts, e.g., linguistic, visual, acoustic. Thus, for Vygotsky, linguistic signs are never arbitrary. They are created, used, borrowed, and interpreted by the individual for the purposeful actions in which he/she is engaged. Language emerges from social and cultural activity, and only later becomes an object of reflection.

Vygotsky's semiotic theory, that provides a link between psychological processes *within* the individual and cultural forms of behavior *between* individuals, is summed up in the following statement: 'The internalization of cultural forms of behavior involves the reconstruction of psychological activity on the basis of sign operations' (Vygotsky 1978: 57). In other words, we learn language not by memorizing arbitrary linguistic shapes and sounds and then putting them to use in goal-oriented activities, but rather, we primarily engage in social activities like schooling, shopping, conducting conversations, responding to teachers' questions. These activities are mediated by all kinds of material signs like gestures, facial expressions, linguistic shapes, and sounds. Through these mediational means, or 'sign operations', external social interactions become 'internalized', i.e. reconstructed internally, as psychological processes—ways of thinking, modes of learning.

What do these 'sign operations' consist of? For Vygotsky, 'signs are artificially created stimuli, the purpose of which is to influence behavior' (cited in Wertsch 1985a: 91). Let us consider each of these terms in turn.

Signs are created

Unlike natural signals that can be recognized by animals and humans as evidence of natural phenomena (for example a wet street is a signal or evidence of rain), signs are human creations (for example, I make the wet street into a sign of rainy weather and I interpret it as my needing an umbrella). James Wertsch comments: 'The fact that humans can create stimuli to regulate their behavior rather than being controlled solely by stimuli existing in the environment is of crucial importance in Vygotsky's definition of higher mental processes' (Wertsch 1985a: 91). Anything in the universe can be a signal that elicits a 'contagious' or instinctive reaction (Vygotsky cited in Wertsch 1985a: 96), but only humans can make sound objects or scribbles on a page into things that point to other things than themselves. The linguistic sign is one of many kinds of signs that can be created and perceived by the senses, be they verbal, acoustic, visual, olfactory, touch-related. Even silences or blank spaces on a page can be made into signs. But what some people interpret as signs, others perceive as white noise or meaningless scribbles, for example, as when we hear or see a language that we do not understand.

One could argue that language learners do not create the foreign linguistic signs that they use and that, furthermore, their non-linguistic signs (the way they dress or their body language) are for the most part conditioned by their environment, not created by them. While it is true that linguistic codes and much of non-linguistic behavior are handed down by the group, individual learners always have the capacity to choose from among the increasing arsenal of signs that they acquire throughout their study those that best fit their communicative needs. Moreover, as we see below, by relating signs to other signs in an utterance, across utterances or across texts, learners do create new signs that may express new meanings (Lantolf 1993). The creation of meaning occurs by combining and recombining already existing signs.

Signs are stimuli

According to Vygotsky, linguistic signs have two functions: (a) they can refer to the context in which they occur, i.e. they have an 'indicative' or indexical function. The relationship between the sign, for example: *water*, and the object it indexes, for example: *rain*, is dependent on the context, for example: a rainy day; (b) they can operate independently of the context in which signs occur, and refer to other signs with which they enter into relationships that are constant across contexts of use. For example, I can see a wet umbrella in the corner of the room and see it as a sign that it is or has been raining outside. In that case, the wet umbrella has a 'symbolic function', i.e. it is a symbol for other signs such as general weather conditions, or ruined vacation. These two types of functions correspond to two ways in which signs relate to the world. They can either refer to objects in the world (what Vygotsky calls *reference*) or they can enter into relationships with other linguistic or non-linguistic signs (what Vygotsky calls *meaning*). Beginning language learners often think that a word is just a label with a relatively fixed referent, for example, that the lexical label for water that falls from the sky is *rain*; but they soon realize that this referent is not the word's meaning. If reference brings together a sign and its object in the real world, for example, the word *rain* and a pool of water, meaning emerges from bringing together one sign and another sign, for example, rain and ruined vacation, or rain and bountiful crops. Meaning varies depending on which sign one puts into relation with which other sign.

To further understand the relation between signs, Vygotsky's semiotic analysis can be usefully supplemented by some of the distinctions made at the turn of the century by Charles S. Peirce (1839–1914). Peirce, writing some thirty years before Vygotsky, argued like him that signs are always oriented toward someone who is likely to decode them: 'A sign … is something which stands to somebody for something in some respect or capacity' (Peirce [1902] 1955: 99). But in specifying the nature of the relation between a sign and the objects it stands for, Peirce went beyond the reference/meaning distinction made by Vygotsky. Like Vygotsky, he called 'index' the indicative function of signs, but he broke down the symbolic function into 'icon' and 'symbol', using the former for a relation of resemblance between sign and object, the latter for a relation of arbitrary cultural convention. For example, smoke or flames index, i.e. point to or evoke fire; the photograph of a fire is an icon, or image, of the fire itself, and the letters F-I-R-E constitute the conventional English symbol for fire.

Any linguistic sign can be seen as a combination of index, icon, and symbol. For example, the utterances produced by language learners can be viewed in three ways: (a) as indexing a certain reality, (b) as being icons or metaphors for the reality they refer to, (c) as enacting the arbitrary conventions of the code and its socially conventionalized uses (Kramsch 1998). As we shall see in the study below, depending on whether students' linguistic signs are read as indices, icons, or symbols, students' texts can be interpreted as either expressing an external reality (the topic or *what they talk about*), or as being iconic of certain values, attitudes, and beliefs (the style or *how they talk about it*), or as reproducing or subverting certain conventionalized rules of use (the genre, ideology, or *why they talk about it in that way*).

Signs are artificial

According to Vygotsky, sign types and their systemic interrelationships are 'artificial', i.e. they can be abstracted from their original context of use and applied across contexts, as when rain is given a different meaning in the context of a tourist's vacation and in the context of farmers concerned about their crops. Signs can thus serve as objects of reflection in themselves. For example, a learner of English can take the linguistic sign *rain* encountered in a short story on a tourist's vacation, and use it in a text she is writing herself on her life on a farm, where rain had a positive, not a negative meaning. It is through her choice of signs put in relation with one another that the writer displays an identifiable subject position. Texts position their narrators both as individuals and as social actors *vis à vis* the events they are narrating. Through the conventional genres they belong to, texts also position their readers in variously conventional ways that imply different possibilities of reader responses (Kress 1988: 107).

Signs are used for a purpose

Signs do not just stand there. They stand for something; they point to something, and in that pointing there is by definition a directionality that veers attention away from itself and toward something else. Vygotsky calls signs 'activity-oriented' or 'goal-directed'. These two terms need to be used with caution in a Western context.

- 'activity' (*deyatel'nost'*) for Vygotsky is not action as opposed to thought or mental processes, but, rather, a 'frame', or sociocultural interpretation that the participants construct of the events in their context of occurrence. To be engaged in a particular activity only means that the individual is functioning in some socioculturally defined context (Kozulin 1986).
- 'Goal' (*tsel'*) in Vygotsky's nomenclature is not restricted to the management of a 'task' or the solving of a 'problem' as the English term might suggest. Rather than 'goal' that evokes for English speakers a stable external target

of which one is conscious ahead of time and that one attempts to 'reach' or 'fulfill' by travelling along a time or space line, better words for the Russian *tsel'* might be 'orientation' or 'directionality'. These terms allow for a dialogical view of consciousness, where consciousness is reorganized and the goal is changed and re-defined in the course of reaching it (Gal'perin 1969; Davydov and Radzikhovskii 1985).

Terms like 'orientation' and 'directionality' capture the physical, phenomenal aspect of signs. Signs as stimuli are grounded in a speaker's/writer's place and point of view; the very use of signs by a sign maker changes how a speaker or a writer orients him/herself in relation to others. Because signs point to other signs, the mere act of using signs reorients the whole field of action, like a magnetic field, and thereby makes things happen. It creates new things, states, and events.

The term 'orientation' also reflects the fact that signs are motivated, non-arbitrary representations of reality (Friedrich 1979; Karcevskij 1982; Hanks 1996; Shore 1996). A sign is always a sign to someone; it is used for a social purpose, and that social purpose is not exhausted in the original intention of the sign maker. For example, a poem gives a new orientation to familiar reality, and this orientation may mean more or different things to a particular reader than was originally intended by the author.

Signs influence behavior

In Vygotsky's goal-oriented semiotics, signs are a means of regulating others' and one's own behavior. Because much of language teaching considers language structures as so many tools to be used in communication, it is important here to distinguish between signs and tools. Vygotsky makes the difference between signs and tools in the way they orient human behavior: tools serve to master nature; signs serve first to influence others, then to master oneself.

> The tool's function is to serve as the conductor of human influence on the object of activity; it is externally oriented; it must lead to changes in objects ... The sign, on the other hand, changes nothing in the object of a psychological operation. It is a means of internal activity aimed at mastering oneself; the sign is internally oriented.
>
> (Vygotsky 1978: 55)

As Lantolf explains in the introduction to this volume, Vygotsky posited that the creation of signs from the given environment first occurs on the inter-psychological, then on the intrapsychological plane. Thus, for example, language learners first use the newly acquired linguistic structures as tools to master a given written assignment, and, in a communicative context, as signs to convey meanings to their readers. In time, their very use of these signs is likely to influence the way they view the reality they are writing about (see Grabois 1997). In the study below, learners of English used English words as tools, to master a certain assignment. Indeed some learners believed that this was all there was to the assignment. But as soon as their texts were read by the class as a whole and thus entered the dialogic, public domain, what they had considered as tools got read and interpreted by the teacher and their fellow students as so many signs, which could be interpreted and put in relation with other signs, and in turn influence the production of other texts, other utterances.

Signs are reversible

Through its repetition over time in conjunction with other signs, the creation of one sign affects the sign giver as well as the sign reader. According to Wertsch (1985b: 81), 'signs have the quality of reversibility. They can act upon the agent in the same way they act upon the environment or others.' This is a most important point in sign theory and one that is most often neglected by language teachers and learners. Learning a new language is not an innocent relabeling of the familiar furniture of the universe (Kramsch and McConnell-Ginet 1992a). It reconfigures one's whole classification system, as many linguists (for example, Whorf 1956; Lakoff 1987) and philosophers of language (Foucault 1970) have argued:

> The use of signs leads humans to a completely new and specific structure of behavior, breaking away from the traditions of biological development and creating for the first time a new form of a culturally based psychological process.
>
> (Vygotsky 1978: 40)

One could say that L2 learners, through the use of a foreign semiotic system, have the possibility of putting a new context or semiotic frame around past events, and thus of preparing a new frame within which to interpret future events. For example, a Vietnamese in Saigon who might have talked in Vietnamese about 'going' or 'e-migrating' to America, once in America refers to himself and other refugees in English as 'im-migrants' who have 'come' to the US, thus putting around the same events two different frames, and taking two different narrative perspectives, as I discuss below.

Sign mediation is a dialogic process

A corollary to Vygotsky's definition of signs is the mutual effect of the use of signs on communities of sign users. In verbal exchanges, be they spoken or written, different signs are used by the different participants or interlocutors because of their different definitions of the communicative situation. In the face of various interpretations of the situation, communication can take place only if the participants agree to understand each others' signs for all practical purposes within 'a temporarily shared social reality' (Wertsch 1985a: 160). Or, to cite Rommetveit: 'The two [interlocutors] are jointly committed to a temporarily shared social world, established and continually modified by acts of communication' (cited in Wertsch 1985a).

As we have seen, for both Peirce and Vygotsky, meaning emerges by an interpretive process that consists of putting a sign in relation with other signs. But to prevent any possible misunderstanding associated with transplanting Vygotsky's sign theory into the positivistic tradition of the late twentieth century, we need to relate it to a concept that was of prime importance to many linguists and literary scholars in the Soviet Union of the 1920s: that of dialogism.

Many psychologists, linguists, and philosophers in the intellectual ferment of the Soviet revolution, among whom Vygotsky, Karcevskij, Jakobson, Vološinov, and Bakhtin, rejected the binary oppositions of mind and body, individual and society, text and context, Self and Other. For them, the great question was: 'What is it in language that binds individuals into groups and at the same time enables individuals to exist as selves?' (Holquist 1990: 57). In a world of motivated and reversible signs, everything co-exists with everything else and acquires meaning, i.e. existence, only through its relation with others. Vygotsky, like Bakhtin, was interested in a unit of analysis that preserved the fundamental essence of consciousness and thus argued against the reductivism of his time that insisted on breaking things down into elements. Bakhtin's concept of 'dialogism' offered a way of thinking about oneself and the world not as two separate entities in interaction with each other, but as two sides of the same coin, relative to and constitutive of each other. Dialogism emphasizes the fact that every utterance is a response to other, prior or potential utterances, i.e. is characterized by 'addressivity' (Bakhtin 1986: 99). Addressivity, 'the quality of turning to someone' (*ibid.*), is a constitutive feature of utterances, which are always addressed to someone in response to someone. For Bakhtin and Vygotsky, we do not just use language in context; we shape the very context that shapes us. 'Each time we talk, we literally enact values in our speech through the process of scripting our place and that of our listener in a culturally specific social scenario' (Holquist 1990: 63). Language learners' utterances address and respond not only to their current teachers' questions and assignments, but also to former teachers' expectations and demands, to prior utterances heard or read, to imagined reactions of potential listeners or future readers.

The study

The advantage of taking semiotic theory as a point of departure for studying language learning is that learning another tongue can be seen as another way of creating, conveying, and exchanging signs, not primarily of acquiring new grammatical and lexical tools that are then put to use in a social context. The meaning of these signs can be viewed as indexical, iconic, or symbolic, but it has to be viewed within a dialogic framework, in which each spoken or written utterance is a response to others and thereby fundamentally multivalent (Kramsch and von Hoene 1995).

In the following study, I describe the acquisition of meaning in ESL writing as a process of acquiring another system of signs and of reflecting on their relationships. Through a stylistic analysis of students' foreign language productions, the dialogic aspects of Vygotsky's theory of signs can be brought to the fore and their implications explored for language teaching.

The text
Crickets by Robert O. Butler

Twenty-six students in two intermediate-level ESL writing classes at UC Berkeley were given to read the short story *Crickets* by Robert O. Butler (1992). The narrator is a Vietnamese-American, formerly called Thieu in Vietnam, now Ted in the US, who came to Louisiana ten years ago with his newly married wife. They had a son to whom they gave the American name Bill. Seeing that his son is bored, Ted tries to interest him in a game he used to play with his friends when he was a boy in Vietnam. They would search for crickets, the big and slow charcoal crickets and the small and smart firecrickets, and they would have them fight each other in teams. At first the son is interested and father and son go searching for crickets. Unfortunately they can only find one kind, the big slow charcoal crickets. The father thinks his son shares in his disappointment, when he realizes the boy is only furious at having stained his brand new Reeboks. As the boy leaves, the father calls after him, 'See you later, Bill.'

The assignment

The 13 students in each class came from a variety of East-Asian and Latin-American countries. In class A, all but one were foreign born, most having emigrated to the US three to five years ago. In class B, by contrast, all but three were American-born from parents who had themselves emigrated to the US, mostly from Asian or Latin-American countries.

The students were asked to summarize the story in their own words in four to five sentences on index cards. Six or seven of these summaries were then rewritten by their authors on the blackboard for general comparison and discussion. Student narrators in turn were to read their summaries aloud, explain any changes they might have made from their cards to the blackboard, and each was to say what they thought were common and divergent features between their own and others' summaries. The purpose was to make students conscious of the motivated semiotic choices they had made, how these choices constructed a meaning to the story, and how those meanings in turn affected the various readers in the class.[2]

The reason I chose a summary over, say, a piece of creative writing, was that it provided for a common semiotic world of signs from which the students could construct their own. A 'summary' can be viewed as the creation by a student of a textual sign or a cluster of textual signs oriented to imaginary or real readers. It can index an original story through direct reference or indirect reference to the events in the story or to the textual aspects of its narration. But it can also be an icon of the theme or the structure of the original text. It can finally be a symbol in the Peircean sense, i.e. the product of societal conventions of what a summary is supposed to be. As a sign, a summary creates in the mind of its reader other signs that enable the reader to make sense of the story told by the original text. The purpose of this study was to make these semiotic processes visible to the students. Making students conscious of their motivated semiotic choices is precisely what, according to Vygotsky, leads learners to higher forms of mental development.

Meaning in the making
From reading to writing on paper

As the students were given ten to fifteen minutes to write their summary in class, they made frequent use of erasures, corrections, substitutions on their index cards. Not knowing who their reader would be or whether they would have any reader other than the teacher, if at all, the changes they made reflect their concern to make their texts as coherent, precise, and accurate as possible and to avoid any ambivalence of meaning. Here are a few examples:

1 One student first started his summary with:

Ted, formerly of nation of South Vietnam …

but changed it to:

Ted, of the former nation of South Vietnam …

thus making the statement politically more accurate.

2 Another student started his second sentence as follows:

Since Bill is already ten year-old …

but changed it to:

Since Bill was born in America he didn't seem to interest in the cricket fight.

thus showing a concern for the logic of the story and for the cohesion of his own summary, which he had started with a sentence in the past tense. But the student appeared to have been dissatisfied with even this second draft, for he changed the sentence once again to:

Since Bill was born in America and became a typical American, he didn't seem to interest in the cricket fight.

thus more clearly making the point of the story.

3 An American student of Vietnamese parentage ended her summary as follows:

Perhaps his resentment to the VN gov't causes him to ~~fo~~

> stop
> ~~not~~ practic~~i~~ing his culture (VN) and ∧ ~~pass~~ it
>   ~~not~~ hesitate
> along to his children? He's confused and continues to struggle.

This student's semantic struggle to find the right words reflects an awareness of the potential misunderstandings caused by the wrong choice of words. Various versions are selected and then discarded: *causes him to forget* becomes *causes him to not practice*, which in turn is discarded in favor of *causes him to stop practicing*. Each of these versions represents a sharpening of factual accuracy with relation to the original text. *To stop practicing* implies a break with a previous practice, whereas *to not practice* might mean that the father had not practiced his culture, even in Vietnam, which is clearly not true. We also see a concern for grammatical congruence, for example, the agreement of the gerund *practicing* to match the verb *stop*. The successive corrections at the end of this sentence index a syntactic confusion that ends up saying the opposite of what the student might have intended to say. But they might also be interpreted as an icon of the deeper confusion experienced by this Vietnamese-American student. From *causes him to not practice his culture and pass it along*, to *causes him to stop practicing his culture and not pass it along*, to *causes him to stop practicing his culture and hesitate*, we see a desire to shape grammatically a complex social and cultural context of experience that is both precise and in conformity with standard English grammar.

4 We see the same struggle for matching coherent thoughts and coherent syntax in the following excerpt, which ends on an interesting thematic ambivalence:

> The second half of the story was to teach that even if
>   not
> geographics change there somethings will ~~always~~ be the same.

The contradiction between *some things will always be the same* and *some things will not be the same* is iconic of the contradiction between the father's desire for continuity between the old culture and the new, and the son's attitude that things are quite different now that they are in the US.

From writing on paper to writing on the chalkboard

Several changes were made once again in the transfer from the index cards to the chalkboard, but this time, they seem to have been prompted by students' increased awareness of their audience and by their concern with reader perception of truth (brackets indicate additions, crosslines indicate deletions).

The author of summary 5, an Australian immigrant, explained his changes with his desire to focus the chalkboard version more explicitly on the clash between the Vietnamese and the American cultures.

5 The short story, 'Crickets', is about a man's transformation into ~~another country~~ [the United States] … One day Ted decided to show Bill a game from his childhood [and culture]. It turned out that the two never played the game because there was only one kind of crickets, the big, slow, and strong charcoal crickets which symbolize the ~~Americans~~ [people]. The smaller but smarter 'fire' crickets were no where to be found which symbolized a detachement from Ted's country and people.

The author of summary 6, a US born student of Korean ancestry, avoided what could be viewed as undue generalizations.

6 Although Ted tries to teach ~~his son~~ Bill his culture ~~and life in Vietnam~~ (w/ fighting crickets), Bill, ~~the son~~, is unable to learn ~~anything~~ because of new American ~~culture~~ attitude.

When asked why he had made these changes, he answered, looking at the author of summary 5: 'It's not American culture *per se*, just the attitude of some Americans.' Other authors claimed to have more writerly concerns in mind, like the author of summary 7:

7 ~~An excerpt about a man from a different culture and a son who is raised in contrast from the man.~~ AN EXCERPT ABOUT A MAN FROM A DIFFERENT CULTURE AND A SON FROM A CONTRASTING CULTURE.

In this summary, several changes occurred between the index card and the chalkboard. The private text had been written in pencil in small characters, while the public text was written with a chalk in capital letters. The syntactically loose relative clause (*who is raised*) was made into a nominalized clause (*from a contrasting culture*). When asked why he had made these changes, the author shrugged his shoulders and answered: 'I dunno. It's easier to read. It doesn't take up so much space.' What is important is not whether this interpretation is the 'true' reason for these changes, but, rather, that the reason given displays a sensitivity to the readers and to the constraints of the medium.

In all these changes, we see an awareness by the students that their signs are the result of non-arbitrary selections that can influence others and reflect also on themselves. But the full extent of these selections and of the new semiotic frame, or sociocultural interpretation, that each student put on the original story was revealed only through the stylistic analysis that teacher and students engaged in for each of the texts displayed on the board. It is to this joint analysis that I now turn.

Students' semiotic frames

Students' texts displayed a range of semiotic devices that gave meaning to the story, despite the students' limited knowledge of English. Students had first to decide how they were going to name the main character, alternately called in the first paragraph of the text Ted, Thieu, or Mr. Thieu. Various beginnings show the difficulty the students had in making their choice.

8   ~~I tried to~~ Ted tried to give his son, Bill, ...

9   Ted, who has a strong Vietnam background and history, has a child, Bill, born in the U.S.

10   The story was about a man named Thieu

11   A man neme Ted (Thieu) moved to the United States as a chemical Engineer

12   ~~Ted~~ Mr. Thicu was an immigrant who escaped from Vietnam.

Naming patterns were one of the signs that differed significantly from one summary to the next, and, combined with other signs, could yield the particular semiotic pattern of that summary. By shifting the narrator from the text's first person to the third person, the student writers were forced to take a stand *vis-à-vis* the object they were encoding. Feeling that the first-person narration was no longer appropriate for a summary, they decided to switch to the third person (excerpt 8). But then how would they name the father? Calling him *Ted* was adopting an American narrative perspective (excerpts 8 and 9); calling him *Thieu* was adopting a Vietnamese perspective (excerpt 10). Which perspective to take? Narrator 11 tries to use parentheses to solve the problem; narrator 12 decides to use the formal *Mr. Thieu* as a means of distancing himself from the problem.

Student summaries further varied in the way they anchored the reader in the perspective of the narrator through deictics of time, place, and personal stance. This was done first through the presence or absence of temporal or spatial markers. A summary could describe the specific events in their chronological order, as does summary 13.

13   When Ted first immigrated to the States, his American name, Ted, was the only disturbation of his life. As time moves on, he found Louisiana is very much like Vietnam ...

Temporal markers (for example, *as time moves on, one day, in the end, finally*) and spatial markers (for example, *the States, America, Louisiana*) punctuate the telling, establishing the same sequence of events as the original story.

A summary could also attempt to render a universally valid story of immigration, in which case one found in it no particular temporal or spatial sequencing, for example in summary 14 where the sequencing is purely argumentative.

14   This is a story about the transitional phase that a typical immigrant goes through. It talks about how a Vietnamese man adapts to the new environment; his observations and comments. It deals with the gap in his relation with his son; how his son has grown to have very different interests.

Here, nominalizations like *transitional phase, observations and comment, gap in his relation*, serve to make the text abstract, i.e. typical, and therefore generalizable to other immigration situations.

Deictic devices could also indicate the authorial stance or point of view of the narrator. In example 15, phrases like *In Vietnam he struggled ... Now in the US he struggles ...* situate the narrator in the American here-and-now. Similarly, calling Ted *an immigrant* (rather than an *emigrant*) who *comes* or *immigrates* (rather than *goes* or *flees* or *emigrates*) to America, are all indications of a deictic perspective anchored in a narrator living in the United States.[3]

Also relevant was the choice of verb used to depict the main character's coming to America. There is a difference whether Mr. Thieu is said to have *a strong Vietnam background* (excerpt 9), or to have *fled* (excerpt 16) or *escaped* (excerpt 12) from Vietnam, or to be *a refugee from Vietnam*, or whether he is said to have *moved* (excerpt 11) or *immigrated* (excerpt 13) to the United States.

This orientation was further rendered visible through repetitions and parallelisms, for example, the deliberate repetition of the word *struggle* in summary 15 (chosen even the fourth time over the variant *fought*), and the use of parallel constructions in summary 16.

15   This story is about an immigrant from Vietnam. He *struggled* in his native country and now he *struggles* in the U.S. However these *struggles* are very much different. In Vietnam ~~he str fought~~ *struggled* for his life, for his freedom. Now in the U.S. he *struggles* to try to find a balance between cultural values ... He's confused and continues to *struggle* (my emphasis)

16   Ted, Vietnese, had a son name Bill with his wife when he fled to the states. Bill, growing up in Louisiana, adapted to the American culture. Ted, fearful that his son would lose touch with their original culture, wanted to show what their culture was like. Therefore, Ted attempted to show his son a game that he used to play with crickets. However, Bill showed no interest and Ted realized that like the land, the two cultures are different and require a different lifestyle.

The rhetorical movement of this last summary (1 Ted ... Bill 2 Bill, growing up ... 3 Ted, fearful ... 4 Therefore ... 5 However...), with its parallel constructions in 2 and 3, and its cohesive markers in 4 and 5, represents iconically the problematic polarity, or dilemma, expressed in the story.

Summary 17, by contrast, uses lack of cohesion as an effective rhetorical device.

17   However he realized that the game is not just boring for the son but also that he lost a lot more than just his Vietnamese name. His cultural identity.

The sudden cohesive rupture between the first and the second sentence both indexes the empathy of the narrator for the father and serves as an icon for the abrupt loss of cultural identity that he has incurred.

Students' summaries further showed clear evidence of the subject positions of their narrators. These were either expressed indirectly from within the story, as in summary 18:

18   A man neme Ted (Thieu) moved to United States as a chemical Engineer *after leading a tough childhood in Vitname* [my emphasis].

or from outside the story as in the following two summaries:

19   It turned out that the two never played the game because there was only one kind of crickets, the big, slow, charcoal crickets which *symbolize the American people*. The smaller, but smarter 'fire' cricket, were nowhere to be found *which symbolized a detachment from Ted's country and people* [my emphasis].

20   It was hard for Bill to attain the values and attitude from his father's culture. *I was glad that Ted realized it, because I've seen a lot of foreigner parents who don't* [my emphasis].

We have seen how students' summaries encoded meanings both indexically and iconically. They also made use of conventional ways of talking about immigration, especially those authors who were US born and had thus grown up with a US American, Californian 'cultural model' (Shore 1996: 44). Expressions like *clash of cultures, cultural ancestry, generation gap, cultural gap, cultural identity, traditional culture,* that were found in many of the summaries, echo prior texts taken from the current US-American discourse on immigration and ethnic difference, as are also phrases like [the father] *wants to show his son his roots in the Vietnamese culture; the first generation ... cannot share its identities* (sic) *as Vietnamese with the second generation;* [the father] *is confused ; he gives up trying to communicate with his son; he accepts his son the way he is; different cultures require different lifestyles.* All these phrases, which are not in the original text, are like so many conventional symbols used by the American media and pop psychology to talk about the problems of immigrants and ethnic minorities. They require no further explanation because the authors can rely on the common American context of the classroom to be understood by their readers. By using these symbols, that 'animate' or echo the words and utterances of prior speakers and writers (Goffman 1981:144), students give additional meaning to the original story.

Making further use of conventionalized signs, various students drew on prior school socialization to interpret the genre 'summary' the way they had been taught. Compare summary 14 above with the following summary:

21   When Ted first immigrated to the States, his American name, Ted, was the only disturbation of his life. As time moves on, he found Louisiana is very much like Vietnam. However because of the incident he shared with his America born son, he realized the difference between United States & Vietnam. He said there are only 'charcoal crikets' here in the States.

Summaries 14 and 21 seem to be operating according to two different conceptions of what a 'summary' is. For the first author, a summary should render the main idea. She explains: 'Names are of no interest. The main thing is the larger issue. I tried to capture the essential of what the story means.' For the second, a summary should recapitulate the main facts and events in the order in which they happen in the story; a summary should not contain any explicit opinion or interpretation. This is why the author put the word 'charcoal crickets' in quotation marks, because, he said, 'they are only a symbol for the things and the people that you find in the United States', but he avoided saying that explicitly in his summary. By contrast, summary 16 above was both factual and interpretive, and kept to the original order of events. All three narrators seemed to follow a conventional text type they learned in school, even if they gave it their own idiosyncratic twist.

The dialogic nature of meaning

Class interpretation and discussion of each of the student texts encouraged students to give additional meaning to what they had written, as we can see in the following exchange:

22   Ming and Allan read their respective summaries aloud.
Ming (born in China, three years in US): A man neme Ted (Thieu) moved to United States as a chemical Engineer after leading a tough childhood in Vitname …
Allan (born in Taiwan, three years in US): Ted is a Vietnamese refugee from the Vietnam war, who had immigrated to Louisiana. He is the most intelligent worker in his company … Ted tried to share his childhood experience (i.e. Cricket fighting) with Bill …
T (to Ming): Is it significant that you called him Thieu in parentheses?
Ming: Yes, he was called Thieu before he moved to the United States.
T: You mean you used the name 'Thieu' before it says in your summary that he moved to the US. After that in the last sentence you call him 'Ted'.
→ **Ming** (smiling): Yeah because then I have to give him his American name.
  T: Is it important that he is a chemical engineer?

Ming: Yes he is not just any immigrant with a menial job, he is a successful engineer!

T (to class): Is it better to write 'chemical engineer' like in Ming's summary or 'the most intelligent worker in his company' like Allan did?

Freddy (from Guatemala): It is more significant that he is intelligent than what job he has …

Allan: I really wanted to focus on the general problem of the immigrant not on the crickets.

T: Is that why you put the crickets in parentheses '(i.e. cricket fighting)'?

→**Allan** (smiles and nods)

When asked to interpret the texts on the board, students usually do not view themselves as authors, but merely as scribes of a pre-determined 'story' (Ming) or as live characters in a real-life event (Freddy). The reason Ming gives for calling the character Thieu, for instance, refers to the chronology of the story as told by Butler. Ming responds to the teacher's questions as if she had been the witness to real events, or as if she were a character in the plot, not as the narratorial persona that she is herself. Freddy adduces his own personal experience to justify Allan's choice of words. When, however, the teacher rephrases Ming's and Allan's responses as *authorial responses*, she invariably elicits smiles of recognition from the students for her pedagogic tactic (see markers). The students then seem ready to assume authorial responsibility. Tim even finds the appropriate metalanguage for that authorial role:

23   **Tim** (reads his summary aloud) 'The short story, "Crickets" is about a man's transformation into the United States. Ted, (Mr.Thieu) is from Vietnam and fled to America because of all the problems in his country …

  T (to Tim): What distinguishes your summary from that of others?

  Tim: I'm interested in the transformation of an immigrant to another country=

  T: =that you represent in your text by keeping the two names, Ted and Thieu, transformed one into the other?

→   **Tim** (smiles): Yeah, it's the transformation that you see playing a symbolic role.

But not all learners are equally open to this quest for rhetorical symbolism. Some are in fact explicitly reticent to read more into their texts than the referential meanings of the words.

24   **Jeff** (born in Burma, two years in US): reads his summary on the board 'Mr. Thieu was an immigrant who escaped from Vietnam. He and his wife and American-born child, Bill lived in LA where Mr. Thieu was called Ted as he worked in a refinery. When Ted saw that his son was bored, he tried to introduce the idea of fighting crickets but as he and his son searched for crickets, they only found one type which made the

whole game uninteresting and Ted was sorry that he had introduced the idea to his son.'

T: How does your summary compare to the others?

Jeff: Mine doesn't include attitudes ... mine is pretty shallow ... I think ... You asked us to summarize, so I just summarized, I really didn't think about it.

T: Anyone else wants to comment on Jeff's summary?

Edmond (reading Jeff's summary): He ends with Ted being 'sorry that he had introduced the idea to his son' even though he wanted it ... I see there the idea of pain. I was just wondering ... Although he claimed he didn't intend to put any attitudes in there he did end his summary in a pretty sad way ... sort of open-ended, like the story itself.

T (to Jeff): Your summary says he worked in a refinery. The others didn't mention where he worked. Is that important?

Jeff: The people at work respect him.

T: Is it significant that he works in a refinery?

→ **Jeff:** Hm (ponders) yeah! (his face lights up) ... because he is smarter, like the crickets.

Like Ming in excerpt 22, Jeff rejects in the beginning any attempt by the teacher to make him into a responsible narrator, a creator of signs in his own right ('I really didn't think about it'). No doubt the genre summary encourages that attitude. But Jeff seems to be less responding to the constraints of the genre than performing an obligatory act of compliance to school routine ('You asked us to summarize, so I just summarized'). However, once he realizes that the name of the game is not compliance, but interpretation, and that the teacher's questions are not requests for information or knowledge display, but, rather, invitations to interpret his own signs, Jeff smiles and invents in his last rejoinder a rationale for his rhetorical choice, playing on the double connotation of 'working in a refinery', that could mean 'holding a good job' and 'being a finer, i.e. smarter, person'.

These three examples show that learners are eminently able to construct a semiotic universe that links linguistic signs not only to their dictionary referents, but also to these learners' knowledge of the world, and to other linguistic signs as well. However, the traditional emphasis on requests for or display of information in instructional settings, and the lack of an appropriate meta-language, put constraints on the amount of semiotic activity that students are able or willing to engage in in language classrooms.

In each of these exchanges, the students first seem to prefer to remain on the level of the story. The reasons they give for their rhetorical choices are the causes of events or motives of actions within the story, or their own general life experience. It is only through the patient encouragement of the teacher that they seem ready to access the semiotic 'pleasure of the text' itself (Barthes 1975) and the pleasure of constructing themselves as authorial or discursive selves.

Pedagogical implications

An analysis of the various summaries has shown that the students made ample use of semiotic devices to reframe the story on their own terms. Because the genre that had been assigned to them ('summary') greatly restricted what they could say, their choices of what to say and how to say it became all the more significant. The rich semiotic contexts in which this exercise was carried out further imbued students' choices with meaning.

There was first the prior semiotic context of the original story or plot, as well as the text itself written by Robert Butler, and each student's prior educational and life experiences. There was, in addition, the triple semiotic context of the exercise at hand that consisted of three consecutive conditions of enunciation: individual students writing on individual index cards for a non-specified reader, individual students writing with chalk on the chalkboard for public display before an audience of teacher and peers, texts on the chalkboard as objects of joint oral discussion. At each of these junctures semiotic choices were made, in which participants took on various roles: authors of their words on the index cards, narrators and animators of their words on the board, 'principals', to use Goffman's term, when orally suggesting meanings with the authority of expert critics (see Goffman 1981: 144).[4]

Within these semiotic contexts, students made use of linguistic signs of an indexical, iconic, and symbolic nature and of paralinguistic signs such as handwriting, erasures, corrections, punctuation, and the like. They were encouraged to give meaning to their use of these signs.

Although the students' summaries showed a wealth of semiotic devices, most of these devices were used to link signs and their contextual referents, found in the context of the story and the context of their own experience. Indeed, some students seemed to use words mostly as tools to accomplish a writing assignment, as in Jeff's self-assessment. One cannot say that theirs was not a goal-oriented activity, as they were certainly 'doing school', but it did not have the dialogic character typical of sign operations. For many of them, it was a problem-solving task that required linguistic tools, not signs. As the exercise proceeded, however, students were more and more encouraged to link textual sign to textual sign and to consider not only the indicative function of their texts, but their symbolic function as well.

In each of these exchanges the teacher transformed linguistic tools into signs by imbuing them with addressivity, by transforming sentences into utterances created with a communicative purpose and by making explicit their narrator's subject position. By bringing out the purpose or orientation of the students' signs, i.e. not so much what the students had intended to mean, but the potential meanings of what they ended up writing, the teacher tried to make the students conscious of the way they had reencoded the original story and how their reencoding provided a frame for the interpretation of other students' encodings. For example, when Tim read his summary aloud in excerpt 23, his bold and explicit acknowledgment of the story's political symbolism shocked the rest of the class into various gasps, and encouraged subsequent symbolic readings like the one offered by Edmond in 24.

Since the students reencoded the original story by placing it within the context of their own life experiences, each of these summaries indexed the worldviews of their writers as well. Most of the students who were foreign born and were recent immigrants to the US wrote summaries that indexed sympathy with the father's plight, whereas the summaries of students who were born and raised in the US by foreign parents indexed in most cases impatience with the father and identification with the American youngster.

Vygotsky's semiotic analysis can serve to explain the aesthetic pleasure obviously experienced by the students when they discover both the semiotic potential of their own texts and their own discursive roles as narrators. But it can also illuminate the processes by which second language students acquire the ability to make meanings that are both private and public. Private, because they are able to recast in their own words experiences that only non-native speakers, immigrants, have gone through. Public, because they are able to choose words and combinations of words that can pass on that experience to a larger audience of English speakers. Second language acquisition is precisely this process by which learners acquire ever greater conscious control of the semiotic choices offered by the foreign language.

It is through the dialogic construction of rhetorical roles through the written and the spoken medium that students experience themselves as both private, individual, and public, social sign makers, and that they appreciate the fluidity of meanings they can attribute to themselves and others. Like Goffman later on, Vygotsky insisted on the notion of 'role' (Vygotsky 1989), a social performance-related concept far different from the currently fashionable notion of 'identity'—a dialogic notion of self in other and other in self, creating themselves and others through signs. The teacher in both these classes contributed actively to move consistently the students from their 'true' self to their 'narrator' or 'author' self, showing them, in effect, that, in a language class, they are who they say they are, no more, no less (Kramsch 1989), and that the search for the true and original authorial intention is less interesting than the one they are willing to construct after the fact (Widdowson 1992: x).[5]

As the examples above show, students are not used to seeing themselves are 'merely' playing a narrative role. They think they have to put their 'true' self on the line and report on what they 'intended' to say. The teacher here, by contrast, approached both the classroom dialogue and the students' culturally marked texts as discourse processes, i.e. she viewed the students as narrators of someone else's story, a process through which they also narrated themselves.

Conclusion

In second language acquisition research, Vygotsky's cognitive theory and his theory of tool-mediated action have taken precedence over his theory of signs. The reason why it has found such resonance might be that it has filled a need to take the sociocultural context of learning into account without putting in question the dominant view of communication as a problem to be solved with the help of linguistic 'tools'. But Vygotsky was careful to show that language, unlike other, natural, signals found in the environment, is both a tool and a sign. As James Wertsch writes in light of Vygotsky's work:

> While one cannot understand tool-mediated action without understanding its origins, one cannot reduce a tool-mediated action to its origins. An adequate analysis of action must take into account … the transformation it undergoes as a result of becoming intertwined with a sign system.
>
> (Wertsch 1985a: 206)

Vygotsky, like Bakhtin, whose vision he shared to a large extent, as A. A. Leontiev points out (1995), sees human personality made up of different roles that get played out in dialogic situations. It is in the context of dialogic relationships that signs get emitted, received, and exchanged; meanings proliferate and are constrained by custom and institutional control. Vygotsky's broadly interdisciplinary work enables us to add to the cognitive also the semiotic dimension of language acquisition. This dimension is both linguistic and eminently aesthetic, inasmuch as it deals with the perception of form not as separate from, but as another word for 'content' (White 1987). It can account for the linguistic pleasure experienced by the students in this study and for their growing ability to enter various discursive roles as authors, narrators, interpreters, and critics. (For other similar studies, see Kramsch 1995c, 1996.) This ability, in turn, leads to ever greater cognitive development.

Vygotsky's semiotic analysis can offer a suitable pedagogic framework to teach language and culture as a system of linguistic and non-linguistic signs intertwined in a socially and historically situated environment. Such a pedagogy is timely as it echoes post-structuralist trends in the humanities and gives prominence to a view of the language learner as someone who creates new signs by manipulating signs created by others.

Notes

1 A shorter report on this study appeared in Kramsch 1995c.
2 Of course, one of the main constraints is that language learners cannot always write (and speak) about what they would like to but about what they are able to write and talk about. This constraint is different in degree, but not in nature from that imposed on any speaker/writer who has to make sure that his/her ideas are expressed in the right words for the right audience.
3 The original text, narrated in the first person, enables a shift in perspective from Vietnam to the United States when Thieu and his wife decide to leave Saigon and 'end up' in Louisiana. The text does not use words like

'emigrating', 'immigrating', or 'fleeing'. Instead it reads: 'And then there were Thai Pirates in the South China Sea and idiots running the refugee centers ... to find a place for me and my new bride, who braved with me the midnight escape by boat and the terrible sea and all the rest. We ended up here in the flat bayou land of Louisiana ...' Whether the students knew the difference between 'emigration' and 'immigration' and thus were able to make a conscious choice of one over the other, is not relevant here. More important is the perspectival frame that this choice places on the text and the effect it might have on readers.

4 In *Forms of Talk* (1981) Erving Goffman distinguishes three kinds of stances a speaker can take *vis-à-vis* the production of his/her utterances. The speaker can be an 'author', i.e. someone who has selected the sentiments that are being expressed and the words in which they are encoded; the speaker can be an 'animator' of the words uttered, i.e. 'an individual active in the role of utterance production', even if these words are borrowed from someone else, as when one learns a foreign language; the speaker can be a 'principal', i.e. 'someone whose position is established by the words that are spoken' (1981: 144), as when a writer assumes authorial responsibility and expertise.

5 Within a semiotic framework, the question is not what the student intended to mean prior to choosing any of these terms, but what effect these terms now have on the reader once they are put in relation with other terms chosen in this and other summaries, and what they say about the general orientation of the student text.

7   Second language learning as participation and the (re)construction of selves[1]

Aneta Pavlenko
Temple University

James P. Lantolf
The Pennsylvania State University

Introduction

This chapter is about second language learning not as the acquisition of a new set of grammatical, lexical, and phonological forms but as a struggle of concrete socially constituted and always situated beings to participate in the symbolically mediated lifeworld (see Habermas 1987) of another culture. These individuals have intentions, agency, affect, and above all histories, and are frequently, though not always, known as people.[2] Our discussion of second language learning as the struggle for participation, and its potential consequences, is informed by sociohistorical and social constructionist theories, which are still very much situated on the margins of our field—a field in which the preeminent metaphors are computationalism (see Lantolf 1996) and the mind as a container (see van Lier this volume).

Sfard (1998), in fact, observes that a new metaphor, *participation* (PM), has emerged in the education literature not as a replacement for, but as a complement to, the traditional learning as *acquisition* metaphor (AM), often associated with computer and the container metaphors. Leaving aside the informative details of her analysis of the two metaphors, we wish to highlight those aspects of her discussion that are relevant to our current project. AM, according to Sfard (*ibid.*: 5), compels us to think of knowledge as a commodity that is accumulated by the learner and to construe the mind as the repository where the learner hoards the commodity. In SLA such an approach allows us to see language as a set of rules and facts to be acquired and permits us to discuss learner language in all its complexity. PM, on the other hand, obliges us to think of learning 'as a process of becoming a member of a certain community' (Sfard 1998: 6), which entails 'the ability to communicate in the language of this community and act according to its particular norms' (*ibid.*).

Applying such an approach to SLA involves shifting the focus of investigation from language structure to language use in context, and to the issues of affiliation and belonging. Moreover, while AM is about states and the permanence implied by related terms such as 'having', and 'knowledge', PM is characterized by terms such as 'doing', 'knowing', and 'becoming part of a greater whole' (*ibid.*). AM implies somewhat discrete learning stages with a well-defined end point; PM 'leaves no room for halting signals' (*ibid.*). As Hanks (1996: 222) puts it, viewing language learning as participation, 'does not involve acquiring rules or codes, but ways of acting and different kinds of participation.' Thus, we can summarize by saying that AM focuses on the individual mind and the internalization of knowledge, which is crucial for the study of the *what* in SLA, while PM stresses contextualization and engagement with others (see van Lier this volume) in its attempt to investigate the *how*.

We want to make it clear, however, that neither we nor Sfard are prepared to propose the new metaphor as a replacement for the acquisition metaphor. Rather it is intended as a complement to the older metaphor, since, as we will show, it makes visible aspects of second language learning that the acquisition metaphor leaves hidden. Both metaphors have a role to play in explicating the processes entailed in learning a second, or for that matter, a first, language. Having two different perspectives at our disposition allows us to engage productively in the study of learner languages, on the one hand, and in the study of language socialization on the other. As our chapter focuses on the latter, we chose the PM metaphor as more appropriate for the analysis we wish to develop.

The data we wish to consider—first-person narratives—have, until only recently, been marginalized by the social and human sciences as legitimate data and to a large extent are still not part of the mainstream in our own field (some exceptions are Peirce 1995; Polanyi 1995; Siegal 1995 and 1996; Norton 1997; Schumann 1998).

In our view, two principal reasons explain this marginalization. First of all, there is a strong belief in the discursive space we refer to as science, that first-person tellings are less reliable and less valid than third-person tellings. Therefore, such tellings are assigned the status of 'anecdotal': perhaps interesting but potentially incomplete, if not erroneous, unless, of course, they are produced by researchers themselves and even then they are not granted the same legitimacy as third-person accounts.[3] Here we mention the well-known introspective studies of Schumann and Schumann (1977), who recorded their acquisition of Arabic, Bailey's (1983) analysis of competitiveness and anxiety in her beginner's French class, Schmidt's and Frota's (1986) account of Schmidt's first steps in learning Portuguese in and out of the classroom in Brazil, and Neu's (1991) investigation of her study of Polish. Although interesting and insightful, these and other similar studies have a relatively narrow scope in that their focus is on the initial stages of acquisition of linguistic structures, primarily in the classroom, of people whose goal seems to be restricted to developing some degree of proficiency in language as a code, but not to cross the border into the domain where selves and worlds are reconstructed. As Searle so cogently notes:

> in ways that are not at all obvious on the surface, much of the bankruptcy of most work in the philosophy of mind and a great deal of sterility of academic psychology over the past fifty years, over the whole of my intellectual lifetime, have come from a persistent failure to recognize and come to terms with the fact that the ontology of the mental is an irreducibly first-person ontology.[4]
>
> (Searle 1992: 95)

We also believe, as one of the present authors has argued elsewhere (Lantolf 1996), that SLA researchers, like our colleagues working in other human and social sciences, have found the stunning achievements of the natural sciences over centuries an irresistible attraction, and so what could be more natural (pun intended) than to 'reshape all inquiry, and all of culture, on its model' (Rorty 1979: 367). Hence, over the course of the present century, the social and human sciences, and, in particular, psychology, along with its derivative and related disciplines, have subscribed uncritically to the rationalist epistemology and experimental methodology of the hard sciences.[5] Among the many problems created by this move is the conversion of first-person into third-person research in the name of objectivity.[6] What seems to have been lost in all of this is just what a first-person account of the physical world would look like in the first place (or should we say in the third place)! However, in recent years narrative approaches and first-person tellings have found their way back into a variety of disciplines, including anthropology and psychology (for example, Smith, Harré, and Van Langenhove 1995a). Below we will argue that in the human sciences first-person accounts in the form of personal narratives provide a much richer source of data than do third-person distal observations.

The second reason for marginalizing the particular type of narrative we discuss here is that they are about the experience of becoming and being bilingual and have been produced by people who themselves are frequently marginalized. Linguistic theories, including those prevalent in SLA research, have traditionally assumed monolingualism to be the unmarked case. As a result 'SLA researchers seem to have neglected the fact that the goal of SLA is bilingualism' (Sridhar and Sridhar 1986: 5) of any kind, let alone the late bilingualism we consider here (for the few exceptions, see Coppieters 1987; Birdsong 1992; Ioup *et al.* 1994). It is therefore not too surprising that the personal narratives of bilinguals have not found their way into mainstream linguistic or SLA research.[7]

Outside of the field of SLA, however, there is an abundance of autobiographic narratives in which the stages of second language learning are recounted by adult immigrants, whose goal often is to become assimilated and acculturated. The memoirs of these bicultural bilinguals in general and of bilingual writers in particular constitute a rich, compelling, and informative source of evidence about the process of adult second language learning (for a detailed analysis see Pavlenko 1998). While the tradition of hermeneutic research in SLA is rich and longstanding, up until now it has mainly considered the 'here-and-now' or 'in process' descriptions of second language learning process by learners and researchers. Our intent then in the present chapter is to establish 'retroactive' first-person narratives[8] as a legitimate source of data on the learning process by teasing out in a theoretically informed way insights provided by the life stories of people who have struggled through cultural border crossings.

Narrativity and the human sciences

George Mead (1977), the pragmatist and social psychologist, recognized early on that people played an active role in constructing their own lives.[9] Mead, in many ways a proponent of the scientific tradition with roots in Vico, argued that because of the personal agency involved in shaping a life, it was necessary to develop a methodology 'that would provide information about the person's own self-interpretation of his or her actions' (Polkinghorne 1988: 104).[10]

At about the same time that Mead was developing his theories, the Russian scholar, Mikhail Bakhtin, was developing his views on the self constituted as a story, through which happenings in specific places and at specific times are made coherent (Holquist 1990: 37). Jerome Bruner, one of the founders of modern cognitive psychology, recognizes that the doxology of the scientific method—'thou shalt not indulge self-delusion, nor utter unverifiable propositions, nor commit contradiction, nor treat mere history as cause' (Bruner 1996: 132)—is unable to describe the basis on which ordinary people go about making sense of their and others' activities. The problem, in Bruner's view, is that the ways in which people make sense of their experiences and themselves in the everyday world cannot be formulated as 'testable propositions' (*ibid*.). Consequently, the quest for the causes of human sense making itself makes little sense, and therefore, the logico-scientific mode of conducting research requires a complementary mode—a mode that searches for *reasons* rather than causes. Thus, Bruner was instrumental in introducing a narrative-based research methodology into psychology. According to Bruner (1986: 11), each of the two research modes 'provides a distinctive way of ordering experience, or constructing reality. Each has operating principles of its own and its own criteria of well-formedness. They also differ radically in their procedures for verification' (see below). A fundamental difference between narrative knowing and categorical knowing is that the former takes as essential an awareness that 'time is the major dimension of human existence' (Polkinghorne 1988: 20) and recognizes the indispensable role of situatedness in human life activity, including what is mental, while the latter type of knowing is assumed to be impervious to the effects of time and space, thus giving rise to the sweeping foundational claims typical of traditional scientific theorizing.

In recent years narrative genre and personal narratives *per se* have gained increasing stature in psychology, sociology, sociolinguistics, and anthropology as legitimate and rich data sources for a variety of investigations, including that of narrative construction of selves and realities (Polkinghorne 1988; Bruner 1990, 1991; Rosenwald and Ochberg 1992; Josselson and Lieblich 1993; Linde 1993; Johnstone 1996; Bamberg 1997; Ochs 1997). We are not going to argue that personal narratives should replace observational/experimental research; rather we believe they bring to the surface aspects of human activity, including SLA, that cannot be captured in the more traditional approach to research. On the other hand, we also want to underscore that there is no compelling reason to favor one type of data over the other and to rank methods. The hegemony currently enjoyed by experimental/observational methodologies is linked in large part to the successes these methodologies have achieved in the hard sciences. However, it has also been observed that

> experimental methods strip behavior of its social context, substituting an artificial environment that may have little generalizability; and, secondly, that these methods are inherently hierarchical, with a powerful researcher observing, manipulating, and sometimes deceiving 'subjects' who are denied their subjectivity.
>
> (Crawford 1995: 172)

According to Rorty (1979: 362), if we jettison the essentialist Cartesian 'mind as mirror' metaphor and look at things from an existentialist/hermeneutic perspective, we come to see the descriptions of ourselves formulated in the language of the natural sciences 'as on a par with alternative descriptions offered by poets, novelists, depth psychologists, sculptors, anthropologists, and mystics' and that both types of descriptions (i.e. categorical and narrative) are 'simply among the repertoire of self-descriptions at our disposal'. Furthermore, we find it difficult to dispute Polkinghorne's (1988: ix) incisive, although we suspect for some, controversial observation, that the social sciences have not manifested the same level of accomplishments as the hard sciences, despite nearly a century-long love affair with their methodology and discourse. As Polkinghorne (1988) writes,

> I do not believe that the solutions to human problems will come from developing even more sophisticated creative applications of the natural science model, but by developing additional, complementary approaches that are especially sensitive to the unique characteristics of human existence.
>
> (Polkinghorne 1988: x)

Shore (1996) makes an important distinction between *actors'* and *observers'* *models* when developing accounts of human behavior. Unlike observers' models, which are organized 'more in terms of categories, permitting mutual rather than just personal orientation,' actors' models 'employ symbolic forms that are dynamic and graded, permitting the representation of an individual's changing relationships to any phenomenon ... they are dynamic ecological models that govern the negotiation of a changing landscape' (*ibid.*: 56). Included among actors' models are narratives, which Shore (1996) characterizes as verbal formulas that are either conventional or personal in nature and which people use to 'continually make sense of their worlds on the fly' (*ibid.*: 58). Furthermore, through narrative 'experience is literally talked into meaningfulness' and 'the strange and the familiar achieve a working relationship' (Shore 1996: 58). Narratives take on an especially clear function when people are confronted with disturbing and anomalous circumstances, such as a natural disaster, an assassination of a community leader, etc. In such cases, 'people generally become talkative' and they continue to tell the story 'until the events are gradually domesticated into one or more coherent and shared narratives that circulate in the community' (Shore 1996: 58). Bruner (1996: 90), citing Kierkegaard, stresses that 'telling stories in order to understand is not mere enrichment of the mind: without them we are, to use his phrase, reduced to fear and trembling.'

While communities construct narratives that often become conventionalized and integrated into the community fabric as cultural models that provide cohesion for the community, individuals also construct their own personal narratives, based on the conventionalized models, which allow them to make their own lives cohesive; that is, to understand what they are and where they are headed (Polkinghorne 1988; Linde 1993). The cohesive glue that imbues the narrative with significance is the plot which gives meaning to the events of the narrative and which in turn allows people to make sense of their own actions and those of others (Polkinghorne 1988: 21). The events that happen to people can only make sense if they can be fitted into an existing plot or if the plot itself can be reconfigured or replaced. This latter possibility usually only happens with considerable difficulty and resistance, since most people try very hard to maintain their current plot even if it means ignoring or distorting the new happenings (Polkinghorne 1988: 182). In her ground-breaking research on life stories of middle class Americans, Linde (1993: 221) suggests that at the base of their stories are coherence systems, 'social systems of assumptions about the world that speakers use to make events and evaluations coherent'. Failure to integrate new events into these systems of coherence or to alter the plot of a life story appropriately, frequently results in confusion, strangeness, and conflict and can, on occasion, lead to deep cognitive and emotional instabilities that end tragically (Harré and Gillett 1994).

While scientific understanding is established on the basis of laws of patterns of relationship across categories that have been abstracted from their spatial and temporal contexts, narrative understanding is quintessentially explanation based on the events that take place in a particular place and time and that can be integrated into the plot recognized as belonging to a specific life (Polkinghorne 1988: 21). Narrative explanation, unlike predictive logico-mathematical explanation, is retroactive in that it clarifies events with respect to the outcome that follows from the events; hence, it is about reconstruction (Polkinghorne 1988: 27). Narrative explanation cannot be any other way because the outcome of the narrative is unknown until it occurs.

As with other scientific research, narrative-based research entails detection, selection, and, above all, interpretation of data, but unlike the logico-mathematical approach, intentionality is at the heart of the interpretation process. This clearly distinguishes human actions from mere physical occurrences, since it acknowledges that people make things happen by intervening in events and that actions are generally undertaken with a preconceived end in mind (Polkinghorne 1988: 169).

Finally, narrative-based research, like its logico-mathematical counterpart, addresses questions of validity, reliability, and significance, although these concepts are understood in a different way than they are in traditional scientific research. Significance is not about probability due to chance in a random sample, but about meaningfulness or importance (Polkinghorne 1988: 175). And reliability is not about the consistency and stability of measuring instruments that always result in the same score, but it is about the dependability of the data and the strength of the analysis of the data (Polkinghorne 1988: 176). Finally, validity is based on a well-grounded conclusion, but it does not presume certainty; rather it proposes likelihood, since narrative research deals with open rather than the closed systems of traditional scientific research (Polkinghorne 1988: 175). Most importantly, narrative-based theory and research also has ecological validity as that which 'has something to say about what people do in real, culturally significant situations' (Neisser 1976: 2).

The stories

With the above in mind, we now turn to consideration of the border crossings of late/adult bilinguals as told in personal narratives. We will examine autobiographic work of several American and French authors of Eastern European origin, all of whom learned their second language (in which they work today) as adults: Polish-English bilinguals Eva Hoffman (*Lost in Translation. A Life in a New Language*) and Anna Wierzbicka (*The Double Life of a Bilingual: A Cross-Cultural Perspective*), Romanian-English bilinguals Andrei Codrescu (*The Disappearance of the Outside*) and Marianne Hirsch (*Pictures of Displaced Girlhood*), Czech-English bilingual Jan Novak (*My Typewriter Made Me Do It*), Bulgarian-French-English trilingual Tzvetan

Todorov (*Dialogism and Schizophrenia*), and Russian-English bilinguals Helen Yakobson (*Crossing Borders. From Revolutionary Russia to China to America*), Natasha Lvovich (*The Multilingual Self. An Inquiry into Language Learning*), and Cathy Young (*Growing Up in Moscow. Memories of a Soviet Girlhood*). These Eastern European experiences are echoed in a memoir of a Japanese-English bilingual Kyoko Mori (*Polite Lies. On being a Woman Caught Between Cultures*).

We chose to work with these particular authors in order to investigate an area of second language learning about which very little is known: an atypical experience of adults who attempt to become native speakers of their second language. This experience differs in many ways from that of growing up as a bilingual (see Zentella 1997).[11] It also differs from a more typical outcome of second language learning in adulthood whereby the learners achieve 'some level of proficiency'. As we argue elsewhere (Lantolf and Pavlenko 1998), people are agents in charge of their own learning, and most frequently they decide to learn their second language 'to a certain extent', which allows them to be proficient, even fluent, but without the consequences of losing the old and adopting the new ways of being in the world.

The second aspect that the narratives have in common is the relationship between the dominant language (English or French spoken in a Western country) and the minority Slavic language (spoken in what at the time were communist countries of Eastern Europe), whereby the dominant language affords both power and prestige to its speakers. An analysis of these unique stories of language learning 'to the point of no return' in their sociohistoric context has important implications for reconceptualizing notions of agency, success, competence, and fluency in a second language and also provides insights into the consequences of border crossings for the relationship between language and identity.

Our analysis demonstrates that the narratives of the bilingual writers in themselves represent a space where identities are reconstructed and life stories retold in the security of the double displacement granted by writing in a second language (see Hoffman, p. 121). We identify particular sites of reconstruction of identity, many of which are marked by internal conflicts between dominant monolithic ideologies of language learning and the authors' day-to-day experiences of participation in new discursive practices. We further suggest self-translation as a unifying metaphor, which, unlike the acquisition metaphor, entails a phase of continuous loss and only later an overlapping second phase of gain and reconstruction (Pavlenko 1998).

The initial phase of loss can be segmented into five stages:

– loss of one's linguistic identity ('careless baptism', according to Hoffman 1989)
– loss of all subjectivities

- loss of the frame of reference and the link between the signifier and the signified
- loss of the inner voice
- first language attrition.

The phase of recovery and (re)construction encompasses four critical stages:

- appropriation of others' voices
- emergence of one's own new voice, often in writing first
- translation therapy: reconstruction of one's past
- continuous growth 'into' new positions and subjectivities.

Before we consider how the above stages play out in the stories to be told here, it is necessary to define, as precisely as we can, just what a *self* is. An important first step is to distinguish a self from a *person*. According to Harré (1987: 110), a person is 'the publicly recognized human individual who is the focus of overt practices of social life', while a self is 'the still centre of experience' to which various conscious states, including organizations of memory, perception, and agency, are attributed. A self is composed of 'four coordinated manifolds' (Harré and Gillett 1994: 104): a location in space or a point of view; a location in time, or a 'trajectory or path through time'; a location of responsibility, or agency; and a social location in a 'manifold of persons, ordered by status, age, reputation, and the like'.

A self is a coherent dynamic system (Penuel and Wertsch 1995: 89) that is in 'continuous production' (Harré and Gillett 1994: 111), and which emerges as the individual participates in the (most especially, verbal) practices of a culture. Thus, for children, growing up culturally is about engaging in activities, depending on the culture, such as seeing movies, watching television, listening to music, viewing art, playing games, reading and listening to stories about others as well as themselves (*ibid.*). These activities are most often created by others displaced in time and space and thus, importantly, provide the means through which 'history and historical processes find their way to the core of individual identity' (*ibid.*). As children participate in such daily activities, they appropriate the signs (i.e. culturally constructed semiotic artifacts) incorporated by others 'into the flow of action' to talk about and thus, think about, themselves (Penuel and Wertsch 1995: 91). The question we ask and try to answer in what follows, is, what happens to a self when an individual moves from participation in the discursive practices of one culture, in this case, the native culture, to those of another culture ?[12] In examining the processes entailed in border crossings, our focus will fall on two of the central manifolds of a narratively constituted self—time and agency.

Second language learning: phase of loss

We will discuss the above stages relying on all sources, but primarily on the most detailed and insightful description of second language socialization and acculturation to date, Eva Hoffman's *Lost in Translation. A Life in a New Language* (1989). Currently an American writer, Hoffman was thirteen when her Polish-Jewish family emigrated from Poland to North America in 1959. Her autobiographic book provides a penetrating account of a gradual personality change, together with deep insights into Polish and Anglo cultural attitudes and norms that have clashed in her personal experiences.

The first step on the route to self-translation, identified by Hoffman (1989), is a name change, often imposed. Due to this 'careless baptism' from Ewa and Alina, the author and her sister become 'Eva' and 'Elaine'. What follows is a shattering loss of their linguistic identity:

> Nothing much has happened, except a small, seismic mental shift. The twist in our names takes them a tiny distance from us—but it's a gap into which the infinite hobgoblin of abstraction enters. Our Polish names didn't refer to us; they were as surely us as our eyes or hands. These new appellations, which we ourselves can't yet pronounce, are not us. They are identification tags, disembodied signs pointing to objects that happen to be my sister and myself ... [They] make us strangers to ourselves.
>
> (Hoffman 1989: 105)

Similar comments are made by another Polish-English bilingual, the well-known linguist, Anna Wierzbicka (1985), by Marianne Hirsch (1994), the Romanian-English scholar, and by the Russian-American bilingual, Helen Yakobson, who poignantly attests to the catastrophic consequences of her 'Americanization':

> My 'Americanization' took place at all levels of my existence; in one sweep I had lost not only my family and my familiar surroundings, but also my ethnic, cultural and class identity.
>
> (Yakobson 1994: 119)

At stake in the renaming process is, as Hoffman's commentary especially makes transparent, not merely a phonological problem to be overcome with some practice. It is about the conversion of subjects, actively embedded in their world, into objects no longer able to fully animate that world. In other words, it is about loss of agency in the world—an agency, in large part, constructed through linguistic means.

According to Harré and Gillett (1994: 106), first and second person pronouns are part of the *indexical* system of a language (other indexicals include *now*, *here*, *this*, *that*). Unlike anaphoric pronouns (*he* and *she*), which stand for some other word, usually a proper name, indexicals, above all, index the content or social force of an utterance with the spatial, temporal, moral, and social manifolds of a self. Through the indexical pronoun, the speaker experiences the world from a unique spatial (i.e. bodily) and temporal location, and he or she acts in relation to others. Most importantly, for our purposes, the speaker also implicates him- or herself as an agent responsible for actions, both physical and symbolic, that contribute to the formation and re-formation of the world inhabited by objects as well as other agents (Harré and Gillett 1994: 107). Our thesis here is that the shift from Ewa and Alina to Eva and Elaine represents the loss of social manifold affiliated with their respective indexical 'I's'. The mapping of their first person indexical, which was a Polish 'I', onto their social, now North American, manifestation of this 'I' was ruptured as a consequence of their having been relabeled.

Loss of agency is not only about severing one's union with the world inhabited by others, it is, and perhaps more profoundly so, about losing the connection to one's own inner world—the world of the mind. This is attested in several of the writers we examined, but it is most explicitly, and painfully, evidenced in the words of Hoffman:

> I wait for that spontaneous flow of inner language which used to be my nighttime talk with myself … Nothing comes. Polish, in a short time, has atrophied, shriveled from sheer uselessness. Its words don't apply to my new experiences, they're not coeval with any of the objects, or faces, or the very air I breathe in the daytime. In English, the words have not penetrated to those layers of my psyche from which a private connection could proceed.
>
> (Hoffman 1989: 107)

The two great Russian scholars, Vygotsky and Bakhtin, both assigned inner speech a central role in their respective theorizing about the nature of human mental life. For Vygotsky, inner speech is semantically dense (as Lantolf and Appel 1994, describe it as 'a semantic black hole') personal meaning (or *smysl*), and for Bakhtin it is a private dialogue in which the self simultaneously plays the role of speaker and listener (Wertsch 1991). For both thinkers, inner speech functions to organize and make sense of a person's experiences of the world. Just as social speech mediates the individual's relationship to the world of others and objects, private speech, its derivative, mediates the relationship between the person and his or her inner mental order, or what Vygotsky called consciousness (Frawley 1997).

In the above passage Hoffman seems to be in a semantic twilight zone in which her inner speech in Polish has ceased to function, while the inner speech sparked by English, her new language, has yet to emerge. From a sociohistorical perspective, then, she has no way of organizing and making sense of her experiences. In some sense, she has no experiences, because, as both Vygotsky and Bakhtin agree, it is through inner speech that we create our experiences; that is, in inner speech we organize and integrate the events that occur in space and time into the plot of our life narrative. Without inner speech, this organization and integration are impossible.

Mori (1997), who emigrated from Japan to the United States at the age of twenty, upon returning to Japan after nearly twenty years of residency in North America, no longer has a Japanese voice and is compelled to rely on her English, inner and social, voices to participate in the discursive practices of her former native language.

> In Japanese, I don't have a voice for speaking my mind. ... Trying to speak Japanese in Japan, I'm still thinking in English. I can't turn off what I really want to say and concentrate on what is appropriate. Flustered, I try to work out a quick translation, but my feelings are untranslatable and my voice is the voice of a foreigner.
>
> (Mori 1997: 16–17)

For a time, Hoffman's heroine is forced to live in a split universe, where the signifier has become severed from the signified. Ewa deeply mourns her inability to describe the world around her; her new words are simple referents without any conceptual systems or experiences to back them up:

> The words I learn now don't stand for things in the same unquestioned way they did in my native tongue. 'River' in Polish was a vital sound, energized with the essence of riverhood, of my rivers, of my being immersed in rivers. 'River' in English is cold—a word without an aura. It has no accumulated associations for me, and it does not give off the radiating haze of connotation. It does not evoke.
>
> (Hoffman 1989: 106)

Often, the inability of the 'new' language to intimately name the world (both inner and outer) is accompanied by a deterioration of that same ability in the native language. While native language attrition is dispassionately documented (i.e. third-person stance) in the scientific literature (see Seliger and Vago 1991; Waas 1996), it is dramatically experienced (i.e. first-person viewpoint) in the narratives of the writers under consideration as loss of self and identity. Jan Novak, a Czech-American, portrays his native language attrition as follows:

> ... my Czech had begun to deteriorate. There were times now when I could not recall an everyday word, such as 'carrot', 'filer', or 'sloth'. I would waste the day probing the labyrinthine recesses of my memory because to get help from the dictionary seemed only to legitimize the loss. ... Computers, graft, football and other things were becoming easier to talk about in English. Most disturbingly, however, now and then a straightforward Czech phrase would suddenly turn opaque and abstract on me. To comprehend it, I would have to replay it in my mind as if it reached me wrapped in a thick, unfamiliar accent. I would not be sure whether it was correctly put; there was a sense that something was wrong with it, but I could not say what. The fleeting glimpses of Czech as a foreign language unnerved and depressed me ... gradually I realized when drafting [my poems] that I was now explaining things that a Czech reader would know. I had started to write for Americans; my linguistic transformation was under way. It was to happen in three delicately unburdening stages, as I moved from writing in

Czech about Czechs for Czechs to writing for Americans in English about Americans.

(Novak 1994: 263–4)

Mori (1997) writes of her loss of pragmatic competence in Japanese:

> ... the symbolic invitations in the Midwest don't confuse me; I can always tell them apart from the real thing. In Japan, there are no clear-cut signs to tell me which invitations are real and which are not. People can give all kinds of details and still not expect me to show up at their door or call them from the train station. I cannot tell when I am about to make a fool of myself or hurt someone's feelings by taking them at their word or by failing to do so. ... I can only fall silent because thirty seconds into the conversation, I have already failed an important task: while I was bowing and saying hello, I was supposed to have been calculating the other person's age, rank, and position in order to determine how polite I should be for the rest of the conversation.

(Mori 1997: 10–11)

The impact of the unraveling of a self is forcefully captured in Hoffman's words:

> Linguistic dispossession is a sufficient motive for violence, for it is close to the dispossession of one's self. Blind rage, helpless rage is rage that has no words—rage that overwhelms one with darkness. And if one is perpetually without words, if one exists in the entropy of inarticulateness, that condition itself is bound to be an enraging frustration.

(Hoffman 1989: 124)

Recovery and (re)construction: second language becoming

The initial step toward recovery and reconstruction of a self, according to the authors in question, is the appropriation of others' voices, or speaking personally created, and in the case of late bilinguals, recreated, through appropriation (or in Bakhtin's terms, 'ventriloquation') of the voices of others (Wertsch 1991). We observe the beginnings of the recreation process in the following excerpt from Hoffman:

> All around me, the Babel of American voices, hardy midwestern voices, sassy New York voices, quick youthful voices, voices arching under the pressure of various crosscurrents. ... Since I lack a voice of my own, the voices of others invade me as if I were a silent ventriloquist. They ricochet within me, carrying on conversations, lending me their modulations, intonations, rhythms. I do not yet possess them; they possess me. But some of them satisfy a need; some of them stick to my ribs. ... Eventually, the voices enter me; by assuming them, I gradually make them mine.

(Hoffman 1989: 219–220)

Frequently, recovery takes place through friendships, as the US Russian immigrant, Lvovich tells us:

> I reinvented myself in these friendships, becoming American: We laugh, make jokes, exchange news, cry on each other's shoulders and talk a lot … These friendships helped me to move away from immigration as a micro-life aside from other lives and to realize that I am like everybody else now.
>
> (Lvovich 1997: 81)

Eventually, a new voice and with it a self gradually emerges. At first the voice is often captured in writing, in many cases in a diary, a private activity conducted in a public language, which grants 'the double distance of English and writing' (Hoffman 1989: 121). For Hoffman her diary is a crucial stepping stone toward recovery of agency. It bestows upon her a new, English, 'written self' (*ibid.*). Because this self exists primarily in writing, it is experienced not as a fully agentive self, but as an 'impersonal' and 'objective' self, and even though Hoffman remarks that 'this language is beginning to invent another me' (*ibid.*), she is at first unable to deploy the quintessential indexical pronoun of agency, 'I'. Instead she is 'driven, as by a compulsion, to the double, the Siamese-twin "you" (*ibid.*).' Although at this point in her story, she acknowledges Eva as her public persona, she has not yet identified Eva with 'I' in her private mental domain.

The need for repositioning *vis-à-vis* one's own life and experiences comes through compellingly in all of the narratives. Many of the authors write about (or, in effect, rewrite) their childhood experiences in the new language. Elsewhere, Pavlenko (1998) argues that this rewriting of one's life story in another language represents more than anything translation therapy, the final stage of the healing process, prompted by the need to translate oneself, to ensure continuity by transforming and reintegrating one's childhood into one's new past. Without this move, one would be left with an unfinished life in one language, and a life, begun at midstream, in another. The necessity of binding the two halves together prompts the authors to look into their past from a position of double displacement: in time as well as in cultural space.

Step by step, Hoffman's Ewa/Eva discovers and inhabits the new cultural space, learning to preserve appropriate distances, read subtle nuances, and act according to new cultural scripts. Slowly Ewa's second voice acquires increasing strength; Eva becomes a person in her own right, arriving at the realization that

> This goddamn place is my home now … I know all the issues and all the codes here. I'm as alert as a bat to all subliminal signals sent by word, look, gesture. I know who is likely to think what about feminism and Nicaragua and psychoanalysis and Woody Allen. … When I think of myself in cultural categories—which I do perhaps too often—I know that I'm a recognizable

example of a species: a professional New York woman ... I fit, and my
surroundings fit me.

(Hoffman 1989: 169–170)

The new linguistic identities, just as the original, are co-constructed with
others; thus, Lvovich (1997) 'becomes American' on her trip to Canada:

> The funniest outcome was that I represented in Calgary not only the far
> away, almost nonexistent Europe, but the border between the United
> States and Canada: an American, a New Yorker. I was the symbol of the
> huge, the messy, the dirty, the aggressive New York, the capital of the
> world, with its dangers and its opportunities. Because they identified me
> with that mysterious life in the melting pot, imaginable only from
> television or movies, I suddenly felt that I really belonged to that life, that
> after years of wandering, I finally had landed in the right place, as
> diversified as my background of intercultural adventures and fantasies and
> as challenging as my intellectual interests. With the eyes of my cowboys, I
> saw myself as an American, a New Yorker ...

(Lvovich 1997: 69)

Ultimate attainment?

Even though our discussion of personal narratives has been necessarily brief,
it does point to several conclusions. First, these memoirs as artifacts created
in the writers' second languages establish that linguistic border crossing in
adulthood is possible, critical age notwithstanding. They lead us to join a
number of other scholars (Singh 1998) in an attempt to problematize and to
deconstruct the concept of *native speaker*, a cornerstone of modernist
linguistics. In order to do that we separate two important issues: being born
in a certain geographic place versus having a participant status in a discursive
community. While the authors considered here were born elsewhere and,
depending on their personal histories and linguistic ideologies, may forever
claim allegiance to the place of their birth, they also undeniably belong in their
second self-chosen world, not as observers but as full-fledged participants.
Moreover, these individuals often occupy discursive spaces that are far from
marginal, as is the case with many of the writers (Codrescu, Mori, Novak)
and scholars (Wierzbicka, Todorov, Hoffman, Hirsch, Yakobson). In particular,
Codrescu, professor of English at Louisiana State University, whose novels,
poems, essays, films, and commentaries on National Public Radio are an
important part of contemporary American culture, has achieved status akin
to a cult figure.

We would also like to argue that the ultimate attainment in second language
learning relies on one's agency (see also Pavlenko 1997, 1998). While the first
language and subjectivities are an indisputable given, the new ones are
arrived at by choice. Agency is crucial at the point where the individuals must

not just start memorizing a dozen new words and expressions but have to decide on whether to initiate a long, painful, inexhaustive and, for some, never-ending process of self-translation. From this perspective, we suggest that 'failure' to attain 'ultimately' in a second language is an issue that arises from the imposition of the third-person objectivist perspective informed by a particular linguistic ideology based on the NS/NNS dichotomy. Seen through a different lens, however, those who do not become members of another culture, never set out to translate themselves in the first place, never intended to fit into the new social networks, to negotiate new subjectivities of gender, adulthood, parenthood, etc. of the host culture.[13]

If we transcend the domain of phonology and morphosyntax and move into the domain where meanings and selves are constituted by language—ultimate attainment and failure to 'ultimately attain' lose much of their mystery, as agency and intentionality take center stage. The individual may feel comfortable being who he or she is and may not wish to 'become' a native of another language and culture. Thus, negotiation of new meanings and construction of new subjectivities may be irrelevant to her/his personal agenda. It is not accidental that many immigrants settle in communities in which they continue to live, as closely as possible, the lives they led in their native countries in order to follow their own customs and traditions, while at the same time benefitting politically and economically from being elsewhere. This is not to say that they do not learn the language of the community, since many do develop functional proficiency in the new language. Attempts to learn the majority language are usually limited to functional use only, since most of their quotidian interactions are, by choice, with members of their own group.

The decision to preserve one's identity in a foreign environment applies not only to short-term visitors (for example, immigrant workers in Germany, France, Kuwait, or Saudi Arabia), who adjust 'as little as possible so as to make the return less difficult' (Grosjean 1982: 159), but also to long-term, or even permanent, residents of the new community. Kozulin and Venger (1994: 234–5), for example, report that Russian Jews who emigrated to Israel following the collapse of the Soviet Union show a stronger tendency to integrate into institutional and (particular) quotidian spheres (for example, living in Israeli rather than immigrant neighborhoods) of Israeli life, but resist cultural integration, opting to preserve the Russian language for themselves and their children and thus maintain integrity of the self as Russian. Importantly, the immigrants showed a strong positive attitude toward life in their new country; yet, contrary to what Schumann's well-known acculturation model argues, they chose not to become fully part of this life. This is because the integration process is much more complex than the model assumes. As Kozulin and Venger summarize the Russian immigrant situation,

> afraid of losing their self-integrity, the new immigrants responded by reverting to the familiar split between cultural and other spheres. Russian

culture is supposed to safeguard self-integrity, while gradual acceptance of Israeli norms in the institutional and quotidian spheres is supposed to guarantee their adaptation.

(Kozulin and Venger 1994: 237)

It is ultimately through their own intentions and agency that people decide to undergo or not undergo the frequently agonizing process of linguistic, cultural, and personal transformation documented in the preceding narratives. This decision may be influenced by various factors, including one's positioning in the native discourse and the power relations between the discourses involved. If we assume the social constructionist view that identities do not exist within people but are constructed between them in interaction, then, in one case the individuals undertake the construction of new identities, appropriate to the new surroundings, while in another they assume an overarching identity as non-native speakers—legitimate but marginal members of a community (see Lave and Wenger 1991).

Activity theory and narrativity: an explanatory framework

It seems clear from the foregoing discussion that human beings have the capacity to control much of their own behavior, mental as well as physical, not on the basis of biological urges that arise from the inside, but from the outside through the creation and use of material and symbolic artifacts (Kuutti 1996: 26). Many of the artifacts we use to construct our worlds and mediate our relationships to these worlds are often created by other individuals; some are our contemporaries, but importantly, there are also those who preceded us in time and space. Thus, in regulating our own activities through artifacts, we benefit not only from our own experience but from that of our forebears (Cole and Engestrom 1993: 9). Hence people in the present as well as in the past 'play a crucial role in the formation of human cognitive capacities' (Cole and Engestrom 1993: 6). Reflecting the viewpoint of Vygotsky and the sociohistorical school of psychology, Cole and Engestrom (1993: 9) see culture as a mode of development that is unique to our species and which permits the achievements of previous generations to find their way into the present. In essence, culture is 'history in the present' (*ibid.*). This history in the present, or culture, is not merely the situation in which human ontogenetic and microgenetic development take place. It is a functional organ, or as some characterize it, an activity system, composed of historically organized social relations created by humanity with the power to penetrate into itself (Zinchenko 1996: 313).

Personal narrative, patterned after culturally constructed conventional narratives (Linde 1993; Shore 1996), is an important verbal artifact for bringing past events (i.e. occurrences involving other people) into the present and for projecting the present into the future. In so doing, people are able to make sense, that is, make meaning, of what they do and of what others do with them. A simple, yet powerful, illustration of how projection might work is provided by Cole and Engestrom (1993). Studies of parents' reactions to discovering the sex of their newborn child, include comments such as 'We shall be worried to death when she's eighteen' and 'It can't play rugby', both utterances said of girls. According to Cole and Engestrom (1993: 18), the adults who generated these utterances were interpreting the biology of the child in terms of their own culturally constructed past (i.e. their own personal narratives as well as conventional cultural narratives). Hence, for the parents, it is the case that female offspring, according to 'conventional knowledge', do not play rugby and will become the object of boys' sexual interest upon reaching adolescence. Parents then use this cultural knowledge from their own past in projecting a probable future for their daughters and then undertake to organize the plot of their daughters' personal narratives to ensure that the projected future is actualized.

With regard to the bilinguals' narratives considered here, we believe that the problem confronting these individuals is the conflict that arises when they attempt to bring their past into the present. Their personal narratives and, consequently, their 'self' were constructed in a time and place constrained by conventions that differ from conventions of their present time and place. Thus, they have no way of making sense of the present and this, in turn, gives rise to the cognitive and affective dissonances reported in the narratives. (For a detailed treatment of such clashes in *récit d'enfance*, see Valenta 1991.) To overcome this difficulty, they are forced to reorganize, and, in some cases, organize anew, the plots of their life stories in line with the new set of conventions and social relationships sanctioned by the new community in which they find themselves. The result is the formation of new ways to mean (i.e. make sense of their experiences and of who they are). Without this restructuring, these individuals would remain on the margins of the new community in which they reside (but not live). A linguistic cross-over is from the perspective of sociohistorical theory an intentional renegotiation of one's multiple identities, which are reconstructed in communications with members of another discourse. Marginal participation, on the other hand, entails a struggle to maintain previously constructed and assumed identities in the face of a new present (see Siegal 1995, 1996).

Evidence for the interpretation we are proposing comes from the narratives in question. At one point in her story Hoffman writes that her parents, unlike the parents in the situation presented by Cole and Engestrom, in their new Anglo cultural setting express their frustration at no longer knowing how to rear their own children:

> They don't try to exercise much influence over me anymore. 'In Poland, I would have known how to bring you up, I would have known what to do,' my mother says wistfully, but here, she has lost her sureness, her authority. She doesn't know how hard to scold Alinka [Eva's sister] when she comes

home at late hours; she can only worry over her daughter's vague evening activities.

(Hoffman 1989: 145)

At another point, Hoffman talks specifically about her loss of past and being trapped in the present and thus being unable to make full sense of her world and her place in it:

I can't afford to look back, and I can't figure out how to look forward. In both directions, I may see a Medusa, and I already feel the danger of being turned into stone. Betwixt and between, I am stuck and time is stuck within me. Time used to open out, serene, shimmering with promise. If I wanted to hold a moment still, it was because I wanted to expand it, to get its fill. Now, time has no dimension, no extension backward or forward. I arrest the past, and I hold myself stiffly against the future; I want to stop the flow. As a punishment, I exist in the stasis of a perpetual present, that other side of 'living in the present', which is not eternity but a prison. I can't throw a bridge between the present and the past, and therefore I can't make time move.

(Hoffman 1989: 116–17)

In a similar vein, Mori (1997) describes how her choice of an American rather than Japanese female identity led her to avoid speaking Japanese altogether:

I don't like to go to Japan because I find it exhausting to speak Japanese all day, every day. What I am afraid of is the language, not the place. Even in Green Bay, when someone insists on speaking to me in Japanese, I clam up after a few words of general greetings, unable to go on. ... Talking seems especially futile when I have to address a man in Japanese. Every word I say forces me to be elaborately polite, indirect, submissive, and unassertive. There is no way I can sound intelligent, clearheaded, or decisive. But if I did not speak a 'proper' feminine language, I would sound stupid in another way—like someone who is uneducated, insensitive, and rude, and therefore cannot be taken seriously. I never speak Japanese with the Japanese man who teaches physics at the college where I teach English. We are colleagues, meant to be equals. The language I use should not automatically define me as second best.

(Mori 1997: 10–12)

This type of positioning is especially interesting because it parallels Siegal's (1995 and 1996) account of Western women's resistance to perform Japanese gender identities despite the interactional difficulties it caused them.

Based on the personal narratives discussed above, we would like to suggest that while a person may become a functional bilingual either by necessity or by choice, as an adult she or he becomes a bicultural bilingual by choice only. More than anything else late or adult bilingualism requires agency and intentionality (similar to crossing class lines): it is through intentional social interactions with members of the other culture, through continuous attempts to construct new meanings through new discourses, that one becomes an equal participant in new discursive spaces, but apparently not without a cost.

Conclusion

We are convinced that the full force of the participation metaphor and the derivative metaphors of 'becoming' and 'border crossing' can be most profitably explored within the framework of activity theory and social constructionist approaches with their focus on the role of cultural resources and history in the organization and mediation of mind. Participation for those whose narratives we have explored is not just about taking part in new cultural settings; it is about a profound struggle to reconstruct a self. The narratives depict the experiences of people who have both physically and symbolically crossed the border (Anzaldúa 1987) between one way of being and another and perceive themselves as becoming someone other than who they were before. Entailed in the crossing was the active and intentional (re)construction of a history. Without a new narrative the crossing would not have been possible. Put another way, crossing a cultural border is about 'renarratizing' a life. Moreover, the border crossings considered here have strong parallels in Vygotsky's thinking on the ontogenetic development of children into adults (Kozulin and Venger 1994: 237). In both cases, the individual's mental organization changes through the appropriation of the mediational means made available in social interactions.[14]

Recently, one of the present authors had a conversation with a well known and respected member of the SLA community about the relevance of personal narratives of the type examined in the present study for SLA research. This researcher remarked that while such data might very well be interesting and relevant to our enterprise, were he/she to include them in a scholarly paper, he/she would not be taken seriously by our colleagues. We believe that our analysis further widens the space within second language research for first-person tellings as legitimate data, explored in the work of McNamara (1987) and (1997), Hall (1995b), Peirce (1995), Tarone and Swain (1995), Norton (1997) and Kalaja and Leppänen (in press).

While additional research on L2 narratives is clearly in order, it should not be restricted to the written accounts of people of letters. Perhaps in some way writing about the struggle allows the individual to attain what Bakhtin calls *transgredience* (Holquist 1990: 32–3), or the ability to perceive interactional events from outside of the event itself and in which attention is focused on the resources and indentities involved in the events (Hall 1995b: 225); so, transgredience then becomes a way of facilitating the difficult and complex process of crossing a border and achieving full and legitimate participation in a new community. An interesting and important question is to what extent and by what means do the countless others who have attempted to cross borders, but who have not, or cannot write about it, achieve transgredience? A related, and no less important, set of questions also demands investigation: who does and who does not attempt border crossings? Do all those who attempt border crossings experience the intense personal reconstruction documented in the present study? Do the status of the community and the role of the language within the community which the individual aspires to affect the border crossing process? How and to what extent do people participate without reconstructing their identity? How successful are individuals at maintaining their original narratives and with them their L1 selves, while immersed in the second cultural milieu? What is the role of dominant linguistic ideologies in how people perceive themselves and their life stories? How and to what extent is the participation metaphor implicated in classroom second language learning (see Donato this volume) and how does this relate to participation outside of the classroom?

Finally, in supporting the participation metaphor, we are not proposing abandonment of the acquisition metaphor, nor are we claiming a dichotomous relationship between the two. Much important SLA research has been and remains to be done under the sway of this metaphor. We are saying, however, that the new metaphor allows for the opening of a new discursive space in which first-person tellings are as legitimate and revealing as third-person accounts of learning.

Notes

1   An earlier version of this chapter was presented at the colloquium on sociocultural theory and second language learning held in conjunction with the annual conference for the American Association for Applied Linguistics in Orlando, Florida, March 1997.

2   A common practice in cognitive psychology and linguistics has been to ascribe such phenomena as agency and intentions to all kinds of devices and mechanisms, except those of the embodied and embedded kind (i.e. people). According to Searle (1992: 79), while it might be convenient to talk about things like thermostats as perceiving temperature fluctuations, and carburetors as knowing how much air and fuel to mix, and computers as having memories, 'these attributions are psychologically irrelevant, because they do not imply the presence of any mental phenomena. The intentionality described in all of these cases is purely *as-if*' (italics in original). Interestingly, even in those cases in which intentions and agency are at least affiliated in some way with people, there continues to be a reluctance to decouple the constructs from the mechanistic discourse of computationalism. This point is nicely illustrated in a recent paper by de Bot (1996: 541–2), who, in trying to provide a psycholinguistic account of Swain's *output hypothesis*, provides the following revealing

characterization of a bit of think-aloud data drawn from a study by Swain and Lapkin (1995): 'this is a particularly interesting example because it shows that after a given number of trials the *system decides* (italics added) that it will not be able to find the target item, and feeds this information back to the conceptualizer, *who* (italics added) then has to come up with a different phrasing in which the French word for *lazy* (italics added) does not appear.' (For an enlightening discussion of how such anthropomorphic language is used by scholars, often unreflectively, to construct rather than reflect reality, see Potter (1996).)

3   Danziger (1990) presents a very enlightening history of how the shift from first-person to third-person research took place in psychology.

4   The great Italian humanist, Giambattista Vico, was among the first in the West to propose the necessity of first-person accounts of human mental activity as an anodyne response to the dominant Cartesian third-person scientific tradition (see Berlin 1976). As Searle (1992: 94) points out, there is absolutely no reason to assume that the statement 'I now have a pain in my lower back' is subjective, despite the fact that 'the actual pain itself, has a subjective mode of existence'. Interestingly, psychology has attempted to 'objectivize' the mode of existence of such phenomena as pain, or light intensity, by convincing people to assign a number on a scale, say from 1 to 5 (Danziger: 1990). This may have a great deal to do with the strong belief in the West, especially in the US, that phenomena do not exist unless they can be measured and if something can be measured it follows that it must exist (for example, IQ) (see Stewart and Bennett 1991: 31–2).

5   For interesting accounts of how the 'science' of psychology was constructed on the natural science model and the efforts of scholars such as Vico, von Humboldt, Dilthey, and Gadamer, among others, to resist what they saw as a misguided approach to the study of humans as interpretive language animals, see the following works: Obird (1976), Taylor (1985), Soyland (1994), Cole (1996), and Danziger (1997).

6   We think it fair to say that on most accounts, 'objective' is construed to mean something like 'accurately reflecting or representing the object of study'. This, of course, presumes the truth of the Cartesian metaphor of the 'mind as mirror of reality' (Rorty 1979: 3). According to Rorty (1979: 337), the only usable way to understand 'objective' is as 'agreement', arising from a 'consensus of rational discussants'. Subjectivity, then, for Rorty, enters the picture when someone dares to introduce into the discussion considerations which are unfamiliar to the other participants or which are deemed by these others to be irrelevant.

7   To be sure, some theorizers, such as Pinker (1994), have at least acknow-ledged the presence among us of such individuals, but even here only the most exceptional cases are recognized—Conrad, Nabokov, Beckett, and Ionesco.

8   Not all first-person accounts constitute narratives, of course. In the early days of laboratory psychology, researchers such as Wundt and his colleagues relied on introspective statements of their subjects, including in the early days the researchers themselves, to investigate such phenomena as the perception of light intensity, emotions, and personality traits (Danziger 1990). Use of introspection as a research instrument fell into disfavor during the heyday of behaviorism and was recently reintroduced into cognitive research by Simon and Newell in the 1980s and has become a favorite tool of SLA researchers studying such processes as reading, learning and communication strategies, test-taking strategies, and even pragmatics.

9   Despite his widespread influence on sociology and psychology, Mead failed to publish a single book and only managed to put out a few major papers. Following his death in 1931, however, his papers and notes were compiled by several of his students and published in a variety of venues.

10   Despite the similarities between Mead and Vygotsky, there exists a fundamental theoretical distinction between the thinking of the two scholars. For Mead, human interaction is socially situated, but for Vygotsky this interaction is historically positioned (Robbins 1997).

11   For a superb account of how selves are performed differently in the languages of childhood French-Portuguese bilinguals, see Koven (1998).

12   As Henry Widdowson (personal communication, March 1997) suggested to us, movements across discursive practices are not always culture crossings, but may also occur across academic disciplines or from the world defined by one academic theory to that of another within the same discipline, as for instance happened when some linguists abandoned their work in so-called descriptive linguistics and embraced Chomsky's theory. We suspect, but we have no clear evidence at this point to support our suspicion, that such crossings, like the culture crossings examined here, may also entail struggle, emotion, and reconstruction of an (academic) self. A hint that we may be correct comes from a few of the comments from a linguist, reported in Swales *et al.* (1988), who, in fact, abandoned transformational-generative theory and took up a life as a functionalist.

13   For an insightful and in-depth discussion of questions relating to failure, nativeness, and non-nativeness, see Singh (1998).

14   The present chapter focuses on the consequences of border crossings for the reconstruction of a self. Research by Pavlenko (1997), Grabois (1997), and Lantolf (1999) shows that participation can also lead to changes in what is more traditionally dealt with under the heading of cognition and cognitive mediation.

8 Side affects: The strategic development of professional satisfaction

Deryn P. Verity
St. Michael's College

Introduction

As teacher education has come to adopt a sociocultural perspective, the practices of reflection, self-assessment, and narrative have gained widespread legitimacy (Kramp and Humphreys 1994; Sperling 1994; Olson 1995; Cummings 1996; Antonek *et al.* 1997). The stories of teachers and learners, of life both inside and outside the classroom, are becoming increasingly respected as tools for investigating how and why the development and transformation of expertise proceeds (Peirce 1995; Bailey and Nunan 1996; Borg 1998). It is difficult, in such a fast-growing field of qualitative research, to characterize in a helpful but brief way the wide range of issues covered by teacher narratives: for example, Bailey and Nunan identify at least five different themes among their contributors, ranging from teacher decision-making in class to political concerns. However, at least one fundamental if not hard and fast division between categories of narratives is important to note: they either serve to stimulate thought or action on a given issue or they reveal what would otherwise be the private reality of the writer/participant. As Olson suggests, 'narratives of experience can be used to confirm what we already know or to lead to new insights' (1995: 121), while Borg (1998: 11) claims that 'the goal ... is to understand the inner perspectives on the meanings of the actions of those being studied.' Whether presenting a narrative of description or a narrative of explanation, to use Polkinghorne's similar dichotomy (1988), all such studies contribute to our increasing recognition of the complexity of the functional system formed by the interdependent process of *teaching* and *learning*. Not only language learners but also language teachers change over time; reading teacher narratives illuminates the idea that articulating personal history helps shape how we understand the 'plot' of our activity through time (Pavlenko and Lantolf, this volume). 'It is with the aid of language that we bridge different aspects of our existence: the past, the present, and the future,' writes John-Steiner, in her seminal study of the entanglement of language, thought, and creative production (John-Steiner 1985).

Bailey and Nunan's 'collection of international stories' (1996: xi) is so far the densest and widest-ranging single source of such narrative explorations. However, on a smaller scale, individual writers' accounts are scattered throughout the professional literature. Reflecting what Olson terms the 'paradigmatic' function of narrative, i.e. providing a kind of annotated template for future praxis in similar situations (1995: 121) are, for example, the numerous accounts provided by Anglo-American teachers of their attempts to use an interactive, 'communicative' style of teaching with Asian students (for example, Kemp 1995; Miller 1995; Ryan 1995; Sullivan 1996b and this volume; Korst 1997). These writers ultimately aim, through description and commentary, to help teachers who might follow in their footsteps to prepare for obstacles that are typically faced in a given sociocultural context. To this end, little attempt is made to reconstruct from an 'inner perspective' the personal or professional transformation that resulted from the writers overcoming the obstacles they encountered. Instead, salient cultural and psychological features of the Asian students' unfamiliar, and often unsettling, behavior are discussed, and the writer advances ethical and procedural advice on adapting Western pedagogies in ways that avoid both capitulation (Miller 1995) and imperialism (Ryan 1995). Though some retrospective personal details are often included ('I vacillated between feeling myself a failure as a teacher and judging my students to be thick-headed and, despite their pleasant demeanor, unco-operative,' recalls Miller 1995), they tend to be subordinated to the writer's goal of digesting his or her own experiences for the future benefit of the reader (who presumably is preparing to undergo a similar experience). By contrast, another type of narrative, typically first-person, is retroactively interpretive rather than predictive. This kind of story aims to reconstruct and reconfigure past events through the retelling of them. Such narratives 'sort out the multitude of events and decisions that are connected ... [and] select those which are significant in light of the ... conclusion. The story highlights the significance of particular decisions and events and their roles in the final outcome' (Polkinghorne 1988: 170).

As the narrative of an American teacher in Japan, the story recounted in this chapter eschews advice for the introspective goal of reconstruction and interpretation (DiCamilla and Lantolf 1994: 347). Much as Peirce's extensive narrative studies of immigrant language learners explore the concept of social identity as a site of struggle and change (Peirce 1995), the episode described here illustrates the notion that professional identity is a zone of historically situated activity vulnerable to external conditions and influences which may require strategic maintenance, rather than a fixed state of being whose continuity is assured. As an essay in retrospective interpretation, this episode offers little in the way of object lessons, except perhaps to give some insight into the tools teachers have at their disposal for constructing and sustaining a coherent sense of professional expertise and the satisfactions connected to that expertise, even under debilitating external conditions. The reversion of an expert to a state of novicehood, though not inevitable or even common, is dismaying when it occurs: what this chapter suggests is that feeling like a novice again is not just embarrassing or annoying, it actually impedes expert activity by fragmenting cognitive functioning. Few studies have looked at the social origins of affect and its dynamic relationship to cognitive development (though see Gillette 1994). Vygotsky, whose theories so crucially inform the sociocultural paradigm, felt that emotions deserved theoretical status equal to that of cognition (Wertsch 1985a: 189); he claimed that the tendency to focus on thought without reference to the affective-volitional web that embeds it was a fundamental flaw of traditional psychology (Vygotsky 1986: 10). His early death prevented him from pursuing this interest, so, while the neo-Vygotskian paradigm of investigation of cognition thrives, our understanding of affect lags behind. As Peirce (1995: 10) points out, affective variables have tended to be ascribed to a unidimensional personality which exists in dichotomous contrast to an external social context. However, my experience of losing all ability to take satisfaction from my work when my expert cognitive functioning regressed to a novice-like state suggests that affect is, by being enmeshed with cognition, inextricably linked to context as well.

Defining 'professional satisfaction' is tricky. For purposes of this discussion I leave aside external issues of social status, monetary compensation, and job security, and define satisfaction in subjective terms: it means leaving most classes, on most days, in most semesters, feeling good about a job well done. From this perspective, a major reward of teaching well is the pleasure inherent in the activity itself; it serves as a creative enterprise, which, like other forms of creative activity, 'gives meaning to experience, [providing] a sense of purpose that confers dignity' upon us and what we do. The expert teacher enjoys the 'contradictory pulls of joy and discouragement, of sudden bursts of insight and tiring efforts of execution, of process and product' (John-Steiner 1985: 79). In brief, liking one's work makes one good at it, and, in the reiterative spiral of expertise, being good at one's work in turn makes one like it more. As a creative activity, teaching balances the intellectual and the affective, the self and the other. Good teachers use their knowledge and skills for the benefit of their students, but also for their own benefit, deliberately creating settings and eliciting interactions that engender and sustain their own sense of doing a good job (Cummings 1996). Ideally, a teacher develops a personal style which allows affective rewards to appear consistently, avoiding stagnation on the one hand and burn-out on the other. Normally, once this level of expertise has been attained, most professional teachers look only ahead, not back. They may, of course, face a difficult class in a given semester or pursue further education and have to take on a student role temporarily, but few revisit the experience of being professional novices for any length of time, except, briefly and virtually, when training, supervising, or otherwise working with newcomers to the field. Indeed, the experience of being thrust unexpectedly back into the chaos of novicehood sounds so rare as to be almost hypothetical. The ordinariness of the following narrative—American-trained ESL teacher and teacher trainer working overseas in what was essentially a benign environment—suggests that it might not be uncommon. What is often dismissed as 'culture shock', that nebulous collection of changes and stresses that affect people as they adapt to life in a new cultural context, may in fact be linked with facing specific challenges to one's professional identity.

The loss of self-regulation

In fact, in theory a reversion to novicehood is quite possible. It is a tenet of the genetic basis of the Vygotskian paradigm that development is neither uniform nor unidirectional. According to the principle of continuous access (Frawley and Lantolf 1985), even a fully self-regulated expert may, in the face of debilitating stress, revert to novice-like dependence upon help (regulation in the task) from objects and others in the external environment. Such reversion signals a breakdown in the person's normally skilled, automatic engagement in the activity.

My first semester of teaching English at a large national university in Japan was a textbook illustration of this principle at work. Previous experience had led me to believe that I was, with all due humility, an expert teacher of English. A native speaker and trained teacher, I was experienced, flexible, and skilled, my activity routinized but not fossilized; I was well-versed in traditional practice but creative in adapting innovative techniques. I enjoyed teaching oral skills particularly, had had extensive contact with Japanese students and had taught large, monolingual classes in EFL settings before. Indeed, when informed that, due to delays in ordering, I should count on having no textbooks for the first semester, I was pleased: I saw myself as having such a flexible and contingent style that I would prefer to prepare my own materials. (The duties of the position included teaching seven 90-minute weekly classes of general English skills to first- and second-year students.)

Thus, in my head, I felt prepared to deal with the teaching environment in Japan; if I had been asked to provide techniques for confronting any of the predictable challenges of this famously challenging environment, I could have rattled off several. Affectively, however, I was unprepared for the distress I felt when I confronted *myself* in this new setting. Over the years, I had developed a style of teaching that drew heavily on what I considered a good sense of student response. I was used to teaching 'off' my students, rather than 'to' them. I had always thrived upon, as I interacted with a group of learners over the course of a semester, the challenge of calibrating and adapting my chosen methods, materials, and goals to the various signals of attention, orientation, understanding, and enthusiasm they emitted. Consciously or unconsciously, much of the satisfaction I drew from my professional activity was due to pride in the way I put the concept of teaching as responsive assistance into practice. The apparent irrelevance of this skill in the new setting made those first weeks in Japan devastating: although I 'knew' I was an expert, I 'felt' like a novice.

As the principle of continuous access predicts, in the face of failure, I reverted to a novice-like search for external mediation to regain control of my activity. Where I had been self-regulated, that is, able to achieve every teaching goal I set for myself more or less effortlessly, having no conscious memory or awareness of the ZPDs I had had to traverse to attain those goals initially, I was now floundering in the depths of a vast, forgotten zone of earlier, less-complete, development. What had been automatic, subtle, and fun was suddenly obscure, laborious, and worrisome. While I had been anticipating being alphabetically illiterate in Japan, the shock of being professionally illiterate, of being unable to penetrate—indeed, unable even to recognize—the text of student response, was profound. Unexpectedly, I was thrown back in time to an era, barely remembered, when I did not know what I was doing.

However, I had committed myself to fulfilling the expectations of the job. Though I had the emotions of a novice, I still had, or believed I had, the cognition of an expert. These simultaneous and often conflicting modes of perception made me behave in ways that felt fragmented and aimless at first; by the end of the semester, I had managed to construct and pursue a new goal, one that had never been necessary before: the reintegration of cognitive with affective proficiency at a level, previously taken for granted, which allowed me once again to enjoy teaching and derive creative satisfaction from it.

Talking to myself: looking for the 'other'

As anyone who makes regular diary entries knows, writing things down is a way of giving one's thoughts a more objective reality. Such 'jottings to the self', as John-Steiner calls them (1985: 112) serve both planning and creative functions (*ibid.*: 114), helping us prepare and interpret our actions and reactions. This kind of self-directed writing is, like its oral counter-part, private speech, typically elliptical and telegraphic in form, lacking many of the elements of successful communicative writing; however, as one study of novice writers at work shows, private writing should not be judged as a deficient, or failed, form of social writing (DiCamilla and Lantolf 1994: 353), but rather read in terms of the mediating function it serves. Private writing, like private speech, allows the self to act as a temporary 'other'. Writers, experts as well as novices, use self-directed writing to consider 'possible answers to [their] own internally self-addressed queries' (*ibid.*: 354). What appears in private writing is 'cognitive, not communicative', reflecting the writer's mental processes, not the writer's concern for a future reader (*ibid.*: 364).

This description fits both the existence and the contents of a teaching diary I kept during that first semester in Japan. Originally, I had planned to keep a record of successful and less successful lessons in order to be better prepared in future semesters, what Olson calls a paradigmatic record, with a future-time, practical orientation (Olson 1995: 121). (I planned to stay at the job for at least three years, and knew that the teaching duties would not vary much.) As early as the second entry, however, even a quick perusal reveals the diary's true function: writing in it was, in DiCamilla and Lantolf's phrase, a 'cognitive act' I performed to guide myself through the suddenly unfamiliar task of teaching (1994: 360). It became a zone for thinking, where, through externalizing and making explicit my thoughts and feelings, I struggled to regain a sense of control in my activity, to sort through the voices, facts, memories, skills, and resources that constituted my shattered sense of expertise (McCafferty 1994b: 14). It was private speech, typically ephemeral and relevant only in terms of the immediate context, made tangible and reaccessible.

Indeed, the very existence of the diary is the clearest sign of the disintegration of my self-regulation; although I had been, up to then, a most unreliable journal-keeper, I made regular and frequent entries in the diary for fourteen weeks. The zone of proximal development, that central Vygotskian arena of transformation, functions not only as a mediational space for the completion of particular tasks, but also as a place for the learner to confront, practice, and internalize strategies for the completion of other similar tasks (Lantolf and Appel 1994a: 10). It is where instruction manuals are accessed: under stress, we take a quick peek into our codified knowledge to remind ourselves of what we know. My teaching diary reveals someone who is trying not merely to peek into the instruction manual, but to write it all over again.

Perhaps the canonical form of private writing is the list. This 'staccato, thinking-aloud manner' of putting cognition onto paper is a common mnemonic tool (John-Steiner 1985: 112). Even an experienced teacher will jot a brief list of planned activities before going into class. The first entry in the diary, made before the first class meeting, is the proleptic memo of a confident expert, summarizing not only plans for tomorrow's lesson, but a semester's worth of follow-up activities. (Numbers following each entry refer to the week of the semester in which the entry was made.)

Today I start with the famous 'who am I?' exercise ... can picture using [it] for a variety of exercises:

> *interview the person in the picture*
> *have a conversation between two pictures*
> *describe the person, have the student holding the picture identify his picture from the description*
> *paste on back, guess who am I that way*
> *write a letter to that person*
> *self-introductions of people in photos*

pick from a group which person you would most want to:

> *be stuck on a desert island with*
> *marry*
> *have as a father/mother*
> *meet*
> *have dinner with*
> *(also least want to; would be afraid to; etc.)*
> *and, most important, WHY? Justify all choices.(1)*

My 'advance picture' of the possibilities, however, was embarrassingly at odds with the difficulty I faced the next day trying to implement even the basic form of the exercise (small groups, questioning one member about a celebrity face on a card hidden from public view). The challenges of organizing and animating small-group work with large classes of students who appeared reluctant to move their chairs, reluctant to speak English with each other, and reluctant to try a new type of exercise, made the idea of monitoring whether they explained 'why' and 'justifying their choices' ridiculous. The blow to my self-confidence at having so badly misjudged the possibilities of the situation is clear in the deflated tone of subsequent lists, which, minimalist in form, completely lack any of the enthusiastic scope of that first entry. Rather than examples of expert display, they seem to be reluctant reminders of ways to fill class time:

> *Do person out of room; back to back; I spy; identify from description. (3)*
> *For following week, handout ... describe neighborhoods; describe pictures, abstract and realistic. (4)*
> *First, dictation. A very tough one ...; Second, a worksheet on rhyming sounds ...; Third, the jumbled story worksheets. (5)*

By the sixth week, the very activity of making the list was becoming as burdensome as the teaching of the items within it:

> *Many tasks to describe. Here goes: 'Listen ... write ... cloze ... match ... listen ... match ... (6)*

Obviously, lists and other mnemonic tools are indispensable to efficient teaching. From grade books to lesson plans, written records help the teacher do her job. They are fully functional, however, only if they are used for their intended purpose. I rarely managed to implement all the activities suggested by my carefully constructed lists; their primary function was affective. Starting out as memos oriented to future action, they quickly became past-oriented symbolic tools in my struggle to remind myself of what I knew how to do in class (recalling John-Steiner's note (1985: 115) that writers often use notebooks for the purpose of 'purging worn-out intentions'). On paper, if not in the classroom, I could still muster impressive professional resources and flexibility.

It was almost as if I were saying to myself, 'Well, if the students aren't impressed with me, at least I'm impressed with me.'

Clearly, I was uncomfortable at having regressed to a much earlier stage of what had become a gaping zone of proximal development. In its depths, I was driven by the unfamiliar and unsettling need for mediation. As the theory states, besides being a forum for testing what one knows, the ZPD is an arena of distributed knowledge and responsibility (Lantolf and Appel 1994a). In the ZPD, the novice seeks semiotic mediation from external sources, often other people. The dialogic forms that characterize the early entries reflect my need for other-regulation, the urge to bounce ideas and questions off a virtual interlocutor. As was true of DiCamilla and Lantolf's subjects, private writing, in this case my diary, served to focus my attention on the many (and suddenly overwhelming number of) discrete items I had to keep control of in my teaching activity (1994: 363):

> *If 24 people need so much logistical flexibility (and we have moveable desks in that room) think about managing with 50 or more ... (1)*
> *If they asked twenty questions, it was twenty questions in an hour of class for 53 students. That's not too bad, is it? (3)*
> *Obviously, [the test] will have dictation, clothing and description vocabulary ... but what can it really test? And how can I really grade them? (4)*
> *Is it possible to even vaguely monitor the activities of so many students— will they actually tell the story ... ? (5)*
> *They should do the questions in groups. I wonder how? (7)*

Being my own 'other' meant that these questions were directed at myself; besides asking, I also had to answer. Accordingly, the 'expert-I' offered philosophy, advice, and opinions to the newly 'novice-I', musing on judgments 'she' had made. Expert judgment is ideally neither rigid nor inflexible, and certainly not infallible, but it should be at least efficient. The unfamiliar fragmentation of thought from feeling made my mental actions slow. The entries of the first few weeks of the semester reflect the alternating confidence and insecurity with which I advanced, and judged, rejected, and accepted my own ideas. The vacillating, tentative reflections of these entries illustrate how crucial the diary was for helping me examine not only what I planned, and what I did, but how I felt about what I did. Especially in the first difficult weeks, it served as a kind of semiotic workshop, where I could reorganize and refamiliarize myself with my own private array of psychological tools:

> (before class): *I really believe ... that it is more important to review and stimulate basic conversational confidence than it is to try to introduce abstruse concepts and pose intellectual challenges. (1)*
> (after class): *Maybe I can ask people to sit in corners. (1)*
> *... It's hard to keep a sense of how things are going in the really big classes. (2)*

> *... having the focal words and concepts written down helps them, though it encourages them to write translations immediately. (3)*
> *... the worksheet was kind of a shot in the dark, not really useful or interesting ... I really don't think the rhyming worksheet is particularly promising or useful ... maybe the clue is to give only one worksheet for every five students, so they have to speak (5)*
> (before class): *I went overboard and mixed everything up, out of order, too so it is even harder than it should be ... Anyway, we won't get through more than two or three of the exercises, especially if we stop to check answers after each one, which we should really do ... [the exercise] is even harder than it should be. Probably too much. (6)*
> (after class): *I like it, and will definitely continue with the more difficult exercises next week ... but it showed me to lower expectations for the other, less skilled classes. (6)*
> *I think [the lessons] were moderately popular. Probably it would be better to use more content and less [sic] numbering and cloze type exercises ... (7)*

Although I consciously remember experiencing strong emotions most of that first semester, there are in fact very few explicitly emotional comments in the diary, though I do criticize myself rather sharply once or twice:

> *I forgot to bring the dictation, so I had to improvise a sentence, which was really stupid ... it's hard to keep a sense of how things are going in the really big classes. (1)*
> *Whether the large classes can handle the circulation and understanding [what they are supposed to do] is beyond me. I will wait and see. (3)*

I *'hijacked'* (5) some ideas from a file; the choice of word conveys the panic and loss of control I was feeling; otherwise, my comments were humorously negative, either overstating—the lesson was *a general disaster* (5)—or understating—*I am not looking forward to this* (7)—my reactions.

This joking tone, more appropriate to a social, i.e. interpersonal rather than self-directed, conversation, must have served to help me distance myself from unfamiliar and thus disturbing feelings of incompetence:

> *The big problem this week is making up an exam ... Gag. (6)*
> *What a disaster that test was (for me, not them)! ... What to do for next week? ... I'll think about it tomorrow ... Gag. (8)*

There was only one dramatic outburst:

> *This is the last day, thank god, of a boring lesson ... [and, thinking about next week's lesson] ... I don't know. It's hard to care, even after just 8 weeks. I wonder what it feels like after 8 years??!! (8)*

As this last comment indicates, the strongest and most debilitating effect the new setting had upon my teaching was that it shifted my orientation from the higher-level abstract activity of teaching (an activity that I had been able to expertly manipulate to fulfill both other people's and my own cognitive and affective needs) to the much less elegant and satisfying activity of trying to get myself to be able to teach (struggling to engage a series of semi-coherent actions in ways that were at best incompletely remembered from an earlier level of expertise). Like the novice writers in DiCamilla and Lantolf's study whose writing reflects their attempts to write, not what they are trying to communicate to their intended readership (1994: 363), my comments show that my attention was on how to get through the task of teaching rather than on what I, as a professional, normally paid attention to, namely, the students' reactions, needs, and engagement with the language. I had arrived in Japan feeling fully competent, with the broad perspective and skilled judgment of an expert, functioning at a high level of integrated autonomy. After a few weeks there, expertise had fragmented: my perspective had shrunk to the next lesson, my judgments seemed irrelevant, if not useless, and my autonomy was curtailed to the point where I had to create an 'other' to talk to. Indeed, not only was I other-regulated by the students' apparent lack of response to my teaching, I was, like any novice learning the ropes, inappropriately object-regulated by some of the material elements of the new teaching environment.

Taking action: object- and other-regulation

The stress of feeling cognitively clumsy made me physically and logistically inept as well. Where I had in previous teaching settings led lively, active oral lessons with a variety of exercise types and interactions, in Japan I found myself struggling simply to handle the physical materials of teaching. To use Wertsch's apt metaphor (1991: 93), I was having trouble with the tool kit. For example, a bitterly humorous comment early on displays my sense of being object-regulated by the unfamiliar administrative demands of large classes: *Major thing to remember: take roll slowly, it uses up time! (2)*

I also had problems with my voice for the first time in my career. Other-regulated by the students' impassive silence when I tried to direct questions or instructions to them, I became impatient with myself for being unable to arouse a familiar response from them: consequently, I spoke more, and with less effect, than ever before. My hitherto expert intuition as to how much and what kind of mediation would work best for any given group, moment-to-moment, regularly let me down. More than once, I even reverted to that time-honored method of insuring comprehension, speaking louder. My excessive in-class explanations of what to do and how to do it were, I see with hindsight, essentially private speech, externalized cognition to keep myself on track, though I made sure to sprinkle these pedagogically unsound monologues with superficially appropriate features—reduced speed, simplified vocabulary—as a gesture towards my student audience. Perhaps I was trying to fool myself that I was actually talking to them, not myself. Most of my conscious attention, however, was on my dismay over the physical demands my incompetence was putting on my throat:

> *This will be a hard lesson for some of them, but it will save my voice … in fact, we probably won't get to all three parts in most of the classes, and that's OK too. As long as I don't have to wear my voice out. (4)*
> *I look forward to using these materials because it will save my voice (maybe, if I don't have to spend the whole class explaining things). By Friday I am quite worn out vocally; actually, by the end of Tuesday as well. (6)*

Organizing even the familiar artifacts of the classroom became laborious. To keep at least the superficial appearance of expertise intact, I took to writing myself full instructions for using the materials of each lesson:

> *Maybe I should give out more cards, so groups will be smaller. (1)*
> *If time/atmosphere permits, I will use the back-to-back exercise as well … maybe make one person leave the room at first—better whole group focus … (3)*
> *Plan is to have three kinds of listening exercises, all taped … (4)*
> *… maybe for the larger classes, I should have some kind of follow-up where five randomly selected students have to tell the story in front of the class. (5)*

When the need to design and give a mid-term test to the 300-plus students in my classes loomed, it became a nightmare of conceptual and logistical complexity. Having no idea whether the students cared about having a test (although the English classes were required, the grades did not count towards graduation, and students could usually retake a class freely), I decided to go forward with making one because (a) I had promised them a mid-term test, and part of my image of myself as a professional was to keep my promises to the class, and (b) it represented a relatively concrete, if daunting, task, as opposed to the fluid and formless flow of daily lessons. Again, I used the diary to lay out the administrative details for myself very explicitly:

> *The big problem this week is making up an exam that is reasonable, easy to grade and flexible for all these levels. (6)*
> *I am not looking forward to this [exam], but I did tell them I would give them exams, so I have to do it … in the larger classes, it will be a zoo … The exam is printed on one large sheet, which makes transportation of it much easier; I think I will ask them to fold it in half when they receive it, to keep eyes from wandering. I have pre-counted the exams into separate folders, and I will pass them out individually, asking the S[tudents]s not to turn them over until everyone has one. (7)*

The entry made after the exam was given reveals that I was still defining the test-giving process, once routine, in terms of obstacles. However, the entry reveals the glimmerings of self-awareness, too. For the first time, I articulate in the diary what it was that I actually missed in this new, unimproved version of my teaching: being able to rely on my subjective judgments, however faulty, of the students. I simply could not use my well-honed teaching antennae in these large classes:

> *The worst thing about the exam is correcting it ... I wonder how I can avoid this tedium in the future ... how would one assess the larger classes except subjectively? That's faulty enough in a small class where you can more accurately judge who people are and how much they are participating. (7)*

Nevertheless, succeeding in the task of preparing and giving the test helped propel me toward my goal of feeling professional again. A week after the test, I felt self-confident enough to risk abandoning the strategy I had used up until now of preparing over-planned, laboriously formulated lessons. While it is hardly a model of pedagogical form, what I did represents a strategic step toward recovering my once-expert ability to teach responsively. As if daring myself to be the engaged, flexible teacher I knew I could be, I arrived at the campus one day completely unprepared:

> *Well, this is the first time I have ever showed up at the Faculty only a few minutes before class and with no idea in my head about what I want them to do ... I got a brainstorm to use the little flip booklet of cards I made with different topics. A full description of the improvised game follows. There was a lot of laughter and some English spoken, so I guess it was moderately successful. (8)*

A further comment notes that despite the happy success of the improvisation, the pressure of preparation has hardly eased off:

> *... but now I have to think of something to do next week—I wish the weeks wouldn't come so quickly. Just as I am getting one lesson down I feel like I have to prepare another one. (8)*

This episode seems to have been an affective turning point of the semester; the first seven weeks, culminating with the midterm exam, had represented a stage of activity within which I maintained a rather hollow professional veneer, but internally felt random, chaotic, and inept. The emotional states I had experienced during this period were not only negative, but more inappropriately, oriented mostly toward myself and my failure to extract satisfaction from my activity. Although I had fulfilled a certain intellectual contract with the students, by providing them with apparently purposeful, if discrete and fragmentary, lessons, I had hardly engaged with them in any motivating or responsive way. In that I had denied them, and myself, any chance of experiencing the satisfaction that comes from engaging in a well-structured lesson taught by an alert, responsive teacher. It was only in this semi-improvised experience of the eighth week that I tested my fragile autonomy by taking a tentative step toward feeling self-regulated, i.e. flexible and responsive, in the face of teaching that material to those students.

Self-mediation in the ZPD: reinventing the wheel, rewriting the story

No matter how much I had read before coming to Japan about what teaching there would be like, I was unprepared for the experience of being *me* in Japan: the shock woke me up from my slumber of unanalyzed expertise. Olson, in her discussion of the uses of narrative in teacher education, notes that 'surprise can awaken each of us to new ways of storying experience and constructing knowledge' (1995: 131), echoing Polkinghorne's characterization of narrative as 'reconstructive … and retrodictive' (1988: 120). The experience of losing self-regulation and regaining it in a new setting helped me to become, literally, newly authoritative. I wrote the story as I reconstructed it. The experience recounted here is not just an episode newly told about my history: it is part of the new story of that history, given meaning precisely in the telling. As mentioned earlier, narratives of explanation impart significance to events from the perspective of the final outcome; at the time I kept the diary, I had little idea that it in fact told the story of somebody strategically (well, at times randomly) creating a new ZPD with the aim of mining its resources. It has been suggested that the appropriate question to ask of a narrative is what the events 'have meant to someone' (Polkinghorne 1988: 160). Looking at the semester recounted in this chapter through a sociocultural prism illuminates the 'plot' of that segment of my professional story, even, by extrapolation, all of it. As a language teacher committed to the principles of the Vygotskian paradigm, I look back and see myself attempting to mediate my activity strategically. The feeling of fragmentation I had in fact of the new educational culture was not entirely metaphorical; there were indeed two 'selves' who needed to communicate: the temporarily eclipsed expert and the long-dormant novice who had suddenly been thrust to the foreground. Knowing this now helps me understand what I went through then.

The telling of the story does not immediately explain its meaning or its function. There is no recipe or template that can be directly extracted for use in another situation. Indeed, the strategies I used to effect this reconstruction are not completely transparent to me, several years later, even with the benefit of hindsight and a relatively detailed record. Certainly, its genesis incorporated different kinds of actions: the conscious choices of someone who deliberately informs her professional activity with the tenets of sociocultural theory, whose awareness of the ZPD as a functional system motivated her to seek and create forms of self-mediation in a new and challenging environment; the instinctive actions of an expert under stress, of someone whose professional identity was important enough to her that she would expend significant energy to sustain and renew it; and the somewhat random acts of a desperate person (the title of a paper recently published in Japan comes to mind:

'Answer, please answer!' (Korst 1997)). What is obvious to me now, however, looking back, is that these various moves were integrated by a mostly un-articulated, but unifying, idea, developed over previous years of professional activity, of what good language teaching was *when I did it*. In other words, thanks to years of successful and satisfying teaching, I had a deeply-rooted sense of what my own expert teaching activity should look and feel like, that is, responsive, contingent, energetic, and deeply satisfying in the visible assistance it gave to my students. I could call upon this (at times obscured) remembered image as I floundered in the new setting.

By engaging in actions I *knew* were right, even when they did not necessarily *feel* right, by outperforming my competence in those incompetent times, I managed to exploit the duality of knowing one way (like an expert) and feeling another (like a novice). While coping with the affective burden of feeling like a failure much of the time, I could turn the cognitive tasks of teaching over to the essentially automatic guidance of the expert putative 'other' who had been created in internal dialogue. This strategy worked for two reasons. First of all, the internal expert worked much more efficiently than a literal, i.e. external, other could have, because 'she' had access to my entire history of knowing-about-teaching. I did not have to attempt to explain my reactions or meanings to her; she could immediately be put to work drawing upon that pool of knowledge, slightly muddied though it was with stress. Second, though this awareness is keener in hindsight than it was at the time, it was somehow clear to me—possibly because of my Vygotskian inclinations—that I did not need to know *more* to succeed in the new environment: I needed to know *differently*. It was this conviction that the very act of engaging with my sense of failure would transform it, not stubborn independence, that caused me to turn inwards rather than outwards for help.

Thus, I did not seek advice from colleagues in the department, whose orientations and teaching styles were extremely different from my own, or turn to the relatively large number of resource books and materials that were readily available in the staff library. Rather, I chose to use internally-created tools, which had been forged through previous experience, and, more importantly, through successful and satisfying experience. The place I felt most like a failure was in the space where my professional satisfaction had always been most nourished, namely, my ability to teach responsively and contingently, according to the demands of a given situation. Failing to recognize, much less respond to, the demands of the students in the new teaching situation, I turned instead to the demands I could satisfy, and indeed felt strongly that I should satisfy, namely those of my suddenly voluble inner novice. The expert half of myself, I realize upon reading the diary, tried to make sure that the students' needs were at least minimally fulfilled, freeing the unsettled novice to cope with the difficulty of learning to use tools strategically in the new context. This meant, in practice, reinventing the wheel, in a sense. It was not that what I knew about teaching was useless in the new situation, but that my relationship with what I knew had to be restructured.

For the most part, this meant using pedagogical activities familiar from many previous teaching contexts. In fact, rereading the diary, I find that almost all of my lessons were constructed from exercises that I knew very well. Whenever I planned a lesson, I tried to use 'old favorites', language practice activities which were extremely well known to me, and, importantly for maintaining my sense of professionalism, were at the same time 'good' language learning activities, i.e. student-centered, communicative, interactional, open-ended, etc. In addition, I always tried to use these exercises with several, or even all, of my seven classes. This way, while providing them with communicative, interactive practice in English, I could separate the low-level procedural task of running the exercise from the higher-level analytical and interpretive tasks of observing how the specific students of each class responded to a given lesson in their culturally and individually determined ways. This internal duality of purpose permitted me to sharpen my informal assessment skills, which felt so blunt in the new environment, while not abdicating entirely my pedagogical commitment. Although the diary tends to be a record of my immediate subjective frustrations I felt when familiar actions produced unfamiliar results, rather than of the more objective analyses of student responses, the internally-created expert was always at work: each class period became an opportunity for observation and understanding. Having read the requisite books and articles on interpreting Japanese student behavior, I was less interested in analyzing why they seemed unresponsive, or reluctant to speak, or unable to express a firm personal opinion, than in *what* they actually did in response to what I said and did. Since I could not entirely abrogate my teaching responsibilities for observation, I chose techniques and procedures that I could carry out—even under affective stress—relatively automatically.

It was in this doubly coded space that I learned to appreciate what the students were doing, instead of simply being frustrated by what they were not doing. By rotating a lesson through several different classes, I began to be able to tell a co-operative group from a recalcitrant group, one that was able to react to my relatively intense and verbal style of teaching and one that was intimidated by it, one that was resisting the exercise from one that was just waiting for me to shut up so they could get on with it. In other words, I became more able to decode student response and, in turn, respond to it in the new context. 'Recalcitrant' in an American ESL context might look like 'wildly eager' in Japan, as I learned to see.

The success of this strategy is apparent in several early entries, though in fact, I have no actual memory of feeling successful. Indeed, positive assessments appear consistently from the earliest entries, demonstrating that the affective pressures were destructive enough to my rational judgment that I was unable to understand the import of these markers of success even as I recorded them.

Although student reaction was subtle, compared to what I would have preferred, even I could see that the students enjoyed many of the activities I presented them with:

> *They were relatively lively and the plans went well ... (1)*
> *This class went pretty well ... it is ... a smaller and more motivated crew ...*
> *Dictation went well, since I remembered to bring it ... three classes very long, things went well ... there were no abject failures so far this week (1)*
> *Three classes today; the first one, despite its relatively large size, goes well because they are pretty motivated ... the first class to use the worksheets went very well—they really seemed interested in the topic ... they delved right in, and spoke a lot of English, at least in asking the questions. (2)*
> *It went pretty well, considering. They did kind of get into it, and most of them tried, at least in asking the questions, to actually use English ... what I really liked was the enthusiasm of the classes—I could sit back a bit. (3)*

There were even moments when success appeared in familiar guise, that is, when the class took off with a minimum of guidance from me:

> *The most important thing is that they got the idea instantly, so I didn't have to stand around doing a lot of explaining. (3)*

Expertise regained: the new story

Although I remember the semester as uniformly difficult and unsatisfying, the story suggested by the diary is that the first eight weeks were by far the hardest time. Entries for the second half of the semester indicate some recuperation of both a sense of satisfaction and, particularly important for my personal style of teaching, a renewed flexibility and awareness in my interactions with the students:

> *The main note for this week is that the Friday 1st period class, which usually ... tend[s] to be quiet and sullen ... wasn't too bad today. I expect more of them since they are scientists, and supposedly intelligent ... [but] I made a deliberate attempt to be more gentle, in part to cover [a] truly foul mood, and it kind of worked. (9)*

Although problems did not disappear after the 8th week, I noted them with greater complacency:

> *... some of them seemed to drop out ... so I went around and tried to get those particular students to tell me their stories. All in all, less enthusiasm and sense of accomplishment in the larger classes, but not too bad. (9)*
> *... it went well, though a bit slower than I feared. In fact, my first instinct was right ... they really did seem to get the point. The focus of the week is to insist on the fact English must be used, not just memorized ... I wonder*

*how it will go? It won't go at all if they don't bring enough dictionaries ...
We'll see. (10)*

A late-semester entry reveals that I was able to confess explicitly my
dissatisfaction with the fragmented and low-level focus of my professional
activity:

*Another idea came to me while I was walking around [town] this noontime
... how about a defining exercise, forcing them to use their logical skills at
finding and making meaning? It would need quite a bit of preparation on
my part, but that's OK because I have a quiet weekend this time and also
because I really need to put some mental work into my teaching for once.
(9)*

A list of eight possible exercises follows, fully annotated; not only do I impress
myself again, I display direct access again to the (relative) depths of my expert
knowledge and experience of language teaching.

By the eleventh week, when another test loomed, no agitated notes were
made, just a list of the test components, and a comment afterwards about
how well it went. More revealingly, I include an explicit piece of data from
my small but growing pool of expert knowledge about students in this
environment:

*Second exam: given with no hitches ... the test ended up being pretty much
what I wanted (12)* followed by a detailed description of each part of the
test, including ... *Part Four: formal to informal [registers]. Kind of fun ...
When it suits ... and helps them, they pay attention, retain instructions and
follow them. (12)*

During this final week before the long summer holiday, the diary virtually
ignores the cognitive and affective difficulties of the previous three months.
Did I really not remember them? It is more likely that the entry reflects a
newly forward-looking orientation in my professional activity:

*Well, that's essentially one semester gone, though it drags ... through
September for no obvious reason. Teaching wise, I think I hit a lot of high
spots and made some good impressions, maybe convinced few [sic] people
that English wasn't totally a dull language. It became much less wearing
and dragging after a few weeks ... I should be able to re-use much [sic] of
this semester's lessons next year in the larger classes. (12)*

The last two entries of the semester, made in September after the long summer
break, rather anticlimactically note that the summer vacation has ended, I am
preparing a final exam, this time to be done in groups, and that I will use the
last two meetings of the semester to rehearse for it and give it:

*I have decided to use the first meeting to practice the exam style and the
second meeting to give a kind of exam: a listening/recreate the story/*

collective work exam which should pull together the dictations, the vocabulary, the thinking, the text-oriented stuff we did all semester. (13)

This comment indicates a stronger sense of self-regulation for the task of making up an appropriate test: the tone is calmly assertive, indicating an integrated, i.e. more expert, perspective on the tasks practiced in the semester just past. Most interestingly, the entry provides evidence that I was, after the vagaries of the shakedown period, able to feel confident choosing a preferred and familiar evaluation tool, the group test. I defined the test event from the perspective of what *I* believed would serve the goal of language learning best, rather than from the other-regulated perspective of desperately, if minimally, trying to fulfill a promise. Finally, I had reoriented my teaching activity back toward what I had arrived in Japan thinking it should be oriented toward, namely, the learners and the language, and away from myself and my attempts to cope with the demands of the task.

Concluding remarks

'In order for experience to be educative, we need to be able to ... be awake enough to attend carefully to the meanings we construct from our experience,' says Olson (1995: 123). Creating a chapter from this episode woke me up in many ways. Faced with its loss, I learned how enmeshed my sense of professional expertise is with the pleasure I get from being able to teach in my preferred and familiar, i.e. responsive and contingent, way. I became newly cognizant that for professional satisfaction to be sustained, it is insufficient to avoid visible failure. I, and perhaps others, need to keep to a minimum the discouraging feeling *as if* we are failing. Choosing to rely on myself for strategic mediation in the zone of sudden and unexpected incompetence not only helped me ultimately to calibrate my teaching to a specific new environment; it also reconfirmed my sense of expertise by alerting me to the fact that I still had access to the tools of this expertise, despite having temporarily lost mastery of them. Had I in fact turned outwards for help, I suspect that I would not have been able to follow other people's advice, even had they offered any. I needed instead to hear more clearly my own voice, which, I must have been unconsciously aware, is in sociocultural terms an aggregate of the many voices out of which I had originally constructed my expertise. In Vygotskian terms, rather than take in new information, I needed to restructure my relationship with old information, i.e. identify again what was salient, relevant, and important in the new context. Routine, suddenly failing me, had to be recoded. In an abbreviated form, this semester permitted, or forced, me to relive the history of my professional expertise and renew my investment in what had become an automatized, but unarticulated, expert style of work.

The sociocultural paradigm accepts that all strategic activity, including ostensible failure, is potentially revelatory. As the world becomes ever smaller, as language teachers move even more easily from culture to culture, and as the classroom becomes more and more an arena for cultural confrontation and potential conflict (Fried 1994), teacher education programs can only be strengthened by investing their participants' stories—those of experts who fail as well as novices who succeed—with authority. Researchers like Bailey and Nunan (1996), who elevate the voices and insights of working teachers to a level where they can receive the kind of serious reception typically accorded only to more traditional research projects, provide important support for the acceptance of narrative ways of knowing. It is important, further, to recognize the complexity of the act of telling itself: while narratives are highly accessible, they are far from transparent. What we seek to learn from a first-person narrative like this one might be a useful lesson, such as the reminder that we all carry traces of our multiple origins within us, a lesson which gives even the most staunchly self-reliant professional permission to call upon the other selves that constitute a current expert identity. On the other hand, the power of a story might be less easily transferable, except in principle: the very act of telling is an act of transformation. Speaking as a trainer of teachers who will go on to teach ESL in many corners of the world, I believe that the loss of self-regulation, the fall from expert to novice, and the climb back again to a newly authored expertise was a lesson much more about myself and my professional identity than about Japan or the dangers of culture shock. Creating the story by interpreting the written record of a past episode has strengthened my conviction that my students will benefit not so much from reading about *my* experience but from getting practice creating stories about themselves and their teaching. As a teacher trainer, I find it all too easy to forget what it felt like to know how, and what, a novice knows. Looking into this 'notebook of my mind' gave me the chance to renew a sense of immediacy by recollecting my own beginnings (John-Steiner 1985: 79). The experience recounted here is the story of an opportunity—however unsought or unwelcome at the time—to understand better, by having regained them, the sources and satisfactions of success.

9 The appropriation of gestures of the abstract by L2 learners

Steven G. McCafferty
University of Nevada, Las Vegas

Mohammed K. Ahmed
International University of Japan

Introduction

Nonverbal elements have been considered important to second language (L2) concerns for a long time. However, most of the research in the area has focused on testing. As yet, there has been little interest in the acquisition, or appropriation of nonverbal forms by learners. It seems likely that this inattention is at least in part due to the perspective of language as a disembodied set of linguistic rules as inherited from the study of formal linguistics.

We of course realize that in face-to-face interactions the use of nonverbal expression is an important dimension. (Some researchers suggest that communication is actually largely conveyed nonverbally.) However, it is also true that even when others are not present such as on the telephone or when talking to an object, for example a computer, we continue to use nonverbal forms of expression. Moreover, in the process of writing or when involved in some other reflective activity we also at times gesture to ourselves. With this in mind, it needs to be brought out that language is not just a set of linguistic rules, that it is *embodied*. Indeed, in relation to communicative interaction, Poyatos (1980: 114) notes *kinesic*, *kinetic*, *vocal*, *chemical*, *thermal*, and *dermal* 'Body Communication Channels' for 'emission' and *visual*, *auditory*, *olfactory*, *dermal*, and *kinesthetic* channels for 'perception'. Also, he goes on to suggest that these channels are interconnected with sociocultural elements which together function as communicative systems, and that 'the study of any one system by itself is totally shortsighted' (1980: 117).

Within the Vygotskian perspective, the theoretical framework for this study, speech and thought are considered to become 'intertwined' at a point in intellectual development. McNeill (1992), and elsewhere, demonstrates that speech and gesture arise together in ontogenesis, and furthermore, he argues that speech and gesture are intertwined, the former providing the linguistic and the latter the imagistic element to thought. Further, McNeill (1987: 89) directly links inner speech, as described by Vygotsky, to gesture, suggesting that 'inner speech is the smallest unit in which imagistic and syntactic thinking come together'. As such, there would seem to be an interconnection between inner speech, gesture, culture, and conceptualization as all of these are integral to each other from a Vygotskian point of view.

The question then arises whether gestures that are particularly associated with cultural expression, that is, metaphoric gestures, change with exposure to a new language/culture. For example, a common metaphoric gesture in America (and elsewhere) for 'transition' is deployed when the hands, palms facing the body, rotate around one another, accompanying, for instance, the word 'working' in the utterance 'Well, we're working on it'. If gestures of this type are appropriated by L2 learners, given the interconnections discussed above, it would seem possible that aspects of inner speech change as well, and moreover, that the concepts imaged by gesture in connection with inner speech change as part of a process of remediation involving use of the second language within the settings of the culture.

Although this perspective constitutes an important aspect of the chapter, the primary focus of the study is on appropriation, that is, to see if second language learners appropriate metaphoric and other gestures of the abstract. However, first we examine inner speech in relation to both first language (L1) and second language (L2) concerns, provide a brief overview of gesture as a phenomenon, examine the connection between gesture and inner speech, and review the relevant studies on gesture and L2 acquisition.

Inner speech

Within Vygotskian theory, a central element in the development of human intellectual capacity is speech for the self or *private speech* (called 'egocentric' speech by Vygotsky, following Piaget), and when private speech eventually 'goes underground', inner speech. The precursor to speech for the self is of course social speech. Through interacting with members in particular socioculturally situated contexts, children begin to appropriate the intellectual world around them. This is done primarily with the use of language, the most powerful of mediational means at our disposal. According to Vygotsky, when a child starts to use language for thinking purposes (private speech), he or she has shifted to an intrapersonal psychological plane where the use of speech now functions to help with problem solving and other metacognitive activities as well as for interpersonal functions.

At around age seven, the use of private speech turns inward, the child beginning to 'think words' instead of producing them (Vygotsky 1986: 230). As such, private speech is transitional, although it continues to 'resurface' in the face of demanding circumstances. Inner speech becomes the dominant mode of verbal thought and remains a central fixture governing our higher mental functions such as planning, guiding, and monitoring the course of activity. In characterizing this level of thought it is important to consider both its psycholinguistic attributes and how it operates in relation to other realms of thought. In this second regard, Vygotsky wrote:

> In inner speech words die as they bring forth thought. Inner speech is to a large extent thinking in pure meanings. It is a dynamic, shifting, unstable thing, fluttering between word and thought, the two more or less stable, more or less firmly delineated components of verbal thought.
>
> (Vygotsky 1986: 249)

The special linguistic properties that Vygotsky attributed to inner speech are related to two different dimensions. The first has to do with syntax, there being an abbreviated, disconnected, and incomplete quality to inner speech when compared to external speech. This compilation of characteristics is considered to be the outcome of a process of ellipsis: the least important elements with regard to meaning are eliminated, leaving only those grammatical elements that are salient to the contexts. As an example, Vygotsky provides the situation of people waiting for a bus:

> No one will say, on seeing the bus approach, 'This bus for which we are waiting is coming.' The sentence is likely to be an abbreviated 'Coming,' or some such expression, because the subject is plain from the situation.
>
> (Vygotsky 1986: 236)

This reduction of syntax is termed 'predicativity'; however, as pointed out by Wertsch (1991: 41), this term should not be confused with sentence-level linguistic analysis, but is rather of a functional nature, meaning that those elements that are known within the context are not brought out; rather it is what is not understood that becomes salient, thus it is a *psychological predicate* that is being referred to.

Inner speech is also defined semantically in ways that set it apart from interpersonal speech. First of all, words (utterances) at this level are filled with *sense*, that is to say, that the meaning as recognized in outward usage is of much less importance than its many psychological associations. Vygotsky acknowledges Frederic Paulhan in this regard, from whom he suggests comes the notion that 'The sense of a word ... is the sum of all the psychological events aroused in our consciousness by the word' (Vygotsky 1986: 244).

The second semantic quality is termed *agglutination* and is compared to processes found in synthetic languages which form word meaning in such a way that several words can be merged into one; 'the new word not only expresses a rather complex idea, but designates all the separate elements contained in that idea' (Vygotsky 1986: 246). The third semantic characteristic of inner speech relates to the notion of an 'influx of sense' into words in which

'The senses of different words flow into one another—literally 'influence' one another—so that the earlier ones are contained in, and modify, the later ones'. The word *green* demonstrates this phenomenon with its current social, political, environmental, and economic overtones.

If indeed inner speech takes on specific sociocultural attributes and at the same time performs functions related to self-regulation, it would not be surprising to surmise that our thinking is influenced by the particular elements exerted by the first language as embedded within the activity of its use. In turn, it would seem likely that inner speech and the L1 are connected to how we think about things as well, as part of the overall process of semiotic mediation.

It is also interesting to note in relation to inner speech that although Sokolov (1972) researched cerebral activity and inner speech, with the use of magnetic imaging there is now 'hard' evidence of its occurrence. Paulescu, Firth, and Frackowiak (1993) recorded a brain scan of an individual in the process of 'quiet mental rehearsal' (no vocalization) (found in Baars 1997: 75). The scan shows 'bright spots (areas of high brain activity) in the two parts of the brain known to be involved in speech input and output'. It is also interesting that Baars goes on to suggest that this inward practice facilitates outward expression by the very fact that the same area of the brain is involved in both (although from a Vygotskian developmental point of view, the emphasis would be placed the other way around—how the interpersonal affects the intrapersonal).

Inner speech and L2 learning

With regard to how inner speech is related to second language learning, it is first of all important to consider studies of L2 private speech as there are strong connections, functionally, between private and inner speech. These studies (see McCafferty 1994a for a review) indicate that learners do not usually resort to their L1, but do so at times, perhaps when they feel most challenged. However, it also appears that for some cultures people may not express themselves using overt forms of private speech, instead possibly engaging in L1 inner speech during pauses they take when engaged in verbal problem-solving situations in the L2 (Appel 1986).

There is also evidence of the tie between concepts and the L1 with regard to L2 lexical acquisition. For example, Bates and McWhinney (1981) found that even after 25 years of residence in a country in which the L2 is the primary means of communication, and with people who actively participated in all levels of the culture through the L2, when given an association task their associations, even though in the L2, were more like native speakers of their L1 than native speakers of the L2. However, Grabois (1997: 164–5) in a more recent study that also examined lexical organization found that 'long term residents of a second language culture do reorganize their lexicons in the

L2 in a way which progressively approximates the organization of native speakers ... and is probably the result of not only a great deal of time spent in the target culture, but also of personal commitment and favorable attitude toward the language learning process.'

In the only study that we know of that directly addresses the relationship between inner speech and L2 acquisition, Ushakova (1994: 155) notes the importance of the first language in 'establishing inner speech mechanisms' that then serve to guide the L2 learning process. In her words, this process is one of 'plugging the newly established structures into the ones worked out earlier, as well as employing already existing verbal skills'. In this model the primary role of inner speech in the L1, that is, inner self development, no longer applies; instead these same mechanisms are turned toward the goal of language learning. Grabois (1997: 35), however, points to 'methodological problems' with this study, bringing some of its claims into question. Moreover, Grabois suggests in relation to inner speech that:

> ... one could argue that consciousness and cognition are situated; they are dynamic processes which are inseparable from the activities which the individual is involved in; not simply abilities possessed by the individual and to be employed at her discretion. This line of thinking would occur when the L2 comes to serve as a linguistic tool for the mediation of conceptual organization.

> (Grabois 1997: 35)

Although Grabois does not conclude that this is in fact what happens, he is clearly open to the possibility that inner speech can change through mediation of the L2.

Gesture

Vygotsky gave gesture an important role in the development of language, noting that intentionality develops out of indicatory gestures in conjunction with a child's first words, and indeed that 'The word, at first, is a conventional substitute for the gesture: it appears long before the child's crucial "discovery of language" and before he is capable of logical operations' (Vygotsky 1986: 65). This of course indicates that gestures are where the child first comes into contact in a meaningful way with semiotic mediation, and thus with this essential aspect of being human.

Some of the more salient characteristics of gesture in relation to speech follow. Gestures for the most part are synchronized with the speech they accompany or occur just before it. Over 90 per cent of gestures accompany speech whether there is an interlocutor present or not. From about age two onward speech and gesture develop together, both basically moving from the referential to the abstract. Unlike speech, there are no standard forms of gesture, excluding emblems (waving 'hi', for example) that a speaker needs to conform to, so there tends to be a great deal of idiosyncrasy at the level of the individual, despite strong cultural influences for some types of gesture.

There are areas of contention with regard to the research on how speech and gesture interface, and of special interest to the current study is the debate concerning the connection between thinking, speaking, and gesturing. Although there is little argument that speech and thought are interconnected at some level, this is not true concerning thought and gestures. There are those who do research on gesture who regard it exclusively from an interpersonal perspective, having to do only with communicative practices between interlocutors. Perhaps most investigators, however, find a role for both individual and social dimensions, and indeed, from a Vygotskian perspective, this would necessarily be so.

David McNeill (1987), and as found in his book on the subject, *Hand and Mind* (1992), has particularly concentrated on how thought, gesture, and language are interrelated at the intrapersonal level. McNeill (1992: 245) contends that speech and gesture are 'dialectically' engaged—gesture providing imagery and speech the verbal or linguistic structure to thought. He also argues that those gestures connected with the germination of thought come at the early stages of an utterance and may not be recognizable to an interlocutor in terms of any 'outward' meaning.

Gesture and inner speech

As gestures tend to represent the 'whole' of an idea they are different from language which is of a hierarchical nature, one structure building on the next in order to make meaning. Gestures are thus synthetic, representing a compilation of elements (McNeill 1992: 19). As such, McNeill suggests they tend to reveal a speaker's psychological predicate (above) in conjunction with inner speech. Using an example from an earlier study (McNeill 1985), McNeill (1987: 91) notes with the utterance 'and he finds a big knife' that with the word *finds* the speaker produced the following gesture: 'His hand, taking the form of a grip, groped behind him as though picking something up'. In explicating the relationship between the gesture and the utterance McNeill writes:

> We infer that the inner speech symbol was *finds*. This is based on the assumption that the symbol and image remained together through the entire development of the surface sentence. The gesture showed (1) the act of picking up the knife, (2) that the knife was picked up from the rear, and (3) that the shape of the knife's handle was round. Yet the gesture synchronized with the single word *finds*, a word that conventionally carries none of this information.
>
> (McNeill 1987: 91)

Importantly, gestures are also capable of expressing the psychological predicate in ways not available in speech. In fact, sometimes, as in the case of a lexical deficiency, gestures must be used to bring out a missing property if it is key to the expression of the speaker's intent. McNeill (1992: 129) uses English verbs to illustrate this point, few of which signify the shape of a moving object, *drip* being one instance of where this does happen since only liquids are considered to have this shape when in motion. In further support of this claim, McNeill provides evidence, again from his own work, which shows that when gesture is explicitly prohibited in narrative settings where there is an interlocutor then speech becomes more complex (1992: 283).

Of further interest is the fact that gesture occurs at high points of *communicative dynamism*, which McNeill, following Firbas (1964, 1971), defines as 'the extent to which the message at a given point is "pushing the communication forward"' (1992: 207). If the speaker is at a point in his/her narration, for example, where there is a crossroads as to what element of the narration is to be concentrated on, this represents a point of 'high' communicative dynamism. High communicative dynamism is tied by McNeill to Vygotsky's consideration of the psychological predicate:

> Thus, a gesture should occur exactly where the information conveyed is relatively unpredictable, inaccessible, and/or discontinuous, viz., where CD (communicative dynamism) is increasing and with what Vygotsky regarded as the psychological predicate (parentheses added).
>
> (McNeill 1992: 208)

Given the above, it is not surprising that McCafferty (1998) found a high correspondence between forms of private speech and the use of gesture for L2 learners.

Gesture and L2 learning

A good deal of interest has been generated with regard to L2 gestures, although in fact most of this work has concentrated on the need to assess this dimension and/or suggestions for doing so (for example, Canale and Swain 1981; Bachman 1990, 1991; Neu 1990; Kellerman 1992; Al-shabbi 1993). Additionally, there have been attempts to study L2 learners' comprehension of gestures; for example, Mohan and Helmer (1988) found a positive effect for the comprehension of gesture for children who had had a good deal of exposure to the L2 in naturalistic conditions. However to date, little work has been done on whether or not learners not only comprehend but also appropriate, or acquire nonverbal elements.

In one such study, McCafferty (1998) found that Japanese learners even with relatively brief periods of exposure to American culture produced forms of the 'I don't know'/uncertainty gesture (arms spread outward from the body, palms up), although this is not a Japanese gesture. The fact that this form of gesture was found in conjunction with private speech, that is, at an intrapsychological level, provides support for the notion that learners do appropriate L2 gestures, although in this case, only with regard to this particular emblem.

Bilingual children in Canada have been studied regarding 'kinesic variation in code switching' (von Raffler-Engel 1976: 235). Results, although 'scanty', did find that in a retelling task both Anglophone and Francophone children tended to accommodate the interlocutor nonverbally to some extent, adopting some forms of gesture different from those found when interacting with children from the same language/cultural background. However, von Raffler-Engel reports that she did not observe this same accommodation in the case of adult bilinguals.

The study

Purpose

The purpose of this study was to investigate whether exposure to a second language under two different learning conditions, *naturalistic* (residing in a country where the L2 is the everyday language of use) and *instruction only* (where the L2 is learned as a foreign language primarily through instruction) would lead to the appropriation of gestures of the abstract (below). Because these gestures, or at least some forms, are not easily assigned meaning by an interlocutor, even native speakers generally having little or no metagestural awareness of them, it seemed unlikely that they would simply be 'picked up' in the way an emblem might be. It was of course expected that if the appropriation of these gestures was found, this would happen in the case of the naturalistic learners with extensive L2/culture experience.

It is also important to mention that although the study tallied the frequency of use for the gestures of the abstract selected for study, there was no attempt to use inferential statistics owing to the fact that data collection was done through recording discussions which lasted varying lengths of time depending on how interested the participants were in pursuing the topic. Also, the production of these forms could not be 'controlled' as their use hinged on the particulars of the interactional contexts in relation to the individuals involved.

Gestures of the abstract used in the study

Metaphoric gestures are of a 'pictorial' nature but instead of presenting an object, the image represents an idea. For example, with the utterance 'the movie I saw ...' the gesture could image *movie* as a rounded object held out in front of the body between the hands, like a ball: in this case, termed a *bounded container* gesture (Figure 9.1a).

Another variation of the bounded container gesture takes the same form as the 'I don't know'/uncertainty emblem as found in American culture, i.e. the arms at the elbows are horizontal and held apart out wider than the body with the palms up and fingers outstretched. However, in this case the gesture signals possibility or potential, as when found accompanying the utterance 'Well, what could I do?' (labeled a *potential* gesture (Figure 9.1b)). *Unbounded* container gestures are also produced, and McNeill suggests that these are found in 'non-Western' cultures, and are formed with the palms down, the 'object' represented below the speaker and as such 'unsupported' (Figure 9.1c).

Another form of gestures of the abstract is *splitting the gesture space*, and is used when comparing and contrasting ideas. The speaker partitions the immediate space in front of him or her, designating the left side for one idea and the right side for the other as found, for instance, with the utterance 'The monkeys don't care because the monkey's a different society', the speaker in this case moving his arms, bent at the elbows, palms down, up and down out of sync with each other in front of him (McCafferty 1998: 86) (Figure 9.1d).

Beats are the sharp up and down movement of a hand or tapping of the foot. McNeill (1992) explains their basic function by comparing them to highlighting words in a written text. In both cases there is an emphasis that makes the chosen word(s) stand apart from the rest of the text. In a further treatment, McNeill, Cassell, and Levy (1993: 10) indicate that a beat can also function metapragmatically, that it 'indexes the word or phrase it accompanies as being significant not purely for its semantic content, but also for its discourse–pragmatic content'.

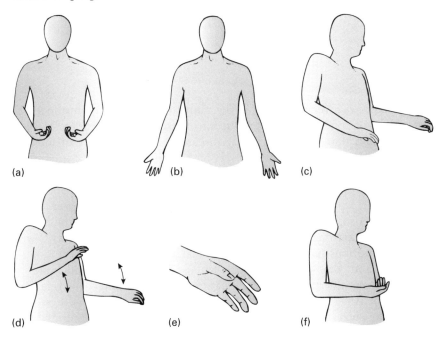

Figure 9.1: Illustration of gestures

Participants

The study involved 36 participants from four different language contexts: (1) eight advanced Japanese speakers of English as a second language with their primary exposure to the language through naturalistic contexts, which in the case of these people involved living in the US and/or Canada, and for a period of at least three years—although many had done so for much longer. (Table 9.1 presents background information concerning these people.) These data were collected in the US: (2) ten Japanese advanced speakers of English as a second language exposed to the language largely through instruction-only contexts (though some had used English on vacation, spending a month or two outside of Japan) (data collected in Japan), (3) Twelve largely monolingual native speakers of American English (data collected in the US), and (4), eight largely monolingual speakers of Japanese (data collected in Japan). Each of the four groups contained both men and women who ranged in age from their 20s to their 50s.

	Sex	Age	Nationality of spouse	Number of years spent in North America.
1	w	46	Japanese	16
2	m	44	Japanese	6
3	w	37	American	5
4	w	30	not married	3
5	m	50	Canadian	30
6	w	35	American	12
7	m	43	Japanese	12
8	w	40	American	18

Table 9.1: Naturalistic participants

Instrument

It was necessary given the nature of the study to determine circumstances for data collection conducive to the production of gestures of the abstract. McNeill (1992) found that when informally discussing various topics of interest, speakers tended to produce a relatively high frequency of these forms. With this in mind, marriage was chosen as a discussion topic for the study, as in addition, there are strong cross-cultural differences between Japanese and American perceptions and practices with regard to virtually all aspects of this institution. Also, there are conceptual metaphors which represent the cultural expression of marriage. For example, MARRIAGE IS AN INVESTMENT with verbal realizations such as 'And that was really something that we got out of marriage' and 'I'm scared it's going to cost me too much and leave me without being able to stay in the relationship' was found to be one such schema for Americans discussing this topic (Quinn 1987: 177). It seemed likely that such conceptual metaphors might vary cross-culturally, and moreover, that the naturalistic learners might possibly have appropriated such underlying conceptual schemas. This notion is supported by Pavlenko (1996), who found that Russian speakers of English living in the US used American verbal metaphors of privacy to describe various situations in a silent film, despite the lack of such metaphors in Russian.

Procedures

Participants were paired within each of the four groups. Each person was acquainted with the other in the pair. This was considered important primarily as the sensitivity of the topic necessarily called for some 'feeling out' of personal history. Some pairs were, however, clearly more familiar with each other than others. An attempt was made to pair two men, two women, and a man and a woman in each group, but this was not always possible. As it turned out, some people were married and some were not among the Japanese participants, while for the Americans some were also divorced. It did not seem to matter what the mixture was for each pair regarding marital status as both differences and similarities in background led to an exchange of ideas and experiences.

Each pair was asked to consider a list of seven discussion questions, all of which aimed at eliciting opinions and beliefs about some central aspect of marriage (Appendix, p. 219). After having a chance to familiarize themselves with the items, each pair was asked to sit down on chairs turned at a three-quarter angle toward a video camera so that each participant was situated halfway between facing his or her partner and the camera. They were told that the discussion might go on up to ten minutes or so, and that they would be video-recorded during that time. In fact, some pairs took much less time than this and some much more. All participants except the monolingual Japanese used English exclusively in their discussions. It is also important to point out that none of the participants had any idea that the study involved nonverbal communication, nor did the researchers interact with the participants.

Data analysis

The recorded data were gone over, and each instance of the use of one of the gestures of the abstract included in the study was identified by examining the relationship between the gesture and the verbal content that it accompanied. The characterization of the gesture, i.e. the various, finger, hand, and arm configurations over the course, or 'stroke phase' of each gesture was coded in relation to the accompanying verbal element. In most cases this process required multiple viewings, often done in slow motion. The frequency of each gesture type was then tallied for the purpose of providing descriptive statistics. It should also be mentioned that in many cases gestures expressed more than one element, for example beats often co-occurred with other gesture types.

Results

Findings indicated that the naturalistic learners had appropriated American forms of gesture as recorded for the monolingual American participants in relation to container and potential gestures, and beats to some extent as well. Also, the instruction-only learners were much more like the monolingual Japanese speakers than the naturalistic learners in their use of the gestures studied despite their advanced English proficiency. The specifics of the findings for each gesture type follow.

Unbounded container gestures

Unbounded container gestures were produced among all three groups in which the Japanese participants were involved. Unexpectedly, however, seven of the 12 American participants also used this gesture, although at comparatively low levels of frequency in relation to the Japanese groups in the study (Table 9.2). However, there were pronounced differences between the Japanese and American versions of unbounded gestures, the Japanese deploying a form with the palms parallel to the ground, while the Americans generally tilted their palms slightly upwards (Figure 9.1e). Additionally, in all instances except one the Americans used only one hand in producing this gesture, while the Japanese tended to use both hands.

	Pair 1	Pair 2	Pair 3	Pair 4	Pair 5	Pair 6	Total
Am. NS	w / w 0 1	w / w 0 1	w / m 2 2	m / m 1 0	w / w 0 4	w / w 0 1	12
J. NS	w / w 2 24	m / m 5 0	m / w 6 0				37
J. Class.	w / m 7 10	w / m 0 0	w / w 0 5	m / m 8 11	w / w 3 7		51
J. Nat.	w / m 3 1	w / w 3 4	m / w 3 1	m / w 0 19			34
Grand total	134						

Table 9.2: Unbounded container gestures

Little difference was found for the use of unbounded container gestures between the Japanese monolinguals and the instruction-only learners. On the other hand, only one of the eight naturalistic learners used a two-handed-palms-down form of this gesture, and the other participants from this group who produced this gesture deployed the one-handed variation described above for the American monolinguals. It is also interesting to note that the two-handed form was much more common among the women than the men for the Japanese participants.

Bounded container gestures

Unexpectedly, bounded container gestures were found among all three of the Japanese groups; only three participants failing to produce any. The American participants used this gesture at levels of frequency comparable to the Japanese in the case of two-handed forms, but tended to use a one-handed version (Figure 9.1f) a great deal more often than did the monolingual and instruction-only participants. However the naturalistic learners produced the one-handed form at about the same level of frequency as the Americans (Table 9.3).

There were also qualitative differences, the Japanese women in both the monolingual and instruction-only groups tending to use a more restricted version of the gesture than either the Americans or naturalistic learners, in general creating smaller bounded 'objects', and when using two hands, the fingers of both hands either touching, or almost touching.

	Pair 1	Pair 2	Pair 3	Pair 4	Pair 5	Pair 6	Total
Am. NS	w / w	w / w	w / m	m / m	w / w	w / w	
	27 11	6 18	0 11	15 6	0 19	9 7	129
J. NS	w / w	m / m	m / w				
	19 15	1 0	1 15				51
J. Class.	w / m	w / m	w / w	m / m	w / w		
	9 7	10 9	3 0	17 8	12 9		84
J. Nat.	w / m	w / w	m / w	m / w			
	27 4	8 9	31 11	12 0			102
Grand total	366						

Table 9.3: Bounded container gestures

Potential gestures

Three of the twelve monolingual American participants used potential gestures, as did six of the eight naturalistic learners. No forms were recorded for the Japanese monolinguals, but two of the ten instruction-only learners also deployed this gesture (Table 9.4 on p. 212).

Splitting the gesture space

The partitioning of space to show contrast between one idea and another was found for all four groups in the study. The naturalistic learners displayed the lowest levels of frequency (Table 9.5). There were no particularly noticeable qualitative or gender differences across groups.

	Pair 1	Pair 2	Pair 3	Pair 4	Pair 5	Pair 6	Total
Am. NS	w / w 3 0	w / w 0 0	w / m 0 0	m / m 1 0	w / w 0 0	w / w 2 0	6
J. NS	w / w 0 0	m / m 0 0	m / w 0 0				0
J. Class.	w / m 0 0	w / m 0 1	w / w 1 0	m / m 0 0	w / w 0 0		2
J. Nat.	w / m 1 0	w / w 4 1	m / w 2 3	m / w 2 0			13
Grand total	21						

Table 9.4: Potential gestures

	Pair 1	Pair 2	Pair 3	Pair 4	Pair 5	Pair 6	Total
Am. NS	w / w 14 4	w / w 2 3	w / m 2 0	m / m 5 0	w / w 0 8	w / w 5 2	45
J. NS	w / w 2 3	m / m 0 0	m / w 6 1				12
J. Class.	w / m 1 0	w / m 3 2	w / w 1 3	m / m 7 1	w / w 3 3		24
J. Nat.	w / m 6 0	w / w 0 0	m / w 0 0	m / w 0 0			6
Grand total	87						

Table 9.5: Partitioning space gestures

Beats

All participants produced beats, this category proving to have the highest relative levels of frequency for most of the people in the study (Table 9.6, p. 213). However, there were noticeable qualitative differences. Most striking was the wavy/shaky character of beats on the part of the Japanese, and particularly the women in the monolingual and instruction-only groups. Only one of the four women in the naturalistic group displayed these characteristics and none of the men. This 'accent' was also found for the American monolinguals, although it happened rarely and did not differ with regard to gender. Also, for the Japanese, this kind of beat was more common with container gestures than with the other forms included in the study.

	Pair 1	Pair 2	Pair 3	Pair 4	Pair 5	Pair 6	Total
Am. NS	w / w	w / w	w / m	m / m	w / w	w / w	
	34 19	35 75	4 13	39 2	41 53	30 15	360
J. NS	w / w	m / m	m / w				
	27 40	27 22	50 53				219
J. Class.	w / m	w / m	w / w	m / m	w / w		
	81 101	57 58	18 32	102 36	25 36		546
J. Nat.	w / m	w / w	m / w	m / w			
	74 23	5 11	36 27	52 17			245
Grand total	1370						

Table 9.6: Beats

Verbal metaphors and accompanying gestures

Only one shared conceptual metaphor was found between the Americans and Japanese in the study: MARRIAGE IS A MANUFACTURED PRODUCT. One of the American monolinguals said, 'you can just build right on to it', when referring to a 'good marriage', moving his arms up from stomach to chest level, palms facing, thumbs and fingers rounded inward, as if sliding up a cylinder. Also a naturalistic learner, while saying, 'build ideal family', created a pyramid-like form, her hands stacking one 'brick' on the next, first with one hand then the other to the top of the imagined structure. She used a similar form of gesture when also speaking about family 'goals' and 'working together' as a family. This is of interest as, although not in the verbal message, the underlying conceptual metaphor was still that of 'building' as conveyed through gesture (the psychological predicate), and in this case through gestural forms that appear iconic, but which because they represent abstract ideas are metaphoric.

Other nonverbal elements

Although the study specifically looked for transformations in the use of gestures of the abstract for learners exposed to naturalist contexts, some of the other nonverbal forms of expression found in the study for the naturalistic learners also proved in some cases to be strikingly similar to those of the American monolinguals. These features are considered below.

Both the Japanese monolingual and instruction-only participants showed little movement of the shoulders when speaking while both the American monolinguals and naturalistic learners shrugged their shoulders on occasion and were more flexible in their upper body movements in general than the Japanese participants in the other two groups. The notion of flexibility also applies to how people sat. Women in the Japanese monolingual and instruction-only groups sat in a particular, culturally-sanctioned way with hands on the lap and legs either crossed or held together with feet flat on the floor. (Ramsey 1984 notes a number of nonverbal traditions which Japanese women conform to.) However, regardless of gender, the naturalistic learners mostly sat in less fixed postures, legs crossed in various positions or with the heels of their shoes resting a few inches up on the leg of the chair, for example, as did the American monolinguals.

In addition, the Japanese are noted for an almost constant nodding of the head and/or the use of verbal means to indicate appreciation and encouragement for what is being said (Maynard 1989, 1990). Nonverbal backchanneling was indeed quite frequent among the Japanese monolingual and instruction-only participants. However, except for one pair, both women in their 30s, the naturalistic learners behaved in a manner similar to the American monolinguals, who generally had less pronounced and less frequent nodding of the head.

The touching of conversation partners proved to be a major nonverbal difference between the naturalistically exposed participants and the rest of the Japanese in the study. None of the people in the monolingual or instructed groups ever touched one another. However, two of the women in the American group did so as did two of the women in the naturalistic group. It is also important to note in this latter case that the recipients were men as this is particularly uncommon in Japan (Ramsey 1984; von Raffler-Engel 1980a).

Facial expression proved to be another domain of similarity for the naturalistic learners and the American monolinguals. Basically, there was greater animation and expression on the part of participants in these two groups than for the Japanese monolinguals and the instruction-only participants. The one exception to this was a woman in the instruction-only group who had spent considerable time living in Jordan. Kunihiro (1980: 331) points out that traditionally American facial expressions tend to be more expressive than Japanese, suggesting that freely showing one's emotions is considered as 'a sign of immaturity' by the Japanese.

There were also instances where both the American monolinguals and naturalistic learners acted out the part of people outside of the immediate situation, and in doing so, portrayed the nonverbal expressions of that person as well. This did not happen at all with the other two groups of Japanese participants.

Discussion

The finding that both the Americans and the Japanese in the study used unbounded and bounded container gestures alike is surprising in relation to McNeill's (1992) notion that bounded forms of this gesture are 'Western' and unbounded forms 'non-Western'. However, the combined use of unbounded metaphoric gestures on the part of the Americans was low in comparison to the Japanese in the study. Also, the gestural form differed, the Americans for the most part using one hand to form this gesture and rarely using a common feature of the Japanese, namely, the palm(s)-down position in a largely unbounded manner. It is also important to note in relation to appropriation that only one of the naturalistic learners used the unbounded Japanese form above; the other people in the group produced forms similar to those for the American participants.

In relation to bounded container gestures, only one of the four women (the same person who used the Japanese version of unbounded gestures), and none of the men in the naturalistic group used the 'restricted' form of this gesture, a common feature among the Japanese participants in the other two groups. Also, the strongest evidence of appropriation for container gestures lies with the single-handed, bounded form which was found at a much higher degree of frequency for the monolingual Americans and naturalistic learners than for the other two groups in the study.

Findings for use of the potential gesture also tend to point to its appropriation by the naturalistic learners as there were only two recorded instances of its use for participants in the Japanese monolingual and instruction-only groups but multiple forms were found for each of four of the naturalistic learners. There is a difficulty associated with this finding, however, in that the form this gesture takes is in fact the same as that for the 'I don't know'/uncertainty emblem, and it does seem possible that the emblematic meaning was appropriated first and the 'potential' meaning gained through extension, although there is still quite a distinct difference in meaning between the two.

The fact that no discernible differences were found for gestures of the abstract that partition space for the comparison of concepts is of interest only to the extent that this variety of gesture appears to be common in both cultures. Beats, on the other hand, proved to be interesting at a qualitative level as the Japanese tended to have a different way of showing emphasis with them. It is important to point out, in reference to appropriation, however, that the same naturalistic learner who was the only person to produce two-handed unbounded container gestures and to use the restricted form of bounded containers was also the only person in this group to produce wavy/shaky beats. Therefore she was responsible for much of what was nonverbally Japanese among the naturalistic participants.

The use of gesture in accompanying verbal metaphors proved to be interesting as well, although only one shared verbal conceptual metaphor was found between the Americans and the Japanese. However, this one example is significant, as despite the absence of a complementary verbal counterpart at one point, the use of gesture continued to indicate the underlying conceptual element.

However, it is important to point out that Quinn's (1987) idea concerning the use of conceptual metaphors as a way of understanding cultures is controversial. Gibbs (1994), for example, objects to Quinn's notion that the specific use of metaphor is less important than how it supports abstract categories of understanding:

> My response to Quinn is that much of our cultural understanding of marriage is motivated by metaphor. We may be able as analysts to abstract from people's metaphorical understanding of their experience and provide a detailed idealized, even culturally sensitive, model that appears independent of metaphor. Yet we don't know if these idealized cultural models are constitutive of individuals' ordinary experiences: They might be convenient fictions created by scholars to suggest regularities in human experience that are really motivated by figurative schemes of thought.
>
> (Gibbs 1994: 206)

The one example from this study concerning the concept MARRIAGE IS A MANUFACTURED PRODUCT would seem to support Gibbs's notion that the metaphor is very much realized in the thinking of the participants in addition to cultural contexts. Gibbs also explicitly acknowledges the importance of gesture in relation to conceptualization, citing McNeill's (1992) work on metaphoric gestures, and noting that 'Nonverbal gestures exhibit people's metaphorical conceptions of experience' (1994: 164). Indeed it would seem that further research into the use of gesture in relation to conceptual metaphors is warranted.

The fact that the naturalistic learners were found to have appropriated a number of nonverbal interactional features, overall appearing much more like the Americans in the study than the Japanese in the other two groups, is also of relevance to the concerns of the study. First of all, as pointed out by von Raffler-Engel (1980a), there are 'low kinesic cultures' in which, for example, the vast majority of nonverbal behaviors are not explicitly taught to children as a part of growing up, while in others, and the Japanese are cited as an instance of this, nonverbal elements are formally attended to. von Raffler-Engel provides the example of how even at the age of two a Japanese girl had internalized the act of bowing to such an extent as to do so while speaking on the telephone (1980a: 144).

Furthermore, Ramsey (1984: 157) provides many examples of how the Japanese as a culture value *synchronony*, the ability to join with others. This has both a kinesic dimension, as in the case of the frequent nodding of the head as a form of backchanneling, and a psychological dimension as demonstrated in the concept *omoiyari* which basically entails a 'willingness to feel what others are feeling'. With regard to how deeply seated this cultural-historical predilection is, nonverbally, Ramsey states:

> among group members, the nonverbal communication of the message 'with' can supersede messages of agreement, disagreement or concern about task completion. The creation of harmony, flowing from attention to 'withness', greatly influences the dynamics of interpersonal interaction
>
> (Ramsey 1984: 162)

Therefore, the naturalistic learners may have had a cultural predisposition toward creating intersubjective states with members from their new communities. If so, this may have aided them with regard to appropriating nonverbal elements as a part of accommodating to their new surrounds.

Conclusion

Findings for the use of gestures of the abstract in the study offer support for the idea that some of these forms had been appropriated by the naturalistic learners. Also, the rather striking evidence of the extent to which the naturalistic learners had appropriated other nonverbal forms related to North American culture adds support to the notion that nonverbal elements in general proved to be a significant aspect of acculturation for them. It is important to reiterate in relation to this that the naturalistic participants were not interacting with monolingual Americans but with other Japanese with similar backgrounds—albeit in English—yet still they did so nonverbally in a manner in many ways different from their shared cultural origins.

As for the question of a transformation of inner speech in relation to gesture: it seems unlikely that the naturalistic learners had simply adopted different gestural forms to represent established concepts without any change in 'sense', given the interconnectedness of thought, language, and gesture established above in addition to the relative opaqueness of meaning for some of the metaphoric gestures in the study. Rather, our belief is that the high degree of functional English proficiency of these people together with their level of experience within cultural settings created grounds for remediation.

However, it also needs to be kept in mind that apparently the Japanese grow up with a meta-awareness of the use of nonverbal means of communication; moreover, Japanese culture prizes a sense of being in tune with others. Therefore, it may be that the naturalistic learners adopted even less than transparent gesture types as a part of fitting in; although even in this case, with time and experience it is not unreasonable to think that the 'new' nonverbal elements may have become 'infused with sense'. However, further study is obviously required to explore this and other issues in the study, and to better understand the relationship of nonverbal elements to second language learning in general.

Appendix: discussion questions

What do you think of the idea of arranged marriages?

What do you think the benefits of marriage are? What about the limitations?

What do you think is the role of each partner with regard to the other in a marriage?

What factors do you think lead couples to become frustrated with one another, estranged, separated, or divorced?

How do you think people can best resolve the difficulties they encounter in a marriage?

How do you think marriage differs in the short term than in the long term?

What would you see as the 'ideal marriage'?

10 Second language acquisition theory and the truth(s) about relativity

Steven L. Thorne
The Pennsylvania State University

*'In a language encrusted world, the situation at hand is hard
to get at.'*

(A. L. Becker 1982)

Introduction

This chapter provides a framework which, to paraphrase Bourdieu, attempts
to objectify the process of objectification itself.[1] I will argue that responsible
theorizing in second language acquisition (SLA) embraces both relativism[2]
and essentialism[3]. The trick, and there is always a trick, is to do so strategically.
Within a recursive framework, I attempt to illustrate the bounded and historically
contingent nature of theoretical work as a rationale for the continued
pluralism of SLA research foci and methods. The bulk of these comments
highlight approaches to SLA which foreground the situated and historical
qualities of human activity, specifically sociocultural theory and its reliance
on an expanded formulation of linguistic relativism. Research by communication
theorists, linguistic anthropologists, SLA researchers, and psychologists will
be drawn together in a multi-stranded discussion supporting a few issues
which I believe current SLA research is just beginning to take seriously.
Among these are that human actions and social identity articulate ecologically
with social-material, historical, and discursive contexts. An exploration of
the social formation of mind, recognizing certain ontogenetic, neurobiological
limits, and linking key ideas to SLA, comprises a second theme. I conclude
with a broadened notion of linguistic relativism as the key to understanding
how, and why, sociohistorical, cultural, and linguistic contexts do indeed co-
construct, in symphony with yet-to-be-explained biological material and
inclinations, durable social practices of mind and activity. A corollary to this
latter point is that cognitive processes, in many instances (conversation for
example), are usefully viewed as distributed rather than individually bound
activity.

The relative nature of theoretical work

A review of recent SLA journals shows heated debate between cognitive and social theories of SLA, and perhaps more importantly, a tension concerning what constitutes productive research within the field. In a special issue of *Applied Linguistics* focused on theory building, Long (1993) stated the need for theory culling within SLA. Block (1996) entered what had become an escalating intra-field debate and asked what 'the ontological parameters of the [SLA] field are to be. In simple terms, what counts as SLA or SLA-related research and what does not?' (*ibid.*: 75) Implicit in Block's question was a yet more important question—who gets to decide these things for the field? In opposition to Long (1990, 1993) and Beretta (1991) as proponents of a unified theory of SLA, Block argued for theoretical pluralism and challenged the 'mainstream' SLA preoccupation with cognitive factors. Other skirmishes include Lantolf (1996), who provides a postmodern argument for a pluralist approach to the exploration of SLA, and a published response to Block's (1996) article supporting the rationalist scientific substrate to much of SLA by Gregg *et al.* (1997). The current public forum engagement of these issues is a paper by Firth and Wagner (1997) accompanied by six supporting and contrary response articles. Firth and Wagner stress that the SLA literature is dominated by a focus on individual cognitive issues and a corresponding ellipsis of attention to context and sociocultural–historical issues. They argue that an emphasis on individual cognition within SLA fails to account for a large number of sociolinguistic and communicative dimensions of language use, including the roles of context, discourse, and interaction, and the flat social identity of 'learner' and 'native speaker' as they are used as research proxy for human agents. Each of these turns-at-talk within the SLA literature offer polarized and highly charged metanarratives illustrating the politics and truths of the state of SLA theory building. I will argue for a position that cross-linguistic research in first language socialization and linguistic anthropology effectively demonstrate—that relativism is an undeniable quality of the linguistic, social, and conceptual world(s) of human beings.[4] This would include humans-as-theorists who, within historical and particular discursive contexts, most often produce field-commensurate metaphors to work by.[5]

Developing and/or supporting a theoretical perspective requires stating clearly what the theory in question is a theory of (Bialystok 1990). If, as Williams has argued, '[a] definition of language is always, implicitly or explicitly, a definition of human beings in the world' (1977: 21), then the dominant core of current theories of SLA are for the most part defining a world of a-historical, decontextualized, and disembodied brains. It is my belief that such a theory does not fit the evidence. My numerous years as a language learner (and user) have universally (and I use this term consciously) included rich and specific historical situatedness, webs of social interactivity, context contingent identity work, and as far as I am aware, my brain has invariably remained an organic component of my body. These qualities of historical, contextual, and social situatedness are the 'universals', in all their many forms, that need explicating in any account of the processes of second language acquisition.

The argument

Psychological and cognitively oriented approaches to SLA represent but one dimension of the complex of phenomena and their interrelationships which need to be grouped together under the label of SLA. I wish to problematize strict distinctions between individual cognition and sociohistorical and socio-cultural contexts. By hermetically compartmentalizing individual cognition, we may mask the very processes we seek to describe. To put a more radical spin on this, aspects of what is often labeled cognition may be usefully understood in part as sociocultural practices. In other words, 'cognition' is historically and contextually co-constituted *in combination with*, not merely derived from, neurobiological factors local to individual brains (see Frawley 1997 for efforts to create a commensurate syncretism of Vygotskyan psychology and cognitive science). Though the balance of this co-construction is not yet clear (Schumann 1990), there is evidence supporting the need for, and validity of, contextual approaches to learning, language, and activity (Cole and Engestrom 1993; Salomon 1993; Hutchins 1995).

In this chapter, the theoretical perspectives I bring to bear on second language acquisition stress (a) sociocultural[6] views of psychology and learning (the historical and situated quality of 'cognition'), and to a lesser extent, social practice theory (the dialectic interrelations between individual and cooperative practices and the construction of social context), (b) linguistic relativity (here understood as the influences of language on perception and activity), and (c) distributed cognition (evidence that units of analysis for the study and description of second language learning ought to extend beyond the confines of individual brains to include joint activity, within communities of practice, and mediation, through artifacts). In expressing these views I am argumentative on a few fronts, but I wish to underscore that my intention is to show the compelling potential of sociocultural approaches to SLA and not to discredit other paradigms. It is after all the 30-plus year history of largely experimental research that has established SLA as a respected discipline. All in the SLA community are indebted to this history as it formed a field which we now, not always harmoniously, seek to advance. It is my hope that the existence of distinct and multiple theoretical traditions may help to explicate the processes of SLA, and subsequently, to develop more accurate heuristics which model these processes and conditions.

SLA and applied linguistics as the social science that it is (or should be)

Regardless of whether one finds *any* theory of SLA compelling or not, I wish to underscore the necessarily relative nature of all theoretical work, and the essentialization, though often for needed and useful purposes, that accompanies the conflation of data into categories of more general specification.[7] Vygotsky stated that '[f]acts are always examined in the light of some theory and therefore cannot be disentangled from philosophy' (1986: 11, cited in Lantolf and Appel 1994a: 12). I would add that an instance of theoretical modeling is historically relative in terms of its relational and oppositional construction *vis-à-vis* earlier research, as well as being built from a foundation of referential categories, used to catalogue and group empirical data, which are themselves historically contingent. Theoretical work is necessarily 'observer relevant', and thus implicated in one or a few ideologies.[8] These can be either explicitly stated by the author (the strategic approach, for example, 'I endorse the code model of human communication'), or implicitly assumed in one's work and teaching practices (reliance on a lexicon and methodology that indexes such a belief structure).

Overview volumes (Larsen-Freeman and Long 1991; Ellis 1994) make it clear that, for the most part, SLA researchers do not include relevant intellectual work occurring (and having occurred) in related fields (though Ellis does endorse the metaphor of a prism, where SLA 'is best seen as a complex, multi-faceted phenomenon ... [that affords] different perspectives on the same entity' (1994: 667)). This condition may be due in part to an incommensurability of discourses (Pennycook 1994b and Kramsch 1995a), a condition which has become more exaggerated over time as SLA seeks out its own identity as a freestanding discipline. As Kramsch puts it,

> [b]ecause each discourse domain has its own metaphors, its own categor-izations, its own way of relating the parts to the whole, the broadened intellectual agenda now available to language teachers and applied linguists has made it more difficult to communicate across historically and socially created discourses.
>
> (Kramsch 1995a: 4)

It is ironic that greater access to a 'broadened intellectual agenda' may result in decreased cross-disciplinary fertilization. Yet it is clear, to take an example close to heart, that a significant hurdle to understanding the backdrop against which sociocultural theories of SLA are drawn may be Marxist and critical theory's rhetorical density and specific lexicon. Such challenges notwithstanding, these and other intellectual movements offer significant tactics for self-evaluation which further the hope of linking SLA to our cousin social science disciplines. Though it would be a mistake to overdramatize the issue, the considerable promotion within the mainstream SLA and applied linguistics journals for a culling of exogenous theory may hinder more experimental and social theoretical trends in the SLA field and could engender a complicit hegemony of the Gramscian sort.[9]

To look through another lens, within Bourdieu's (1991) market-place metaphor, discursive fields—including academic specializations such as SLA for example—operate through proper forms of symbolic exchange, and reproduce themselves through a mechanism of selection bias that favors those holding the same or similar categories of perception. Although intended to strengthen the field and research productivity, if 'normal science' approaches to SLA were to become too dominant (for example, Long 1990, 1993; Beretta 1991; Gregg 1993), the result could be to impoverish divergent theoretical positions of the symbolic (and potentially economic) capital necessary for what feminist theorists Bryson and de Castell (1993: 355) term access to 'means of discursive production'. In short, SLA could be intellectually hobbled by an increased insistence on 'accepted facts' (such as they are) and scientific positivist modeling.

A brief look at SLA approaches—from brain to society

SLA theory already comes in lots of flavors, so one might ask—why would we want more? Yet each highlights a certain set of phenomena, each defines 'rigor' by slightly different criteria, and each employs methodologies that aim to provide coherence to particular types of data, and through particular categories of reference. What I see as the core of current SLA theorizing are cognitive processing and information processing approaches, which consider the individual and his or her language-related mental functions, including short- and long-term memory issues, language reception and production processes, and so on (for example, McLaughlin 1987; Anderson 1983). These approaches focus on individual performance and abilities, intrapsychological activity, physical science methodologies, and scientific genre presentation of research results. Cognitively oriented research foregrounds the isolation of variables, favors repeatable experimental design, and may require specific decontextualized and controlled environments.

Though attention to social factors and acculturation are core to Schumann's (1998) work, for example, he comments that a neurobiological component is integral to theories of second language acquisition. As Schumann (1990) points out, however, little conclusive neurobiological research exists. Further thwarting efforts to understand the cognitive dimensions of language acquisition is that SLA research is primarily based on secondary evidence—externalized language activity—followed by after-the-fact reconstructions of the types of processes and mechanisms that *might* have produced such visible activity (vocalization, graphical representations of language, responses to particular stimuli in controlled setting environments). Without wanting to take away from sophisticated research on how the brain stores and processes information (and expresses and comprehends/constructs meaning through language), to understand SLA as it occurs between (and not merely within) people, it is critical to remove 'context' and 'interaction' from the static and superficial 'variable' category, and, with more complexity, to reinterpret 'cognitive issues' as also historical, social, activity-, and context-contingent issues. There is a continuum, then, from information/cognitive processing attentions within SLA to those examining processes of second language interaction and negotiation. This now long-standing interest in negotiation (for example, Hatch 1978; Long 1983b; Long and Porter 1985; Varonis and Gass 1985; Pica 1987; Erlich, Avery, and Yorio 1990) does acknowledge the importance of social and interactional factors for SLA. A diverse group of researchers and agendas are engaged in this area (which shall not be spelled out here), but for the most part, they retain the terminological inertia of the engineering-computational metaphors common to cognitive approaches.

There is a corrective to the limitations of standard cognitive theory (see Lave and Chaiklin 1993 for critiques of cognitive science, and Harré and Gillett 1994 for a look at the 'discursive' or 'second' cognitive revolution), with its isolation of human activity from the contexts of its production and reception, in social practice and sociocultural theories of language, learning, and sociality. In contrast to the engineering-computational metaphor varieties of SLA, which have defined themselves and the processes they look at through terminology such as input, output, uptake, etc. (and the use and learning of language understood as 'information processing'), practice and sociocultural paradigms of learning, though distinct from one another and rooted in divergent intellectual traditions, seek relational, historical, and non-dualist ways of reconceptualizing 'learning' and 'behavior' as 'change' and 'practice'. Hall (1995b), Peirce (1995), Rampton (1995), and Firth and Wagner (1997), for example, offer heterogeneous approaches to, and under-standings of, second language phenomena which may be characterized as 'firmly rooted in contingent, situated, and interactional experiences of the individual as a social being' (Firth and Wagner 1998: 92). Second language learning is a process involving the copresence of intra- and interpsychological activity, environments with histories, and an ongoing negotiation of social identity. Understood in this way, the activity of foreign and second language learning occurs within material and social conditions which must be taken into account in the production of ecologically robust research.

Social practice theory and sociocultural approaches to SLA

Social practice theory, only recently applied to the problems of SLA, most notably by Hall (1995b) and van Lier (1996), attempts to capture the interplay between macro social structures and moment-to-moment practices. At first blush, it would seem that environments—institutional settings for example, such as university classrooms—*are* the context within which activity would take place. But practice theory would take into account additional factors, such as the historical qualities of 'universities', the institutionally defined subject positions of 'student' and 'instructor', and how these subject positions are inhabited (and their resources and constraints) by real people in concrete situations, issues of epistemology, and normative interactional and cultural patterns. Static constructs are problematic and analysis instead begins by framing context dialectically as bidirectionally constructed through the relationships between agent and structure. The sedimented patterns and activities engaged in everyday life are both a product of the constraints and resources that a particular social and institutional setting provides, as well as productive of these very settings, constraints, and resources. In a synopsis of what such an approach might offer to SLA, Hall notes that

> [a] primary interest of [practice theory] is the explication of the interactive processes by which individuals within groups, and groups within communities, (re)create and respond to both their sociohistorical and locally situated interactive conditions, and the consequences—linguistic, social, and cognitive—of their doing so.
>
> (Hall 1995b: 221)

In short, practice theory seeks to unify under a common theoretical umbrella the ways human activity reproduces systems, and how systems may change as a result of human activity (for example, Ortner 1984).

Sociocultural theory is a term applied to the efforts by Vygotsky and his students to formulate 'a psychology grounded in Marxism' (Wertsch 1985a: 7), with an emphasis on locating the individual within collective, material, and historical conditions. The entailments of a sociocultural theory approach foreground sociality to individuality, language as socially constructed rather than internally intrinsic, language as both referential and constructive of social reality, and notions of distributed and assisted activity in contrast to individual accomplishment. There is a general tendency to derive the micro-processes of language learning and use from larger social, political, and historical contexts, and to understand what occurs within these frames of reference as mutually (though not necessarily equally) influencing one another. In contrast to practice theory, sociocultural theory as it is applied in psychology, education, and SLA focuses primarily on human development and learning. Central to this approach is that human activity is mediated by material artifacts and by symbolic sign systems, the most important of which is language. Though the limitations of space preclude a discussion of it here, language as social-semiotic systems, expertly developed in the work of Halliday (for example, Halliday 1978; Halliday and Hasan 1989), is formative to the view espoused in this chapter.

With its commitment to the importance of human agency and societal context in the L2 development process, sociocultural theory is participating in newer genres of SLA research. Representing a variety of research perspectives, one productive new focus looks specifically at the relations between language learning and social identity (Kramsch 1995b; Peirce 1995; Siegal 1996; Norton 1997; McNamara 1997; Pavlenko and Lantolf this volume). An emphasis on the relations between social identity and SLA requires a greater emphasis on context (discussed from a sociocultural perspective by Donato 1994; Platt and Brooks 1994; and from a cultural studies perspective by Kramsch 1993) and a rendering of human agents as more complex than 'students' or 'non-native speakers' (for example, Firth and Wagner 1997).

(Mis)appropriation and (in)commensurability

Sociocultural approaches to learning, based as they are on the central notions of mediation, historical and contextual situatedness, and human action (Wertsch 1985a), have gained some currency in SLA theorists' and researcher's recent work, but often as an add-on to an otherwise epistemologically divergent approach to SLA (for example, psycholinguistic, cognitive, etc.). Vygotsky's zone of proximal development (ZPD), for example, is a popularized and ostensibly accessible dimension of his work that has been widely discussed since the mid-1980s. The use, value, and broad dissemination of Vygotsky's ZPD is not in question, or at least is not the issue I wish to address. The focus here is the degree to which the entailments of a social-Marxist philosophy of mind stop with the ZPD concept, and indeed, reinterpret it to conform to an ideologically commensurate standard (the core principle of which is that learning is primarily an individual activity). An example will best illustrate this point.

Vygotsky's ZPD has of late been unconvincingly equated with Krashen's metaphor of comprehensible input ($i + 1$). The differences between these two concepts have been discussed elsewhere (deGuerrero 1996; Dunn and Lantolf 1998), but briefly, Krashen developed the input hypothesis—the notion that language acquisition occurs when an individual is surrounded by target language input at $i + 1$, where i is the acquirer's current level of competence and $+ 1$ denotes the stage immediately following i in a natural order developmental sequence. The learner moves from stage i to stage $i +1$ by understanding input containing $i + 1$ (Krashen 1982). Vygotsky's ZPD concept, by sharp contrast, involves what an individual can accomplish or perform in collaboration with a more competent other's assistance (or the structural properties of the physical environment, or constructed mediational means and tools, which can carry some of the weight of what is traditionally understood as 'mental' activity). Hence $i + 1$ is a metaphor about language input quality and its effect on language acquisition, and Vygotsky's ZPD a theoretical approach to development based on the close analysis of activity made possible through collaboration. Krashen's $i + 1$ and Vygotsky's ZPD, then, are unrelated in their conceptualization (a passive body listening versus collaborative activity), philosophical underpinnings (learner as autonomous versus personal ability co-constructed through activity with other people and artifacts in the environment), focus processes (childlike learning versus the collaborative accomplishment of a specific task), and generally, their results (though it is certainly possible that a more capable peer could provide linguistically mediated social interaction to the end of assisting someone with language-related tasks and learning).

There are ideological and philosophical entailments to including sociocultural theory in one's teaching and theoretical framework. A mixing of theoretical and pedagogic principles based on divergent ideologies generates a 'cohesion gap' of sorts, and I believe these differences are, or have the potential to be, quite profound. The difficulty with quick appropriations and analog mappings of dissimilar theoretical and pedagogical stances is often due to incommensurable formulations of core concepts such as 'learning', 'language', 'identity', 'activity', and 'interaction', and how important each of these factors is understood to be, if they are addressed at all, in the processes of second language development. While they are certainly problematic, I see these cohesion gaps as potential arenas where discoveries and insights might be produced as a result of the thinking and research catalyzed by these incongruities.

The relative principles of context

'The particular meaning categories configured in the language at any point depend critically upon the social world with which it articulates' (Hanks 1996: 181).[10] Whether it is explicitly stated or tacitly assumed, a theory of communication and a theory of the (un)importance of social context lies beneath whatever SLA research one carries out. Since the inception of modern SLA (Pit Corder's observation of learners' systematic errors—what he termed a learner's 'internal syllabus' (1967)) the preoccupation for the most part has been on interlanguage, learner variation, L1 to L2 transfer, and of course the development of cognitive models of what might be going on inside the head. As SLA researcher Hall points out: 'That our use of language both indexes and creates the social contexts of its use is not a novel idea' (Hall 1995b: 206). Yet despite its long history as a research focus among anthropologists and communication theorists, context has remained little theorized in SLA studies.

Commenting from a sociocultural perspective, Donato offers the following critique of conventional psycholinguistics: 'underlying the construct of L2 input and output in modified interaction (which is said to foster negotiation leading to reorganization of a learner's interlanguage) is the [code] model of communication', which presumes that the goal of communicative language use is the 'successful sending and receiving of linguistic tokens' (1994: 34). The theoretical assumptions of the code model of communication[11] are well formulated by Reddy's (1979) 'conduit metaphor'—IDEAS ARE OBJECTS, LANGUAGE IS A CONTAINER, COMMUNICATION IS SENDING. As SLA theorists and linguists have pointed out (Lakoff and Johnson 1981; Donato 1994; Lantolf 1996), this impoverished understanding of communicative processes too often infiltrates the metaphors through which communication is framed (among native English speakers at least). Primary among the problems of the code model of communication is that it places emphasis on the formal characterizations of language involving the linguistic competence (in Chomsky's sense) to produce grammatical utterances. There is no reckoning of interaction in the code model, and the treatment of message reception/comprehension is anemic due to its basis in the conduit metaphor.

The relevance of communication theory

At the core of each theory of SLA is an assumption about what the communication process involves, and subsequently, the types of exposure and practices that contribute to learning. As asserted above by Donato, many theories and approaches to SLA observe the code model of communication, and as such do not include the interactively constructed and historically conditioned nature of communicative activity and context (local and historical). Also problematic is the strict separation of language use from language acquisition. Arbitrary units for measuring acquisition (for example, written and oral examinations) may in fact be poor indicators of ongoing developmental processes that co-occur with uses of language. The relevance of communication theory to language acquisition theory, then, is profound, for it is through language use that development occurs, and in use that these developmental processes may be most clearly illustrated. Below I attempt to show that an improved understanding of communicative practice has the potential to provide the means for productive research into second and foreign language use and development.

Communication theorists Sperber and Wilson (1986: 118) hypothesize a 'context effect' in which a 'hearer retrieves or constructs and then processes a number of assumptions. They form a gradually changing backdrop against which new information is processed ... This involves the contextual effects of an assumption in a context determined, at least in part, by earlier acts of communication.' Sperber and Wilson emphasize that context is emergent and cumulative based on shared knowledge with an interlocutor, and that communication involves the sending and receiving-constructing of 'assumptions' (rather than stand-alone 'messages'). Through their development of Relevance Theory (rooted in Grice's work 1989), which attempts to account for the fact that semantically sparse utterances invoke determinate meanings within specific contexts, Sperber and Wilson make a case for a pragmatic or 'relevancy'-based approach to communication. Relevancy to an individual, as well as to a community of practice (in the sense of Lave and Wenger 1991), is a primary strength of sociocultural approaches to SLA.

'Temporarily shared social worlds'

To deepen this discussion of the role and characteristics of context, Rommetveit (1974: 3), in a number of works he characterizes as 'exploring [the] subtle relationships between communication settings, tacit presuppositions and what is said', focuses on the notions of ellipsis and prolepsis as they come to constitute intersubjectivity (or 'temporarily shared social world'). It is the dearth of the information-carrying capacity of natural language that requires of any theory of human communication an explanation for our species' communicative successes. Understood is that communicative breakdowns occur, and that such occurrences in fact underscore the need for a workable theory of context, intersubjectivity, or other extralinguistic process to work interdependently with linguistic and paralinguistic communicative practices. Rommetveit turns traditional assumptions about language around, and states—'we may thus reverse the traditional linguistic approach to ellipsis[12]: *ellipsis*, we may claim, *appears to be the prototype of verbal communication under ideal conditions of complete complementarity in an intersubjectively established, temporarily shared social world*' (1974: 29—italics in the original). Or to quote Hanks (1996: 148), '[t]he blank spots (ellipsis) point into the intersubjective context, linking verbal form to the extralinguistic horizon of social knowledge.' Intersubjective states are created, not inherited or presumed, and draw agents together toward a common focus, activity, process, or goal (Rommetveit 1974; Habermas 1984). The dialogic exchange of ellipses and indexicals, universal to both face-to-face and written exchanges, makes possible participation frameworks which build socially distributed perceptions that are, as described by Goodwin, 'situated, context dependent, … and intensely local' (1996: 398).

Rommetveit discusses particular social and pragmatic uses of ellipsis, other than those of economy or the reduction of redundancy, through the notion of prolepsis. Prolepsis involves ellipsis, but is different for the subtle establishment of social inclusion it brings with it. The hearer is 'invited to step into an enlarged common space, and shared background knowledge is thereby created, rather than assumed' (van Lier 1996: 161).[13] The notion that certain presuppositions imposed through discourse, such as mentioning an unknown name or event or place to an interlocutor, may in fact make this person an insider 'precisely because that expanded social reality is taken for granted rather than explicitly spelled out … What is said serves on such occasions to induce presuppositions and trigger anticipatory comprehension, and what is made known will necessarily transcend what is said' (Rommetveit 1974: 88).

Rommetveit argues then that the nesting of an utterance significantly alters its message structure. Hence he moves communication from a system of invariant semantics to one of contextual variability. For speakers to understand one another they utilize an ability to work out messages in relation to specific contexts rather than rely on universally distributed linguistic competence.

Hanks notes that Rommetveit relies on Wittgenstein's notion of language games, wherein participants share or develop an understanding, or set of rules, about how to 'play' when the game is successful communication. Contexts can be characterized as made up of 'metalinguistic contracts, which govern how speakers concretize the indeterminate meanings of the words they use with one another' (Rommetveit 1974: 57, cited in Hanks 1996: 150). This reference to the organization of talk-in-interaction will be expanded upon below.

The essentials of Rommetveit's proposed theory of communication can be summarized as follows: (a) ellipsis is not the exception, but rather the prototype of communication, (b) intersubjectivity is the quality emergent of linguistically mediated communication when it is successfully practiced, (c) prolepsis provides a necessary corrective to flat and static understandings of communication-context relations and illustrates the pragmatic–semantic functions that ellipsis may invoke, and (d) communication is a co-constructed social process and not an act of simple transmission. Thus linguistic interaction is constructive of a 'temporarily shared social reality', and, in reciprocity, such intersubjectivity scaffolds the process of intention–attribution and communicative practice. In this sense, sociocultural approaches to SLA are closely related to social constructivism in interpreting foreign and second language interaction to involve the *creation*, and not mere reflection, of social realities.

At the risk of overstating the obvious, then, there is a strong research tradition within anthropology, sociology, and linguistics which illustrates the contextual relativity of semantic values (for example, deixis and indexicality). Such a reappraisal of communicative practices could precipitate a radical shift within SLA, from an understanding of the language learned as context-independent lexical and grammatical meaning (present in formal theories of language and communication), to an acknowledgment of the relative and context-contingent nature of language-in-use. Hence to take seriously socio-cultural theory and commensurate insights from linguistics, anthropology, sociology, psychology, and communications theory as they pertain to SLA, the following themes arise:

- the interdependences between language and conceptual development,
- language as the principal sign system carrying socio-historical-cultural presence into the moment,
- language as a primary resource through which people interactively construct social reality, and
- the reproduction of individual and community practices due in part to the inertia (e.g. stable and historical qualities) of language constructed social worlds.

What I argue through the rest of this chapter is sociocultural theory's reliance, if you will, on a broadened formulation of linguistic relativism, and how the dynamics of linguistic relativism make evident the significance of a sociocultural approach. Linguistic relativism, in its base form, is the notion that culture, mediated largely by language and communicative practices, affects the way humans think about and organize their world(s).[14] This notion is especially pertinent to neo-Vygotskyan approaches for the emphasis within this method on private and inner speech—the practice of using the semiotic system of language as a tool for self-regulation and cognitive orientation to a task or situation. Linguistic relativism is here expanded to encompass this notion: that language is the medium through which historical, discursive, and cultural resonances lend to particular contexts their texture and working principles, for want of a better phrase. These 'textures' can be multiple, *a priori* shared between interlocutors, or co-constructed in the moment as per Rommetveit's notion of intersubjectivity. I believe a theory of SLA can and should involve these various components, and that the practices of second and foreign language teaching and learning would benefit as a result.

Linguistic relativity and social cognition

Vygotsky's work makes the case that mind is socially constituted 'through mediation via semiotic systems, notably language, that are themselves expressions of socio-historical processes' (Cazden 1993). Sociocultural approaches reverse Piaget's epigenetic constructivist theory of development wherein cognition precedes language acquisition (see Karmiloff-Smith 1992 for a corrective to the standard Piagetian view). Vygotsky in fact reverses Piaget, arguing that speech is initially social, is then internalized, and subsequently leads to inner and private (or egocentric) speech. For Vygotsky, biological, ontogenetically prior developmental dispositions exist, but later higher-order mental functions, of which language use and symbolic and concrete activity are a part, are socioculturally determined (Lantolf and Appel 1994a).[15]

Against the sorts of 'child as autonomous being' construct characterized by Piaget, the 'interactionist' camp (so termed by Gopnik and Meltzoff 1993) posits that children grow up suspended in cultural-linguistic environments which in part influence the direction of their cognitive development. There are a variety of perspectives on the depth and commensurability of human language variation. My argument here is that considerable differences between languages do exist, and hence differences in language-specific world-framing as well. Gopnik and Meltzoff (1993: 220) make the statement clearly: 'Different languages carve up the world in different ways, making certain semantic distinctions obligatory and others optional, or marking certain distinctions by clear morphological variations, while others can only be expressed by complex and indirect means.' Bowerman (1989: 143) comments that 'even though recent research has shown that languages are semantically less varied than had been supposed, they are by no means uniform.' Lakoff (1987), Slobin (1996), and others address the depth of linguistic variation issue through 'grammaticized concepts', that is, concepts that are part and parcel of the grammatical system of language, and thus not generally available to conscious reflection. Fundamental domains (in which 'concepts' can be located), such as time, causality, an emphasis on aspect versus tense, and spatial relations, tend to be grammaticized.

Two first language acquisition studies, the first by Gopnik and Choi (1991) and a second by Gopnik and Meltzoff (1993), provide concrete illustrations useful to this analysis. These first language studies are included not to equate first and second language acquisition, but to demonstrate a specific correspondence between language-culture environment and conceptual development, which serves the greater goal of illustrating the interdependencies of culture, language, context, and social interaction, which I later bring to bear on the problems of SLA research.

Nouns and categorizing: verbs and means–end awareness

The two above-mentioned studies demonstrate that within their subject pool (Korean, Japanese, and English language children), the culture-language environment had demonstrable effects on participating children's conceptual development, showing specific correlations between grammatical characteristics of the languages[16] in question and domain-specific developmental progress. The Korean and Japanese children (in verb-salient linguistic environments) produced verb morphology earlier than English-speaking children (in noun-salient linguistic environments), but in these studies were significantly delayed in performance concerning categorization tasks (and relatedly, at which age they went through the 'naming spurt'[17]). Perhaps linked to their earlier use of verb morphology, the Korean children were in advance of the English children in means–end abilities[18] (Gopnik and Choi 1991; Gopnik and Meltzoff 1993). Thus there are two specific correspondences that emerge: one between noun salience, naming, and categorization, the other linking verb salience and means–end skills (Gopnik and Meltzoff 1993). To account for these data, Gopnik and Meltzoff (1993: 221) developed the 'specificity hypothesis' which states, in accordance with an interactionist perspective, that there is a 'complex bi-directional interaction between conceptual and semantic development.' In their conclusions, Gopnik and Meltzoff (1993: 243) claim that '[c]onceptual developments are not just prerequisites for semantic developments. Instead, linguistic variations may actually influence cognitive developments.' These cross-linguistic studies thus demonstrate that the linguistic environment influences and to some degree shapes perception and cognitive development. Levinson uses the form of the syllogism to summarize a version of linguistic relativity that these studies bear out. It goes like this:

1 languages vary in semantic structure;

2 semantic categories determine aspects of individual thinking;

therefore

3 aspects of individuals' thinking differs across linguistic communities according to the language they speak.

(Levinson 1995: 133)

'Thinking for speaking'

Traditional linguistic relativism is made up of two seemingly static entities, language and thought (or habitual thought). Based on recent research, Slobin and his associates (for example, Berman and Slobin 1994) offer a formulation of the relations between language and thinking which avoids the methodological dilemma of providing rigorous evidence in illustration of a 'world view'. Through his extensive empirical work in cross-linguistic studies of narrative, Slobin has moved from 'thought and language' to the dynamic, in-progress notions of 'thinking for speaking', the specificity of thinking that occurs in the process of verbalizing (or writing) an utterance. 'The expression of experience in linguistic terms constitutes *thinking for speaking*—a special form of thought that is mobilized for communication ... the activity of thinking takes on a particular quality when it is employed in the activity of speaking' (Slobin 1996: 76). 'Thinking for speaking' represents a concise and temporally specific formulation of linguistic relativism, empirically based on speakers of different languages who generated narratives from the same protocol (a picture storybook). In terms of tense/aspect distinctions and spatial organization, Slobin reports that the children and adults within his study observed the 'selective attention' to event construal grammaticized in their native languages, and that speakers rarely generated narratives outside of those that are normative for their speech community. Slobin (1996: 88) carefully summarizes his study thus: 'I am convinced ... that the events of this little picture book are experienced differently by speakers of different languages—*in the process of making a verbalized story out of them*' (emphasis in the original). Slobin avoids questions of difference beyond those that his participants made evident in their representations of events in language. It is here that social practice theory can help make the connection between these first language acquisition studies and the social foundation for the constitution of mind. With its emphasis on the relationships between daily activity (such as talk-in-interaction) and the social-material conditions which inculcate these same activities, social practice theory unveils the dialectic relationship between what people do each day and the social norms and values ('culture', more or less) from which they spring. This is why ideology, or as Bourdieu and Eagleton (1994) would term it, *doxa*—largely unconscious and spontaneous sets of naturalized assumptions about how the world works—is an integral component, wanted or not, in the research and teaching practices of applied linguists.

Slobin (1996: 91) extends his findings in an exploratory way to SLA. He remarks that certain grammaticized categories, such as plural and instrumental markers, involve linguistically encoded points of view that are supported by sensory experience in the world. Such linguistic categories would not present great conceptual difficulty to second language learners regardless of whether one's native language expresses them or not. Slobin gives as an example that 'if your language lacked a plural marker, you would not have insurmountable difficulty in learning to mark the category of plurality in [a] second language, since this concept is evident to the non-linguistic mind and eye' (1996: 91).[19] By contrast, Slobin argues that distinctions such as aspect, definiteness, and voice, which in childhood we are enculturated to represent through the grammaticized categories of a particular language (itself a historical lexico-grammatical set of arbitraries), would be resistant to restructuring (particularly through transmission approaches to teaching and learning).[20] Second language acquisition difficulties are compounded in such areas since *she went to work* or *she has gone to work*, or *a car* versus *the car*, 'are distinctions that can only be learned through language, and have no other use except to be expressed in language. ... It seems that once our minds have been trained in taking particular points of view for the purposes of speaking, it is exceptionally difficult for us to be retrained' (1996: 91). The insight that language is not a transparent medium unproblematically transmitting information raises both issues of pedagogy as well as problems with SLA theories dependent on 'code model' assumptions about communication. This is another point at which strategic reevaluation of base level principles can prove useful to researchers and practitioners alike.

Slobin's 'thinking for speaking' does not occur in a social vacuum, but rather in contexts which themselves are formed by discursive and historical processes. Extending Slobin's 'thinking for speaking' in this way implicates *interactional features* of communication as a larger framework within which to develop a grammar of the communicative process. Slobin's formulation of linguistic relativism is an elegant and demonstrable characterization of the interactional co-construction that will be specific not only to speakers of a language, but also to members of particular speech communities who share discourse strategies, allocation of turns-at-talk (latching versus interruptions for example), and the like. This expanding out of 'thinking for speaking' to encompass the organization of talk-in-interaction will be continued below.

In summary, the key points of this section are that semantic domains are partitioned differently across languages, and that this is accomplished at a level beneath that of our everyday perception—grammaticized in the semantics of morpho-syntactic structures themselves.[21] The first language studies discussed above indicate that language is in a bidirectional relationship with conceptual development and category formation. A temporally specific form of linguistic relativity, such as I have described here based on Slobin's work, is the mechanism by which human communication and cognition can be linked to specific historical and contextually contingent forms of communicative practice. As language-culture environments influence the encoding and construction of experience, the materiality of language encrusts, or symbolically concretizes, the world (to borrow from Becker's 1982 formulation which began this chapter). In essence, social agents constitute themselves in part through the language practices they engage in.

Relativity and talk-in-interaction

We turn now to an extension of grammar which includes the grammar of talk-in-interaction, and by doing so expand linguistic relativity to include inter-actional dynamics. The confluence of Rommetveit's notion of intersubjectivity and the robust, dialectical understanding of context from communication and social practice theory hinge on this broadened notion of linguistic relativity. The arguments and research I have brought forward for the historical, relative, and sociocultural nature of communicative practice indicate that language structure, and to be further developed here, practices of use in communicative activity, have effects on the thinking and speaking that is done there. The genesis of human forms of communication is conversational interaction—the primordial environment for the ontogenetic and phylogenetic use and develop-ment of natural language (Schegloff 1996). Schegloff (*ibid.*: 55) also mentions that the local and interactional nature of talk-in-interaction means that grammatical structures should be understood in part as adaptations to such communicative contexts and partially 'shaped by interactional considerations'.

A system of grammar (or the durable patterns of language that are, for example, abstracted from use in descriptive linguistics), as well as its local instantiation in discourse, stands in a reflexive relationship to the organization of a 'spate of talk'. Situational contingencies shape grammar as it plays out in use, and the grammatical qualities of a particular language, selectively high-lighting certain conceptual principles, contribute to THE organization of turns-at-talk, and more generally, to the way talk-in-interaction is organized (*ibid.*: 56). As mentioned, this extended concept of grammar, to include language-based interaction, is also part of what I would like to subsume under the rubric of linguistic relativism. Though it is not linked with interaction *per se*, Vološinov (1973) and Bakhtin (1986) both commented that grammar can express a good deal, but that style and intonation can do more (see Schultz 1990). Style, intonation, prosody, and talk-in-interaction and its organizational structure (Goodwin 1996; Schegloff 1996) are all implicated in this larger understanding of the organization of communicative practices, their historical and situated qualities, and the dialectical process whereby talk-in-interaction and grammaticized features of a language *are the sociocultural qualities which co-constitute the context within which communicative practices occur*, and reciprocally, the cultural-historical-discursive qualities of social context tend to (re)inculcate communicative practices in their social, ideological, and culturally specific forms.

A sociocultural syllogism in parallel with (and adjunct to) Levinson's for linguistic relativism might go like this:

1 languages and forms of communicative practice vary over speech communities;

2 a socially constructed and distributed resource, language is the principal mediational means constituting individual and collective qualities of 'mind';[22]

therefore,

3 higher-order aspects of individuals' thinking are socioculturally influenced through the situated practices of talk-in-interaction.

Therefore, when SLA researchers attempt to 'get at what's really going on' in processes of second and foreign language learning, the unit of analysis and the context within which such research takes place become crucial for the validity of the results. The concluding remarks below lay out critical issues for thinking about the practice of theorizing in general and SLA theorizing specifically, and why units of analysis ought to include more than individual heads.

Distributed cognition and units of analysis

Calhoun, LiPuma, and Postone (1993: 3), commenting on Bourdieu, argue that 'social life ... must be understood in terms that do justice both to objective, material, social, and cultural structures and to the constituting practices and experiences of individuals and groups.' In contrast to a methodology stressing strict isolation of variables and phenomena, the foundation of sociocultural theory approaches is that context, language (learning and use), and subjectivity are analytically separable, but must be understood holistically and interdependently to make sense of 'situated activity' (Lave and Wenger 1991; Hanks 1996). In a related vein, distributed cognition approaches posit that 'context' is not another variable, but rather is in part productive of, and in part produced by, collective and individual human activity. Hence decontextualized research may isolate a focus phenomenon, but this isolation from typical contexts of occurrence may in turn mutate the phenomenon under surveillance. Akin to Labov's 'observer's paradox', this raises serious methodological issues for SLA researchers as processes such as memory, speech production, sense of social situatedness and social identity and entitlement, and the presence or absence of paralinguistic information such as head nodding, facial expressions, and gesticulation, impact and even constitute levels of engagement and performance (Lantolf 1999). Nardi observes that it is not possible to fully understand how people learn and work if the unit of analysis is the uncharacteristic 'unaided individual with no access to other people or to artifacts for the accomplishing of the task at hand' (Nardi 1996a: 69). This observation would seem particularly applicable to second and foreign language acquisition research, given the inherent social-interactive nature of communicative practice.

The strategic use of essentialism

As discussed earlier in this chapter, theory construction—SLA-related or otherwise—is both relative and essentializing. Addressing this issue, critical theorist Gayatri Spivak calls for the 'strategic use of essentialism'. By this she is responding to deconstructionist modes of inquiry, which she says fail in their efforts to decenter both the subject position of the researcher and the object of scrutiny itself. The salient issue to Spivak's proposed use of essentialism for my comments here is that 'since it is not possible not to be an essentialist, one can self-consciously use this irreducible moment of essentialism as part of one's strategy' (Spivak in interview with Harasym—Harasym 1988: 66). Spivak continues to say that 'no representation can take place, no *Vertretung*, representation, can take place without essentialism' (*ibid.*). Of note is that Spivak has commented extensively on subaltern historiography[23] and the efforts within this movement to pluralize and rerepresent historical perspectives to the end of gaining a more complete understanding of typically subaltern, or marginalized and silenced, groups of people. Responsible theorizing, or, paraphrasing Spivak, strategic essentializing, can involve denaturalizing representations of data and category formation, affirming that 'subjects' are people with personal and collective histories, and remaining aware that methodological approaches and data-gathering contexts are historically and discursively specific, with repercussions on human (inter)activity and performance. As SLA is still a developing field in many ways, both a tolerance for a diversity of hypotheses and claims and a self-conscious, political awareness of how theory builders are socially, ideologically, intellectually, and institutionally located, seems a fruitful and necessary approach to understanding SLA in all its contingent and contextually diverse conditions.

A relative conclusion

Language patterns of some durability are the sedimented product of historical and sociocultural activity, which in part structure current contexts, and reciprocally, such contexts in turn co-structure interactional and communicative practices. Through the here-expanded principles of linguistic relativism, context is bound not just to communicative practice, but to thinking and cognitive activity as well. In terms of theory building within SLA, a 'strategic use of essentialism' would spell out as clearly as possible the foundational attributes upon which higher-level analyses are built. A broad intellectual framework would be critical for interconnections with findings in other fields. I have also tried to point out that a strategic and responsible unit of analysis should account for social situatedness (role/identity/subjectivity issues), cognitive activity, discursive and local context, and attempt to address how these phenomena mutually influence one another.

What would SLA efforts gain from a relativist approach to theorizing? How deep can the antagonisms and incommensurabilities go while still remaining a productive, intellectual community? These are difficult questions, but historically, the outliers within intellectual communities have both hurtled off in retrospectively wrong directions while also producing, in other instances, discoveries that led to paradigm shifts (Kuhn 1970) and improved understanding of the social and material worlds we share. As Geertz (1973: 88) stated in reference to the field of anthropology in the 1970s, there is always a danger of stagnation due, in part, to the 'dead hand of competence'. Thus I propose a practice of SLA theorizing which embraces pluralism, makes known its relativism, and which underscores SLA research as a 'process of exploration' (Schumann 1993). This includes the consideration of the historical, discursive, and contextual situatedness of people within talk-in-interaction, the distributed nature of mediational resources (most notably language), and the sociohistorical constitution of sedimented practices of mental activity (in other words a rethinking of cognition). SLA is complex, and perhaps made more so given Bakhtin's (1986) view that there can be no single (universal) truth due to our differential positioning. At the same time, and endorsed here, is that truth(s) bringing together neurobiology and historical-contextual contingency may in fact be obtainable, but will require a plurality of efforts to be realized.

Notes

1   Bourdieu notes that the process of constituting an academic study 'as a representation capable of being the object of a story, description, or account, and secondarily [as] an interpretation, produces an essential distortion which has to be theorized if one is to record in the theory the effects both of the act of recording and of the theory' (Bourdieu 1990: 101). Bourdieu underscores the confounding of the actions of agents in the world with 'philological relations', or the work of researchers, and suggests an academic method which takes 'as its object the very operation of objectification' (*ibid.*).

2   Relativism is here understood, paradoxically, as a human absolute, due to the limitations, if you take the standpoint theorist side, or the specificity, if you take the sociocultural other, of the human conceptual and perceptual apparatus. Bourdieu also discusses in great detail the constructed and relative nature of categories of perception, which he argues arise from socially (experientially) constituted generative dispositions (*habitus*).

> Constructing the notion of habitus as a system of acquired dispositions, functioning on the practical level as categories of perception and assessment or as classificatory principles as well as being the organizing

principles of action, meant constituting the social agent in his true role as the practical operator of the construction of objects.

(Bourdieu 1990: 13)

Here Bourdieu presents a formulation for the constructed nature of social reality. Historically, Bourdieu is responding to Kant's arguments for *a priori* categories of perception (which he discusses in considerable detail in *Distinction* 1979).

3   Essentialism is an unavoidable feature of theory building, as individual data are 'typed', represented by numbers or language, and organized in categories of broader description. This holds from 'thick description' ethnography to hard science research. Problems arise when category users and developers (theorists and researchers) naturalize their representations, models, and categories.

4   For extensive anthropological inquiry into language socialization and cultural difference, see the work of Schieffelin (1990), Ochs (1988), and Schieffelin and Ochs (1986).

5   In an illustration of cross-perspective harmony, McLaughlin (1987, 1990) renders a clear assessment of issues in theory building that are much in line with those I present here.

6   There has been considerable discussion about the term 'sociocultural'— what it means, who it belongs to, and the intellectual lineage it is emergent of. For a historical assessment, see Wertsch, del Rio, and Alvarez (1995), who discuss at length the intellectual antecedents to 'sociocultural' approaches to understanding human activity. They describe (with an excluded caveat) the neo-Vygotsky project this way: 'the goal of sociocultural research is to understand the relationship between human mental functioning, on the one hand, and cultural, historical, and institutional setting, on the other' (1995: 56). Later, Wertsch adds that neo-Vygotskyan scholars (Rogoff is named) disagree with the 'evolutionist assumptions indexed by the terms "sociohistorical" and "cultural-historical" ' thus for Wertsch at least, the term 'sociocultural' refers to the Vygotskyan tradition while also to a contemporary and altered version of it (according to Wertsch, Vygotsky himself did not use the Russian equivalent of 'socio-cultural'). Lastly, in reference to not invoking Vygotsky's name as the progenitor of sociocultural theory, Wertsch states that all sociocultural (for example, Wertsch 1985a), and socio-cultural-historical (Cole 1996) research involve two principal themes, those of '*human action* and *mediation*', and that these are the 'defining moments of sociocultural research' (and which are, in fact, directly linked to Vygotsky's work, for example, 1978). This project is broadly in line with Wertsch's emphasis on 'human action' and 'mediation', here more specifically characterized as language-based social interaction and the mediational qualities of human language.

7   Fowler, discussing linguistic relativism (with which I believe theoretical category formation is tightly related), provides an elegant formulation

of this process, that a 'code simplifies knowledge and behavior by allowing particulars to be recognized as instances of a category' (1986: 31).

8   Searle's distinction of 'intrinsic' vs. 'observer relative' phenomena offers a useful way to frame both categories of reference and theory building itself. Though certain phenomena do appear to be 'intrinsic' (Searle mentions photosynthesis as an example), our systems of explanation and classification of such phenomena are observer relative (1992).

9   Antonio Gramsci's notion of hegemony moves beyond the term's usual meaning of domination to include consensual acquiescence. Gramsci describes this idea as, in part, 'the "spontaneous" consent given by the great masses of the population to the general direction imposed on social life by the dominant fundamental group; this consent is "historically" caused by the prestige (and consequent confidence) which the dominant group enjoys because of its position and function in the world of production' (Gramsci 1971: 12, in *Selections from the Prison Notebooks of Antonio Gramsci*, edited and translated by Quintin Hoare and Geoffrey Nowell Smith. New York: International Publishers).

10   A decade ago, I studied for a year at Banaras Hindu University. I focused on language study: Hindi, Urdu, a local vernacular called Kashike Bhojpuri, and worked on a linguistics project that a year later became my first conference presentation (on sexual puns in Kashike Bhojpuri). The insights I gained drinking endless cups of tea in male-clientele *chai* shops had mostly to do with the wit and complexity of the *double-entendre* language games my friends would play on each other, and often on me as the 'least capable peer'. But as my language awareness developed, I began to catch the simpler of the interactively constructed moments during which either a pun would work or not. Those verbal performances that flopped failed to take sufficient account of the reception necessary by non-addressed insiders, for this pun game had more to do with speaking indirectly to Goffman's 'legitimate bystanders' (1967), those in-the-know sitting around waiting for a laugh, than to the hoped-for brunt of the joke. As a second language learner in this situation, the interactional dynamics constituting these complex plays on words, and my involvement there, were formative to my current interest in social context and its importance to SLA.

11   Sperber and Wilson (1986: 2) claim that from

> Aristotle through to modern semiotics, all theories of communication were based on a single model, ... the code model.
>
> (Sperber and Wilson 1986: 2)

> Yet the code model of verbal communication is only a hypothesis, with well-known merits and rather less well-known defects. Its main merit is that it is explanatory: utterances do succeed in communicating thoughts, and the hypothesis that they encode thoughts might explain

how this is done. Its main defect … is that it is descriptively inadequate: comprehension involves more than the decoding of a linguistic signal.
(Sperber and Wilson 1986: 6)

They developed 'relevance theory' to try to account for the cognitive, contextual, social, and interactional features of human communication, emphasizing that 'human cognition tends to be geared toward the maximization of relevance' (1986: 261).

12 The conventional linguistic perspective is that *ellipsis* refers to an utterance where, for reasons of economy, emphasis, or style, part of its structure, expressed previously, has been omitted.

13 Rommetveit discusses this point via the disclosure of a personal letter he received from his friend Willem Hofstee (who originally proposed the term and notion of prolepsis):

> … Today I walked with one of the psychologists here past the Mayflower cinema in Eugene, where Bergman's latest film movie is being shown. He asked me whether I had seen it. I said no, and asked if he had. He said yes, he had. I asked him how he liked it, and he said 'I liked it very much, but Mary Ann did not'; without ever explicitly having 'made known' to me that he is married and that his wife's name is Mary Ann, that they went to see the film together, and a lot of other things—and (if I am correct) without assuming that I knew all this. His utterance was proleptic in that it triggered a search on my part for a shared social reality which in turn would provide a basis for understanding the sentence. Incidentally, it would have been barbaric and pedantic to say, 'Oh, Mary Ann is your wife'. To be precise, prolepsis here served to establish a relationship between his wife and me as persons who should at some time get together. My comment would have been a crude rejection of that implication.
> (Rommetveit 1974: 87–8)

14 Linguistic relativism is the focus of a long debate, which Gumperz and Levinson (1996) date back to St. Augustine, and in modern times to Humboldt's *Weltanschauung* ('worldview'). Linguistic determinism, such as is generally attributed to Whorf, has been shown to be untenable (Gumperz and Levinson 1996).

15 Linguistic anthropologists Ochs and Schieffelin put it this way: 'Sociocultural systems are to be considered as one force influencing language acquisition. Biological predispositions, of course, have a hand in this as well' (1984: 309).

16 Background knowledge on the languages in question, English, Korean, and Japanese, is necessary for understanding these studies as they relate language structure with perceptual and semantic development. English, as a subject–verb–object language, is noun-salient ('salient' in the linguistic sense of '+stress'). Utterance final position, usually the object

of the clause in English, therefore stands out to the young learner. As Slobin illustrated through his extensive cross-linguistic first language acquisition research, postposed markers and clause final position have proven +salient to young learners. Imagine a parent pointing to a picture of a dog in a picture book and saying 'look at the DOGGY' (upper case = + stress). By contrast, Korean and Japanese are verb-salient languages, are verb final (subject–object–verb word order), rely on complex verb morphology in the generation of semantic values, and observe frequent noun ellipsis (when compared to English).

17   The 'things have names' stage, also referred to as the 'naming spurt', typically occurs between nine and 13 months. By 13 months, the child has 'objectified' the referent–vehicle (sign) relationship, and realizes she or he can substitute a sign for a thing in communication, while at the same time realizing the referent and sign are not the same.

18   Examples of means–end tasks Gopnik and Meltzoff employed are 'using a string vertically to obtain an object attached to it'; 'using a stick to obtain an out-of-reach object'; and 'stacking a set of rings on a post, avoiding one solid ring'. The authors note that 'these tasks may be solved using either a trial-and-error groping or immediately, in an insightful manner', and that for their study, 'only immediate, insightful solutions were counted' (Gopnik and Meltzoff 1993: 226).

19   Slobin is emphasizing the learning of L2 conceptual categories in adult populations. He cautiously proposes that plural and instrumental markers would not be particularly difficult on a conceptual level since they 'may be obvious on non-linguistic grounds'. This does not imply that adult second language learners will necessarily remember to mark obligatory categories in their L2, a separate issue Slobin addressses as the matter of 'automizing attention' (Slobin 1996: 94).

20   In a related vein, Kramsch discusses the problem that too often, language 'teachers teach language and culture, or culture in language, but not language as culture' (Kramsch 1995b: 83).

21   Berlin and Kay (1969) point out evidence for parameters constraining the semantics of color terms. But as Hanks (1996) notes, the Berlin and Kay study, important as it is, disproves linguistic determinism rather than substantively addresses the concept of relativity. In other words, semantic universals and language differences influencing habitualized perceptions of the world are not exclusive to one another.

22   I use 'mind' following Wertsch (1991: 14), who describes it thus: 'mind is viewed here as something that "extends beyond the skin" in at least two senses: it is often socially distributed and it is connected to the notion of mediation ... mental functioning is viewed as being shaped or even defined by the mediational means it employs to carry out a task.'

23   Subaltern historiography is an intellectual project aimed at articulating the hidden players in history, usually women, the lower classes, and

generally less represented communities. Edward Said describes it thus: 'Subaltern studies represents a crossing of boundaries, a smuggling of ideas across lines, a stirring up of intellectual and, as always, political complacence' (1988: x). It is in the spirit of crossing boundaries and forging novel alliances that I reference subaltern studies/historiography.

11 From input to affordance: Social-interactive learning from an ecological perspective

Leo van Lier
Monterey Institute of International Studies

Introduction

In this chapter I want to present some arguments for an ecological way of researching, practicing, and conceptualizing language learning (first, second, and foreign). In themselves my proposals may not be very revolutionary, since they refer to well-established traditions in various fields, though perhaps less so in educational linguistics. However, I wish to suggest that an ecological approach can unite a number of well-established views on language learning, especially when this ecological approach is anchored in an ecological worldview. In particular I will suggest that the work of Vygotsky and Bakhtin, dating from the early decades of the twentieth century, illustrates an ecological approach to cognition, learning, and language.

An ecological approach to language learning questions some basic assumptions that lie behind most of the rationalist and empiricist theories and practices that dominate in our field, and offers fresh ways of looking at some old questions that have been around for a long time. I will argue that ecology is a fruitful way to understand and build on the legacy that Vygotsky, Bakhtin, and also their American contemporaries Peirce, Mead, and Dewey, left for us.

My arguments for an ecological approach are based on a critique of three premises underlying standard scientific thinking. The first premise is that behind the diversity in language learning theories and teaching procedures there lies, as a rarely questioned backdrop, the scientific perspective that has dominated Western civilization since the days of Galileo and Descartes. According to this perspective, scientific work must have the following three characteristics (cf. Checkland 1981):

1 in order to conduct coherent investigations it is necessary to simplify and select from the infinite variety of the real world;

2 in accordance with Occam's razor, the simplest explanations that minimally account for the data are to be preferred;

3 problems must be broken down into their component elements and these must be analyzed one by one.

The scientific approach has led to enormous advances in physics, engineering, technology, and other 'hard' fields of inquiry. As a result the science of physics has served as an example for all other sciences and would-be sciences in terms of precision, rigor, and success. As the New Zealand physicist Lord Rutherford put it, 'There is physics, and there is stamp collecting' (Checkland 1981: 52). The supremacy of physics is no longer as strong now, and it has arguably been eclipsed in recent decades by biology, necessitating a reexamination of the methods by which scientific research is conducted (Capra 1996).

The second premise is that, regardless of the particular views of teaching and learning that are espoused by language learning professionals, it is generally taken for granted that learning takes place in the brain, by means of computational mechanisms that process information that is received by the senses. Whether the perspective is constructivist, behaviorist, or nativist, the underlying view of learning is that information is received and subsequently processed in the brain and incorporated into mental structures providing knowledge and skills of various kinds (cf. Donato's term 'input crunching', 1994: 34).

The third and final premise, related to the previous one, is that activity and interaction, or in general the contexts in which learning takes place, relate to learning in indirect ways, by feeding into the cognitive processes that are going on in the brain and mind of the learner, the mind being basically the same as the brain, but at some abstract level.

An ecological approach to language learning challenges the three premises that I have briefly described above. First, it shifts the emphasis from scientific reductionism to the notion of emergence. Instead of assuming that every phenomenon can be explained in terms of simpler phenomena or components, it says that at every level of development properties emerge that cannot be reduced to those of prior levels. Second, ecology says that not all of cognition and learning can be explained in terms of processes that go on inside the head. Finally, an ecological approach asserts that the perceptual and social activity of the learner, and particularly the verbal and nonverbal interaction in which the learner engages, are central to an understanding of learning. In other words, they do not just facilitate learning, they *are* learning in a fundamental way.

From an ecological perspective, the learner is immersed in an environment full of potential meanings. These meanings become available gradually as the learner acts and interacts within and with this environment. Learning is not a holus-bolus or piecemeal migration of meanings to the inside of the learner's head, but rather the development of increasingly effective ways of dealing with the world and its meanings. Therefore, to look for learning is to look at the active learner in her environment, not at the contents of her brain. To borrow a quote from Mace (1974), 'Ask not what's inside your head, ask what your head's inside of' (quoted in Reber 1993: 58).

This does not mean that learners are merely empty heads[1] that reverberate harmoniously with the environment. Rather, it means that cognition and learning rely on both representational (schematic, historical, cultural, and so on) and ecological (perceptual, emergent, action-based) processes and systems (Neisser 1992). Language itself is therefore also both representational and ecological. Its definition, its structure, and its use are inherently dialogical, as Bakhtin already saw (1981), and as was immanent, if not always explicit, in Peirce's semiotic scheme (Merrell 1997b).

In the following pages I will sketch some of the major features of an ecological approach to language learning, and show how it relates to the Vygotskyan sociocultural theory illustrated in the other chapters of this book. I will argue that it is necessary to reconceptualize language, context, and learning in profound ways if we wish to reap the benefits of the visions presented at the beginning of the twentieth century by Bakhtin, Dewey, Peirce, Vygotsky, and others, whose message has once again become prominent. I will also argue that an ecological approach suggests new ways of doing research. As a starting point I will examine the notion of interaction, since its importance for learning is an area of common ground for most perspectives on language learning, however different their explanations and procedures might otherwise be.

Interaction

The role of interaction is prominent in most current perspectives on SLA (for recent overviews see Long 1996; Gass 1997). Interaction is of course also a central ingredient in sociocultural theory and in the ecological perspective I advance in this chapter. However, the nature of the role of interaction, or the precise ways in which it relates to SLA, are interpreted in different ways by these perspectives.

The best-developed perspective on interaction, illustrated in the work of Gass (1997), Long (1996), Pica (see Pica *et al.* 1996, for a recent study) and others, adheres to the three premises I stated in the introduction. From all the complex phenomena that may occur in interaction, the notion of negotiation of meaning is highlighted as being indicative of learning processes at work, or at least as a likely candidate for learning opportunities. The reason is that in negotiating meaning a piece of language that was not comprehensible before, now becomes comprehensible as a result of negotiation work and can thus be incorporated into the learner's target-language repertoire. But in addition, as Long points out in his 'updated version of the interaction hypothesis' (1996: 453),

> ... negotiation for meaning, and especially negotiation work that triggers interactional adjustments by the NS or more competent interlocutor, facilitates acquisition because it connects input, internal learner capacities, particularly selective attention, and output in productive ways.
>
> (Long 1996: 451–2)

Negotiation of this kind therefore bestows three benefits upon SLA: improved comprehensibility of input, enhanced attention, and the need to produce output. A further assumption is that the learner can learn best from negotiating with a native speaker or a more competent interlocutor, presumably because knowledge has to come from one who knows or can do more. Interestingly, in a study by Pica *et al.* (1996), some suggestions surface that may indicate that learners can be effective in assisting each other in communicating meaningfully. However, here too the effectiveness of the learners' inter-actions with one another is evaluated by comparing them to equivalent interactions with NS, and the latter are thus treated as the yardstick of what has 'been shown to be effective' (Pica *et al.* 1996: 79). This leaves open and unaddressed the possibility that in learner–learner interaction other meaning-making and language-learning processes may occur that are different from, but not necessary less beneficial than, those in NS/NNS interaction.[2]

Occam's razor states that simpler explanations are to be preferred over more complex ones, so long as they account for the data. But the razor is in fact a double-edged sword, since in practice there may be a 'conspiracy' effect between the explanation and the data. The 'simplest explanation that accounts for the data' is applied to data that have been extracted from complex processes because of prior assumptions regarding their (the data's) significance. Thus the data encourage the 'simplest explanation' and the 'prior assump-tions' to become identical. As a result research runs the danger of becoming locked into a reductionism from which it may be hard to break away.

The simplest explanation in this case would be to expect evidence of learning in learners' utterances subsequent to, and as a result of, negotiation cycles. Both Long (1996: 449) and Pica (1992: 227) point out the dangers inherent in this, and they stress that only longitudinal data can show evidence of sustained acquisition. The problem is that once the longitudinal evidence is in, it will be very difficult to link it incontrovertibly to the negotiation work of yesteryear.

Compounding the problem is the fact that prior theoretical assumptions lead to the selection or design of interactional contexts that favor the occurrence of phenomena that are theoretically assumed to be valuable. In this case, the assumption is that learning occurs when something that is defective is replaced with something that is fixed or improved. This replacement is possible as a result of the transfer of information from a person who knows more (an NS, or a more competent NNS) to the learner, who knows less. Learning occurs when the learner receives and processes information that comes from an interlocutor who has knowledge and skills at a higher level than the learner does.

From this perspective, tasks that require a great deal of negotiation—in the sense of interactional work aimed at resolving communication problems—provide more learning opportunities than general conversation. As Long puts it:

> ... the role of free conversation is notoriously poor as a context for driving interlanguage development ... in contrast, tasks that orient participants to shared goals and involve them in some work or activity produce more negotiation work ... When working cooperatively on certain kinds of problem-solving tasks ... participants' conversational feet are held to the fire ... .

(Long 1996: 448)

To illustrate some of the issues involved, let us look at some examples of learner interaction. First, here is an extract illustrating negotiation of meaning between an NS and an NNS engaged in a two-way communication gap task, from Pica.

(1)   NNS: so there's a cross in the center of the paper
      NS: what do you mean by cross?
      NNS: traffic cross
      NS: oh, where people can cross or a traffic light
      NNS: yes

(Pica 1992: 218)

By way of comparison, here is an extract from a conversational interaction between two learners, from van Lier and Matsuo:

(2)   424 Y: Wow, how long does it take to from here?
      425 I: Ah, ten years about ten years.
      426 Y: ͤto Korea. About ten years? About ten days?
      427 I: Ten days. (laughter) I'm very (xxx)
      428 Y: Yeah, ten days.
      429 I: ͤten days.
      430 Y: Wow, it's airmail?
      431 I: Yes.
      432 Y: O::h, that's long time.
      433 I: Yes. Very long time. I-
      434 Y: From here to Japan, about it takes about 5 day—usually 5 days
      435   or 6 days
      436 I: ͤo::h, very fast.

(van Lier and Matsuo 2000)

And finally, an extract from a conversation between a learner and a native speaker:

(3)   NS: So what made you decide to get into journalism?
      NNS: Um, I think, uh, if I may be a journalist
      NS: Uh-huh
      NNS: so I can I can work by myself. Uh, I mean, uh, I don't need to, uh
             work for a company?

(van Lier and Matsuo 2000)

We note that in (1) there is a clear example of negotiation for meaning. In (2) there is also such a negotiation (in 425–8). However, in the second extract this negotiation is embedded in a lot of other talk involving comparisons between airmail to two countries, expressions of surprise, evaluations of content, and so on. If that is common in conversation (van Lier and Matsuo 2000 suggest that it is), then given an arbitrary piece of discourse, there may be more instances of negotiation of this type (repair negotiation, as it is called in Nakahama, Tyler, and van Lier 1998), in communication gap tasks, since in conversation such negotiations tend to be part of a lot of other talk, because there is much more work to be done in conversation than exchanging inform-ation to be entered on a piece of paper.

Looking next at (3), we see here no instance at all of repair negotiation. However, that does not mean that the interlocutors are doing no work. In fact, the NNS is doing considerable linguistic work here explaining why she wants to be a journalist. In addition, she is negotiating her social self, her identity, establishing who she is and why she makes the choices in her life that she makes. I would say that her conversational feet are in fact held to the fire here. Indeed, if I may elasticize Long's metaphor, the NNS here wants to make sure she does not put her conversational feet in her mouth, because there is a personal investment in the information she constructs for her interlocutor.

To sum up, the ecological approach faces a considerable challenge. By studying the interaction in its totality, the researcher must attempt to show the emergence of learning, the location of learning opportunities, the peda-gogical value of various interactional contexts and processes, and the effectiveness of pedagogical strategies. No ready-made research procedures exist for this sort of work (the ethological approach to biological research in particular ecosystems may come closest), but it is my assumption that it is worthwhile to look for such an approach, and I assume further that the work of Vygotsky, Bakhtin, C. S. Peirce and others at the beginning of the twentieth century is going to be of considerable value in this pursuit. In the following section I will sketch some of the main features of an ecological approach to language learning research.

Ecology

The field of ecology[3] dates back to at least around the middle of the nineteenth century, when the term was invented by the German biologist Ernst Haeckel (1886; see Arndt and Janney 1983) to refer to the totality of relationships of an organism with all other organisms with which it comes into contact. Its core meaning relates to the study and management of the environment (ecosphere, or biosphere) or specific ecosystems. However, it is also used to denote a worldview that is completely different from the scientific or rational one inherited from Descartes, which assumes that it is the right and destiny of the human race to control and exploit the earth and all its inanimate and animate resources (the *anthropocentric* worldview). The ecological worldview is, by contrast, *ecocentric* or *geocentric*, and it assumes, similar to the belief systems of indigenous peoples, that humans are part of a greater natural order, or even a great living system, Gaia or living earth (see Lovelock 1979; Capra 1996; Goldsmith 1998). This view of ecology is called *deep ecology* by the Norwegian philosopher Arne Naess, and is contrasted with *shallow ecology*, which merely studies ways of controlling ecosystems and managing them, including the prevention and treatment of environmental damage and disasters (Allen and Hoekstra 1992).

The reader may well ask at this point, what does this have to do with language learning? An idealistic answer might be: 'Everything' and a practical answer might be: 'Nothing', but this is not a debate I wish to enter into here.[4] Rather, I will focus on ecology as a specific way to study cognition, language, and learning.

There are several influential psychological approaches that have been referred to as ecological. Among the best-known ones are Gibson's theory of visual perception (1979), Bronfenbrenner's approach to the study of child development (1979), and Lewin's pioneering studies of social contexts (for example, the 'life space') through action research (1943). Recent ecological work in psychology and learning includes Neisser (1992), Bronfenbrenner and Ceci (1994), Cole (1996), and Reed (1996).

In linguistics, early references relating ecology and language are Trim (1959) and Haugen (1972), and recent work explicitly using the ecological label includes Makkai (1993) and Mühlhäusler (1996). Other approaches to linguistics with a strong ecological 'flavor'[5] include Halliday (1994), Yngve (1996), and Lamb (1999).

An ecological linguistics is a study of language as relations (of thought, action, power), rather than as objects (words, sentences, rules). It also relates verbal utterances to other aspects of meaning making, such as gestures, drawings, artifacts, etc. (Kress, Martins, and Ogborn 1998; McCafferty 1998; McCafferty and Ahmed this volume). So, when a young woman explains to her friend how she and her boyfriend moved a new bathtub into a small bathroom (they are remodeling their apartment), she not only uses words to explain how they did this, but she makes a drawing on a piece of paper, and uses frequent gestures to indicate turning over, moving sideways, tilting, bumping into and damaging walls, and so on. Her interlocutor, likewise, uses words, backchannels, gestures, and expressions of empathy to indicate appreciation, understanding, or the need for more elaboration. The totality of meaning-making in this conversation is not merely linguistic; it is semiotic.

In terms of learning, language emerges out of semiotic activity. The context is not just there to provide input (linguistic models or objects) to a passive recipient. The environment provides a 'semiotic budget' (analogous to the energy budget of an ecosystem) within which the active learner engages in meaning-making activities together with others, who may be more, equally, or less competent in linguistic terms. The semiotic budget does not refer to the amount of 'input' available, nor the amount of input that is enhanced for comprehension, but to the opportunities for meaningful action that the situation affords.

I will return to this notion of ecological learning later in this chapter, but first I will explore the notion of *affordance* as an alternative to *input*.

Affordance

The word affordance was coined by the psychologist James Gibson to refer to a reciprocal relationship between an organism and a particular feature of its environment (1979). An affordance is a particular property of the environment that is relevant—for good or for ill—to an active, perceiving organism in that environment. An affordance affords further action (but does not cause or trigger it). What becomes an affordance depends on what the organism does, what it wants, and what is useful for it. In the forest a leaf can offer very different affordances to different organisms. It can offer crawling on for a tree frog, cutting for an ant, food for a caterpillar, shade for a spider, medicine for a shaman, and so on. In all cases, the leaf is the same: its properties do not change; it is just that different properties are perceived and acted upon by different organisms. Parallels to language can easily be drawn. If the language learner is active and engaged, she will perceive linguistic affordances and use them for linguistic action.

In Gibson's ecological theory of perception, an affordance is a property of neither the actor nor of an object: it is a relationship between the two. Many such relationships have been researched since Gibson's pioneering work with airforce pilots during the 1940s and 1950s. One example is the simple action of walking through a doorway. It appears that people rotate their shoulders before going through a doorway if the doorway is less than 1.3 times the width of their shoulders. So, doorways afford passing, but the way that they do this depends on their size as well as ours. Another example is a hermit crab looking for a bigger home. Hermit crabs are vulnerable animals that live in shells that they find on the ocean floor. When they grow too big for their shell they have to look for a bigger one. When they encounter a potential new home, they will first crawl over it a number of times, then turn it around and around, examine it from all angles, then probe its insides, and finally make a judgment regarding its suitability. This is a high-stakes pursuit, because if the new shell does not fit, the crab might not be able to make a swift move, and it is likely to end up as another animal's meal. The crab's activity, then, explores the affordances of the manipulated object.

The construct of affordance is relevant to language learning in several different ways. As I indicated above, an ecological view of language is a relational, not a material one. This means that language learning is not a process of representing linguistic objects in the brain on the basis of input received. But it is easier to say what language learning is not than what it is, in ecological terms. What does it mean to know a language, if not to possess a store of linguistic structures, rules, words, phrases, and so on? What are the linguistic contents of the mind? This is not an easy question to answer, either for the cognitivist or for the ecologist. I suppose that the ecologist will say that knowledge of language for a human is like knowledge of the jungle for an animal. The animal does not 'have' the jungle; it knows how to use the jungle and how to live in it. Perhaps we can say by analogy that we do not 'have' or 'possess' language, but that we learn to use it and to 'live in it'. Taking a semiotic perspective, we might amplify, and place language inside a more general scheme of sign-making systems.

The centrality of interaction in the concept of affordance is highlighted in the description given in Varela, Thompson, and Rosch: 'affordances consist in the opportunities for interaction that things in the environment possess relative to the sensorimotor capacities of the animal' (1991: 203). In terms of language learning, the environment is full of language that provides opportunities for learning to the active, participating learner. The linguistic world to which the learner has access, and in which she becomes actively engaged, is 'full of demands and requirements, opportunities and limitations, rejections and invitations, enablements and constraints—in short, affordances' (Shotter and Newson 1982:34). From the pedagogical perspective, the message may be to provide a rich 'semiotic budget', as I called it above, and to structure the learner's activities and participation so that access is available and engagement encouraged. This brings ecological language learning in line with proposals for situated learning (and 'legitimate peripheral participation') by Lave and Wenger (1991), and the guided participation, apprenticeship, and participatory appropriation described by Rogoff (1995).

In Gibson's ecological psychology, as in the work of Vygotsky, Bakhtin, and their respective followers, the unit of analysis is not the perceived object or linguistic *input*, but the active learner, or the *activity* itself.[6] As Vygotsky put it, eyes, hand, and speech unite when the child is engaged in practical tasks, and it is this 'newborn unity of perception, speech and action' that 'constitutes the real and vital object of analysis' (Vygotsky and Luria 1994: 109). This view brings Vygotsky close to the ecological psychology of Gibson.

Language learning, context, and complexity

In Vygotsky's vision of human development, language and thought emerge (and merge) through the child's engagement in human activity, both with physical objects and artifacts (tools), and with social, historical, and cultural practices (signs). The development of higher mental functions is possible because of an increasing interdependence of speech and thought, and because it is mediated by signs (including, but not only, linguistic ones). This development proceeds through the internalization of activities that are first realized in social interaction (Bakhurst 1991: 83).

A number of researchers in developmental psychology see the context in which development and learning take place as crucial and even defining. This trend, which diverges from the highly acclaimed cognitive revolution that started in the 1960s, has led to a debate between cognitive and situative (or contextualized) perspectives on learning research (Greeno 1997). The former are often called constructivist, Piagetian, or neo-Piagetian approaches that place an emphasis on the computational processes that happen in the brain, whereas the latter are social-constructivist or constructionist approaches that see a strong role for social and other contextual processes. Bakhtin's dialogical view of language, Vygotsky's sociocultural theory, and the various manifestations of ecological theory are at the contextual or situative end of the spectrum, even though they do not necessarily deny a central role to cognitive processes (Neisser 1992).

As I mentioned in the introduction, a scientific approach to language learning research assumes that learning is the result of computational processes in the brain. An ecological alternative to such a view of learning as brain-resident is the bioecological model developed by Bronfenbrenner (Bronfenbrenner 1979, 1993; Bronfenbrenner and Ceci 1994). Bronfenbrenner has developed a model of hierarchically nested ecosystems, and a methodology for investigating contextualized learning that has the notions of person, process, context, time, and outcome as a checklist of concerns. Learning contexts are described in this work as proximal processes, analogous to Vygotsky's Zone of Proximal Development (the ZPD). In the bioecological model, such contexts are effective if they encourage the realization of

1 differentiated perception and response

2 directing and controlling one's own behavior

3 coping successfully under stress

4 acquiring knowledge and skill

5 establishing and maintaining mutually rewarding relationships

6 modifying and constructing one's own physical, social, and symbolic environment.

These features of proximal learning contexts can serve as a guide for the identification of learning opportunities in classrooms, particularly if the research is conducted in the framework of Bronfenbrenner's 'PPCT' recommendations, in which an integral focus on *person, process, context,* and *time* is emphasized (Bronfenbrenner 1993).

Ecological research asks the questions. How does learning emerge? What are the overt signs of its processes at work? What evidence can be gathered to document learning? One of Wittgenstein's dictums is that 'there are remarks that sow and remarks that reap' (1980: 78). In our language learning research we have traditionally tended to look for evidence of the 'reaping' kind, tangible and countable linguistic objects of some kind. However, it seems to me that we need to learn to identify 'sowing' events, which lead to the emergence of complex language as a result of activity in proximal contexts such as those that Bronfenbrenner describes. Vygotsky's innovative use of experiments is an illustration of such a focus on emergent qualities of learning. He believed that mental abilities should be studied by analyzing their development in the context of interaction with others. The ZPD was created as a context in which careful intervention would stimulate internalization, and the insights were reported by the detailed description of particular cases rather than quantification and statistical analysis (Bakhurst 1991: 83).

What are the patterns of emergence of language? Gibson notes two broad organizational phases of language: the indicational and the predicational phase (Reed 1996). I think it is reasonable to add another phase before that: the intersubjective phase. The first significant linguistic activity of a child is intersubjective dyadic interaction (through gestures, gaze, vocalizations) with a caregiver (Trevarthen 1990). At around nine months a new ability emerges: triadic interaction, or the ability to focus jointly with a caregiver on an object or event, and with increasing mobility (the child can now move around and go to and around objects) this turns into various kinds of dynamic interaction (Reed 1996). Indicational language is characterized by selecting and pointing out objects and events in social interaction, and sharing the affordances of the environment. At around two years of age, language is beginning to be used in predicational ways. Children begin to use speech to express their needs, plans, rules of games, and conversations, etc., and are confronted with the needs, plans, etc. of others. The largely lexical composition of the indicational phase is now transformed and grammar emerges, spurred by the use of specific verbs for specific purposes (Tomasello 1992; Reed 1996).

This short account of language development as consisting of intersubjectivity, indicativity, and predicativity places language development within the bodily, social, and mental development of the child. It is ecological and semiotic in the sense that it is perceptual, contextual, social. It relates the emergence of language both to social relationships and to the developing skills of movement around objects and into different physical and social spaces, and to gestures. It suggests a broad development from firstness (quality, feeling—or iconicity) to secondness (change, reaction, recognition, comparison—or indexicality) to thirdness (rule, reason, habit—or symbolicity) in the Peircean sense, though the growth of signs is certainly far too complex and dynamic to be expressed so simply in three large blocks.

If first language development proceeds somewhat in the manner depicted here, this does not of course mean that second language development should proceed in a similar manner. However, there are several interesting possibilities that ecological research can investigate. One is the relation between gestures and developing second language speech. At the indicational level, for example, the use of pointing to objects as related to vocabulary development can be explored. This may seem rather a 'Me Tarzan, You Jane' approach, but in the context of collaborative work at the computer I have noted a great deal of this indicational (deictic, indexical) work going on at the early stages of second language development. Gestures, pictures, and objects all blend with language in the communicative context, and even first language use can be seen as a semiotic system that supports emerging second language use (Brooks, Donato, and McGlone 1997).

Setting up tasks and activities to promote triadic and dynamic interaction rather than dyadic interaction may be an interesting avenue to explore. We may find, for example, that many of the two-way communication tasks that are popular in second language classrooms are essentially dyadic. Even though there may be a picture that needs to be matched, the view of the partner's picture is often blocked so that only the partner's face is visible. This makes indicational language processes difficult and tortured, and that which would normally be accomplished in a triadic format is forced into a dyadic format. This may be considered an advantage, in that it forces participants into a predicational mode (they *have* to use grammar) since they cannot rely on an indicational mode (communicating by pointing), yet we must consider the possibility that predicational processes do not automatically emerge when indicational resources are perceptually curtailed.

Such observations open up new avenues for research. However, the way in which to research them is by no means clear-cut. Here again we can get useful ideas from Vygotsky. It has often been noted that his descriptions of experiments are highly unorthodox and lacking in apparent rigor. However, as Bakhurst points out, Vygotsky was focused on the emergence of capacities, not their products, and this led him to introduce interventions and to describe the results of those interventions in detail (Bakhurst 1991: 83). His research was therefore ecological, and similar in many respects to Lewin's action research.

Recent developments in systems theory and complexity theory (Larsen-Freeman 1997) offer a range of suggestions to develop new approaches to research which build on Vygotsky's pioneering experiments. I have already mentioned Bronfenbrenner and Ceci's indicators of effective functioning in proximal contexts, and their investigative principles of *person, process, context* and *time* (and a later addition, *outcome*). I have suggested elsewhere that these principles can be productively combined with a systems approach to education, using the practical model developed by systems analyst Peter Checkland, which consists of a range of procedures to be applied in cyclical or parallel fashion: perceiving, predicating, comparing, deciding, acting, and evaluating (Checkland 1981; van Lier 1999).

We are some distance away from developing effective research procedures and strategies for ecological research, though this should not deter us from exploring in the directions outlined above. Indeed, only by investigating language learning in context, and documenting this context as carefully as possible, can we find out what the value of an ecological approach might be. In this endeavor we can find considerable inspiration in the research practices of Vygotsky himself, as well as a number of different strands of research in the decades following him, by developmental researchers, educational anthropologists, psychologists, discourse analysts, etc. (see Wold 1992a; Wozniak and Fischer 1993) as well as work in sociocultural theory itself (Moll 1990; Lantolf and Appel 1994b; and studies in this volume).

Conclusion

In this chapter I have drawn connections between Vygotskyan approaches to learning and an ecological-semiotic framework based on the work of Bakhtin, Bronfenbrenner, Gibson, Peirce, among others. Currently, most of the discussion in our field is based on an input–output metaphor of learning and cognition, in which mind and brain are seen as the 'containers' of both learning processes and learning products.

The ecological perspective questions the common assumption that language, cognitions, memories, and intelligence are uniquely contained inside the brain, and that learning consists of various ways of putting them there. We have to learn to understand what Harold Garfinkel meant when he said that, to find answers to our questions, 'there is no reason to look under the skull since nothing of interest is to be found there but brains' (1963: 190).

I have suggested that the notion of input can be replaced by the ecological notion of affordance, which refers to the relationship between properties of the environment and the active learner. Two important concepts for investigation in an ecological view are perception and action (and the relations between them). Speaking of young children, Butterworth puts the issue as follows:

> On the ecological view, perception is necessarily situated within the ecology since it consists in obtaining information from the active relation between the organism and a structured environment. Indeed, it is the process of perception that situates the organism in the environment. The evidence from infancy suggests that perception is a 'module' or component of the

cognitive system that is antecedent to thought and language and that may contribute to the mastery of reasoning.

(Butterworth 1992: 3)

We must not assume that adults learn language the same way that children do, nor of course that L1 learning is the same as L2 learning. Vygotsky found that, whereas children showed both unmediated and mediated attention in their activities, for adults all attention was mediated (van der Veer and Valsiner 1991: 236). Along similar lines, Gibson (1979) argued that all linguistic affordances are socially mediated. This does not mean, in my view, that direct perception of linguistic and more generally semiotic signs is not available to L2 learners and adults. Communicative actions and events are directly perceived, and carry deep meanings at emotional and intuitive levels (Vygotsky 1978). However, these direct perceptions of meanings in the environment—'firstnesses' in Peirce's scheme—are combined with, folded into, and integrated in social, cultural, and symbolic meanings that are largely brought along and shaped by language itself. This is precisely the power of the Peircean semiotic: the fluidity and transformative quality of the sign, which is always engendered into more complex signs, which in turn can be de-engendered into simpler signs, so that, for example, a simple artifact or saying can grow into a cultural symbol, and this in turn can condense into a cultural icon (Merrell 1997a).

I assume that the indexical plane is the way into language, the 'workbench' so to speak: the first job for language is to indicate and index the world (Vygotsky 1978: 35). Soon however, more complex symbolic meanings enter into the picture, both in terms of linguistic normativity (habit and structure) and linguistic creativity (variety and invention), roughly paralleling Bakhtin's centripetal and centrifugal forces of language (1981).[7] At the same time, however, the iconic plane remains very much a vital force, even though it appears to run underground and often defies verbalization. The iconic qualities of language speak through gestures and expressions, but also of course through creative language use, from banter and puns to poetry and songs. For the newborn infant, however, the iconic qualities of language are all there is to language, and this iconic substrate may do more to shape our semiotic world than we can ever know.

To end on a more practical note, an ecological approach to language learning avoids a narrow interpretation of language as words that are transmitted through the air, on paper, or along wires from a sender to a receiver. It also avoids seeing learning as something that happens exclusively inside a person's head. Ecological educators see language and learning as relationships among learners and between learners and the environment. This does not deny cognitive processes, but it connects those cognitive processes with social processes. Language is also connected with kinesic, prosodic, and other visual and auditory sources of meaning, and as a result of this contextualized and process-oriented thinking new ways of practicing and theorizing language education will emerge.

The ecological perspective thus places a strong emphasis on contextualizing language into other semiotic systems, and into the contextual world as a whole. It also calls for a reexamination of assessment practices that attempt to locate success in the solitary performance of a learner, and of teaching practices that are cast in the form of 'instructional delivery systems'. Perhaps, after all, we 'learn' language in the same way that an animal 'learns' the forest, or a plant 'learns' the soil.

Notes

1 Nor that heads come fully loaded (for example, with a linguistic 'instinct', see Pinker 1994), as some innatists believe, and only need minimal triggering from the environment to grow to their full functionality.
2 For examples and discussion of learner–learner interaction in L1 settings, see Barnes and Todd 1978; Mercer 1995; for L2 settings, see Brooks, Donato, and McGlone 1997; van Lier and Matsuo 2000.
3 The word *eco* is derived from a Greek word meaning *household*.
4 I do not wish to deny the importance of this question. The relationships between ecology and education are explored in the work of C. A. Bowers (Bowers 1993; Bowers and Flinders 1990), which is strongly influenced by Gregory Bateson (1979).
5 Systemic networks, patterning, and linguistic relations between speakers and their environment are all aspects of an ecological way of looking at language. One might of course argue that all study of language and context (hence, all of sociolinguistics, discourse analysis, and pragmatics) is ecological in some sense, but this might be carrying the ecological metaphor too far. To be useful and distinctive, ecological linguistics may start off by defining language as the totality of linguistic activities and relationships among speakers and between speakers and the physical, social, personal, cultural, and historical world they live in. A ramshackle enough definition, but one that I believe does not violate the work of the linguists mentioned.
6 Both Vygotsky and Bakhtin often use the *word* as a unit of analysis. However, the term word often appears to be coterminous with utterance, discourse, and activity in their definition (in line with the original meaning of the Greek word *logos*).
7 Bakhtin considered the struggle between centripetal and centrifugal forces the energizing principle of all linguistic life. Centripetal forces are those that pull 'inwards', toward homogeneity, unification, habits, prescriptive-ness, etc., whereas centrifugal forces are those that pull 'outwards', toward diversity, creativity, variety, etc. (Bakhtin 1981); see also van Lier 1996: 183–4).

Bibliography

Ahmed, M. 1988. *Speaking as Cognitive Regulation: A Study of L1 and L2 Dyadic Problem-solving Activity.* Unpublished doctoral dissertation. University of Delaware: Newark, DE.

Ahmed, M. K. 1994. 'Speaking as cognitive regulation: A Vygotskian perspective on dialogic communication' in J. P. Lantolf and G. Appel (eds.): *Vygotskian Approaches to Second Language Research.* Norwood, NJ: Ablex.

Alderson, J. C., C. Clapham, and D. Steel. 1998. 'Metalinguistic knowledge, language aptitude and language proficiency'. *Language Teaching Research* 1: 93–121.

Aljaafreh, A. and J. P. Lantolf. 1994. 'Negative feedback as regulation and second language learning in the zone of proximal development'. *The Modern Language Journal* 78: 465–83.

Allen, T. F. H. and T. W. Hoekstra. 1992. *Toward a Unified Ecology.* New York, NY: Columbia University Press.

Al-shabbi, A. E. 1993. 'Gesture in the communicative language teaching classroom'. *TESOL Journal* 2: 16–19.

Anderson, J. 1983. *The Architecture of Cognition.* Cambridge, MA: Harvard University Press.

Antón, M. and F. DiCamilla. 1998 'Socio-cognitive functions of L1 collaborative interaction in the L2 classroom'. *The Canadian Modern Language Review* 54/3: 314–42.

Antonek, J. L., D. E. McCormick, and R. Donato. 1997. 'The student teacher portfolio as autobiography: Developing a professional identity'. *The Modern Language Journal* 81: 15–27.

Anzaldúa, G. 1987. *Borderlands/La Frontera: The New Mestiza.* San Francisco, CA: Spinsters/Aunt Lute.

Appel, G. 1986. *L1 and L2 narrative and expository discourse production: A Vygotskian analysis.* Unpublished doctoral dissertation, University of Delaware, Newark, DE.

Appel, G. and J. P. Lantolf. 1994. 'Speaking as mediation: A study of L1 and L2 recall tasks'. *The Modern Language Journal* 78/4: 437–52.

Arievitch. I. and R. van der Veer. 1995. 'Furthering the internalization debate: Gal'perin's contribution'. *Human Development* 38: 113–26.

Arndt, H. and R. W. Janney. 1983. 'The duck-rabbit phenomenon: Notes on the disambiguation of ambiguous utterances' in W. Enninger and L. M. Haynes (eds.): *Studies in Language Ecology.* Wiesbaden: Franz Steiner Verlag.

Auerbach, E. 1989. 'Toward a socio-contextual approach to family literacy'. *Harvard Educational Review* 59: 165–81.

Baars, B. 1997. *In the Theater of Consciousness.* New York, NY: Oxford University Press.

Bachman, L. F. 1990. *Fundamental Considerations in Language Testing.* Oxford: Oxford University Press.

Bachman, L. F. 1991. 'What does language testing have to offer?' *TESOL Quarterly* 25: 671–704.

Bailey, K. 1983. 'Competitiveness and anxiety in adult second language learning: Looking at and through the diary studies' in H. Selinger and M. Long (eds.): *Classroom Oriented Research in Second Language Acquisition*. Rowley, MA: Newbury House.

Bailey, K. M. and **D. Nunan** (eds.) 1996. *Voices from the Language Classroom*. Cambridge: Cambridge University Press.

Bakhtin, M. 1981. *The Dialogic Imagination, Four Essays by M. M. Bakhtin*. M. Holquist (ed.) and C. Emerson (translator). Austin, TX: University of Texas Press.

Bakhtin, M. 1986. *Speech Genres and Other Late Essays*. Austin, TX: University of Texas Press.

Bakhurst, D. 1991. *Consciousness and Revolution in Soviet Philosophy. From the Bolsheviks to Evald Ilyenkov*. Cambridge: Cambridge University Press.

Bamberg, M. 1997. 'Oral versions of personal experience: Three decades of narrative analysis'. *Journal of Narrative and Life History* 7: 1–4.

Barnes, D. and **F. Todd.** 1978. *Discussion and Learning in Small Groups*. London: Routledge.

Barthes, R. 1975. *The Pleasure of the Text*. New York, NY: Hill and Wang.

Bates, E. and **B. McWhinney.** 1981. 'Second language acquisition from a functionalist perspective: Pragmatics, semantics and perceptual strategies' in H. Winitz (ed.): *Annals of the New York Academy of Sciences Conferences on Native Language and Foreign Language Acquisition*. New York, NY: New York Academy of Sciences.

Bateson, G. 1979. *Mind and Nature: A Necessary Unity*. London: Fontana.

Bauman, R. 1986. *Story, Performance and Event: Contextual Studies of Oral Narrative*. Cambridge: Cambridge University Press.

Beach, K. 1995. 'Activity as a mediator of sociocultural change and individual development: The case of school-work transition in Nepal'. *Mind, Culture, and Activity* 2: 285–302.

Becker, A. L. 1982. 'Beyond translation: Esthetics and language description' in H. Byrnes (ed.): *Contemporary Perceptions of Language: Interdisciplinary Dimensions*. Georgetown University Round Table on Languages and Linguistics 1982. Washington, DC: Georgetown University Press.

Bellah, R., R. Madsen, W. Sullivan, A. Swidler, and **S. Tipton.** 1985. *Habits of the Heart. Individualism and Commitment in American Life*. Berkeley, CA: University of California Press.

Bereiter, C. 1994. 'Implications of postmodernism for science, or, science as progressive discourse'. *Educational Psychologist* 29: 3–12.

Beretta, A. 1991. 'Theory construction in SLA: Complimentarity and opposition'. *Studies in Second Language Acquisition* 13: 493–511.

Berlin, I. 1976. *Vico and Herder*. New York, NY: Viking Press.

Berlin, B. and **P. Kay.** 1969. *Basic Color Terms: Their Universality and Evolution*. Berkeley, CA: University of California Press.

Berman, R. A. and **D. I. Slobin** (eds.). 1994. *Relating Events in Narrative: A Crosslinguistic Developmental Study*. Hillsdale, NJ: Lawrence Erlbaum Associates, Publishers.

Bialystok, E. 1990. 'The competence of processing: Classifying theories of second language acquisition'. *TESOL Quarterly* 24: 635–48.

Birdsong, D. 1992. 'Ultimate attainment in second language acquisition'. *Language* 68: 706–55.

Blakar, R. and **R. Rommetveit.** 1975. 'Utterances in cavuo and context'. *International Journal of Psycholinguistics*. 2/2: 5–32.

Block, D. 1996. 'Not so fast: Some thoughts on theory culling, relativism, accepted findings and the heart and soul of SLA'. *Applied Linguistics* 17/1: 63–83.

Bond, M. H. and K-k. Hwang. 1986. 'The social psychology of the Chinese people' in M. H. Bond (ed.): *The Psychology of the Chinese People*. Hong Kong: Oxford University Press.

Borg, S. 1998. 'Teachers' pedagogical systems and grammar teaching: A qualitative study'. *TESOL Quarterly* 32: 9–38.

Bourdieu, P. 1979a. *Distinction: A Social Critique of the Judgement of Taste*. Cambridge, MA: Harvard University Press.

Bourdieu, P. 1979b. *Outline of a Theory of Practice*. Cambridge: Cambridge University Press.

Bourdieu, P. 1990. *In Other Words: Essays Towards a Reflexive Sociology*. Stanford, CA: Stanford University Press.

Bourdieu, P. 1991. *Language and Symbolic Power*, Cambridge, MA: Harvard University Press.

Bourdieu, P. and T. Eagleton. 1994. 'Doxa and common life: An interview' in S. Zizek (ed.): *Mapping Ideology*. New York, NY: Verso.

Bourdieu, P. and J. C. Passeron. 1977. *Reproduction in Education, Society and Culture*. London: Sage.

Bowerman, M. 1989. 'Learning a semantic system: what role do cognitive predispositions play?' in M. L. Rice and R. J. Schiefelbusch (eds.): *The Teachability of Language*. Baltimore: Paul H. Brooks.

Bowers, C. A. 1993. *Critical Essays on Education, Modernity, and the Recovery of the Ecological Imperative*. New York, NY: Teachers College Press.

Bowers, C. A. and D. J. Flinders. 1990. *Responsive Teaching: An Ecological Approach to Classroom Patterns of Language, Culture, and Thought*. New York, NY: Teachers College Press.

Breen, M. 1985a. 'Authenticity in the language classroom'. *Applied Linguistics* 6/1: 60–70.

Breen, M. 1985b. 'The social context for language learning—A neglected situation?' *Studies in Second Language Acquisition* 7: 135–58.

Breen, M. and C. Candlin. 1980. 'The essentials of a communicative curriculum in language teaching'. *Applied Linguistics* 1/2: 89–112.

Broner M. and E. Tarone. 1999. *Is it fun? Language play in a fifth grade Spanish immersion classroom*. Paper presented at the Annual Conference of the American Association for Applied Linguistics. Stamford, CT. March 1999.

Bronfenbrenner, U. 1979. *The Ecology of Human Development*. Cambridge, MA: Harvard University Press.

Bronfenbrenner, U. 1993. 'The ecology of cognitive development: Research models and fugitive findings' in Wozniak and Fischer.

Bronfenbrenner, U. and S. J. Ceci. 1994. 'Nature–nurture reconceptualized in developmental perspective: A bioecological model'. *Psychological Review* 101: 568–86.

Brooks, F. P. 1992. 'Communicative competence and the conversation course: A social interaction perspective'. *Linguistics and Education* 4: 219–46.

Brooks, F. P. 1993. 'Some problems and caveats in communicative discourse: Toward a conceptualization of the foreign language classroom'. *Foreign Language Annals* 46: 635–52.

Brooks, F. P. and R. Donato. 1994. 'Vygotskyan approaches to understanding foreign language learner discourse during communicative tasks'. *Hispania* 77: 262–74.

Brooks, F. P., R. Donato, and J. V. McGlone. 1997. 'When are they going to say "it" right?: Understanding learner talk during pair-work activity'. *Foreign Language Annals* 30: 524–41.

Brown, A. and A. Palincsar. 1981. 'Inducing strategic learning from texts by means of informed, self-controlled training'. *Topics in Learning and Learning Disabilities* 2: 1–17.

Brown, H. D. 1994. *Teaching by Principles: An Interactive Approach to Language Pedagogy.* Englewood Cliffs, NJ: Prentice Hall Regents.

Bruffee, K. 1994. 'Collaborative learning and the "conversation of mankind" '. *College English* 46/7: 635–52.

Brumfit, C. 1984. *Communicative Methodology in Language Teaching.* Cambridge: Cambridge University Press.

Bruner, J. S. 1973. *Beyond the Information Given: Studies in the Psychology of Knowing.* New York, NY: Norton.

Bruner, J. S. 1975. 'The ontogenesis of speech acts'. *Journal of Child Language* 2: 1–19.

Bruner, J. S. 1983. *Child's Talk: Learning to use Language.* New York, NY: Norton.

Bruner, J. S. 1986. *Actual Minds, Possible Worlds.* Cambridge, MA: Harvard University Press.

Bruner, J. S. 1990. *Acts of Meaning.* Cambridge, MA: Harvard University Press.

Bruner, J. S. 1991. 'The narrative construction of reality'. *Critical Inquiry* 18: 1–21.

Bruner, J. S. 1996. *The Culture of Education.* Cambridge, MA: Harvard University Press.

Bruner, J. S. and V. Sherwood. 1976. 'Peekaboo and the learning of rule structures' in J. S. Bruner, A. Jolly and K. Sylva (eds.): *Play: Its Role in Development and Evolution.* Harmondsworth: Penguin.

Bryson, M. and S. de Castell. 1993. 'En/gendering equity: On some paradoxical consequences of institutionalized programs of emancipation'. *Educational Theory* 43: 341–55.

Buchler, J. (ed.). 1955. *Philosophical Writings of Peirce.* New York, NY: Dover Books.

Burgess, A. 1993. 'Reading Vygotsky' in H. Daniels (ed.): *Charting the Agenda: Educational Activity after Vygotsky.* New York, NY: Routledge.

Burnaby, B. and Y. Sun. 1989. 'Chinese teachers' views of western language teaching: Context informs paradigms'. *TESOL Quarterly* 23: 219–38.

Butler, R. O. 1992. *A Good Scent from a Strange Mountain.* New York, NY: Penguin Books.

Butterworth, G. 1992. 'Context and cognition in models of cognitive growth', in Light and Butterworth.

Calhoun, D., E. LiPuma, and M. Postone. 1993. *Bourdieu: Critical Perspectives.* Chicago, IL: University of Chicago Press.

Canale, M. and M. Swain. 1981. 'Theoretical bases of communicative approaches to second language teaching and testing'. *Applied Linguistics* 1: 1–47.

Capra, R. 1996. *The Web of Life: A New Scientific Understanding of Living Systems.* New York, NY: Anchor Books.

Carruthers, P. and J. Boucher. 1998. 'Introduction: Opening up options' in P. Carruthers and J. Boucher (eds.): *Language and Thought. Interdisciplinary Themes.* Cambridge: Cambridge University Press.

Cazden, C. B. 1981. 'Performance before competence: Assistance to child discourse in the zone of proximal development'. *The Quarterly Newsletter of the Laboratory of Comparative Human Cognition.* 5/1: 5–8.

Cazden, C. B. 1988. *Classroom Discourse: The Language of Teaching and Learning.* Portsmouth, NH: Heinemann.

Cazden, C. B. 1993. 'Vygotsky, Hymes and Bakhtin: From word to utterance and voice' in E. N. Minick and E. Forman (eds.): *Contexts for Learning: Sociocultural Dynamics in Children's Development.* New York, NY: Oxford University Press.

Checkland, P. 1981. *Systems Thinking, Systems Practice*. New York, NY: Wiley.

Cheng, C.-Y. 1987. 'Chinese philosophy and contemporary human communication theory' in D. L. Kincaid (ed.): *Communication Theory: Eastern and Western Perspectives*. San Diego, CA: Harcourt Brace Jovanovich.

Chomsky, N. 1972. *Language and Mind*. San Diego, CA: Harcourt Brace Jovanovich.

Cobb, P. 1998. 'Learning from distributed theories of intelligence'. *Mind, Culture, and Activity: An International Journal* 5: 187–204.

Codrescu, A. 1990. *The Disappearance of the Outside*. Boston, MA: Addison-Wesley.

Cole, M. 1996. *Cultural Psychology: A Once and Future Discipline*. Cambridge, MA: Belknap Press.

Cole, M. and Y. Engestrom. 1993. 'A cultural-historical approach to distributed cognition' in G. Solomon (ed.) 1993: *Distributed Cognition. Psychological and Educational Considerations*. Cambridge: Cambridge University Press.

Cole, M. and K. Traupmann. 1981. 'Comparative cognitive research: Learning from a learning disabled child' in W. A. Collins (ed.): *Aspects of the Development of Competence*. Hillsdale, NJ: Lawrence Erlbaum Associates, Publishers.

Cook, G. 1997. 'Language play, language learning'. *English Language Teaching Journal* 51: 224–31.

Cook, G. 2000. *Language Play, Language Learning*. Oxford: Oxford University Press.

Coppieters, R. 1987. 'Competence differences between native and non-native speakers'. *Language* 63: 544–74.

Corder, S. P. 1967. 'The significance of learners' errors'. *International Review of Applied Linguistics* 5: 161–9.

Coughlan, P. and P. Duff. 1994. 'Same task, different activities: Analysis of a second language acquisition task from an activity theory perspective' in Lantolf and Appel 1994b.

Craven, E. 1991. 'Teaching Chinese teachers to teach English writing' in Thao Le and McCausland.

Crawford, M. 1995. *Talking Difference. On Gender and Language*. London: Sage Publications.

Creswell, J. W. 1994. *Research Design: Qualitative and Quantitative Approaches*. Thousand Oaks, CA: Sage Publications.

Creswell, J. W. 1998. *Qualitative Inquiry and Research Design: Choosing Among Five Traditions*. Thousand Oaks, CA: Sage Publications.

Crookes, G. and S. M. Gass (eds.). 1993a. *Tasks and Language Learning: Integrating Theory and Practice*. Clevedon, N. Somerset: Multilingual Matters.

Crookes, G. and S. M. Gass (eds.). 1993b. *Tasks in a Pedagogical Context*. Clevedon, N. Somerset: Multilingual Matters.

Cummings, M. C. 1996. 'Sardo revisited: Voice, faith, and multiple repeaters' in Bailey and Nunan.

Dalton, S. and J. Sison. 1995. *Enacting instructional conversations with Spanish-speaking students in middle school mathematics*. The National Center for Research on Cultural Diversity and Second Language Learning, research report 12. Santa Cruz, CA.

Danziger, K. 1990. *Constructing the Subject. Historical Origins of Psychological Research*. Cambridge: Cambridge University Press.

Danziger, K. 1997. *Naming the Mind. How Psychology Found Its Language*. London: Sage Publications.

Davies, B. and R. Harré. 1993. 'Positioning: The discursive production of the selves'. *Journal for the Theory of Social Behavior* 20/1: 43–63.

Davydov, V. V. and L. A Radzikhovskii. 1985. 'Vygotsky's theory and the activity-oriented approach in psychology' in Wertsch (ed.): 1985b.

de Bot, K. 1996. 'The psycholinguistics of the output hypothesis'. *Language Learning* 46: 529–55.

de Bot, K. and B. Weltens. 1995. 'Foreign language attrition'. *Annual Review of Applied Linguistics* 15: 151–64.

de Guerrero, M. 1996. 'Krashen's i + 1 and Vygotsky's ZPD: Really two very different notions'. *TESOL-GRAM*, p. 9.

Diaz, R. M. and L. E. Berk (eds.). 1992. *Private Speech: From Social Interaction to Self-Regulation*. Hillsdale, NJ: Lawrence Erlbaum Associates, Publishers.

DiCamilla, F. J. and J. P. Lantolf. 1994. 'The linguistic analysis of private writing'. *Language Sciences* 16: 347–69.

DiNitto, R. In press. 'Can Collaboration Be Unsuccessful? A Sociocultural Analysis of Classroom Setting and Japanese L2 Performance in Group Tasks.' *Journal of the Association of Teachers of Japanese*.

Donato, R. 1988. *Beyond group: A psycholinguistic rationale for collective activity in second-language learning*. Unpublished doctoral dissertation, University of Delaware, Newark, DE.

Donato, R. 1994. 'Collective scaffolding in second language learning' in Lantolf and Appel 1994b.

Donato, R. and R. B. Adair-Hauck. 1992. 'Discourse perspectives on formal instruction'. *Language Awareness*, 1/2: 73–89.

Donato, R., J. L. Antonek, and G. R. Tucker. 1994. 'Multiple perspectives on a Japanese FLES program'. *Foreign Language Annals* 27/3: 365–78.

Donato, R., J. L. Antonek, and G. R. Tucker. 1996. 'Documenting and assessing a Japanese FLES program: Ambiance and achievement'. *Language Learning* 46/3: 497–528.

Donato, R. and J. P. Lantolf. 1990. 'The dialogic origins of L2 monitoring'. *Pragmatics and Language Learning* 1: 83–97.

Doughty, C. and E. Varela. 1997. 'Communicative focus on form' in Doughty and Williams.

Doughty, C. and J. Williams (eds.). 1998. *Focus on Form in Classroom Second Language Acquisition*. Cambridge: Cambridge University Press.

Dreyfus, H. L. and S. E. Dreyfus. 1986. *Mind over Machine. The Power of Human Intuition and Expertise in the Era of the Computer*. New York, NY: The Free Press.

Dunn, W. E. and J. P. Lantolf. 1998. 'Vygotsky's zone of proximal development and Krashen's i + 1: Incommensurable constructs; incommensurable theories'. *Language Learning* 48: 411–42.

Edwards, D. 1997. *Discourse and Cognition*. London: Sage Publications.

Ellis, G. 1996. *The significance of cultural influences within EFL in Vietnam*. Paper presented at meeting of the Applied Linguistics Association of Australia (ALAA). Sydney.

Ellis, R. 1994. *The Study of Second Language Acquisition*. Oxford: Oxford University Press.

Ellis, R. 1997. *SLA Research and Language Teaching*. Oxford: Oxford University Press.

Ellis, R. 1998. 'Teaching and research: Options in grammar teaching'. *TESOL Quarterly* 32/1: 39–60.

Ellis, R., Y. Tanaka, and A. Yamazaki. 1994. 'Classroom interaction, comprehension, and the acquisition of L2 word meanings'. *Language Learning* 44: 449–91.

Engestrom, Y. 1999. 'Innovative learning in work teams: Analyzing cycles of knowledge creation in practice' in Y. Engestrom, R. Miettinen, and R-L. Punamaki (eds.): *Perspectives on Activity Theory*. Cambridge: Cambridge University Press.

Engestrom, Y. and D. Middleton (eds.). 1996. *Cognition and Communication at Work*. Cambridge: Cambridge University Press.

Erlich, S., P. Avery, and C. Yorio. 1990. 'Discourse structure and the negotiation of comprehensible input'. *Studies in Second Language Acquisition* 11: 397–414.

Faerch, C. and G. Kasper. 1986. 'The role of comprehension in second language acquisition'. *Applied Linguistics* 7: 256–74.

Fairclough, N. 1989. *Language and Power*. London: Longman.

Firbas, J. 1964. 'On defining the theme in functional sentence analysis'. *Travaux linguistiques de Prague* 1: 267–80.

Firbas, J. 1971. 'On the concept of communicative dynamism in the theory of functional sentence perspective'. *Philologica Pragensia* 8: 135–44.

Firth, A. and J. Wagner. 1997. 'On discourse, communication, and (some) fundamental concepts in SLA research'. *The Modern Language Journal* 82: 91–4.

Firth, A. and J. Wagner. 1998. 'SLA property: No trespassing'. *The Modern Language Journal* 81: 285–300.

Forrester, M. A. 1992. *The Development of Young Children's Social–Cognitive Skills*. Hove, NJ: Lawrence Erlbaum Associates, Publishers.

Foster, M. 1989. ' "It's cookin' now": Performance analysis of the speech events of a Black teacher in an urban community college'. *Language in Society* 18: 1–30.

Foster, P. 1998. 'A classroom perspective on the negotiation of meaning'. *Applied Linguistics* 18/1: 39–60.

Foucault, M. 1970. *The Order of Things*. New York, NY: Vintage.

Fowler, R. 1986. *Linguistic Criticism*. Oxford: Oxford University Press.

Frawley, W. 1987. *Text and Epistemology*. Norwood, NJ: Ablex Publishing Corporation.

Frawley, W. 1992. *Linguistic Semantics*. Hillsdale, NJ: Lawrence Erlbaum Associates, Publishers.

Frawley, W. 1997. *Vygotsky and Cognitive Science. Language and the Unification of the Social and Computational Mind*. Cambridge, MA: Harvard University Press.

Frawley, W. and J. P. Lantolf. 1984. 'Speaking as self-order: A critique of orthodox L2 research'. *Studies in Second Language Acquisition* 6: 143–59.

Frawley, W. and J. P. Lantolf. 1985. 'Second language discourse: A Vygotskyan perspective'. *Applied Linguistics* 6: 19–44.

Freed, B. (ed.). 1995. *Second Language Acquisition in a Study Abroad Context*. Amsterdam: John Benjamins.

Fried, J. 1994. 'Bridging emotion and intellect; Classroom diversity in process'. *College Teaching* 41: 123–8.

Friedrich, P. 1979. 'The symbol and its relative non-arbitrariness' in *Language, Context, and the Imagination*. Stanford, CA: Stanford University Press.

Gal'perin, P. Ya. 1967. 'On the notion of internalization'. *Soviet Psychology* 5: 28–33.

Gal'perin, P. Ya. 1969. 'Stages in the development of mental acts' in M. Cole and I. Maltzman (eds.): *A Handbook of Contemporary Soviet Psychology*. New York, NY: Basic Books.

Garfinkel, H. 1963. 'A conception of, and experiments with, "trust" as a condition of stable concerted actions' in O. J. Harvey (ed.): *Motivation and Social Interaction*. New York, NY: Ronald Press.

Gass, S. M. 1991. 'Grammar instruction, selective attention and learning processes' in R. Phillipson, E. Kellerman, L. Selinker, M. Sharwood Smith, and M. Swain (eds.): *Foreign/Second Language Pedagogy Research: A Commemorative Volume for Claus Faerch*. Clevedon, N. Somerset: Multilingual Matters.

Gass, S. M. 1997. *Input, Interaction and the Second Language Learner*. Mahwah, NJ: Lawrence Erlbaum Associates, Publishers.

Gass, S. M. and C. Madden (eds.). 1985. *Input in Second Language Acquisition.* Rowley, MA: Newbury House.

Gass, S. M. and E. M. Varonis. 1985. 'Variation in native speaker speech modification to non-native speakers'. *Studies in Second Language Acquisition* 7: 37–58.

Gee, J. P. 1994. 'Discourses: Reflections on M. A. K. Halliday's "towards a language-based theory of learning"'. *Linguistics and Education* 6: 33–40.

Geertz, C. 1973. *The Interpretation of Cultures.* New York, NY: Basic Books.

Gibbs, R. W. 1994. *The Poetics of Mind: Figurative Thought, Language, and Understanding.* Cambridge: Cambridge University Press.

Gibson, J. J. 1966. *The Senses Considered as Perceptual Systems.* Boston, MA: Houghton Mifflin.

Gibson, J. J. 1979. *The Ecological Approach to Visual Perception.* Boston, MA: Houghton Mifflin.

Gillette, B. 1994. 'The role of learner goals in L2 success' in Lantolf and Appel 1994b.

Giroux, H. and P. McLaren. 1989. 'Introduction' in H. Giroux and P. McLaren (eds.): *Critical Pedagogy, and Cultural Struggle.* Albany, NY: SUNY Press.

Goffman, E. 1967. *Interaction Ritual: Essays in Face to Face Behavior.* Garden City, NY: Free Press.

Goffman, E. 1974. *Frame Analysis.* New York, NY: Harper & Row.

Goffman, E. 1981. *Forms of Talk.* Philadelphia, PA: University of Pennsylvania Press.

Goldenberg, C. 1991. *Instructional Conversations and Their Classroom Application.* Santa Cruz, CA: National Center for Research on Cultural Diversity and Second Language Learning.

Goldsmith, E. 1998. *The Way: An Ecological World View.* 2nd ed. Athens, GA: University of Georgia Press.

Goodwin, C. 1996. 'Transparent vision' in Ochs, Schegloff, and Thomas.

Gopnik, A. and S. Choi. 1991. 'Do linguistic differences lead to cognitive differences?: A cross-linguistic study of semantic and cognitive development'. *First Language* 10: 199–215.

Gopnik, A. and A. N. Meltzoff. 1993. 'Words and thoughts in infancy: The specificity hypothesis and the development of categorization and naming' in C. Rovee-Collier and L. P. Lilpsett (eds.): *Advances in Infancy Research* 8: 217–49.

Gordon, I. E. 1989. *Theories of Visual Perception.* Chichester, VT: Wiley.

Grabois, H. 1996. 'Distributed cognition and participation in second language discourse'. *Cornell Working Papers in Linguistics* 14: 1–21.

Grabois, H. 1997. *Love and power. Word association, lexical organization and second language acquisition.* Unpublished Ph.D. dissertation, Cornell University, Ithaca, NY.

Graf, C. 1991. 'Developing a culturally appropriate syllabus for a TEFL methodology course: A case study from China' in Thao Le and McCausland.

Gramsci, A. 1971. *Selections from the Prison Notebooks of Antonio Gramsci.* Quintin Hoare and Geoffrey Nowell Smith (editors and translators). New York, NY: International Publishers.

Green, J. 1983a. 'Exploring classroom discourse: Linguistic perspectives on teaching–learning processes'. *Educational Psychologist* 18: 180–99.

Green, J. 1983b. 'Research on teaching as a linguistic process: A state of the art' in E. Gordon (ed.): *Review of Research in Education,* 10. Washington, DC: American Educational Research Association.

Greeno, J. G. 1997. 'On claims that answer the wrong questions'. *Educational Researcher* 26: 5–17.

Gregg, K. R. 1993. 'Taking explanation seriously; or, let a couple of flowers bloom'. *Applied Linguistics* 14/3: 276–94.

Gregg, K., M. Long, G. Jordan, and A. Beretta. 1997. 'Rationality and its discontents in SLA'. *Applied Linguistics* 18/4: 538–58.

Grice, P. 1989. *Studies in the Way of Words*. Cambridge, MA: Harvard University Press.

Grosjean, F. 1982. *Life with Two Languages. An Introduction to Bilingualism.* Cambridge, MA: Harvard University Press.

Gumperz, J. and S. Levinson (eds.). 1996. *Rethinking Linguistic Relativity.* Cambridge: Cambridge University Press.

Habermas, J. 1984. *The Theory of Communicative Action, Vol. 1. Reason and the Rationalization of Society.* Boston, MA: Beacon Press.

Habermas, J. 1987. *Theory of Communicative Action. Vol. 2. Lifeworld and System: A Critique of Functionalist Reason.* Boston, MA: Beacon Press.

Hadley, A. O. 1993. *Teaching Language in Context.* 2nd edition. Boston, MA: Heinle and Heinle.

Haeckel, E. 1886. *The History of Creation: Or the Development of the Earth and Its Inhabitants by the Action of Natural Causes.* New York, NY: D. Appleton.

Hall, J. K. 1995a ' "Aw, man, where you goin'?": Classroom interaction and the development of L2 interactional competence'. *Issues in Applied Linguistics* 6: 37–62.

Hall, J. K. 1995b '(Re)creating our worlds with words: A sociohistorical perspective of face-to-face interaction'. *Applied Linguistics* 16/2: 206–32.

Hall, J. K. and F. B. Brooks. 1996. *An integrative framework linking classroom interaction, interactive practices, and the development of L2 interactional competence.* Unpublished manuscript.

Halliday, M. A. K. 1970. 'Language structure and language function' in J. Lyons (ed.): *New Horizons in Linguistics.* Harmondsworth: Penguin Books.

Halliday, M. A. K. 1978. *Language as a Social Semiotic: The Social Interpretation of Language and Meaning.* London: Edward Arnold.

Halliday, M. A. K. 1994. *Functional Grammar.* London: Edward Arnold.

Halliday, M. A. K. and R. Hasan. 1989. *Language, Context and Text: Aspects of Language in a Socio-Semiotic Perspective.* Oxford: Oxford University Press.

Hanks, W. F. 1992. 'The indexical ground of deictic reference' in A. Duranti and C. Goodwin (eds.): *Rethinking Context: Language as an Interactive Phenomenon.* Cambridge: Cambridge University Press.

Hanks, W. F. 1996. *Language and Communicative Practices.* Boulder, CO: Westview Press.

Harasym, S. 1988. 'Practical politics of the open end: An interview with Gayatri Chakravorty Spivak'. *Canadian Journal of Political and Social Theory* 12: 51–69.

Harré, R. 1987. 'Persons and selves' in A. Peacock and G. Gillett (eds.): *Persons and Personality: A Contemporary Inquiry.* Oxford: Basil Blackwell.

Harré, R. 1995. 'Discursive psychology' in Smith, Harré, and Van Langenhove 1995b.

Harré, R. and G. Gillett. 1994. The Discursive Mind. Thousand Oaks, CA: Sage Publications.

Harré, R. and P. Stearns (eds). 1995. *Discursive Psychology in Practice.* London: Sage Publications.

Hatch, E. (ed.). 1978. *Second Language Acquisition.* Rowley, MA: Newbury House.

Hatch, E., Y. Shirai, and C. Fantuzzi. 1990. 'The need for an integrated theory: Connecting the modules'. *TESOL Quarterly* 24: 697–716.

Haugen, E. 1972. *The Ecology of Language* (Essays edited by Anwar S. Dil). Stanford, CA: Stanford University Press.

Heath, S. B. 1983. *Ways with Words. Language, Life, and Work in Communities and Classrooms.* Cambridge: Cambridge University Press.

Heritage, J. 1984. 'A change-of-state token and aspects of its sequential placement' in J. M. Atkinson and J. Heritage (eds.): *Structure of Social Action*. Cambridge: Cambridge University Press.

Hirsch, M. 1994. 'Pictures of displaced girlhood' in A. Bammer (ed.): *Displacements. Cultural Identities in Question*. Bloomington, IN: Indiana University Press.

Hoffman, E. 1989. *Lost in Translation. A Life in a New Language*. New York, NY: Dutton.

Holliday, A. 1994. *Appropriate Methodology and Social Context*. Cambridge: Cambridge University Press.

Holliday, A. 1997. 'Six lessons: Cultural continuity in Communicative Language Teaching'. *Language Teaching Research* 1(3): 212–38.

Holquist, M. 1990. *Dialogism. Bakhtin and His World*. London: Routledge.

Holunga, S. 1994. *The effect of metacognitive strategy training with verbalization on the oral accuracy of adult second language learners*. Unpublished doctoral dissertation, University of Toronto (OISE), Toronto.

Howatt, A. P. R. 1984. *A History of English Language Teaching*. Oxford: Oxford University Press.

Hutchins, E. 1995. *Cognition in the Wild*. Cambridge, MA: MIT Press.

Hutchins, E. and T. Klausen. 1996. 'Distributed cognition in an airline cockpit' in Engestrom and Middleton.

Hymes, D. 1972. 'On communicative competence' in J. B. Pride and J. Holmes (eds.): *Sociolinguistics*. Harmondsworth: Penguin Books.

Illich, I. and B. Sanders. 1988. *The Alphabetization of the Popular Mind*. San Francisco, CA: North Point Press.

Ioup, G., E. Boustangui, M. E. Tigi, and M. Moselle. 1994. 'Reexamining the critical period hypothesis: A case study of successful adult SLA in a naturalistic environment'. *Studies in Second Language Acquisition* 16: 73–98.

Jacobs, G. 1996. 'The appropriacy of group activities: Views from some Southeast Asian second language educators'. *RELC Journal* 27: 103–20.

Johnson, K. E. 1995. *Understanding Communication in the Second Language Classroom*. New York, NY: Cambridge University Press.

John-Steiner, V. 1985. *Notebooks of the Mind: Explorations in Thinking*. New York, NY: Harper & Row.

John-Steiner, V. 1992 'Private speech among adults' in Diaz and Berk.

Johnstone, B. 1996. *The Linguistic Individual. Self-expression in Language and Linguistics*. Oxford: Oxford University Press.

Jordan, C. 1982. 'Cultural differences in communication patterns: Classroom adaptations and translation strategies' in M. Clarke and J. Handscombe (eds.): *On TESOL '82. Pacific Perspectives on Language Learning and Teaching*. Washington, DC: TESOL.

Jordan, K., H.-P. Au, and A. Joesting. 1983. 'Patterns of classroom interaction with Pacific Islands children: The importance of cultural differences' in M. Chu-Chang (ed.): *Asian and Pacific-American Perspectives on Bilingual Education*. New York, NY: Teachers College Press.

Josselson, R. and A. Lieblich. 1993. *The Narrative Study of Lives*. Volume 1. London: Sage Publications.

Kachru, B. 1986. *The Alchemy of English: The Spread, Functions and Models of Non-Native Englishes*. Oxford: Pergamon Press.

Kalaja, P. and S. Leppänen. In press. 'Heroes in quest of mastery of the English language' in Proceedings of the Fifth International Conference on Narrative, 1997.

Karcevskij, S. 1982. 'The asymmetric dualism of the linguistic sign' in P. Steiner (ed.): *The Prague School. Selected Writings*, 1929–1946. Austin, TX: University of Texas Press.

Karmiloff-Smith, A. 1992. *A Developmental Perspective on Cognitive Science*. Cambridge, MA: MIT Press.

Kellerman, S. 1992. ' "I see what you mean": The role of kinesic behaviour in listening and implications for foreign and second language learning'. *Applied Linguistics* 13/3: 240–58.

Kemp, J. 1995. 'Culture clash and teacher awareness'. *The Language Teacher* 19: 8–11.

King, B. 1995. 'Activity as a mediator of sociocultural change and individual development: The case of school-work transition in Nepal'. *Mind, Culture, and Activity: An International Journal* 2: 285–302.

Korst, T. J. 1997. 'Answer, please answer! A perspective on Japanese university students' silent response to questions'. *JALT Journal* 19: 279–91.

Koven, M. 1998. 'Two languages in the self/the self in two languages: French-Portuguese bilinguals' verbal enactments and experiences of self in narrative discourse'. *Ethos* 26: 410–55.

Kowal, M. and **M. Swain.** 1994. 'Using collaborative language production tasks to promote students' language awareness'. *Language Awareness* 3: 73–93.

Kowal, M. and **M. Swain.** 1997. 'From semantic to syntactic processing: How can we promote metalinguistic awareness in the French immersion classroom?' in R. K. Johnson and M. Swain (eds.): *Immersion Education: International Perspectives*. Cambridge: Cambridge University Press.

Kozulin, A. 1986. 'The concept of activity in Soviet psychology'. *American Psychologist* 41: 264–74.

Kozulin, A. 1990. *Vygotsky's Psychology: A Biography of Ideas*. Cambridge, MA: Harvard University Press.

Kozulin, A. 1998. *Psychological Tools: A Sociocultural Approach to Education*. Cambridge, MA: Harvard University Press.

Kozulin, A. and **A. Venger.** 1994. 'Immigration without adaptation: The psychological world of Russian immigrants in Israel'. *Mind, Culture, and Activity: An International Journal* 4: 230–8.

Kramp, M. K. and **W. L. Humphreys.** 1994. 'Narrative, self-assessment, and the reflective learner'. *College Teaching* 41: 83–7.

Kramsch, C. 1985. 'Classroom interaction and discourse options'. *Studies in Second Language Acquisition* 7: 169–83.

Kramsch, C. 1989. 'Discourse and text: A narrative view of the foreign language lesson' in J. Alatis (ed.): *Georgetown University Roundtable on Language and Linguistics*. Washington, DC: Georgetown University Press.

Kramsch, C. 1993. *Context and Culture in Language Teaching*. Oxford: Oxford University Press.

Kramsch, C. 1995a. 'The applied linguist and the foreign language teacher: Can they talk to each other?' *Australian Review of Applied Linguistics* 18: 1–16.

Kramsch, C. 1995b. 'The cultural component in language teaching'. *Language, Culture and Curriculum* 8: 83–92.

Kramsch, C. 1995c. 'Rhetorical approaches to understanding' in T. Miller (ed.): *Functional Approaches to Written Text: Classroom Applications*. TESOL-France The Journal 2/2: 61–78.

Kramsch, C. 1996. 'Stylistic choice and cultural awareness' in B. Lothar and W. Delanoy (eds.): *Challenges of Literary Texts in the Foreign Language Classroom*. Tübingen: Günther Narr.

Kramsch, C. 1998. *Language and Culture*. Oxford: Oxford University Press.

Kramsch, C. and **S. McConnell-Ginet.** 1992a. '(Co)ntextual knowledge in language education' in Kramsch and McConnell-Ginet 1992b.

Kramsch, C. and **S. McConnell-Ginet** (eds.). 1992b. *Text and Context: Cross-disciplinary Perspectives on Language Study.* Lexington, MA: D. C. Heath.

Kramsch, C. and **P. Sullivan.** 1996. 'Appropriate pedagogy'. *English Language Teaching Journal* 50: 199–212.

Kramsch, C. and **L. von Hoene.** 1995. 'Re-thinking the teaching and learning of foreign languages through feminist and sociolinguistic theory' in M. Bucholtz, A. C. Liang, L. Sutton, and C. Hines (eds.): *Cultural Performances: Proceedings of the Third Women and Language Conference.* Berkeley, CA: Berkeley Women and Language Group.

Krashen, S. D. 1982. *Principles and Practice in Second Language Acquisition.* Oxford: Pergamon.

Kress, G. (ed.). 1988. *Communication and Culture: An Introduction.* Kensington, Australia: New South Wales University Press.

Kress, G., L. Martins, and **J. Ogborn,** 1998. 'A satellite view of language: Some lessons from science classrooms'. *Language Awareness* 7: 63–89.

Kuczaj, S. A. 1983. *Crib Speech and Language Play.* New York, NY: Springer-Verlag.

Kuhn, T. 1970. *The Structure of Scientific Revolutions.* Chicago, IL: University of Chicago Press.

Kunihiro, T. 1980. 'Personality-structure and communicative behavior: A comparison of Japanese and Americans' in W. von Raffler-Engel (ed.): *Aspects of Nonverbal Communication.* Bath: Pitman Press.

Kuutti, K. 1996. 'Activity theory as a potential framework for human–computer interaction research' in Nardi 1996b.

Labov, W. 1970. 'The study of language in its social context'. *Studium Generale* 23: 66–84.

Lakoff, G. 1987. *Women, Fire and Dangerous Things.* Chicago, IL: University of Chicago Press.

Lakoff, G. and **M. Johnson.** 1981. *Metaphors We Live By.* Chicago, IL: University of Chicago Press.

Lamb, S. M. 1999. *Pathways of the Brain: The Neurocognitive Basis of Language.* Amsterdam: John Benjamins.

Lantolf, J. P. 1993. 'Sociocultural theory and the second-language classroom: The lesson of Strategic Interaction' in J. E. Alatis (ed.): *Georgetown University Round Table on Languages and Linguistics 1993. Strategic Interaction and Language Acquisition: Theory, Practice, and Research.* Washington, DC: Georgetown University Press.

Lantolf, J. P. 1994. 'Sociocultural theory and second language learning: Introduction to the special issue'. *The Modern Language Journal* 78: 418–20.

Lantolf, J. P. 1996. 'Second language theory building: Letting all the flowers bloom!' *Language Learning* 46: 713–49.

Lantolf, J. P. 1997. 'The function of language play in the acquisition of L2 Spanish' in A.-T. Perez-Leroux and W. R. Glass (eds.): *Contemporary Perspectives on the Acquisition of Spanish. Vol. 2: Production, Processing, and Comprehension.* Sommerville, MA: Cascadilla Press.

Lantolf, J. P. 1999. 'Second culture acquisition: Cognitive considerations' in E. Hinkel (ed.): *Culture in Language Teaching and Learning.* Cambridge: Cambridge University Press.

Lantolf, J. P. 1999. 'Revisión de la aplicabilidad de la investigación experimental en las clases de segunda lengua' (Rethinking the relevance of experimental research for the second language classroom) in S. Salaberri (ed.): *Lingüística aplicada en la enseñanza de lenguas extranjeras.* Almería: Universidad de Almería.

Lantolf, J. P. and M. K. Ahmed. 1989. 'Psycholinguistic perspectives on interlanguage variation: A Vygotskyan analysis' in S. M. Gass, L. Selinker, and D. Preston (eds.): *Variation in Second Language Acquisition: Psycholinguistic Issues*. Clevedon, N. Somerset: Multilingual Matters.

Lantolf, J. P. and A. Aljaafreh. 1995. 'Second language learning in the zone of proximal development: A revolutionary experience.' *International Journal of Educational Research* 23: 619–32.

Lantolf, J. P. and G. Appel. 1994a. 'Theoretical framework: An introduction to Vygotskian approaches to second language research' in Lantolf and Appel (eds.) 1994b.

Lantolf, J. P. and G. Appel (eds.): 1994b. *Vygotskian Approaches to Second Language Research*. Norwood, NJ: Ablex Press.

Lantolf, J. P. and A. Pavlenko. 1995. 'Sociocultural theory and second language acquisition'. *Annual Review of Applied Linguistics* 15: 108–24.

Lantolf, J. P. and A. Pavlenko. 1998. *(S)econd (L)anguage (A)ctivity: Understanding learners as people*. Paper presented at the 1998 Annual Meeting of the American Association for Applied Linguistics. Seattle, Washington.

LaPierre, D. 1994. *Language output in a cooperative learning setting: Determining its effects on second language learning*. Unpublished thesis, University of Toronto (OISE), Toronto.

Larsen-Freeman, D. 1997. 'Chaos/complexity science and second language acquisition'. *Applied Linguistics* 18/2: 141–65.

Larsen-Freeman, D. and M. H. Long. 1991. *An Introduction to Second Language Acquisition Research*. New York, NY: Longman.

Lave, J. and S. Chaiklin (eds.). 1993. *Understanding Practice: Perspectives on Activity and Context*. Cambridge: Cambridge University Press.

Lave, J. and E. Wenger. 1991. *Situated Learning: Legitimate Peripheral Participation*. Cambridge: Cambridge University Press.

Leontiev, A. A. 1981. *Psychology and the Language Learning Process*. Oxford: Pergamon Press.

Leontiev, A. A. 1995 'ECCE HOMO'. *Journal of Russian and East European Psychology* 33/4: 35–46.

Leontiev, A. N. 1978. *Activity, Consciousness and Personality*. Englewood Cliffs, NJ: Prentice Hall.

Leontiev, A. N. 1981. 'The problem of activity in psychology' in Wertsch 1981.

Levinson, S. C. 1983. *Pragmatics*. New York, NY: Cambridge University Press.

Levinson, S. C. 1995. 'Interactional biases in human thinking' in E. Goody (ed.): *Social Intelligence and Interaction: Expressions and Implications of the Social Bias in Human Intelligence*. Cambridge: Cambridge University Press.

Lewin, K. 1943. 'Defining the "field at a given time" '. *Psychological Review* 50: 292–310.

Light, P. and G. Butterworth (eds.). 1992. *Context and Cognition: Ways of Learning and Knowing*. New York, NY: Harvester Wheatsheaf.

Lightbown, P. and N. Spada. 1990. 'Focus on form and corrective feedback in communicative language teaching: Effects on second language learning'. *Studies in Second Language Acquisition* 12: 429–48.

Linde, C. 1993. *Life Stories. The Creation of Coherence*. Oxford: Oxford University Press.

Linell, P. 1998. *Approaching Dialogue. Talk, Interaction, and Contexts in Dialogical Perspectives*. Amsterdam: John Benjamins.

Littlewood, W. 1981. *Communicative Language Teaching*. Cambridge: Cambridge University Press.

Long, M. H. 1981. 'Input, interaction, and second language acquisition'. *Annals of the New York Academy of Sciences* 379: 259–78.

Long, M. H. 1983a. 'Linguistic and conversational adjustments to nonnative speakers'. *Studies in Second Language Acquisition* 5: 177–93.

Long, M. H. 1983b. 'Native speaker/non-native speaker conversation and the negotiation of comprehensible input'. *Applied Linguistics* 4: 126–41.

Long, M. H. 1985. 'Input and second language acquisition theory' in Gass and Madden.

Long, M. H. 1990. 'The least second language acquisition theory needs to explain'. *TESOL Quarterly* 24: 649–66.

Long, M. H. 1993. 'Assessment strategies for SLA theories'. *Applied Linguistics* 14: 225–49.

Long, M. H. 1996. 'The role of the linguistic environment in second language acquisition' in W. C. Ritchie and T. K. Bhatia (eds.): *Handbook of Second Language Acquisition*. San Diego, CA: Academic Press.

Long, M. H. and P. Porter. 1985. 'Group work, interlanguage talk, and second language acquisition'. *TESOL Quarterly* 19: 207–28.

Long, M. H. and C. Sato. 1984. 'Methodological issues in interlanguage studies' in A. Davies, C. Criper, and A. Howatt (eds.): *Interlanguage*. Edinburgh: Edinburgh University Press.

Lovelock, J. 1979. *Gaia*. Oxford: Oxford University Press.

Luke, A. 1996. 'Text and discourse in education: An introduction to critical discourse analysis' in M. W. Apple (ed.): *Review of Research in Education* 21. Washington, DC: American Educational Research Association.

Luria, A. R. 1973. *The Working Brain. An Introduction to Neuropsychology*. New York, NY: Basic Books.

Luria, A. R. 1976. *Cognitive Development: Its Cultural and Social Foundations*. Cambridge, MA: Harvard University Press.

Luria, A. R. 1979. *The Making of Mind. A Personal Account of Soviet Psychology*. Cambridge, MA: Harvard University Press.

Luria, A. R. 1981. *Language and Cognition*. New York, NY: Wiley.

Luria, A. R. 1987. *The Mind of a Mnemonimist*. Cambridge, MA: Harvard University Press.

Lvovich, N. 1997. *The Multilingual Self. An Inquiry into Language Learning*. Mahwah, NY: Lawrence Erlbaum Associates, Publishers.

Lyster, R. and L. Ranta. 1997. 'Corrective feedback and learner uptake: Negotiation of form in communicative classrooms'. *Studies in Second Language Acquisition* 19: 37–66.

Mace, W. M. 1974. 'Gibson's strategy for perceiving: Ask not what's inside your head but what your head's inside of' in R. Shaw and J. Brandsford (eds.): *Perceiving, acting and knowing*. Hillsdale, NJ: Erlbaum.

Mackey, A. 1995. *Stepping up the pace: Input, interaction and second language development. An empirical study of questions in ESL*. Unpublished doctoral dissertation, University of Sydney, Sydney.

Makkai, A. 1993. *Ecolinguistics. Toward a New Paradigm for the Science of Language?* London: Pinter Publishers.

Malinowsky, B. 1923. 'The problem of meaning in primitive languages' in C. Ogden and I. Richards (eds.): *The Meaning of Meaning*. New York, NY: Harcourt, Brace, and World.

Markova, I., C.F. Graumann, and K. Foppa (eds). 1995. *Mutualities in Dialogue*. Cambridge: Cambridge University Press.

Maynard, S. K. 1989. *Japanese Conversation: Self-contextualized Through Structure and Interactional Management*. Norwood, NJ: Ablex Press.

Maynard, S. K. 1990. 'Conversation management in contrast: Listener response in Japanese and American English'. *Journal of Pragmatics* 14: 397–412.

McCafferty, S. G. 1994a. 'Adult second language learners' use of private speech: A review of studies'. *The Modern Language Journal* 78/4: 421–36.

McCafferty, S. G. 1994b. 'The use of private speech by adult ESL learners at different levels of proficiency' in Lantolf and Appel 1994b.

McCafferty, S. G. 1996. 'The use of non-verbal forms of expression in relation to L2 private speech'. *Cornell Working Papers in Linguistics* 14: 101–24.

McCafferty, S. G. 1998. 'Nonverbal expression and L2 private speech'. *Applied Linguistics* 19/1: 73–96.

McCone, T. 1993. *Speaking as regulation: Psycholinguistic aspects of student speech in the presence of foreign and native teaching assistants*. Unpublished doctoral dissertation, University of Delaware, Newark, DE.

McCormack, W. C. and S. A. Wurm. 1976. *Language and Man: Anthropological Issues*. The Hague: Mouton.

McLaughlin, B. 1987. *Theories of Second Language Learning*. London: Edward Arnold.

McLaughlin, B. 1990. '"Conscious vs. unconscious" learning'. *TESOL Quarterly* 24: 617–34.

McNamara, T. 1987. 'Language and social identity: Israelis abroad'. *Journal of Language and Social Psychology* 6: 215–28.

McNamara, T. 1997. 'Theorizing social identity: What do we mean by social identity? Competing framework, competing discourses'. *TESOL Quarterly* 31: 561–7.

McNeill, D. 1985. 'So you think gestures are nonverbal?' *Psychological Review* 92: 350–71.

McNeill, D. 1987. *Psycholinguistics: A New Approach*. New York, NY: Harper & Row.

McNeill, D. 1992. *Hand and Mind*. Chicago, IL: University of Chicago Press.

McNeill, D., J. Cassell, and E. T. Levy. 1993. 'Abstract deixis'. *Semiotica* 95: 5–19.

Mead, G. H. 1977. *George Herbert Mead on Social Psychology. Selected Papers*. Anselm Strauss (ed.). Chicago, IL: University of Chicago Press.

Mehan, H. 1979 *Language Lessons*. Cambridge, MA: Harvard University Press.

Mehler, J. and G. Noizet. 1973. *Textes pour une psycholinguistique*. Paris: Mouton.

Mercer, N. 1992. 'Culture, context and the construction of knowledge' in Light and Butterworth.

Mercer, N. 1995. *The Guided Construction of Knowledge: Talk Between Teachers and Learners in the Classroom*. Clevedon, N. Somerset: Multilingual Matters.

Merrell, F. 1997a. 'Do we really need Peirce's whole decalogue of signs?' *Semiotica* 114: 193–286.

Merrell, F. 1997b. *Peirce, Signs, and Meanings*. Toronto: University of Toronto Press.

Miles, M. B. and A. M. Huberman. 1994. *Qualitative Data Analysis*. Thousand Oaks, CA: Sage Publications.

Miller, G. A. and P. N. Johnson-Laird (eds). 1976. *Language and Perception*. Cambridge: Cambridge University Press.

Miller, T. 1995. 'Teacher–student interaction: A cross-cultural perspective'. *Speech Communication Education* 8: 155–72.

Mohan, B. and S. Helmer. 1988. 'Context and second language development: Preschoolers' comprehension of gestures'. *Applied Linguistics* 9/3: 275–92.

Moll, L. C. (ed.). 1990. *Vygotsky and Education: Instructional Implications and Applications of Sociohistorical Psychology*. Cambridge: Cambridge University Press.

Mori, K. 1997. *Polite Lies. On Being a Woman Caught Between Cultures*. New York City: Henry Holt.

Mühlhäusler, P. 1996. *Linguistic Ecology: Language Charge and Linguistic Imperialism in the Pacific Region*. New York, NY: Routledge.

Munby, J. 1978. *Communicative Syllabus Design*. Cambridge: Cambridge University Press.

Nakahama, Y., A. Tyler, and **L. van Lier.** 1998. *Negotiation of meaning in tasks and conversations*. Unpublished paper. Georgetown University, Washington, DC.

Nardi, B. A. 1996a. 'Studying context: A comparison of activity theory, situated action models, and distributed cognition' in Nardi 1996b.

Nardi, B. A. (ed.). 1996b. *Context and Consciousness: Activity Theory and Human–Computer Interaction*. Cambridge, MA: MIT Press.

Nassaji, H. and **M. Swain.** 2000. 'A Vygotskian perspective on corrective feedback in L2: The effect of random versus negotiated help on the learning of English articles'. *Language Awareness* 9: 34–51.

Neisser, U. 1976. *Cognition and Reality*. San Francisco, CA: Freeman.

Neisser, U. 1992. 'Two themes in the study of cognition' in H. L. Pick, P. van den Broek, and D. C. Knill (eds.): *Cognition: Conceptual and Methodological Issues*. Washington, DC: American Psychological Association.

Neu, J. 1990. 'Assessing the role of nonverbal communication in the acquisition of communicative competence' in R. C. Scarcell, E. S. Anderse, and S. D. Krashen (eds.): *Development of Communicative Competence in a Second Language*. New York, NY: Newbury House.

Neu, J. 1991. 'In search of input: The case study of a learner of Polish as a foreign and second language'. *Foreign Language Annals* 24: 427–42.

Newman, D., P. Griffin, and **M. Cole.** 1989. *The Construction Zone: Working for Cognitive Change in School*. Cambridge: Cambridge University Press.

Newman, F. and **L. Holzman.** 1993. *Lev Vygotsky: Revolutionary Scientist*. New York, NY: Routledge.

Newsom, J. 1996. 'Integrating technology with instruction: One district's experience' in S. T. Kerr (ed.): *Technology and the Future of Schooling. Part II*. Chicago, IL: National Society for the Study of Education.

Nguyen, P. (ed.). 1980. *Language in Vietnamese Society: Some Articles by Nguyen Dinh-Hoa*. Carbondale, IL: Asia Books.

Norton, B. 1997. 'Language, identity, and the ownership of English'. *TESOL Quarterly* 31: 409–29.

Novak, J. 1994. 'My typewriter made me do it' in M. Robinson (ed.) 1994: *Altogether Elsewhere. Writers on Exile*. New York, NY: Harcourt, Brace & Company.

Nunan, D. 1989. 'Research on negotiation: What does it reveal about second-language learning conditions, processes, and outcomes?' *Language Learning* 44: 493–527.

Obird, O. 1976. *Cultures in Conflict. An Essay in the Philosophy of the Humanities*. Notre Dame, IN: University of Notre Dame Press.

Ochs, E. 1979. 'Transcription as theory' in E. Ochs and B. B. Schieffelin (eds.): *Developmental Pragmatics*. New York, NY: Academic Press.

Ochs, E. 1988. *Cultural and Language Development: Language Acquisition and Language Socialization in a Samoan Village*. New York, NY: Cambridge University Press.

Ochs, E. 1990. 'Indexicality and socialization' in Stigler, Shweder, and Herdt.

Ochs, E. 1997. 'Narrative' in T. van Dijk (ed.): *Discourse as Structure and Process*. London: Sage Publications.

Ochs, E., E. Schegloff, and **S. Thomas** (eds.). 1996. *Interaction and Grammar*. Cambridge: Cambridge University Press.

Ochs, E. and **B. B. Shieffelin.** 1984. 'Language acquisition and socialization: Three developmental stories', in R. Shweder and R. LeVine (eds.): *Culture Theory: Essays on Mind, Self, and Emotion*. Cambridge: Cambridge University Press.

Ohta, A. S. 1995. 'Applying sociocultural theory to an analysis of learner discourse: Learner–learner collaborative interaction in the zone of proximal development'. *Issues in Applied Linguistics* 6: 93–121.

Ohta, A. S. 1997. 'The development of pragmatic competence in learner–learner classroom interaction' in L. Bouton (ed.): *Pragmatics and Language Learning*, Monograph Series Volume 8 (223–42). Urbana-Champaign, IL: University of Illinois.

Ohta, A. S. 1999. 'Interactional routines and the socialization of interactional style in adult learners of Japanese'. *Journal of Pragmatics* 31: 1493–1512.

Ohta, A. S. In press. *Second language processes in the classroom: Learning Japanese.* Mahwah, NJ: Lawrence Erlbaum Associates.

Olson, D. R. 1994. *The World on Paper. The Conceptual and Cognitive Implications on Writing and Reading.* Cambridge: Cambridge University Press.

Olson, M. R. 1995. 'Conceptualizing narrative authority: Implications for teacher education'. *Teaching and Teacher Education* 11: 119–35.

Ortner, S. 1984. 'Theory in anthropology since the sixties'. *Comparative Studies in Society and History* 26: 126–66.

Palincsar, A. and A. Brown. 1984. 'Reciprocal teaching of comprehension-fostering and comprehension-monitoring activities'. *Cognition and Instruction* 1: 9–31.

Paulescu, E., D. Firth, and R. S. J. Frackowiak. 1993. 'The neural correlate of the verbal component of working memory'. *Nature* 362: 342–5.

Pavlenko, A. 1996. 'Bilingualism and cognition: Concepts in the mental lexicon'. *Cornell Working Papers in Linguistics* 14: 1–21.

Pavlenko, A. 1997. *Bilingualism and cognition.* Unpublished Ph.D. dissertation, Cornell University, Ithaca, NY.

Pavlenko, A. 1998. 'Second language learning by adults: Testimonies of bilingual writers'. *Issues in Applied Linguistics* 9: 3–19.

Peck, S. 1980. 'Language play in child second language acquisition' in D. Larsen-Freeman (ed.): *Discourse Analysis in Second Language Research.* Rowley, MA: Newbury House.

Peirce, B. N. 1995. 'Social identity, investment, and language learning'. *TESOL Quarterly* 29: 9–31.

Peirce, C. S. 1955. 'Logic as semiotic: The theory of signs' in Buchler.

Pennycook, A. 1989. 'The concept of method, interested knowledge, and the politics of language teaching'. *TESOL Quarterly* 23/4: 589–618.

Pennycook, A. 1994a. *The Cultural Politics of English as an International Language.* New York, NY: Longman.

Pennycook, A. 1994b. 'Incommensurable discourses?' *Applied Linguistics* 15/2: 115–38.

Penuel, W. R. and J. V. Wertsch. 1995. 'Vygotsky and identity formation: A sociocultural approach'. *Educational Psychologist* 30: 83–92.

Petrovsky, A. V. 1985. *The Collective Individual.* Moscow: Progress Press.

Phillips, D. C. 1995. 'The good, the bad and the ugly: The many faces of constructivism'. *Educational Researcher* 24/7: 5–12.

Phillipson, R. 1992. *Linguistic Imperialism.* Oxford: Oxford University Press.

Pica, T. 1987. 'Second language acquisition, social interaction, and the classroom'. *Applied Linguistics* 8/1: 3–21.

Pica, T. 1992. 'The textual outcomes of native-speaker–non-native speaker negotiation: What do they reveal about second language learning?' in Kramsch and McConnell-Ginet 1992b.

Pica, T. 1994. 'Research on negotiation: What does it reveal about second-language learning conditions, processes and outcomes'. *Language Learning* 44: 193–527.

Pica, T., L. Holliday, N. Lewis, and L. Morgenthaler. 1989. 'Comprehensible output as an outcome of linguistic demands on the learner'. *Studies in Second Language Acquisition* 11: 63–90.

Pica, T., R. Kanagy, and J. Falodun. 1993. 'Choosing and using communication tasks for second language instruction and research' in Crookes and Gass 1993a.

Pica, T., F. Lincoln-Porter, D. Paninos, and J. Linell. 1996. 'Language learners' interaction: How does it address the input, output, and feedback needs of language learners?' *TESOL Quarterly* 30: 59–84.

Pinker, S. 1994. *The Language Instinct.* New York, NY: Harper Perennial.

Platt, E. and F. B. Brooks. 1994. 'The "acquisition rich environment" revisited'. *The Modern Language Journal* 78/4: 497–511.

Polanyi, L. 1995. 'Language learning and living abroad: Stories from the field' in Freed.

Polkinghorne, D. E. 1988. *Narrative Knowing and the Human Sciences.* Albany, NY: SUNY Press.

Poole, D. and G. G. Patthey-Chavez. 1994. 'Locating assisted performance: A study of instructional activity settings and their effects on the discourse of teaching'. *Issues in Applied Linguistics* 5: 3–35.

Poster, M. 1989. *Critical Theory and Poststructuralism.* Ithaca, NY: Cornell University Press.

Potter, J. 1996. *Representing Reality: Discourse, Rhetoric and Social Construction.* London: Sage Publications.

Poyatos, F. 1980. 'Man as a socializing being: New integrative and interdisciplinary perspectives through cultural and cross-cultural studies in nonverbal communication' in von Raffler-Engel 1980b.

Prabhu, N. 1987. *Second Language Pedagogy.* Oxford: Oxford University Press.

Prawat, R. S. 1995. 'Misreading Dewey: Reform, projects, and the language game'. *Educational Researcher* 24: 13–22.

Quinn, N. 1987. 'Convergent evidence for a cultural model of American marriage' in D. Holland and N. Quinn (eds.): *Cultural Models in Language and Thought.* New York, NY: Cambridge University Press.

Rampton, B. 1995. *Crossing: Language and Ethnicity Among Adolescents.* London: Longman.

Ramsey, S. 1984. 'Double vision: Nonverbal behavior: East and west' in A. Wolfgang (ed.): *Nonverbal Behavior: Perspectives, Applications, Intercultural Insights.* Lewiston, NY: C. J. Hogefe.

Ratner, C. 1991. *Vygotsky's Sociohistorical Psychology and Its Contemporary Applications.* New York, NY: Plenum.

Reber, A. S. 1993. *Implicit Learning and Tacit Knowledge: An Essay on the Cognitive Unconscious.* New York, NY: Oxford University Press.

Reddy, M. 1979. 'The conduit metaphor' in A. Ortony (ed.): *Metaphor and Thought.* Cambridge: Cambridge University Press.

Reed, E. S. 1996. *Encountering the World: Toward an Ecological Psychology.* New York, NY: Oxford University Press.

Richards, J. and T. Rodgers. 1986. *Approaches and Methods in Language Teaching.* New York, NY: Cambridge University Press.

Robbins, D. 1997. *L. S. Vygotsky's Philosophy-Psychology used as a Metatheory in Defining L2 Classroom Acquisition.* Unpublished Habilitationsschrift. University of Hamburg.

Roebuck, R. 1995. *Private writing and orientation: An activity-based approach to L1 (English) and L2 (Spanish) text recall.* Unpublished doctoral dissertation, Cornell University, Ithaca, NY.

Roebuck, R. 1998. *Reading and Recall in L1 and L2: A Sociocultural Approach.* Stamford, CT: Ablex Publishing Corporation.

Rogoff, B. 1990. *Apprenticeship in Thinking, Cognitive Development in Social Context*. New York, NY: Oxford University Press.

Rogoff, B. 1995. 'Observing sociocultural activity on three planes: Participatory appropriation, guided participation, and apprenticeship' in Wertsch, del Rio, and Alvarez.

Rogoff, B. and J. Lave. (eds.). 1984. *Everyday Cognition: Its Development in Social Contexts*. Cambridge, MA: Harvard University Press.

Rommetveit, R. 1974. *On Message Structure: A Framework for the Study of Language and Communication*. New York, NY: John Wiley & Sons.

Rommetveit, R. 1985. 'Language acquisition as increasing linguistic structuring of experience and symbolic behavior control' in Wertsch (ed.) 1985b.

Rommetveit, R. 1991. 'Psycholinguistics, hermaneutics, and cognitive-science' in G. Appel and H. W. Dechert (eds.): *The Case for Psycholinguistic Cases*. Amsterdam: John Benjamins.

Rommetveit, R. 1992. 'Outlines of a dialogically based social-cognitive approach to human cognition and communcation' in A. H. Wold (ed.): *The dialogical alternative: Towards a theory of language and mind*. Oslo: Scandinavian University Press.

Rorty, R. 1979. *Philosophy and the Mirror of Nature*. Princeton, NJ: Princeton University Press.

Rosenwald, G. and R. Ochberg. 1992. *Storied Lives. The Cultural Politics of Self-Understanding*. New Haven, CT: Yale University Press.

Ryan, S. J. 1995. 'Student behavior: Whose norms?' in G. van Troyer, S. Cornwell, and H. Morikawa (eds.): *On JALT 95: Curriculum and Evaluation*. Tokyo: Japanese Association of Language Teachers.

Sacks, H., E. A. Schegloff, and G. Jefferson. 1974. 'A simplest systematics for the organization of turn-taking in conversation'. *Language* 50: 696–735.

Said, E. 1988. 'Forward to selected subaltern studies' in R. Guha and G. Chakravorty Spivak (eds.): *Selected Subaltern Studies*. New York, NY: Oxford University Press.

Salomon, G. (ed.). 1993. *Distributed Cognitions: Psychological and Educational Considerations*. Cambridge: Cambridge University Press.

Sampson, G. 1984. 'Exporting language teaching methods from Canada to China'. *TESL Canada Journal* 1/1: 19–31.

Samuda, V. 1999. 'Guiding relationships between form and meaning during task performance: The role of the teacher' in M. Bygate, P. Skehan, and M. Swain (eds.): *Researching Pedagogic Tasks: Second Language Learning, Teaching and Assessment*. London: Addison-Wesley Longman.

Sanford, M. 1996. *Yea, but can you do that in French 1? The search for instructional conversation*. Unpublished research report, University of Pittsburgh, Pittsburgh, PA.

Savignon, S. 1983. *Communicative Competence: Theory and Classroom Practice*. Reading, MA: Addison-Wesley Publishing Company.

Saville-Troike, M. 1988. 'Private speech: Evidence for second language learning strategies during the "silent period"'. *Journal of Child Language* 15: 567–90.

Schank, R. 1990. *Tell Me a Story: A New Look at Real and Artificial Intelligence*. New York, NY: Charles Scribner's Sons.

Schegloff, E. 1992. 'In another context' in C. Godwin and A. Duranti (eds.): *Rethinking Context: Language as an Interactive Phenomenon*. Cambridge: Cambridge University Press.

Schegloff, E. 1996. 'Turn organization: One intersection of grammar and interaction' in Ochs, Schegloff, and Thomas.

Schieffelin, B. 1990. *The Give and Take of Everyday Life: Language Socialization of Kaluli Children.* New York, NY: Cambridge University Press.

Schieffelin, B. and **E. Ochs.** 1986. *Language Socialization Across Cultures.* New York, NY: Cambridge University Press.

Schmidt, R. (ed.). 1995. *Attention and Awareness in Foreign Language Learning.* Honolulu: Second Language Teaching and Curriculum Center, University of Hawai'i at Manoa.

Schmidt, R. and **S. N. Frota.** 1986. 'Developing basic conversational ability in a second language: A case study of an adult learner of Portuguese' in R. Day (ed.) 1986: *Talking to Learn: Conversation in Second Language Acquisition.* Rowley, MA: Newbury House.

Schultz, E. 1990. *Dialogue at the Margins: Whorf, Bakhtin, and Linguistic Relativity.* Madison, WI: University of Wisconsin Press.

Schumann, F. and **J. Schumann.** 1977. 'Diary of a language learner: An introspective study of second language learning' in H. D. Brown, R. Crymes, and C. Yorio (eds.) 1977: *Teaching and Learning: Trends in Research and Practice.* Washington, DC: TESOL.

Schumann, J. 1990. 'Extending the scope of the acculturation/pidginization model to include cognition'. *TESOL Quarterly* 24: 667–84.

Schumann, J. 1993. 'Some problems with falsification: An illustration from SLA research'. *Applied Linguistics* 14/3: 328–47.

Schumann, J. 1998. *The Neurobiology of Affect in Language. A Supplement to Language Learning* 48.

Scinto, L. F. M. 1987. *Oral and Written Language Norms and the Growth of the Mind.* New York, NY: Academic Press.

Scollon, R. 1976. *Conversations with a One-Year Old.* Honolulu, HI: University of Hawai'i Press.

Scollon, R. and **S. Scollon.** 1994. 'The post-Confucian confusion'. Research Report no. 37. City Polytechnic of Hong Kong, Department of English.

Scribner, S. 1985. 'Knowledge at work'. *Anthropology and Education Quarterly* 16: 199–231.

Scribner, S. and **M. Cole.** 1973. 'Cognitive consequences of formal and informal education'. *Science* 182: 553–9.

Scribner, S. and **M. Cole.** 1981. *The Psychology of Literacy.* Cambridge, MA: Harvard University Press.

Searle, J. R. 1992. *The Rediscovery of the Mind.* Cambridge, MA: MIT Press.

Seliger, H. W. and **R. M. Vago** (eds.). 1991. *First Language Attrition.* New York, NY: Cambridge University Press.

Sfard, A. 1998. 'On two metaphors for learning and the dangers of choosing just one'. *Educational Researcher* 27: 4–13.

Shieh, R. J. J. and **R. Donato.** 1996. *Discursive positioning in L2 interactions: Conflict and complementarity.* Unpublished research report, University of Pittsburgh, Pittsburgh, PA.

Shore, B. 1996. *Culture in Mind. Cognition, Culture and the Problem of Meaning.* Oxford: Oxford University Press.

Shotter, J. and **J. Newson.** 1982. 'An ecological approach to cognitive development: Implicate orders, joint action and intentionality' in G. Butterworth and P. Light (eds.): *Social Cognition: Studies of the Development of Understanding.* Chicago, IL: University of Chicago Press.

Siegal, M. 1995. 'Individual differences and study abroad: Women learning Japanese in Japan' in Freed.

Siegal, M. 1996. 'The role of learner subjectivity in second language sociolinguistic competency: Western women learning Japanese'. *Applied Linguistics* 17/3: 356–82.

Sinclair, J. and **M. Coulthard**. 1975. *Towards an Analysis of Discourse*. Oxford: Oxford University Press.

Singh, R. (ed.). 1998. *The Native Speaker: Multilingual Perspectives*. New Delhi: Sage Publications.

Skehan, P. 1996. 'A framework for the implementation of task-based instruction'. *Applied Linguistics* 17/1: 38–62.

Slobin, D. I. 1996. 'From "thought and language" to "thinking for speaking"' in Gumperz and Levinson.

Smith, J. 1996. *A seven-minute slice of chaos or I'm puzzling through now*. Unpublished research report, University of Pittsburgh, Pittsburgh, PA.

Smith, J., **R. Harré**, and **L. Van Langenhove** (eds.). 1995a. *Rethinking Methods in Psychology*. London: Sage Publications.

Smith, J., **R. Harré**, and **L. Van Langenhove** (eds.). 1995b. *Rethinking Psychology*. London: Sage Publications.

Sokolov, A. N. 1972. *Inner Speech and Thought*. London: Routledge & Kegan Paul.

Soyland, A. J. 1994. *Psychology as Metaphor*. London: Sage Publications.

Spada, N. and **M. Frohlich**. 1995. *COLT Communicative Orientation of Language Teaching Observation Scheme*. Sydney: National Centre for English Language Teaching and Research, Macquarie University.

Sperber, D. and **D. Wilson**. 1986. *Relevance: Communication and Cognition*. Oxford: Basil Blackwell.

Sperling, M. 1994. 'Moments remembered, moments displayed: Narratization, metaphor, and the experience of teaching'. *English Education* 26: 142–56.

Spivak, G. 1985. 'Subaltern studies: Deconstructing historiography' in R. Guha (ed.): *Subaltern Studies IV*. Delhi: Oxford University Press.

Sridhar, K. K. and **S. N. Sridhar**. 1986. 'Bridging the paradigm gap; second language acquisition theory and indigenized varieties of English'. *World Englishes* 5: 3–14.

Stetsenko, A. and **I. Arievitch**. 1997. 'Constructing and deconstructing the self: Comparing post-Vygotskian and discourse-based versions of social constructivism', *Mind, Culture, and Activity, An International Journal* 4: 159–72.

Stewart, E. C. and **M. J. Bennett**. 1991. *American Cultural Patterns. A Cross-cultural Perspective*. Yarmouth, ME: International Press.

Stigler, J. W., **R. A. Shweder**, and **G. Herdt** (eds.). 1990. *Cultural Psychology: The Chicago Symposium on Culture and Human Development*. Cambridge: Cambridge University Press.

Sullivan, P. 1996a. *English language teaching in Vietnam: An appropriation of communicative methodologies*. Unpublished doctoral dissertation, University of California, Berkeley, CA.

Sullivan, P. 1996b. 'Sociocultural influences on classroom interactional styles'. *TESOL Journal* 6: 32–4.

Swain, M. 1985. 'Communicative competence: Some roles of comprehensible input and comprehensible output in its development' in Gass and Madden.

Swain, M. 1993. 'The output hypothesis: Just speaking and writing aren't enough'. *The Canadian Modern Language Review* 50: 158–164.

Swain, M. 1995. 'Three functions of output in second language learning' in G. Cook and B. Seidlhofer (eds.): *Principle and Practice in Applied Linguistics*. Oxford: Oxford University Press.

Swain, M. 1997. 'Collaborative dialogue: Its contribution to second language learning'. *Revista canaria de estudios ingleses* 34: 115–32.

Swain, M. 1998. 'Focus on form through conscious reflection' in Doughty and Williams.

Swain, M. and S. Lapkin. 1995. 'Problems in output and the cognitive processes they generate: A step towards second language learning'. *Applied Linguistics* 16/3: 371–91.

Swain, M. and S. Lapkin. 1998. 'Interaction and second language learning: Two adolescent French immersion students working together'. *The Modern Language Journal* 83: 320–38.

Swain, M. and S. Lapkin. 2000. 'Focus on form through collaborative dialogue: Exploring task effects' in M. Bygate, P. Skehan, and M. Swain (eds.): *Researching pedagogic tasks: Second language learning, teaching and testing*. Harlow, Essex: Addison-Wesley Longman.

Swales, J. M., U. K. Ahmad, Y.-Y. Chang, D. Chavez, D. F. Dressen and R. Seymour. 1998. 'Consider this: The role of imperatives in scholarly writing'. *Applied Linguistics* 19: 97–121.

Takahashi, E. 1998. 'Language development in classroom interaction: A longitudinal study of a Japanese FLES program from a sociocultural perspective'. *Foreign Language Annals* 31: 392–406.

Talyzina, N. 1981. *The Psychology of Learning*. Moscow: Progress Press.

Tannen, D. 1989. *Talking Voices*. Cambridge: Cambridge University Press.

Tannen, D. 1993a. 'What's in a frame?' in Tannen (ed.) 1993b.

Tannen, D. (ed.) 1993b. *Framing in Discourse*. Oxford: Oxford University Press.

Tannen, D. and C. Wallat. 1993. 'Interactive frames and knowledge schemes in interaction' in Tannen (ed.) 1993b.

Tarone, E. and M. Swain. 1995. 'A sociolinguistic perspective on second language use in immersion classrooms'. *The Modern Language Journal* 79: 166–78.

Taylor, C. 1985. *Human Agency and Language*. Philosophical Papers 1. Cambridge: Cambridge University Press.

Thao, Le and M. McCausland (eds.). 1991. *Language Education: Interaction and Development*. Launceston, Tasmania: University of Tasmania.

Tharp, R. G. and R. Gallimore. 1988. *Rousing Minds to Life: Teaching, Learning, and Schooling in Social Context*. New York, NY: Cambridge University Press.

Tharp, R. G. and R. Gallimore. 1991. *The Instructional Conversation: Teaching and Learning in Social Activity*. Santa Cruz, CA: The National Center for Research on Cultural Diversity and Second Language Learning.

Thorne, S. 1999. *An activity theoretical analysis of foreign language electronic discourse*. Ph.D. dissertation. University of California, Berkeley, CA.

Ting, Y. R. 1987. 'Foreign language teaching in China: Problems and perspectives'. *Canadian and International Education* 16: 48–61.

To Thi Anh. 1974. *Eastern and Western Cultural Values. Conflict or Harmony?* Manila: East Asian Pastoral Institute.

Todhunter, S. 1996. *Discursive authenticity in the interactive practices of a Spanish classroom*. Unpublished research report, University of Pittsburgh, Pittsburgh, PA.

Todorov, T. 1994. 'Dialogism and schizophrenia' in A. Arteaga (ed.): *An Other Tongue. Nation and Ethnicity in the Linguistic Borderlands*. Durham and London: Duke University Press.

Tomasello, M. 1992. *First Verbs: A Case Study in Early Grammatical Development*. New York, NY: Cambridge University Press.

Toulmin, S. 1978. 'The Mozart of psychology'. *New York Times Review of Books*. September.

Trevarthen, C. 1990. 'Signs before speech' in T. A. Sebeok and J. Umiker-Sebeok (eds.): *The Semiotic Web 1989*. Berlin: Mouton de Gruyter.

Trim, J. L. M. 1959. 'Historical, descriptive and dynamic linguistics'. *Language and Speech* 2: 9–25.

Tucker, G. R., R. Donato, and J. L. Antonek. 1996. 'Documenting growth in a Japanese FLES program'. *Foreign Language Annals* 29: 539–50.

Ushakova, T. 1994. 'Inner speech and second language acquisition: An experimental-theoretical approach' in Lantolf and Appel 1994b.

Valenta, E. 1991. *Doubled selves and fractured childhoods: A study of the récits d'enfance in Nathalie Sarraute, Agota Kristof and Claude Esteban*. Unpublished Ph.D. dissertation, Cornell University, Ithaca, NY.

van der Veer, R. and J. Valsiner. 1991. *Understanding Vygotsky: A Quest for Synthesis*. Oxford: Basil Blackwell.

Van Langenhove, L. 1995. 'The theoretical foundations of experimental psychology and its alternatives' in J. A. Smith, R. Harré, and L. Van Langenhove (eds.): *Rethinking Psychology*. London: Sage Publications.

van Lier, L. 1996. *Interaction in the Language Curriculum: Awareness, Autonomy, and Authenticity*. London: Longman.

van Lier, L. 1999. *Computers and language learning: A case study in ecology and complexity*. Presentation at AAAL, March 1999. Stamford, Connecticut.

van Lier, L. and N. Matsuo. 2000. 'Varieties of conversational experience: Looking for learning opportunities'. *Applied Language Learning* 11/2.

Varela, F. J., E. Thompson, and E. Rosch. 1991. *The Embodied Mind: Cognitive Science and Human Experience*. Cambridge, MA: MIT Press.

Varonis, E. and S. Gass. 1985. 'Non-native/non-native conversations: A model for negotiating meaning'. *Applied Linguistics* 6/1: 1–90.

Vološinov, V. N. 1973. *Marxism and the Philosophy of Language*. New York, NY: Seminar Press.

von Raffler-Engel, W. 1976. 'Linguistic and kinesic correlations in code switching' in McCormack and Wurm.

von Raffler-Engel, W. 1980a. 'Developmental kinesics: The acquisition of conversational nonverbal behavior' in von Raffler-Engel 1980b.

von Raffler-Engel, W. (ed.). 1980b. *Aspects of Nonverbal Communication*. Bath: Pitman Press.

Vygotsky, L. S. 1978. *Mind in Society*. Cambridge, MA: Harvard University Press.

Vygotsky, L. S. 1981. 'The genesis of higher mental functions' in Wertsch 1981.

Vygotsky, L. S. 1986. *Thought and Language*. Cambridge, MA: MIT Press.

Vygotsky, L. S. 1987. *The Collected Works of L. S. Vygotsky. Volume 1. Thinking and Speaking*. New York, NY: Plenum Press.

Vygotsky, L. S. 1989. 'Concrete human psychology'. *Soviet Psychology* 27/2: 53–77.

Vygotsky, L. S. 1993. *The Collected Works of L. S. Vygotsky. Volume 2. The Fundamentals of Defectology (Abnormal Psychology and Learning Disabilities)*. New York, NY: Plenum Press.

Vygotsky, L. S. 1997. *Educational Psychology*. Boca Raton, FL: St. Lucie Press.

Vygotsky, L. S. and A. Luria, 1994. 'Tool and symbol in child development' in R. van der Veer and J. Valsiner (eds.): *The Vygotsky Reader*. Oxford: Blackwell.

Waas, M. 1996. *Language Attritition Downunder. German Speakers in Australia*. Frankfurt: Studien Zur Allgemeinen und Romanischen Sprachwissenschaft.

Wajnryb, R. 1990. *Grammar Dictation*. Oxford: Oxford University Press.

Wang, J. 1996. *Same task: Different activities*. Unpublished research report, University of Pittsburgh, Pittsburgh, PA.

Weir, R. 1962. *Language in the Crib*. The Hague: Mouton.

Wells, G. 1994. 'The complimentary contributions of Halliday and Vygotsky to a "language-based theory of learning"'. *Linguistics and Education* 6: 41–90.

Wells, G. 1996. 'Using the tool-kit of discourse in the activity of learning and teaching'. *Mind, Culture, and Activity, An International Journal* 3: 74–101.

Wells, G. 1998. 'Using L1 to master L2: A response to Antón and DiCamilla's socio-cognitive functions of L1 collaborative interaction in the L2 classroom'. *The Canadian Modern Language Review* 54: 343–53.

Wells, G. 2000. 'Dialogic inquiry in education: Building on the legacy of Vygotsky' in C. D. Lee and P. Smagorinsky (eds.): *Vygotskian Perpectives on Literacy Research.* New York, NY: Cambridge University Press.

Wertsch, J. V. 1979. 'The regulation of human interaction and the given–new organization of private speech' in G. Ziven (ed.): *The Development of Self-Regulation Through Private Speech.* New York, NY: Wiley.

Wertsch, J. V. (ed.). 1981. *The Concept of Activity in Soviet Psychology.* Armonk, NY: M. E. Sharpe.

Wertsch, J. V. 1985a. *Vygotsky and the Social Formation of Mind.* Cambridge, MA: Harvard University Press.

Wertsch, J. V. (ed.). 1985b. *Culture, Communication and Cognition. Vygotskian Perspectives.* Cambridge: Cambridge University Press.

Wertsch, J. V. 1991. *Voices of the Mind. A Sociocultural Approach to Mediated Action.* Cambridge, MA: Harvard University Press.

Wertsch, J. V. 1998. *Mind as Action.* Oxford: Oxford University Press.

Wertsch, J. V., P. del Rio, and A. Alvarez. (eds.). 1995. *Sociocultural Studies of Mind.* Cambridge: Cambridge University Press.

Wertsch, J. V. and M. Hickmann. 1987. 'Problem-solving in social interaction: A microgenetic analysis' in M. Hickmann (ed.): *Social and Functional Approaches to Language and Thought.* Orlando, FL: Academic Press.

Wertsch, J. V., N. Minick, and F. J. Arns. 1984. 'The creation of context in joint problem solving' in Rogoff and Lave.

Wertsch, J. V. and C. A. Stone. 1985. 'The concept of internalization in Vygotsky's account of the genesis of higher mental functions' in Wertsch (ed.) 1985b.

Wertsch, J. V., P. Tulviste, and F. Hagstrom. 1993. 'A sociocultural approach to agency' in E. A. Forman, N. Minick, and C. A. Stone (eds.): *Context for Learning: Sociocultural Dynamics in Children's Development.* New York, NY: Oxford University Press.

White, H. 1987. *The Content of the Form.* Baltimore, MD: Johns Hopkins Press.

Whorf, B. L. 1956. *Language, Thought, and Reality. Selected Writings of Benjamin Lee Whorf.* J. B. Carroll (ed.) Cambridge, MA: MIT Press.

Widdowson, H. 1978. *Teaching Language as Communication.* Oxford: Oxford University Press.

Widdowson, H. 1990. *Aspects of Language Teaching.* Oxford: Oxford University Press.

Widdowson, H. 1992. *Practical Stylistics.* Oxford: Oxford University Press.

Widdowson, H. 1994. 'The ownership of English'. *TESOL Quarterly* 28: 377–89.

Wierzbicka, A. 1985. 'The double life of a bilingual' in R. Sussex and J. Zubrzycki (eds.): *Polish People and Culture in Australia.* Canberra: Australian National University.

Wierzbicka, A. 1997. 'The double life of a bilingual: A cross-cultural perspective' in M. Bond (ed.): *Working at the Interface of Cultures. Eighteen Lives in Social Science.* London: Routledge.

Williams, R. 1977. *Marxism and Literature.* Oxford: Oxford University Press.

Wittgenstein, L. 1953. *Philosophical Investigations.* Oxford: Basil Blackwell.

Wittgenstein, L. 1980. *Culture and Value.* Chicago, IL: University of Chicago Press.

Wolcott, H. F. 1994. *Transforming Qualitative Data: Description, Analysis, and Interpretation.* Thousand Oaks, CA: Sage Publications.

Wold, A. H. 1992a. 'Introduction' in Wold (ed.) 1992b.

Wold, A. H. (ed.). 1992b. *The Dialogical Alternative: Towards a Theory of Language and Mind*. Oslo: Scandinavian University Press.

Wood, D., J. S. Bruner, and **G. Ross.** 1976. 'The role of tutoring in problem-solving'. *Journal of Child Psychology and Psychiatry* 17: 89–100.

Wozniak, R. H. and **K. W. Fischer** (eds.). 1993. *Development in Context: Acting and Thinking in Specific Environments*. Hillsdale, NJ.: Lawrence Erlbaum Associates, Publishers.

Yakobson, H. 1994. *Crossing Borders. From Revolutionary Russia to China to America*. New York City: Hermitage Publishers.

Yaroshevsky, M. 1989. *Lev Vygotsky*. Moscow: Progress Press.

Yngve, V. H. 1996. *From Grammar to Science: New Foundations for General Linguistics*. Amsterdam: John Benjamins.

Young, C. 1989. *Growing up in Moscow: Memories of a Soviet Girlhood*. New York City: Ticknor & Fields.

Zentella, A. C. 1997. *Growing up Bilingual: Puerto Ricans in New York*. Oxford: Basil Blackwell.

Zinchenko, P. 1996. 'Developing activity theory: The zone of proximal development and beyond' in Nardi 1996b.

Zinchenko, V. P. 1985. 'Vygotsky's ideas about units for the analysis of mind' in Wertsch (ed.) 1985b.

Index

Page numbers in **bold type** denote main treatments; those followed by *n* refer to end-of-chapter Notes.